NEW VENTURE MANAGEMENT

THE ENTREPRENEUR'S ROADMAP

Donald F. Kuratko, Ph.D.

The Jack M. Gill Chair of Entrepreneurship
The Kelley School of Business
Indiana University—Bloomington

Jeffrey S. Hornsby, Ph.D.

The George and Francis Ball Distinguished Professor of Management
Miller College of Business
Ball State University

D0060814

PEARSON
Prentice Hall

UPPER SADDLE RIVER, NEW JERSEY 07458

Library of Congress Cataloging-in-Publication Data

Kuratko, Donald F.
  New venture management : the entrepreneur's roadmap / by Donald F. Kuratko,
Jeffrey S. Hornsby.
      p. cm.
  ISBN-13: 978-0-13-613032-1 (pbk.)
  ISBN-10: 0-13-613032-1 (pbk.)
  1. New business enterprises.   2. Venture capital.   3. Entrepreneurship.
  I. Hornsby, Jeffrey S. (Jeffrey Scott), 1959– II. Title.

  HD62.5.K853 2009
  658—dc22   2007047119

Editor-in-Chief: *David Parker*
Acquisitions Editor: *Jennifer M. Collins*
Product Development Manager: *Ashley Santora*
Editorial Assistant: *Elizabeth Davis*
Marketing Assistant: *Ian Gold*
Associate Managing Editor: *Suzanne Grappi*
Permissions Project Manager: *Charles Morris*
Senior Operations Supervisor: *Arnold Vila*
Operations Specialist: *Carol O'Rourke*
Senior Art Director: *Janet Slowik*
Cover Design: *Karen Quigley*
Cover Photo: *Angelo Cavalli/Digital Vision/Getty Images*
Composition: *ICC Macmillan Inc.*
Full-Service Project Management: *Winifred Sanchez/ICC Macmillan Inc.*
Printer/Binder: *STP/RR Donnelley/Harrisonburg*
Typeface: 10/12 Times Ten Roman

Credits and acknowledgments borrowed from other sources and reproduced, with permission, in this
textbook appear on appropriate page within text.

Pearson Education LTD.   Pearson Education Australia PTY, Limited
Pearson Education Singapore, Pte. Ltd   Pearson Education North Asia Ltd
Pearson Education, Canada, Ltd   Pearson Educación de Mexico, S.A. de C.V.
Pearson Education–Japan   Pearson Education Malaysia, Pte. Ltd.

10 9 8 7 6 5 4 3 2 1
ISBN-13: 978-0-13-613032-1
ISBN-10:   0-13-613032-1

BRIEF CONTENTS

CONTENTS

PART V   NEW VENTURE GROWTH MANAGEMENT   231

PREFACE

THE EFFECT OF NEW VENTURES IN THE 21ST CENTURY

The United States is a nation of new ventures and small businesses. Today, the entire world economy is focused on entrepreneurship and the development of new ventures. Individuals and giant corporations alike rely on smaller ventures for goods and services. Small entrepreneurial ventures greatly outnumber large businesses, and thousands of new ventures are formed each day in this country. Interest in entrepreneurial ventures continues to grow. Governmental bodies, public and private educational institutions, and a variety of economic development groups have joined the business community in recognizing the importance of entrepreneurial ventures to our country and its economy. As the nation and the world progress through the new millennium, effectively managed entrepreneurial ventures are critical to our economic success.

OBJECTIVES OF THE BOOK

New Venture Management provides an introduction to the world of new and emerging ventures and to the fundamentals of effective new venture management—the fundamentals of such diverse activities as planning, marketing, financing, and growth. The book is designed for collegiate or executive education markets. This text is designed for courses in new ventures that involve three distinct but related constituencies. First, it is designed to be useful to professors who relate the latest research to each topic as they teach the course. Second, it has been written for students to *read*; the subject matter is presented in an interesting and easy-to-understand style. Finally, the specific needs of active new venture owner/managers have been considered. The book's coverage of the key aspects of new venture management will help them to improve their management effectiveness on the job.

DISTINGUISHING FEATURES

A number of distinguishing features make this book informative, up to date, and useful.

COMPREHENSIVE ORGANIZATION

The book has five distinct parts. Each chapter has a unique subtitle to indicate to the practicing entrepreneur what is really involved in the chapter.

The Introduction provides an examination of the *Quiet Giant*—the aggregate picture of new ventures in today's economy. It provides an inside look at the world of new and growing ventures. It also explains the nature of new ventures, the opportunities for new ventures, and the factors that bring success and failure to new enterprises.

Part I discusses the various ways that individuals find venture opportunities—by buying an ongoing concern, by establishing a home-based business, or by purchasing a franchise. We have called the chapters in this section *The Pathways* and *The Hybrid*, respectively.

Part II discusses the start-up concerns faced by new ventures, with specific attention given to developing an effective business plan and the legal forms of organization. We have called the chapters in this section *The Roadmap* and *The Structure*, respectively.

Part III explains the marketing research needed for an emerging venture as well as the strategic pricing needs of new ventures. We call the chapters in this section *The Niche* and *The Hook*, respectively.

Part IV deals with financial challenges. It covers the critical sources of capital, financial statements, record keeping, and financial analysis. We call the chapters in this section *The Injection, The Scorecard,* and *The Gauges,* respectively.

Part V focuses on the challenges of managing new ventures. Attention is directed to unique challenges that confront the growing venture and its human resource management functions. We call the chapters in this section *The People* and *The Future*, respectively.

The subject matter of the book moves from consideration of new ventures in general to the very specific needs of individual owner/managers. The underlying theme is *effectiveness*; that is, the book tells the new venture owners/manager what he or she needs to know to manage a successful venture in the 21st century.

INTEREST-BASED FEATURES

NEW VENTURE PERSPECTIVE

Every chapter features a short informational item—entitled *New Venture Perspective*—that is designed to identify key issues that affect the new venture owner/manager. These helpful hints are adapted from some of the latest publications, and each handbook item relates to the chapter in which it appears.

NEW VENTURE CONSULTANT

At the end of each chapter is a brief but challenging study entitled *New Venture Consultant.* The problems posed by these cases are comprehensive, and they call for the application of all of the material in the chapter as well as the student's experience and prior education.

A COMPLETE BUSINESS PLAN

A complete business plan is provided at the end of the textbook. This is provided as a guide for the entrepreneur who is searching for the exact look and style of a successful plan.

ABOUT THE AUTHORS

Dr. Donald F. Kuratko (Dr. K) is the Jack M. Gill Chair of Entrepreneurship, Professor of Entrepreneurship, and Executive Director of the Johnson Center for Entrepreneurship and Innovation, The Kelley School of Business, Indiana University–Bloomington. Professor Kuratko is considered a preeminent scholar and national leader in the field of entrepreneurship. He has published over 150 articles on aspects of entrepreneurship, new venture development, and corporate entrepreneurship. His work has been published in journals such as *Strategic Management Journal, Academy of Management Executive, Journal of Business Venturing, Entrepreneurship Theory and Practice, Journal of Small Business Management, Journal of Small Business Strategy, Family Business Review,* and the *Journal of Business Ethics.* Professor Kuratko has authored 22 books, including the leading entrepreneurship book in American universities today, *Entrepreneurship: Theory, Process, Practice,* 7th ed. (Thomson/South-Western, 2007), as well as *Corporate Entrepreneurship & Innovation,* 2nd ed. (Thomson/South-Western, 2008) and *Strategic Entrepreneurial Growth,* 2nd ed. (Thomson/South-Western, 2004). In addition, Dr. Kuratko has been a consultant on corporate entrepreneurship and entrepreneurial strategies to a number of major corporations, such as Anthem Blue Cross/Blue Shield, AT&T, United Technologies, Ameritech, Walgreens, and Union Carbide Corporation. Dr. Kuratko also serves as the executive director of the Global Consortium of Entrepreneurship Centers (GCEC), an organization comprised of over 200 top university entrepreneurship centers throughout the world.

Under Dr. Kuratko's leadership and with one of the most prolific entrepreneurship research faculties in the world, Indiana University's Entrepreneurship Program has recently been ranked the #1 graduate business school (public institutions) for entrepreneurship and the #1 undergraduate business school for entrepreneurship (public institutions) by *U.S. News & World Report.* In 2007, Indiana University was awarded the National Model M.B.A. Program in Entrepreneurship for the M.B.A. program in entrepreneurship and innovation developed by Dr. Kuratko. Before coming to Indiana University, he was the Stoops Distinguished Professor of Entrepreneurship and founding director of the entrepreneurship program at Ball State University. The entrepreneurship program that Dr. Kuratko developed at Ball State University attained top national rankings, including #4 in *U.S. News & World Report* (the #1 public university for entrepreneurship) and the #1 regional entrepreneurship program in *Entrepreneur* magazine.

Dr. Kuratko's honors include earning the Entrepreneur of the Year for the state of Indiana (sponsored by Ernst & Young, *Inc.* magazine, and Merrill Lynch) and being inducted into the Institute of American Entrepreneurs Hall of Fame. He has been honored with the George Washington Medal of Honor, the Leavey Foundation Award for Excellence in Private Enterprise, the NFIB Entrepreneurship Excellence Award, and the National Model Innovative Pedagogy Award for

Entrepreneurship. In addition, Dr. Kuratko was named the National Outstanding Entrepreneurship Educator by the U.S. Association for Small Business and Entrepreneurship, and he was selected as one of the Top Three Entrepreneurship Professors in the U.S. by the Kauffman Foundation, Ernst & Young, *Inc.* magazine, and Merrill Lynch. He was also named a 21st Century Entrepreneurship Research Fellow by the Global Consortium of Entrepreneurship Centers. Dr. Kuratko was honored by his peers in *Entrepreneur* magazine as one of the Top Two Entrepreneurship Program Directors in the nation for three consecutive years, including the #1 Entrepreneurship Program Director in the nation in 2003. In 2007, the U.S. Association for Small Business and Entrepreneurship honored him with the prestigious John E. Hughes Entrepreneurial Advocacy Award for his career achievements in entrepreneurship and corporate innovation. In 2007, the National Academy of Management honored Professor Kuratko with the highest award bestowed in entrepreneurship — the prestigious Entrepreneurship Advocate Award—for his contributions to the development and advancement of the discipline of entrepreneurship.

Dr. Jeffrey S. Hornsby is the George and Frances Ball Distinguished Professor of Management and professor of Entrepreneurship and Human Resource Management at Ball State University. His research has concentrated in the areas of corporate entrepreneurship, entrepreneurial motivation, compensation, team building, honesty testing, entrepreneurial motivation, and human resource management practices for emerging businesses. He has authored or coauthored 51 refereed journal articles and 63 proceedings articles that have appeared in the *Journal of Applied Psychology, Strategic Management Journal, Academy of Management Executive, Group and Organizational Management, Journal of Small Business Management, Journal of Business Venturing, Entrepreneurship Theory and Practice, Public Personnel Management, Mid-American Journal of Business, Advanced Management Journal, Small Business Forum, Journal of Leadership Studies,* and the *Journal of Business and Psychology*. He has also written two books entitled *The Human Resource Function in Emerging Enterprises* (Thomson/South-Western, 2002) and *Frontline HR: A Handbook for the Emerging Manager* (Thomson Texere, 2005). Dr. Hornsby is also certified by the Society for Human Resource Management (SHRM) as a senior professional in human resource management (SPHR).

Dr. Hornsby's related experience includes extensive corporate training and consulting in entrepreneurial development, community-based entrepreneurship, team building, corporate entrepreneurship, supervisory management, compensation, market research, and human resource management. He has worked with several firms, including BorgWarner Automotive, Rolls Royce, Bank One, BAA, RCI, Ameritech, Blue Cross/Blue Shield, VEI/IMM (a subsidiary of Community Hospitals), Pathologists Associated, Ontario Systems Corporation, State of Indiana Department of Commerce, Frank Miller Lumber Company, Muncie Power Products, and Pathologists Associates. Dr. Hornsby also coordinates and teaches the SHRM exam preparation course using the SHRM Learning System.

Dr. Hornsby has won several teaching and research awards, including the Dean's Teaching Award for ten consecutive years, three conference Best Paper awards, and the Ball State University 2004 Outstanding Faculty Award.

CHAPTER

NEW VENTURES
THE QUIET GIANT

INTRODUCTION

Free enterprise—the concept that any individual is free to transform an idea into a business—is the economic basis for all entrepreneurial activity. The opportunities for potential entrepreneurs are unlimited. The constantly changing economic environment provides a continuous flow of potential opportunities *if* an individual can recognize a profitable idea amid the chaos and cynicism that permeate such an environment. Thousands of alternatives exist because every individual creates and develops ideas with a unique frame of reference.

During the last 10 years, new ventures have emerged at the rate of 500,000 per year. Entrepreneurs and their new ventures have generated millions of jobs to offset the huge reductions made by Fortune 500 firms. Entrepreneurial ventures such as Apple Computer, Federal Express, Intel, Microsoft, and Google have captured the economic spotlight by demonstrating that new ideas from emerging ventures can create the giant institutions of tomorrow. Harsh lessons have been learned, and corporations have realized that the same entrepreneurial spirit found in people who have developed these new ventures may also be present within organizational boundaries. The entrepreneurial flame has caught on throughout the world, with former socialist economies searching for the free enterprise solution through entrepreneurial development.[1]

NEW VENTURES: ENERGIZING ECONOMIES

The past 15 years have witnessed the most powerful emergence of entrepreneurial activity in the world; many statistics illustrate this fact. For example, during the past 10 years, new business incorporations in the United States averaged 600,000 *per year*. This trend clearly demonstrates the popularity of new venture activity, whether through start-ups, expansions, or development. More specifically, in the new millennium we have witnessed the number of smaller businesses in the United States soar to over 26 million, with a predicted annual growth rate of 2 percent. Collectively, U.S. businesses posted over $20 trillion in annual revenues.[2] Let us examine some of the historical numbers supporting this phenomenon.

Several methods are used to measure the impact of new ventures on the economy—for example, efforts to start a firm (which may not be successful), incorporation of a firm (which may never go into business), changes in net tax returns filed (reflecting new filings minus filings no longer received), and a substantial amount of full-time and part-time self-employment. According to the Small Business Administration, 672,000 new businesses were created in 2005, the largest in U.S. history (even 12 percent higher than the infamous dot-com explosion). More significantly, 74 million Americans stated they plan to start a new venture within the next five years, and an additional 199 million Americans plan to start a venture someday.[3] Women–owned ventures increased from 5.4 million in 1997 to 7.7 million in 2006.[4] The nonprofit Tax Foundation reports that entrepreneurs pay more than 54 percent of all individual income taxes. In addition, 60 percent of all corporate tax returns are from S corporations. Within the highest individual tax bracket, 37 percent of filers are current entrepreneurs.[5] These numbers make it clear that new ventures are dominating the U.S. economy . . . truly an entrepreneurial economy.

New ventures with employees may number more than 600,000 in a given year, and another couple million new business entities—in the form of self-employment—may also come into being each year. Approximately one new firm with employees is established every year for every 300 adults in the United States. Because the typical new firm has at least two owners/managers, one of every 150 adults participates in the founding of a new firm each year. Substantially more—one in 12—are involved in trying to launch a new firm. The net result is that the United States has a very robust level of firm creation.

From a global perspective, we can examine the Global Entrepreneurship Monitor (GEM)—a unique, large-scale, long-term project developed jointly by Babson College, the London Business School, and the Kauffman Foundation. Now reaching 40 countries worldwide, the GEM provides an annual assessment of the entrepreneurial environment of each country. The latest GEM divides countries into middle- and high-income clusters; findings show a strong variation across clusters both in frequency and quality of entrepreneurial activity. Middle-income nations, such as Venezuela (25 percent) and Thailand (20.7 percent), outperformed high-income countries like Japan (2.2 percent) and Belgium (3.9 percent) in early-stage entrepreneurial activity. The political, legal, and cultural environment directly impacts entrepreneurs' activity and ability to contribute to the economic development of their country. A major component of GEM is the platform it provides governments to develop more effective entrepreneurial policies and best practices. In general, countries with healthy and diversified labor markets or stronger safety nets in terms of social welfare provisions can be more selective in the kinds of businesses they choose to start—and they have higher ratios of opportunity to necessity-driven motivation. Denmark comes in first, with a 27:4 ratio of early-stage opportunity to early-stage necessity ventures. Overall, every study continues to demonstrate that entrepreneurs' ability to expand existing markets, create new markets, and establish new ventures at a breathtaking pace impacts individuals, firms, and entire nations.[6]

THE GLOBAL IMPACT OF NEW VENTURES

The world economy has achieved its highest economic performance during the last 10 years by fostering and promoting entrepreneurial activity. This global success has at least three key components.

First, large firms that existed in mature industries adapted, downsized, restructured, and reinvented themselves during the late 1990s and are now thriving. Large businesses have learned to become more entrepreneurial. As large firms have become leaner, their sales and profits have increased sharply. For example, General Electric cut its workforce by 40 percent, from more than 400,000 workers 20 years ago to fewer than 240,000 workers today; meanwhile, sales increased fourfold, from less than $20 billion to nearly $80 billion, during the same period. This goal was accomplished in many cases by returning to the firm's core competencies and by contracting out functions to small firms that were formerly done in-house.

Second, while these large companies have been transforming themselves, new entrepreneurial ventures have been blossoming. Twenty years ago, Nucor Steel was a small steel manufacturer with a few hundred employees. It embraced a new technology called thin slab casting, allowing it to thrive while other steel companies were stumbling. Nucor grew to 59,000 employees, with sales of $3.4 billion and a net income of $274 million. Newer entrepreneurial ventures—some of which did not exist 25 years ago—have collectively created 1.4 million new jobs during the past 10 years.

Third, thousands of new ventures have been founded, including many established by women, minorities, and immigrants. These new ventures have come from every sector of the economy and every part of the United States. Together these new ventures make a formidable contribution to the economy, as many firms have hired one or two employees each to create more than one million net new jobs in the last few years.

In summary, new and emerging ventures make two indispensable contributions to the world economy. First, they are an integral part of the renewal process that pervades and defines market economies. New and emerging firms play a crucial role in the innovations that lead to technological change and productivity growth. In short, they are about change and competition because they change market structure. The world economy has become a dynamic, organic entity that is always in the process of *becoming* rather than an established one that has already arrived. It is about prospects for the future, not about the inheritance of the past. Second, new and emerging ventures are the essential mechanism by which millions enter the economic and social mainstream of our global society. New ventures enable millions of people, including women, minorities, and immigrants, to access the entrepreneurial dream. The greatest source of economic strength has always been the entrepreneurial dream of economic growth, equal opportunity, and upward mobility. In this evolutionary process, new ventures play the crucial and indispensable role of providing the social glue that binds together both high-tech and traditional business activities. New venture formations are the critical foundations for any net increase in global employment.

ENTREPRENEURS AND NEW VENTURES

Today, an entrepreneur is an innovator or developer who recognizes and seizes opportunities; converts those opportunities into workable/marketable ideas; adds value through time, effort, money, or skills; assumes the risks of the competitive marketplace to implement these ideas; and realizes the rewards from these efforts.

The entrepreneur is the aggressive catalyst for change in the world of business. He or she is an independent thinker who dares to be different in a background of common events. Many people now regard entrepreneurship as pioneership on the frontier of business.

In recognizing the importance of the evolution of entrepreneurship into the 21st century, researchers Donald F. Kuratko and Richard M. Hodgetts developed an integrated definition that acknowledges the critical factors needed for this phenomenon.

> Entrepreneurship is a dynamic process of vision, change, and creation. It requires an application of energy and passion towards the creation and implementation of new ideas and creative solutions. Essential ingredients include the willingness to take calculated risks—in terms of time, equity, or career; the ability to formulate an effective venture team; the creative skill to marshal the needed resources; the fundamental skill of building a solid business plan; and, finally, the vision to recognize opportunity where others see chaos, contradiction, and confusion.[7]

Today's younger generation of the 21st century may become known as "Generation E" because they are becoming the most entrepreneurial generation since the Industrial Revolution. As many as 5.6 million Americans younger than age 34 are actively trying to start their own businesses today. One-third of new entrepreneurs are younger than age 30, more than 60 percent of 18- to 29-year-olds say they want to own their own businesses, and nearly 80 percent of would-be entrepreneurs in the United States are between the ages of 18 and 34.[8]

Every person has the potential and choice to pursue a career as an entrepreneur. Exactly what motivates individuals to choose entrepreneurship has not been identified, at least not as one single event, characteristic, or trait. A review of the literature related to entrepreneurial characteristics reveals the existence of a large number of factors that can be consolidated into a much smaller set of profile dimensions. For example, if the work of John Kao is considered, 11 common characteristics can be identified:[9]

- Total commitment, determination, and perseverance
- Drive to achieve and grow
- Opportunity and goal orientation
- Taking initiative and personal responsibility
- Persistent problem solving
- Realism and a sense of humor
- Seeking and using feedback
- Internal locus of control
- Calculated risk taking and risk seeking
- Low need for status and power
- Integrity and reliability

Using the simplest of theoretical forms for studying entrepreneurship, entrepreneurs cause entrepreneurship. That is, $E = f(e)$ states that entrepreneurship is a function of the entrepreneur. Thus, the continuous examination of entrepreneurial characteristics helps in the evolving understanding of entrepreneurship.[10]

Entrepreneurship also has been characterized as the interaction of the following skills: inner control, planning and goal setting, risk taking, innovation, reality perception, use of feedback, decision making, human relations, and independence. In addition, many people believe successful entrepreneurs are individuals who are not afraid to fail. New characteristics are continually being added to this ever-growing list.

Keep in mind that *entrepreneurship* is more than the mere creation of a business. Although that is certainly an important facet, it is not the complete picture. The characteristics of seeking opportunities, taking risks beyond security, and having the tenacity to push an idea through to reality combine into a special perspective that permeates entrepreneurs. An entrepreneurial perspective can be developed in individuals. This perspective can be exhibited inside or outside an organization, in profit or not-for-profit enterprises, and in business or nonbusiness activities for the purpose of bringing forth creative ideas. Thus, the entrepreneurial process is an integrated concept that has revolutionized the way business is conducted at every level and in every country.

A Look Ahead

Larry Dietrick, the owner of Scientel Wireless—a company that designs and builds wireless broadband networks for cities and public agencies—has seen its sales grow from $3.2 million in 2005 to $4.2 million in 2006. However, despite that good news, he has some significant concerns to address to help ensure that his company continues to thrive. First, Scientel Wireless is having trouble locating and hiring qualified employees. In addition, health care costs have continued to climb, which has made it difficult for the firm to offer competitive benefit packages to potential employees. For a smaller firm with limited resources, problems like these are serious.

According to PricewaterhouseCoopers' second annual Entrepreneurial Challenge Survey, two-thirds of entrepreneurs contacted were optimistic about the U.S. economy for 2007. Confidence in the economy is a good sign for growing businesses; according to J. Fentress Seagroves, partner in PricewaterhouseCoopers' Private Company Services practice, "It's meaningful because confidence is a critical indicator of current and future economic activity." However, despite having a positive outlook on the economy, finding qualified employees was the chief concern for the coming year among entrepreneurs. Not having enough employees can result in businesses making unimaginable decisions, such as turning down customers.

The demand for good employees has never been greater than it is right now. Skilled employees are one of the tools a business uses to obtain a competitive advantage, according to Seagroves. One way to locate good employees is by asking current employees to refer people they think would be a good fit for the company. A firm can offer cash or gift certificate incentives to help encourage referrals. Another option to help recruit good employees is through local educational systems. Hiring student interns provides businesses with inexpensive employees and gives the student interns valuable work experience. Plus, it also gives the firm the inside track to hiring the student upon completion of his or her degree.

Another chief concern for entrepreneurs in the Entrepreneurial Challenge Survey was cutting costs. Cutting costs will help a business improve profitability if it is encountering a slow market. Michael McNicholas, president of boiler distributor EnviroMechanical, Inc., tries to save money on office supplies by e-mailing customer invoices instead of mailing paper copies, and by locating a telephone plan that will cut costs. Additionally, rising health care costs have many entrepreneurs concerned. However, Bill Collier—author of *How to Succeed as a Small Business Owner . . . and Still Have a Life!*—says that businesses have options that will help alleviate this pressure. According to Collier, entrepreneurs should take advantage of Section 125 cafeteria plans, health reimbursement accounts, health savings accounts, and flexible spending accounts, all of which can help reduce current health care costs by 20 percent. He also recommends that entrepreneurs invest the time and energy required to become an expert in these areas in order to successfully cut these costs.

Another major concern entrepreneurs had for 2007 were spoilers, or wild cards, which are obstacles that are relevant to one company but may not be to another. Lorraine Kay, CEO of Kay Construction in New Jersey, reported that inflation was a big issue for her; however, inflation was only an issue for 4 percent of other entrepreneurs surveyed. "In my 35 years of doing this, I've seen inflation across the board, not only for products but for labor as well, as we are seeing now," said Kay. She noted that her business is paying 70 percent higher prices for steel after an inflationary explosion. When entrepreneurs face a problem like this, the increased price is often passed to the customer as well.

The last chief concern for entrepreneurs for 2007 was increased competition from an ever-increasing global economy. Some businesses believe that the best way to beat the competition is to offer the best prices. However, others believe that taking care of customers better than other businesses will ensure success. Differentiating yourself by becoming customer focused is a great approach for a service company to take. According to Kay, whose company has a 71 percent repeat customer rate, "You don't always have to be the low bidder to be selected for the next project when you operate with this type of strategy."

Michael Shuman, author of *The Small-Mart Revolution: How Local Businesses Are Beating the Global Competition,* mentions that firms should take advantage of manufacturing networks, producer's cooperatives, and joint local delivery systems. Additionally, lobbying local politicians for tax breaks that currently benefit big companies can help. Shuman also suggests that entrepreneurs should take advantage of their built-in advantages, such as selling directly to local markets. Using this strategy minimizes transportation costs, middleman markups, currency exchange risks, Homeland Security hassles, and other issues that hamper global competitors.

Seagroves reminds entrepreneurs that the most important skills for them to possess are flexibility and agility when facing problems. It is important not to get tunnel vision when dealing with today's problems, because they will eventually pass and a new set of hurdles will arise in their place.

Adapted from Mark Henricks, "A Look Ahead," *Entrepreneur* (January 2007): 70–76.

ENTREPRENEURIAL MOTIVATION

Examining the people who start new ventures and how they differ from those who do not may help explain how the motivation that entrepreneurs exhibit during start-up is linked to the sustaining behavior exhibited later. Lanny Herron and Harry J. Sapienza have stated, "Because motivation plays an important part in the creation of new organizations, theories of organization creation that fail to address this notion are incomplete."[11]

Thus, although research on the psychological characteristics of entrepreneurs has not provided an agreed-upon profile of an entrepreneur, it is still important to recognize the contribution of psychological factors to the entrepreneurial process.[12] In fact, the quest for new venture creation as well as the willingness to *sustain* that venture are directly related to an entrepreneur's *motivation*. One research study examined the importance of satisfaction to an entrepreneur's willingness to remain with the venture. Particular goals, attitudes, and backgrounds were all important determinants of an entrepreneur's eventual satisfaction.[13] In that context, Figure 1-1 illustrates the key elements of an

FIGURE 1-1   A Model of Entrepreneurial Motivation

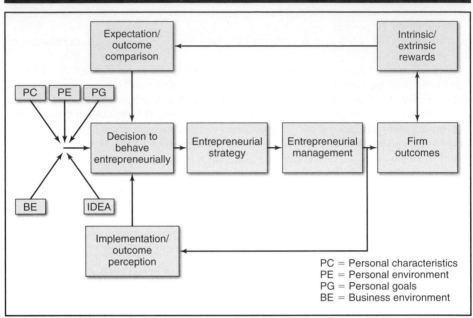

Source: Naffziger, Douglas W., Jeffrey S. Hornsby, and Donald F. Kuratko, "A Proposed Research Model of Entrepreneurial Motivation," *Entrepreneurship Theory & Practice* (Spring 1994): 29–42.

approach or model that examines the motivational process an entrepreneur experiences.[14]

The decision to behave entrepreneurially is the result of the interaction of several factors. One set of factors includes the individual's personal characteristics, the individual's personal environment, the relevant business environment, the individual's personal goal set, and the existence of a viable business idea.[15] In addition, the individual compares his or her perception of the probable outcomes with the personal expectations he or she has in mind. Next, an individual looks at the relationship between the entrepreneurial behavior he or she would implement and the expected outcomes.

According to the model, the entrepreneur's expectations are finally compared with the actual or perceived firm outcomes. Future entrepreneurial behavior is based on the results of all of these comparisons. When outcomes meet or exceed expectations, the entrepreneurial behavior is positively reinforced, and the individual is motivated to continue to behave entrepreneurially, either within the current venture or possibly through the initiation of additional ventures, depending on the existing entrepreneurial goal. When outcomes fail to meet expectations, the entrepreneur's motivation will be lower and will have a corresponding impact on the decision to continue to act entrepreneurially. These perceptions also affect succeeding strategies, strategy implementation, and management of the firm.[16]

Thus, we are experiencing a phenomenon of new venture creation throughout the world today. It has energized economies around the globe and become the most important business concept of the 21st century. Let us examine the advantages and disadvantages associated with starting these new and growing ventures.

ADVANTAGES TO STARTING A NEW VENTURE

Despite the failure record of businesses, the desire for individuals to own and operate their own new venture is still growing. As stated earlier, this continual creation of new businesses is at the heart of a free enterprise system. For individuals pursuing a career in business ownership, numerous benefits can be attained personally as well as professionally. The next section examines the following more common advantages of owning a new venture:

- Independence
- Financial opportunities
- Community service
- Job security
- Family employment
- Challenge

INDEPENDENCE

Most new venture owners enjoy being their own boss; they like the freedom to do things their way. Although a great deal of responsibility often is associated with this independence, they are willing to assume it.

FINANCIAL OPPORTUNITIES

Another major reason for going into business for oneself is financial opportunity. Many new venture owners make more money running their own company than they would working for someone else.

COMMUNITY SERVICE

Sometimes an individual will realize that a particular good or service is not available. If the person has reason to believe the public will pay for such an output, he or she will start a company to provide it.

JOB SECURITY

When one owns a business, job security is ensured. The individual can work as long as he or she wants; no mandatory retirement exists.

FAMILY EMPLOYMENT

Another advantage is the opportunity to provide family members with a place of employment. This has several benefits. First, many owners/managers want to perpetuate their business; how better to do so than to have children or relatives take it over? Second, higher morale and trust usually occur in family-run businesses than in others. Third, in times of severe economic downturn, new venture owners can provide employment for family members.

CHALLENGE

Many new venture owners are lured by the challenge that accompanies going into business for oneself. Research reveals that most successful new venture owners like to feel they have a chance to succeed (they want to know success is possible) and a chance to fail (success is not a sure thing). But one thing is certain: *The final outcome depends heavily on them.* They want to win or lose on their own abilities. This challenge gives them psychological satisfaction.

DISADVANTAGES OF STARTING A NEW VENTURE

Some drawbacks to owning a new venture do exist. Without proper preparation, an individual may find the career path of business ownership frustrating. The major disadvantages of going into business include the following:

- Sales fluctuations
- Competition
- Increased responsibilities
- Financial losses
- Employee relations
- Laws and regulations
- Risk of failure

SALES FLUCTUATIONS

Working for a large firm that pays regularly allows the employee to budget food expenditures, plan vacations, and buy clothing. The venture owner/entrepreneur, however, often faces sales fluctuations. In some months sales are very high, and in others they drop off dramatically. The individual must balance cash inflows with cash outflows so that enough money to meet expenses always exists. Sometimes this will require the owner to take a short-term loan (30 to 90 days) to help the business get through a slack period. Virtually every new venture experiences sales fluctuations. For example, auto dealers have their best sales in months when new models come out (November and December) and in the summer (June and July), when people start thinking about buying a new car. Retail stores find that their greatest sales volume occurs during the end-of-year holiday season. Manufacturers of swimwear obtain their largest sales prior to summer, when they sell their merchandise to wholesalers and retailers. Construction firms have their best months during the summer, when the weather is good.

COMPETITION

A second disadvantage of owning a business is the risk of competition. In particular, an individual may start a business and prosper for three or four years before meeting insurmountable competition. Or changes in market demand may occur, and the owner will find that the new demand is being satisfied by large competitors. For example, small restaurants and diners may lose customers to fast-food chains.

INCREASED RESPONSIBILITIES

New venture owners face many responsibilities, especially as their operations get larger. For example, owners not only have to make more decisions on major matters, they also have to become knowledgeable in many different areas. A successful owner is often a bookkeeper, accountant, salesperson, personnel manager, and janitor all rolled into one. The individual works long hours and, in many cases, six or seven days per week. This is in direct contrast to workers who hold full-time, nine-to-five jobs in which salary is guaranteed and raises and promotions can be counted on.

FINANCIAL LOSSES

When the owner makes all major decisions, inevitably some of them will be wrong. On occasion, inventory will be too high (or low); a product line developed at great expense will not sell; a price reduction will not increase product demand, with a resulting decline in total revenue; an advertising campaign will not pay for itself; or an increase in the sales force will prove to be a mistake, and excess personnel will have to be laid off.

In all of these cases the owner will face a financial loss; if enough of them occur, bankruptcy may result. However, this is not what usually happens. Rather, the owner simply ends up making less money, resulting in a small return on investment for a great deal of effort, work, and risk. Additionally, it is important to note that unless the business is incorporated, the owner is *personally* responsible for all losses. This means the individual could lose everything he or she owns, although in some states the person's home is protected from creditors until the individual chooses to sell it.

EMPLOYEE RELATIONS

The new venture owner also needs to be concerned with employee relations. If the workers are not content, sales will suffer. For example, in many retail stores employees are not allowed to talk or socialize on the job. Workers are expected to remain at their sales counters and stay alert for customers who need assistance. Management believes that if the employees begin talking to one another, they will lose potential sales. On the other hand, research reveals that if employees feel isolated or alone, their attitudes toward the job will decline. This, in turn, will affect their sales ability. They will be rude or curt to the customer, who will then refuse to buy. Thus, a balance must be struck regarding how much socialization can be allowed. Solving this problem requires human relations skills.

Many other employee relations or human resource management issues are also faced by the entrepreneur. For example, friction among workers who do not like each other requires the owner to resolve the conflict either by getting the employees to put aside their personal differences or by firing one or more of them. Another common problem is job assignment—who will do what? The owner must be careful not to overload one person with work while another does virtually nothing. Financial compensation is also an issue. How much should each person be paid? When should raises be given? How large should each raise be? Finally, should salaries be secret, or should the owner let everyone know how much each person is being paid?

Questions such as these exemplify the employee relations problems the owner must resolve. As the enterprise grows and more people are hired, more issues arise. Some of the most common relate to medical insurance, retirement programs, other fringe benefits, and unionization. In short, company growth requires addressing more employee relations issues.

LAWS AND REGULATIONS

New ventures are subject to a multitude of laws and regulations. For example, federal law requires the owner to pay Social Security taxes for all employees as well as to withhold federal taxes from each person's pay and remit these funds to the government. At the state level, in addition to employee taxes, often a state sales tax has to be collected and sent to the proper state agency. Also, for some fields the state required that a license be secured before a business operates; typical examples include restaurants, barbershops, beauty salons, and liquor stores. At the local level, laws often regulate the days of the week and hours of the day during which business can be conducted. In addition, safety and health requirements cover fire prevention and the avoidance of job hazards. Finally, building and zoning regulations limit the type of structures that can be built and where they can be located. For example, in most cities, office and business buildings are not allowed in the same locale as residential homes.

RISK OF FAILURE

The ultimate risk the new venture owner/manager faces is failure, usually with a loss of most, if not all, of the money invested in the enterprise. All entrepreneurs face this risk, and, despite experience and business knowledge, many fail because of factors beyond their control. For example, a major recession hits most new ventures very hard. Meanwhile, despite precautions, every year some companies are forced into bankruptcy because their funds are embezzled by insiders who systematically drain their financial resources. In addition, disasters can strike, such as the terrible hurricanes that have ravaged so many cities (including New Orleans in 2005), totally demolishing many businesses. In each of these cases, the company may be forced to close its doors. In most instances, however, failure is caused by poor management.

NEW VENTURE FAILURE

Every year, many new venture firms cease operations. The most frequent cause is failure to pay debts, in which case it is common for the owners to declare bankruptcy and to seek to accommodate the creditors, such as by paying them 25 cents on the dollar. In other instances, businesses go out of existence because the owners realize that, although they are currently solvent, if they continue operations they will incur debts they cannot meet. In these instances, *business failure* can be defined as "a halt of operations."

SPECIFIC CAUSES OF FAILURE

Year after year, the major reason that businesses fail is incompetence — the owners simply do not know how to run the enterprise. They make major mistakes that an experienced, well-trained entrepreneur would see quickly and easily sidestep.[17]

The second most common reason businesses fail is unbalanced experience the owners do not have well-rounded experience in the major activities of the business, such as finance, purchasing, selling, and production. Because the owner lacks experience in one or more of these critical areas, the enterprise gradually fails.

A third common cause of business failure is lack of managerial experience — the owners simply do not know how to manage people. A fourth common reason is lack of experience in the line; that is, the owner has entered a business field in which he or she has very little knowledge.

Other common causes of business failure include neglect, fraud, and disaster. Neglect occurs when an owner does not pay sufficient attention to the enterprise. The owner who has someone else manage the business while he or she goes fishing often finds the business failing because of neglect. Fraud involves intentional misrepresentation or deception. If one of the people responsible for keeping the business's books begins purchasing materials or goods for him- or herself with the company's money, the business might find itself bankrupt before too long. Of course, the owner can sue the individual for recovery of the merchandise and have him or her sent to jail, but that may happen after the firm's creditors have demanded payment for their merchandise and the owner has had to close the business. Disaster refers to some unforeseen happening or "act of God." If a hurricane hits the area and destroys materials sitting in the company's yard, the loss may require the firm to declare bankruptcy. The same is true for fires, burglaries, or extended strikes.[18]

FAILURE: A LOOK AT THE RECORD

How great has business failure been in the recent past? To answer this question, we must first identify the two types of business failure: firm terminations and business bankruptcies. Firm termination means that an entity no longer exists; this can be for any reason (e.g., the owner grew tired of the business and simply decided to close the doors). However, business bankruptcy is quite different from firm termination. Business bankruptcies result from assets being liquidated and debts owed to creditors—in this case, the owner has no option but to quit the business. Firm terminations in the United States totaled 544,300 in 2004 compared to 544,800 in 2005, an increase of less than one-tenth of a percent. However, business bankruptcy rates increased much more significantly during the same period, totaling 34,317 in 2004 and 39,201 in 2005—an increase of over 14 percent.

Examining such failures more closely leads to two conclusions. First, termination rates vary by region of the country. For example, business terminations in the Mountain states increased by 11.9 percent from 2004 to 2005, whereas those in the Northeast region decreased by 12.6 percent. Business terminations in the West/Northwest region decreased by 7.9 percent from 2004 to 2005, but those in the East Central region increased by 7.4 percent.[19]

The second conclusion that can be reached about business terminations is that survival rates vary by industry. For example, 42 percent of firms in the education and health services sector were still in operation seven years after inception from 1998 to 2005. In contrast, only 25 percent of firms in the information sector were still in existence during the same period.

THE NEW VENTURE SURVIVAL RATE

As a final note in this section, we must acknowledge the surprising rate of survival among smaller ventures. Debunking many myths about failure rates, recent studies are demonstrating a much higher level of survival for these enterprises than ever envisioned. The most recent statistics show an overall 31.2 percent survival rate over a seven-year period, from 1998 to 2005 (see Figure 1-2).[20]

AVOIDING NEW VENTURE MANAGEMENT TRAPS

Over the years, numerous studies of new venture failure have revealed a number of avoidable management traps. The following list provides 10 of the more specific managerial causes of new venture failure, based on a study of businesses that failed.

Inadequate records   Many bankrupt firms simply have inadequate records.

Expansion beyond resources   Some firms grow rapidly, and their bookkeeping systems are not designed to handle dramatic growth. In numerous cases, venture owners simply tried to save money on their bookkeeping system by taking shortcuts—all with disastrous effects.

Lack of information about customers   Unsuccessful firms generally lack information about their customers. For example, one company had been shipping goods to customers without making credit investigations. In many cases, accounts were 90 to 120 days or more in arrears.

Failure to diversify market   A loss of one customer would have a tremendous effect on overall revenue. Some firms contract *all* of their output to one buyer. If that buyer cancels the contract, the company could go bankrupt.

FIGURE 1-2 Survival Rates of New Establishments from Second Quarter of 1998

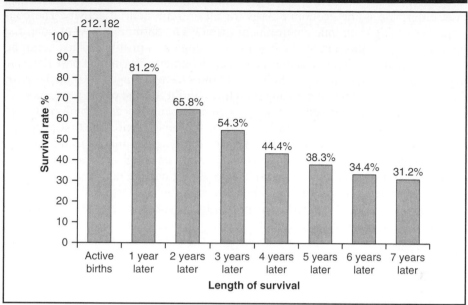

Source: Knaup, Amy E. and Merissa C. Piazza. Characteristics of Survival: Longevity of Business Establishments in the Business Employment Dynamics Data: Extensions. Bureau of Labor Statistics. 2006.

Lack of marketing research   Major ventures are started without any market research being conducted. Changes in market conditions can leave a firm in a very poor position. Lack of market research can be a recipe for disaster.

Legal problems   Saving money on legal fees could be extremely short-sighted. When long, drawn-out patent infringement proceedings become necessary, firms are ill prepared to deal with them. Using the foresight to obtain competent legal advice from the beginning, many problems can be avoided.

Nepotism   Favoritism toward family members could actually cause the enterprise's failure. One of the most typical examples is the practice of carrying family members on the payroll who receive high salaries but contribute little to the overall running of the business.

One-person management   One-person management can lead to company failure. One person's technical genius serving as the reason for the company's success is fine. However, without that person, will the business fail?

Lack of technical competence   Companies suffer from a lack of technical competence when the owners do not understand basic technology or, worse, retain no one on their management team who does.

Absentee management   When the owner stays away for long periods, the operation gradually deteriorates. Financial records can be neglected, taxes may fall behind, customers will be ignored, and so forth. Given such developments, a company will fail.

Summary

Free enterprise is the economic basis for all entrepreneurial activity. The constantly changing economic environment provides a continuous flow of potential opportunities for those individuals who can recognize a profitable idea amid the chaos and cynicism that permeate such an environment. During the past 10 years, new business incorporations in the United States have averaged 600,000 *per year*. The entrepreneurial flame has caught on throughout the rest of the world as well.

New and emerging ventures make two indispensable contributions to the world economy: They are an integral part of the renewal process that pervades and defines market economies, and they are the essential mechanism by which millions enter the economic and social mainstream of our global society.

The entrepreneur is the aggressive catalyst for change in the world of business. *Entrepreneurship* is more than the mere creation of a business; the entrepreneurial process is an integrated concept that has revolutionized the way business is conducted at every level around the globe.

The quest for new venture creation and the willingness to *sustain* that venture are directly related to an entrepreneur's motivation. The decision to behave entrepreneurially is the result of the interaction of several factors, including the individual's personal characteristics, the individual's personal environment, the relevant business environment, the individual's personal goal set, and the existence of a viable business idea.

Individuals who create new ventures experience a number of advantages, including independence, financial opportunities, community service, job security, family employment, and challenges. On the other hand, they also face numerous disadvantages, including sales fluctuations, competition, increased responsibilities, financial losses, employee relations, laws and regulations, and the risk of failure.

In terms of management traps, 10 management-related causes account for most new venture failures. Some of the specific traps are inadequate records, lack of marketing research, legal problems, and lack of information about customers.

When determining whether new venture ownership should be a career goal, a person should carefully weigh the expected growth in a particular industry and analyze why some firms succeed and others fail.

Review and Discussion Questions

1. What is your personal definition of a new venture? What criteria do you use to formulate your definition?
2. Briefly describe what is meant by the term *entrepreneurship*.
3. Describe the predominance of new ventures in the economy.
4. New and emerging ventures make two indispensable contributions to the world economy. Identify each clearly.
5. How would you define an entrepreneur? Use specific characteristics from the chapter.
6. The decision to behave entrepreneurially is the result of the interaction of several factors. Describe these in relation to Figure 1-1.

7. What are the advantages of going into a new venture for oneself? List and explain at least four.
8. What are some of the disadvantages of going into a new venture for oneself? List and explain at least four.
9. Describe the rates of business failure in the United States. Have failures increased or decreased?
10. What are some other major reasons why new ventures fail? Explain them.

NEW VENTURE CONSULTANT

A Business Opportunity?

Calvin Horowitz is thinking about buying a dance studio. He learned about the business opportunity from the owner himself. Calvin takes dancing lessons every Wednesday evening. One night, after finishing his lesson, he was in the hallway having a cup of coffee when the owner, Mark Cecil, came by. Cecil told Calvin that he had been talking to his accountant about selling the business. "I've owned this studio for 23 years," Cecil told Calvin, "and now I want to sell and retire. I'm looking around right now for someone who would like to buy the business." Calvin was excited about the prospect and asked Cecil a lot of questions about the operation.

From what Calvin could determine from the conversation, Cecil has six full-time instructors and nine part-time instructors. Approximately 130 people take lessons each week. Some of these individuals are signed up for 10- and 20-lesson contracts, whereas others walk in off of the street and ask for a particular dance lesson.

Calvin is in the insurance business and does not know a great deal about owning a dance studio. However, he did spend an evening looking over Cecil's operations earlier this week and found that it is very difficult to tell from the records exactly how much revenue Cecil has taken in this year. Some people pay by check and others with cash, and not all of these amounts have been entered in the books. Nor is it possible to pinpoint how many people actually come in for lessons because the instructors sometimes collect the money themselves and—if it is cash—give Cecil his share and pocket the rest. Additionally, Cecil has had three good years and two poor ones during the past five—last year was one of the good ones.

Finally, Cecil does not seem to know (or at least he is not telling Calvin) a great deal about the customers who come in for lessons. However, he does run an ad every week in the Sunday edition of the local paper and believes that this is how people learn about his dance studio, in addition to the word-of-mouth advertising from his clientele. Cecil also believes that he accounts for some of this business himself because he arrives at the studio every day at midmorning and does not go home until after the last lesson. As a result, Cecil knows all of the clients personally and encourages them to keep up their lessons and have their friends come along with them.

After thinking the matter over, Calvin is not sure whether this venture has real potential. He lacks so much information about the business that it will be very difficult to make a decision. However, he has told Cecil that he will let him know within two weeks.

Your consultation: Into which of the management traps discussed in this chapter has Cecil fallen? Explain. What would you advise Calvin to do? Why?

Endnotes

1. Donald F. Kuratko, "A Tribute to 50 Years of Excellence in Entrepreneurship and Small Business," *Journal of Small Business Management* 44, no. 3 (2006): 483–92.
2. www.bizstat.com, June 2005; U.S. Small Business Administration (SBA), www.sba.gov, 2006.
3. SBA, www.sba.gov/advocacy/research, 2006.
4. Center for Women's Business Research, www.cfwbr.org, 2007.
5. The Tax Foundation, www.taxfoundation.org, 2007.
6. M. Minniti and W. D. Bygrave, *Global Entrepreneurship Monitor* (Kansas City, MO: Kauffman Center for Entrepreneurial Leadership, 2004); see also Michael H. Morris and Minet Schindehutte, "Entrepreneurial Values and the Ethnic Enterprise: An Examination of Six Subcultures," *Journal of Small Business Management* 43, no. 4 (2005): 453–97.
7. Donald F. Kuratko and Richard M. Hodgetts, *Entrepreneurship: Theory, Process, & Practice,* 7th ed. (Mason, OH: Thomson/Southwestern, 2007).
8. Bruce Tulgan, "Generation X: The Future is Now," *Entrepreneur of the Year Magazine* (Fall 1999): 42.
9. John J. Kao, *The Entrepreneur* (Englewood Cliffs, NJ: Prentice-Hall, 1991).
10. Benyamin B. Lichtenstein, Kevin J. Dooley, and G. T. Lumpkin, "Measuring Emergence in the Dynamics of New Venture Creation," *Journal of Business Venturing* 21. no. 2 (2006) :153–76.
11. Lanny Herron and Harry J. Sapienza, "The Entrepreneur and the Initiation of New Venture Launch Activities," *Entrepreneurship Theory and Practice* (Fall 1992): 49–55.
12. Kelly G. Shaver and Linda R. Scott, "Person, Process, Choice: The Psychology of New Venture Creation," *Entrepreneurship Theory and Practice* (Winter 1991): 23–45.
13. Arnold C. Cooper and Kendall W. Artz, "Determinants of Satisfaction for Entrepreneurs," *Journal of Business Venturing* (November 1995): 439–58.
14. Douglas W. Naffziger, Jeffrey S. Hornsby, and Donald F. Kuratko, "A Proposed Research Model of Entrepreneurial Motivation," *Entrepreneurship Theory and Practice* (Spring 1994): 29–42.
15. A. Rebecca Rueber and Eileen Fischer, "Understand the Consequences of Founders' Experience," *Journal of Small Business Management* (February 1999): 30–45.
16. Donald F. Kuratko, Jeffrey S. Hornsby, and Douglas W. Naffziger, "An Examination of Owner's Goals in Sustaining Entrepreneurship," *Journal of Small Business Management* (January 1997): 24–33.
17. William P. Sommers and Aydin Koc, "Why Most New Ventures Fail (and How Others Don't)," *Management Review* (September 1987): 35–39.
18. See Harriet Buckman Stephenson, "The Most Critical Problem for the Fledgling Small Business: Getting Sales," *American Journal of Small Business* (Summer 1984): 26–32; and Erkki K. Laitinen, "Prediction of Failure of a Newly Founded Firm," *Journal of Business Venturing* 7 (1992): 323–40.
19. Office of Advocacy of the U.S. Small Business Administration, *The Small Business Economy: A Report to the President* (Washington, DC: Government Printing Office, 2006).
20. Amy E. Knaup and Merissa C. Piazza. *Characteristics of Survival: Longevity of Business Establishments in the Business Employment Dynamics Data—Extensions.* (Washington, DC: U.S. Bureau of Labor Statistics, 2006).

CHAPTER

NEW OR ACQUIRED VENTURES
THE PATHWAYS

INTRODUCTION

The most effective way to approach a new business venture is to create a unique product or service: one that is not being offered today but, if it were, would be in great demand.[1] The next-best way is to adapt something that is currently on the market or extend the offering into an area where it is not presently available. The first approach is often referred to as *new-new,* the second as *new-old.* Remember: Each approach can lead to entrepreneurial success.

APPROACHES TO NEW VENTURE CREATION

NEW-NEW APPROACH

We are always hearing about new products or services entering the market. Typical examples include smartphones, MP3 players, plasma televisions, and global positioning systems (GPSs). All of these products, and more, have been introduced as a result of research and development (R&D) efforts by major corporations; see Table 2-1 for a list of emerging ideas. What we must realize, however, is that unique ideas are not produced only by large companies. Moreover, the rate at which new products enter the market has caused the public to expect many of their household goods to be innovated and improved continuously. Figure 2-1 presents the life-cycle stages of some common products. Note that some are beginning to be accepted, some are in the maturity stage, and others are no longer in demand.

TABLE 2-1   Trends Creating Business Opportunities

Emerging Opportunities	Emerging Internet Opportunities	Emerging Technology Opportunities
Green products	**Mobile advertising**	Nanotechnology
Organic foods	Cell phones	Wireless technology
Organic fibers/textiles	PDAs	
Alternative energy	**"Concierge services"**	
Solar	**Niche social networks**	
Biofuel	Seniors	
Fuel cells	Music fans	
Energy conservation	Groups of local users	
Health care	Pet owners	
Healthy food	Dating groups	
School- and government-sponsored programs	**Virtual economies**	
Exercise	Online auctions	
Yoga	**Educational tutoring**	
Niche gyms	**Human resources services**	
Children	"Matchmaking"	
Nonmedical	"Virtual HR"	
Pre-assisted living	"Online staffing"	
Assisted living transition services		
Niche consumables		
Wine		
Chocolate		
Burgers		
Coffee products		
Exotic salads		
Home automation and media storage		
Lighting control		
Security systems		
Energy management		
Comfort management		
Entertainment systems		
Networked kitchen appliances		

Source: Steve Cooper, Amanda C. Kooser, Kristin Ohlson, Karen E. Spaeder, Nichole L. Torres, and Sara Wilson, "2007 Hot List," *Entrepreneur* (December 2006): 80–93.

FIGURE 2-1   Life-Cycle Stages of Various Products

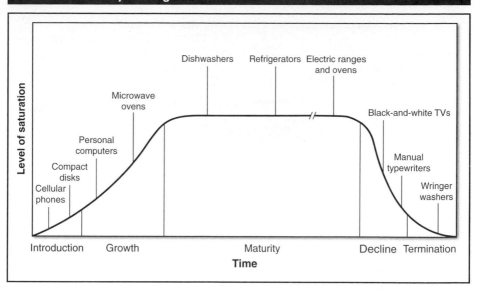

How does one discover or invent new products? One of the easiest ways is to make a list of annoying experiences or hazards encountered during a given period of time with various products or services. Common examples include objects that fall out of one's hand, household chores that are difficult to do, and items that are hard to store. Can innovations alleviate these problems? This is how some people get ideas for new products. As an example, James Ritty once observed the mechanism for recording the revolutions of a ship's propeller. As he watched the device tally the propeller's revolutions, he realized that the idea could be adapted to the recording of sales transactions, a problem he had been trying to solve for some time. The result led to the eventual development of the modern cash register.

Most business ideas tend to come from people's experiences. Figure 2-2 illustrates the sources of new business ideas from a study conducted by the National Federation of Independent Business.

One hot area is Internet social utilities such as Facebook and MySpace. Facebook was founded by Mark Zuckerberg, a Harvard University student who was frustrated by the lack of networking facilities on campus. The company was founded in February 2004 and is now the largest source for photos and one of the most trafficked sites on the Internet. In two short years, the company has received sale offers of $750 million from Viacom[2] and $900 million from Yahoo.[3]

In general, the main sources of ideas to create something new for both men and women are prior jobs, hobbies or interests, and personally identified problems. This indicates the importance of people's awareness of their daily lives (work and free time) for developing new business ideas.

FIGURE 2-2 **Sources of New Business Ideas Among Men and Women**

Sources of new business ideas among men and women

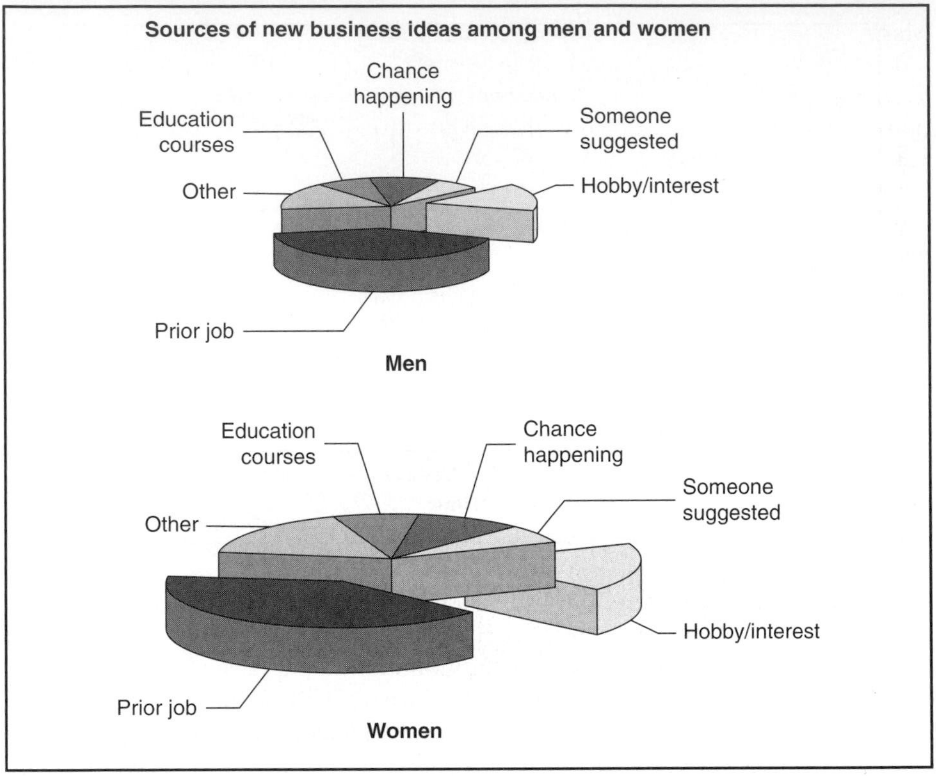

Source: William J. Dennis, *A Small Business Primer* (Washington, DC: National Federation of Independent Business, 1993), 27. Reprinted with permission.

NEW-OLD APPROACH

Most small ventures do not start with a totally unique idea. Instead, an individual "piggybacks" on someone else's idea either by improving a product or by offering a service in an area where it is not currently available. Some of the most common examples are setting up restaurants, clothing stores, or similar outlets in sprawling suburban areas that do not already have an abundance of these stores. Of course, these kinds of operations can be risky because competitors can move in easily. Potential entrepreneurs considering this kind of enterprise should try to offer a product or service that is difficult to copy. For example, a computerized billing and accounting service for medical doctors can be successful if the business has a sufficient number of doctors (18 to 25) to cover the cost of computer operators and administrative expenses in order to turn an adequate profit. Or perhaps another type of enterprise is likely to be overlooked by other would-be entrepreneurs.

Regardless of whether the business is based on a new-new or a new-old idea, the prospective entrepreneur cannot rely exclusively on gut feeling or intuition to get started. Market analysis is the key to a successful venture.

MARKET ANALYSIS

Market analysis can help a prospective business entrepreneur determine whether a demand for a particular good or service exists and whether this demand is sufficient to justify starting a business operation. Large firms do a great deal of market analysis, but such efforts are not restricted to them alone. New smaller ventures can, and must, conduct market research in order to assess the best product or service offerings and acceptable pricing structure.[4] It need not cost much money, for the prospective entrepreneur/manager can perform most of the data gathering and analysis him- or herself.[5] All a person needs to do is accurately formulate the questions that need to be answered and then objectively analyze the data received in response to these questions. In essence, *market analysis* is the application of the scientific method to business problems. The following steps constitute the *scientific method,* which can be used to evaluate a good or a service:

1. State the problem or question in as clear a manner as possible.
2. Gather all the necessary facts about the problem or question.
3. Organize and analyze the facts.
4. Develop one or more courses of action, keeping in mind the pros and cons of each.
5. Select the best alternative and implement it.
6. Observe the progress of this alternative and adjust it as required.

This method can be used not only by people entering a new venture for the first time but also by businesspeople who already are conducting operations and looking at the possibility of expanding their business into new lines or products. However, our attention here is confined to new ventures. The prospective entrepreneur can analyze a business opportunity by breaking the scientific method into four basic steps:

1. Gathering of the facts
2. Organization of the facts
3. Analysis of the facts
4. Implementation of an action plan

GATHERING OF THE FACTS

The first step in analyzing a business opportunity is to gather information about the proposed venture. Who would be attracted to this product or service? How many people in the area would buy it? What market trends may affect the product or service? (See the "New Venture Perspective" box feature on future market trends.) What sales volume would be needed to break even? Do any competitors exist in the area? How well established are they? What does the future of the business look like? Answers to these types of questions can be obtained by reading

---

Trends for Success

She does not use a crystal ball, but Faith Popcorn, a futurist, can see some of the major trends swaying many consumer buying decisions. Popcorn believes that those who understand the future will make fewer mistakes and become more successful. By spotting the trends that will shape marketplaces, she hopes to help entrepreneurs start and grow their businesses. She reaches those entrepreneurs through her marketing consulting firm, Brain-Reserve. How well does Popcorn do at predicting the trends of tomorrow? According to her, she hasn't been wrong about a trend yet.

Popcorn states that, as a marketer, she finds trend knowledgeable invaluable. In her book *Clicking,* she identifies some of the most influential trends driving the marketplace. These are not fads; they are big, sweeping consumer movements that savvy entrepreneurs see as viable opportunities. Since publishing her book, she has provided a yearly set of predictions regarding consumer trends. The following are her predicted trends for the 21st century.

- **Cocooning:** The desire to shelter ourselves from the harsh realities of the outside world.
- **Fantasy adventure:** The need for the new and unconventional. We seek out ways to escape from our problems and experiment with our desires.
- **Skin deeper:** According to Popcorn, our material focus has left us emotionally starved. Due to longer work hours and more emphasis on virtual relationships, we will increasingly want physical contact.
- **BrainFitness:** According to Popcorn, a mental fitness boom is on the horizon. The focus on mental agility will parallel the need for prolonging physical fitness and youthful appearance.
- **Secondhand nostalgia:** As a result of the stresses and concerns of life, we will seek out safe places that allow for a retreat. We will also trend toward activities that were popular during safe times, such as the 1950s (e.g., eating at old-fashioned diners, hiking and camping as outdoor activities, and more community involvement).
- **America's Next Top Surgery:** The rage of reality surgery shows and the increased medical advancements will lead to an obsession with risky surgeries. Also, playing to the fantasy adventure trend, people will be motivated to try new surgeries to cure illnesses and improve appearance.
- **No recognition of age:** The enormous baby boomer market is aging into their 60s and 70s. These boomers view themselves as young and will demand products to meet their needs; however, they will not want products labeled for the elderly. Popcorn suggests that one such outcome could be larger, easier-to-read dials in luxury automobiles such as BMWs and Infinitis.
- **The ease of expertise:** Given the availability of information on the Internet, *expertise* takes on a new meaning. According to Popcorn, "Expertise is no longer earned through years of training; all it takes is a little research." She claims that

we have lost the preferred taste for actual experience and have replaced it with virtual experiences.

- **DeBug–ReBug:** In the past we have focused on removing bad organisms from the environment. Recently, biologists have identified that some organisms can be beneficial and improve health. Popcorn suggests that spas and health care entities will offer "designer" treatments of advantageous organisms.

- **Mood tuning:** According to Popcorn, we now expect that the things we buy will adjust our feelings. We will seek out biologically enhanced purchases that will cause us to feel more confident, sexy, or whatever the situation dictates.

Source: Adapted from "Faith Popcorn's Predictions for 2006," *Arizona Reporter,* www.azreporter.com/news/features/2006/faithpopcorn.shtml (accessed October 10, 2006).

industry journals, obtaining data from the Small Business Association, and talking to a local banker who is knowledgeable about the area.

ORGANIZATION OF THE FACTS

After all of the facts have been gathered, they must be organized in a logical fashion. Facts related to costs and revenues should be kept together, because this information will help the individual compute the breakeven point for operations. Competition and projected sales in the local area should be kept together, because this information can be used to project an estimate of market share. Facts related to industry growth can be used to make projections regarding future sales and profit potential. Organizing the facts in this fashion allows for a more thorough analysis of the information at hand.

ANALYSIS OF THE FACTS

In the analysis stage, the prospective entrepreneur answers the question, "What does it all mean?" In some cases, answering this question is not difficult because the information speaks for itself. For example, is the return on investment in this business high enough to justify the risk? Does the operation's future look promising? Answers to such questions provide the individual with insights about the potential of certain businesses.

Analyses of sales and cost data will provide the would-be entrepreneur with an idea of the profit margin. This can be compared with data on typical profit margins in the industry, which can be obtained from resources found in any business college library or from the Small Business Administration.

Another common analysis involves determining the number of competing firms in the area and the number of total customers. Is the population large enough to support another business? This approach can be used to estimate the potential sales volume of a proposed store.

Still another way to analyze data is to use an index of sales potential, such as an index of consumer purchasing power. For example, *Sales and Marketing*

Management magazine publishes a "Buying Power Index" each year. The magazine also contains information useful for setting sales quotas, planning distribution, and studying sales potential. Information on population and income is provided for every state by county and city. This type of information can help the prospective entrepreneur/manager predict sales in the area and determine whether the business would be an acceptable risk.

Still another type of analysis involves *consumer surveys*. These surveys attempt to learn what customers want. They do not have to be conducted by the prospective entrepreneur; consumer surveys are often conducted by colleges and universities or chambers of commerce and generally are available to the public. These surveys provide important information about local consumer demand, often revealing data that contradict national norms. For instance, although an area may have twice as many outlets as the national average, local consumer demand might be such that room still exists for another outlet.

IMPLEMENTATION OF AN ACTION PLAN

If the analysis reveals that the business venture is a wise one, the entrepreneur can go ahead and begin operations. The specific procedures to follow during this action phase will be discussed in the next section. For the moment, however, it is imperative to remember that the plan may not work perfectly. Some modification may be necessary. Thus, the entrepreneur has to remain flexible in planning. If something does not work out, a contingency or backup plan should be available. The worst thing the entrepreneur could do is adopt an "all or nothing" perspective. After the analysis is complete and the entrepreneur is ready to proceed, an action plan is needed. What will be done, and how will it be done? This plan should cover three areas:

1. The entrepreneur as a person
2. The financial picture
3. Other key factors (e.g., marketing, insurance, building, etc.)

THE ENTREPRENEUR

Before making the final decision about going into business, the entrepreneur needs to ask a number of personal questions. Ten of the most important ones are listed here. As you read, mark the response that best describes you.

1. Are you a self-starter?
   - I can get going without help from others.
   - Once someone gets me going, I am just fine.
   - I take things easy and do not move until I have to.

2. How do you feel about others?
   - I can get along with just about anyone.
   - I do not need anyone else.
   - People irritate me.

3. Can you lead people?
- I can get most people to go along with me once I start something.
- I can give the orders if someone tells me what should be done.
- I let someone else get things done and go along if I like it.

4. Can you take responsibility?
- I take charge and see things through.
- I'll take over if necessary but would rather let someone else be responsible.
- If someone is around who wants to do it, I let him or her.

5. Are you an organizer?
- I like to have a plan before I begin.
- I do all right unless things get too confusing, in which case I quit.
- Whenever I have things all set up, something always comes along to disrupt the plan, so I take things as they come.

6. Are you a hard worker?
- I can keep going as long as necessary.
- I work hard for a while, but then that's it.
- I cannot see that hard work gets you anywhere.

7. Can you make decisions?
- I can make decisions, and they usually turn out pretty well.
- I can make decisions if I have plenty of time, but fast decision making upsets me.
- I do not like to be the one who has to decide things.

8. Can people rely on your word?
- Yes, I do not say things I do not mean.
- I try to level with people, but sometimes I say what is easiest.
- Why bother? The other person does not know the difference.

9. Can you stick with it?
- When I make up my mind to do something, nothing stops me.
- I usually finish what I start.
- If things start to go awry, I usually quit.

10. How good is your health?
- Excellent.
- Pretty good.
- Okay, but it has been better.

Now count the number of checks you made next to the first responses and multiply this number by 3. Count the checks next to the second responses and multiply by 2. Count the number of times you checked the third answer. Total these three numbers. Out of 30 possible points, a successful entrepreneur will have scored at least 25 points. If not, the prospective entrepreneur/manager should consider bringing in a partner or abandoning the idea of going into business alone. The potential entrepreneur should keep in mind these personal factors when formulating the action plan.

THE FINANCIAL PICTURE

The next plan area the prospective entrepreneur/manager must cover is an evaluation of the enterprise's financial picture. How much will it cost to stay in business for the first year? How much revenue will the firm generate during this time period? If the outflow of cash is greater than the inflow, how long will it take before the entrepreneurial venture turns the corner?

Answering these questions requires consideration of two kinds of expenses: start-up and monthly. Table 2-2 illustrates a typical worksheet for making the

TABLE 2-2 Checklist for Estimating Start-Up Expenses			
MONTHLY EXPENSES		**CASH NEEDED TO START THE BUSINESS** (see column 3)	**WHAT TO PUT IN COLUMN 2** (These figures are estimates; the entrepreneur/ manager decides how many months to allow, depending on the type of business)
Item	Estimate based on sales of $___ per year		
	Column 1	Column 2	Column 3
Salary of entrepreneur/ manager	$	$	3 × Column 1
Other salaries and wages			3 × Column 1
Rent			3 × Column 1
Advertising			3 × Column 1
Delivery expense			3 × Column 1
Supplies			3 × Column 1
Telephone and telegraph			3 × Column 1
Other utilities			3 × Column 1
Insurance			6 × Column 1
Taxes, Social Security			4 × Column 1
Interest			3 × Column 1
Maintenance			3 × Column 1
Legal and other professional assistance			3 × Column 1
Miscellaneous			3 × Column 1

TABLE 2-2 (*Continued*)		
START-UP COSTS		
Item	**Estimate**	**TO ARRIVE AT ESTIMATE**
Fixtures and equipment	$	Determine what is typical for this kind of business; talk to suppliers.
Decorating and remodeling		Talk to a contractor.
Installation of fixtures, equipment		Talk to suppliers.
Starting inventory		Talk to suppliers.
Deposits with public utilities		Talk to utility companies.
Legal and other professional fees		Talk to a lawyer, accountant, or other professional.
Licenses and permits		Contact appropriate city offices.
Advertising and promotion		Decide what will be used; talk to media.
Accounts receivable		Estimate how much will be tied up in receivables by credit customers and for how long.
Cash		Allow for unexpected expenses and losses, special purchases, and other expenditures.
Other Expenses		List them and estimate costs.
TOTAL CASH NEEDED TO START	$_____	Add all estimated amounts.

Source: U.S. Small Business Administration, "Management Aids" MA. 2.025 (Washington, DC: U.S. Government Printing Office).

necessary calculations of start-up expenses. Notice that this worksheet is based on the assumption that no money will flow in for about three months; in addition, all start-up costs are totally covered. If the firm is in the manufacturing business, however, it will be three to four months before any goods are produced and sold, so the factors in Column 3 have to be doubled and the amount of cash needed for start-up will be greater. The same may be true for some service businesses.

Much of the information needed to fill in this worksheet already should have been gathered and at least partially analyzed. Now, however, it can be put into a format that allows the entrepreneur to look at the overall financial picture.

At this point, the individual should be concerned with what is called *upside gain and downside loss.* This term refers to the profits the business can make and the losses it can suffer. How much money will the enterprise take in if everything goes well? How much will it gross if operations run as expected? How much will it lose if operations do not? Answers to these questions provide a composite picture of the most optimistic, the most likely, and the most pessimistic results. The entrepreneur has to keep in mind that the upside may be minimal and the downside loss may be great.

It is necessary to examine overall gains and losses. This kind of analysis is referred to as *risk versus reward* analysis and points out the importance of getting an adequate return on the amount of money risked.

OTHER KEY FACTORS

The third planning area with which the prospective entrepreneur/manager must be concerned consists of operational information that will be examined throughout the remainder of this book. However, these factors warrant attention here because of their importance in start-up activities. Some of the major considerations, expressed in the form of questions, include the following:

- *The location/building*

  Is it currently adequate?
  Can it be fixed up without spending too much money?
  Does it have room for expansion?
  Can people get to it easily from parking spaces, bus stops, or their homes?
  Has a lawyer checked the lease agreement and zoning ordinances?

- *Merchandise and equipment*

  Have suppliers who will sell at reasonable prices been located?
  Have the prices and credit terms of suppliers been compared?
  Have all the equipment and suppliers needed for operation been
    purchased?

- *Record keeping*

  Has a record-keeping system been planned for income and expenses,
    inventory, payroll, and taxes?
  Has an accountant been found to help with records and financial statements?
  Have all the financial statements needed for control purposes been identi-
    fied? Does the entrepreneur/manager know how to use them?

- *Insurance and legal concerns*

  Have plans been made for protecting against insurable losses?
  Have all licenses and permits been obtained?
  Has a lawyer been hired to assist with the legal aspects of the operation?

- *Marketing and personnel*

  Have prices for all goods been determined?
  Has a buying plan been worked out?
  Is an advertising program or some form of promotion ready to go?
  Will credit be given to customers? On what basis?
  Will salespeople be used? If so, how will they be recruited? Is a training pro-
    gram planned for them? How much will they be paid?

If questions like these can be answered, the entrepreneur/manager is in a good position to begin. However, in most cases it is necessary for the individual to look more closely into one or more of these operational areas. Perhaps the individual does not fully understand some aspects of the operation.

BUYING AN ONGOING VENTURE

One of the most frequent opportunities undertaken by individuals is the purchase of an ongoing business. In fact, this may be one of the easiest ways for an entrepreneur to get started. A lot of headaches can be avoided with this approach. For example, start-up problems will have been taken care of by previous entrepreneurs. Additionally, the business has a track record the buyer can examine in order to determine the types of products to sell, the prices to charge, and so on. But buying an existing business also has potential pitfalls. Examples include buying a company whose success has been due to the personality and charisma of the former entrepreneur/manager, buying a company when the market for its product has peaked, or simply paying more for a company than it is worth. In this section, we examine the advantages of buying an ongoing business as well as the key valuation methods that help individuals determine a fair price to pay for someone else's business.

ADVANTAGES OF BUYING AN ONGOING VENTURE

Of the numerous advantages to buying an ongoing business, three of the most important are as follows:

1. Because the enterprise is already in operation, its successful future operation is likely.
2. The time and effort associated with starting a new enterprise are eliminated.
3. It sometimes is possible to buy an ongoing business at a bargain price.

Each of these three advantages is discussed next.

LESS FEAR ABOUT SUCCESSFUL FUTURE OPERATION

A new business faces two great dangers: the possibility that it will not find a market for its goods or services and the chance that it will not be able to control its costs. If either event occurs, the new business will go bankrupt.

Buying an existing concern, however, alleviates most of these fears. A successful business already has demonstrated the ability to attract customers, control costs, and make a profit. Additionally, many of the problems a newly formed firm faces are sidestepped. For example: Where should the company be located? How should it advertise? What type of plant or merchandise layout will be the most effective? What type of service does the potential customer base desire? How much should be reordered every three months? What types of customers will this business attract? What pricing strategy should the firm use? Questions such as these already have been asked and answered. Thus, when buying an ongoing operation, the new entrepreneur is often purchasing a *known quantity*. Of course, it is important to check whether hidden problems exist in the operation. Barring something of this nature, however, the purchase of an existing successful operating venture can be a wise investment.

TIME AND EFFORT CAN BE REDUCED

An ongoing enterprise already has assembled the inventory, equipment, personnel, and facilities necessary to run. In many cases, this has taken the entrepreneurs a long time to do. They have spent countless hours "working out the bugs" so that the business is as efficient as possible. Likewise, they probably have gone through a fair number of employees before getting the right type of personnel. Except for the top management in an operating venture, the personnel usually stay following a sale. Therefore, if the new owners treat the workers fairly, they should not have to worry about hiring, placing, and training personnel.

In addition, the previous owners undoubtedly have established relations with suppliers, bankers, and other businesspeople. These individuals often can be relied on to provide assistance to the new owners. The suppliers know the type of merchandise the business orders and how often it needs to be replenished. They can be a source of advice about managing the operation, as can the bankers with whom the enterprise has been doing business. These individuals know the enterprise's capital needs and often provide new owners with the same credit line and assistance they gave the previous owners. The same holds true for the accountant, the lawyer, and any other professionals who served the business in an advisory capacity. Naturally, the new owners may have their own bankers, accountant, or lawyer, but these established relationships are there if the new owners need them.

BUY AT A GOOD PRICE

Sometimes it is possible to buy an ongoing operating venture at a very good price. The entrepreneur may want to sell quickly because of a retirement decision or illness. The entrepreneur may be forced to sell the business in order to raise money for some emergency that has occurred. Or the entrepreneur may seek a greater opportunity in another type of business and therefore be willing to sell at a low price in order to take advantage of the new opportunity. Ideally, when one is looking to buy an ongoing, successful operating venture, one of these three advantages (especially the last one) is present. However, it is uncommon for someone to sell a successful firm at an extraordinarily low price. The entrepreneur of a successful small venture built the enterprise through skillful business practices, knows how to deal with people, and has a good idea of the operation's fair market value. That person will rarely sell for much below the fair market value. Therefore, the prospective entrepreneur must avoid bidding high on a poor investment or walking away from a good bargain because "it smells fishy." The way to prevent making the wrong decision is to evaluate the existing operation in a logical manner.

KEY QUESTIONS TO ASK

When deciding whether to buy, the astute prospective entrepreneur needs to ask and answer a series of "right questions."[6] The following section provides appropriate questions and insights into the types of actions to take for each response. Although some of these questions may be more pertinent to manufacturing ventures, keep in mind that service and Internet operations may benefit from them as well.

WHY IS THE BUSINESS BEING SOLD?

One of the first questions that should be asked is *why* the owner is selling the business.[7] Quite often a difference exists between the reason given to prospective buyers and the real reason. Typical responses include "I'm thinking about retiring," "I've proven to myself that I can be successful in this line of business, so now I'm moving to another operation that will provide me with new challenges," and "I want to move to California and go into business with my brother-in-law there."

Any of these statements may be accurate, and, if they can be substantiated, the buyer may find that the business is indeed worth purchasing. However, because it is difficult to substantiate this sort of personal information, the next thing to do is to check around and gather business-related information. Is the owner in trouble with the suppliers? Is the lease on the building due for renewal and the landlord planning to triple the rent? Worse yet, is the building about to be torn down? Other site problems may relate to competition in the nearby area or zoning changes. Is a new shopping mall about to be built nearby that will take much of the business away from this location? Has the city council passed a new ordinance that calls for the closing of business on Sunday, the day of the week when this store does 25 percent of its business?

Financially, what is the owner going to do after selling the business? Is the seller planning to stay in town? What employment opportunities does he or she have? The reason for asking these questions is that the new owner's worst nightmare is finding that the previous owner has set up a similar business a block away and is drawing back all of his or her customers. One way to prevent this from happening is to have an attorney write into the contract, for a period of at least five years, a *legal restraint of trade* (i.e., an agreement not to compete, or a noncompete clause). This step helps the new owner retain customers.

WHAT IS THE CURRENT PHYSICAL CONDITION OF THE BUSINESS?

Even if the asking price for the operation appears to be fair, it is necessary to examine the *physical condition* of the assets. Does the company own the building? If it does, how much repair work needs to be done? If the building is leased, does the lease provide for the kinds of repairs that will enhance the successful operation of the business? For example, if a flower shop has a somewhat large refrigerator for keeping flowers cool, who has to pay to expand the size of the refrigerator? If the landlord agrees to do so and to recover the investment through an increase in the lease price, the total cost of the additional refrigerated space must be compared to the expected increase in business. Meanwhile, if the landlord does not want to make this type of investment, the new owners must realize that any permanent additions to the property remain with the property. This means that if something cannot be carried out of the building, it stays. Pictures on the walls, chairs, and desks that the previous business owner purchased can be removed. However, new bookshelves nailed to the wall, carpeting attached to the floor, a new acoustic ceiling installed to cut down on noise in the shop, and the new refrigerated area all become permanent property of the building owner. Therefore, the overriding question while examining the physical facilities is, "How much will it cost to get things in order?"

WHAT IS THE CONDITION OF THE INVENTORY?

How much inventory does the current owner show on the books? Does a physical check show that inventory actually exists? Additionally, is inventory *salable,* or is it out-of-date or badly deteriorated?

WHAT IS THE STATE OF THE COMPANY'S OTHER ASSETS?

Most operating ventures possess assets in addition to the physical facilities and the inventory. A machine shop, for example, may have various types of presses and other machinery. An office may have computers, copiers, and other technology belonging to the business. The question to ask about all of this equipment is, "Is it still useful, or has it been replaced by more modern technology?" In short, are these assets obsolete?

Another often-overlooked asset is the firm's records. If the business has kept careful records, it may be possible to determine who is a good credit risk and who is not. Additionally, these records make it easy for a new owner to decide how much credit to extend to prior customers. Likewise, sales records can be very important because they show seasonal demands and peak periods. This can provide the new owner with information for inventory-control purposes and can greatly reduce the risks of over- or understocking.

Still another commonly overlooked asset is past contracts. What type of lease does the current owner have on the building? If the lease was signed three years ago, and it is a seven-year lease with a fixed rent, the price may have been somewhat high when it went into effect but may be on the low side for comparable facilities at the present time. Furthermore, over the next four years the rent should prove to be quite low, considering what competitors will be paying. Of course, if the lease is about to expire, this is a different story. Then the prospective owner has to talk to the landlord to find out what the terms of the lease will be. Additionally, a prospective entrepreneur's lawyer should look at the old lease to determine whether it can be passed on to a new owner and, regardless of the rent, how difficult it is to break the lease should the business begin to fail.

Finally, the prospective buyer must look at intangible assets such as goodwill, patents, franchise rights, and noncompete agreements. *Goodwill* is often defined as the value of the company beyond what is shown on the books. For example, if a software company has a reputation for quick and accurate service, the company has built up goodwill among its customers. If the owners were to sell the business, the buyer would have to pay not only for the physical assets in the software company (e.g., office furniture, computers, etc.) but for the goodwill the firm has accumulated over the years. Patents, franchise rights, and noncompete agreements are also important when valuing a business, but it is very difficult to assess the future value of these assets. The key issue is that these intangible assets could be a major part of a business's value and should not be overlooked.[8] The reputation of a business has its own value.[9]

HOW MANY OF THE EMPLOYEES WILL REMAIN?

It is often difficult to give customers the good service they have come to expect if seasoned employees decide they do not want to remain with the new owner. The owner is certainly an important asset of the firm, but so are the employees; they play a role in making the business a success. Therefore, one question the prospective buyer must ask is, "If some people will be leaving, will enough be left to maintain the type of service the customer is used to getting?" In particular, the new owner must be concerned with key people who are not staying. Key employees are part of the value of the business. If it is evident that these people will not be staying, the prospective buyer must subtract something from the purchase price by making some allowance for the decline in sales and the accompanying expense associated with replacing key personnel.

When purchasing an existing business, you should also conduct an assessment of the current group of employees. Review existing performance evaluations and talk with current owners about the quality of each employee and his or her value to the business. It may be easier to retain valuable employees by seeking them out before the purchase to ensure their feelings of security. As the incoming new owner, interview all of the current employees and make decisions about who to keep and who to let go before you actually take over the enterprise.

WHAT TYPE OF COMPETITION DOES THE BUSINESS FACE?

No matter what goods or service the business provides, the number of people who will want it and the total amount of money they will spend for it are limited.

Thus, the greater the competition, the less the business's chance of earning large profits. As the number of competitors increases, the cost of fighting them usually goes up. More money must be spent on advertising, and price competition must be met with accompanying reductions in overall revenue. Simply too many companies are pursuing the same market.

Additionally, the *quality of competition* must be considered. If nine competitors exist, you could estimate a market share of 10 percent. However, some of these competitors undoubtedly will be more effective than others. One or two may have very good advertising and know how to use it to capture 25 percent of the market. A few others may offer outstanding service and use this advantage to capture 20 percent of the market. Meanwhile, the remaining six fight for what is left.

Next, the location of the competition must be considered. In many instances, a new venture does not offer anything unique, so people buy on the basis of convenience. A service located on the corner may get most of the business of local residents, and one located across town will get virtually none. If a product is the same at each location, no one is going to drive across town for it. This analogy holds true for groceries, notions, drugs, and hardware. If competitors are located near one another, each will take some of the business that the others could have expected, but none is going to maximize its income. However, if the merchandise is items—such as furniture—people will shop very carefully. In this case, a competitor in the immediate area can be a distinct advantage. For example, two furniture stores located near each other tend to draw a greater number of customers than they would if they were located ten blocks apart. When people shop for furniture, they go where a large selection is available. With adjacent stores, customers will reason that if the furniture they are looking for is not in one, it might be in the other. Additionally, since customers can step from one store to the next, they can easily compare prices and sale terms. Finally, the emergence of the Internet has introduced another competitive threat that must be considered. How effective are Internet sales in this particular industry? Are customers likely to "shop at home" using the Internet as their source?

Any analysis of competition should look for *unscrupulous practices*. How cutthroat are the competitors? If they are very cutthroat, the prospective buyer will have to be continually alert for practices such as price fixing and kickbacks to suppliers for special services. Usually, if the company has been around for a couple of years, it has been successful in dealing with these types of practices. However, if some competitors have bad reputations, the new owner will want to know this. After all, over time the customers are likely to form a stereotyped impression of enterprises in a given geographic area and will simply refuse to do business with any of them (e.g., "It's no use looking for clothing in the Eighth Street area"). Customers may retaliate against unethical business practices by boycotting the entire area in which these firms are located. In short, an unethical business competitor can drag down other firms as well.

WHAT IS THE STATUS OF THE FIRM'S FINANCIAL PICTURE?

It may be necessary for a prospective buyer to hire an accountant to look over the company's books. It is important to get an idea of how well the firm is doing financially. One of the primary areas of interest should be the company's *profitability*.[10] Is the business doing anything wrong that can be spotted from the statements? If so, can the prospective buyer eliminate these problems?

Individuals who are skilled at buying companies that are in trouble, straightening them out, and reselling them at a profit know what to look for when examining the books. So do good accountants. Both also know that the seller's books alone should not be taken as proof of sales or profits. One should insist on seeing records of bank deposits for the past two to three years. If the current owner has held the firm for only a short time, the records of the previous owner also should be examined. In fact, it is not out of line to ask for the owner's income tax return. The astute buyer knows that the firm's records reflect its condition.

Another area of interest is the firm's *profit trend*. Is the business making more money every year? More important, are profits going up as quickly as sales, or is more and more revenue necessary to attain the same profit? If the latter is true, the business may have to increase sales 5 to 10 percent annually to net as much as it did the previous year. This spells trouble and is often a sign that the owner is selling because "there are easier ways to make a living."

Finally, even if the company is making money, the prospective buyer should compare the firm's performance to that of similar companies. For example, if a small retail shop is making a 22 percent return on investment this year in contrast to 16 percent two years ago, is this good or bad? It certainly appears to be good, but what if competing stores are making a 32 percent return on investment? Given this information, the firm is not doing as well.

One way to compare a company to the competition is to obtain comparative information put out by firms such as Dun & Bradstreet that gather data on retail and wholesale firms in various fields and provide businesspeople with an overall view of many key financial ratios. For example, one of the most important pieces of information is the comparison of current assets (cash or items that can be turned into cash in the short run) to current liabilities (debts that will be due in the short run). This key ratio reflects a business's ability to meet its current obligations. A second key ratio is the comparison of net profits to net sales (net profit margin). How much profit is the owner making for every dollar in sales? A third key ratio is net profit to net worth (return on net worth). How much profit is the individual making for every dollar invested in the firm? Table 2-3 shows the key ratios and other data for numerous types of businesses.

By comparing the accounting information obtained from a business's books to financial data such as those illustrated in Table 2-3, it is possible to determine how well a business is doing. If the facts look good, the prospective buyer can turn to the question of how much to offer the seller.

Source: For a more thorough and updated analysis, see Steven M. Bragg, *Business Ratios and Formulas: A Comprehensive Guide* (Hoboken, NJ: Wiley, 2002).

TABLE 2-3 Key Data by Business

Line of Business	Quick Ratio (times)	Current Ratio (times)	Collection Period (days)	Accounts Payable to Net Sales (%)	Overall Gross Profit (%)	Net Profit Margin (%)	Asset Turnover (times)	Return on Net Worth (%)
Automotive dealers	0.6	1.8	16.4	4.5	22.5	2.8	5.5	14.6
Bookstores	0.5	2.4	6.9	8.7	36.9	2.9	4.3	12.5
Children's clothing stores	0.6	3.6	6.9	3.8	36.0	4.6	4.2	12.8
Department stores	1.0	3.4	11.7	5.5	32.7	1.7	4.4	6.0
Eating places	0.6	1.0	4.0	3.2	52.6	3.8	74.5	18.5
Employment agencies	2.1	2.4	44.9	1.6	29.6	5.2	109.7	35.4
Fitness facilities	0.7	1.0	24.1	3.3	74.4	5.6	83.1	16.0
Florists	1.1	2.1	18.5	4.0	48.9	4.0	15.3	12.2
Furniture stores	0.9	2.7	25.2	5.0	37.4	3.9	4.8	9.2
Gift and novelty shops	0.7	3.2	6.2	4.4	42.2	5.2	4.7	17.0
Grocery stores	0.5	1.6	2.9	3.2	21.6	1.7	19.2	12.6
Hardware stores	0.7	3.0	18.3	5.2	33.8	3.0	4.5	8.9
Hobby, toy and game shops	0.6	3.1	3.1	4.7	39.9	4.1	4.6	13.2
Hotels and motels	0.8	1.2	9.5	3.1	66.0	8.1	92.2	14.7
Mail-order houses	0.8	2.1	14.1	6.2	38.5	3.3	7.9	17.5
Medical equipment rental facilities	1.5	2.3	63.0	5.0	63.7	6.8	19.1	18.0
Men's and boy's clothing stores	0.9	2.0	32.5	5.7	24.6	3.7	8.1	18.2
Public golf courses	0.8	1.5	6.8	2.8	71.7	3.2	31.3	8.4
Radio, TV, and electronics stores	0.7	2.0	13.5	5.3	35.5	3.8	7.1	17.1
Shoe stores	0.5	3.7	6.2	5.9	37.2	5.0	3.7	14.1
Sporting goods stores	0.8	1.9	35.4	6.8	26.7	2.7	5.8	3.7
Tobacco stores	0.4	2.3	6.6	3.6	31.4	6.6	9.3	44.8
Variety stores	p.8	3.8	4.8	4.4	35.2	4.2	4.7	11.3
Women's clothing stores	0.9	3.7	11.7	4.2	37.4	5.1	5.2	12.3

DETERMINING THE PRICE

After the previously mentioned questions and issues have been resolved, the prospective entrepreneur must answer one final question: "How much are you willing to pay for the business?" This is not an easy question to answer. However, because the enterprise is small, fewer factors need to be considered than if a large corporation were being purchased. Additionally, some commonly accepted indicators can be used to establish an enterprise's value.

ASSESSING THE PRICE

A number of indexes reflect an operating venture's value. Five of the most important follow:

1. Book value
2. Replacement value
3. Liquidation value
4. Past earnings
5. Cash flow

BOOK VALUE

Book value refers to the value of the company's assets from an accounting standpoint. For example, if a firm bought a new machine for $25,000 last year and it has been in operation for one year, its book value would be $20,000, assuming five-year, straight-line depreciation. Likewise, if a business has bought 1,000 shirts for $7 each, they would be carried in the books for $7,000. However, if something has lost value, its book value should be reduced; assets should be carried at *cost* or *present value,* whichever is lower. For example, if an enterprise has just learned that 1,000 shirts it bought are now out of style, it may be lucky to get $4 each for them. The book value of the shirts should be reduced from $7,000 to $4,000.

REPLACEMENT VALUE

Replacement value refers to how much it would cost to buy the same machinery, materials, or merchandise on the market today. In many cases, the use of replacement value increases the asking price for a business. For example, land is seldom in the books at replacement value. If land was bought 10 years ago for $50,000, it may be worth double that today.

LIQUIDATION VALUE

Liquidation value reflects the worth of the business's assets if they were thrown on the market today and purchased by knowledgeable buyers. This value is usually the lowest of those discussed here, because most assets sell for far less than their original purchase price. Consider, for example, that most people expect to buy things at an auction more cheaply than anywhere else. *Auction value* is another term for the liquidation value; it reflects what the owner can get for the assets in a competitive bidding situation.

Past Earnings

Past earnings are important because the bottom-line reason to buy someone's business is to make money. Therefore, the prospective entrepreneur would be wise to choose a business that has been profitable. Of course, to obtain these earning, the *physical assets* (building, machinery, material, inventory) also are needed, but, in the final analysis, the prospective entrepreneur must be concerned with what he or she can earn with these assets.

Cash Flow

Cash flow is still another measure of value. This measure is the most widely used in most service and Internet businesses. Cash flow is equal to net profit after taxes plus any noncash expenses, such as depreciation, depletion, or amortization. *Noncash expenses* are items that can be written off on the company's income tax, thus saving it money while not requiring a layout of cash. These expenses will be discussed later; for the moment, simply keep in mind that they help free up cash for the firm. Many people use cash flow as an index of value because high cash flows are instrumental in reducing debt and helping the firm expand. A company with a high cash flow, therefore, is preferable to one whose cash flow is moderate or low.

None of these five indexes of value is likely to be used exclusively for determining a fair price for an operating venture. However, liquidation value tends to be favored over book value or replacement value if the firm is going out of business. Likewise, in any computation of purchase price, past earnings will play a major role. Before looking at a formula for determining a fair purchase price, however, we must consider asset pricing.

Asset Pricing

A prospective buyer first needs to approach the purchase of a business from a rational standpoint. Some common assets and the ways to evaluate them are discussed here.

- *Building.* If the company owns the building, what value does it have on the company books? Deduct the cost of any repairs or alterations that are needed to keep the facility in working shape.
- *Inventory.* Adjust the purchase price to account for slow-moving or obsolete items.
- *Equipment.* Deduct depreciation of equipment from the purchase price. If some of the equipment is not usable because of age or obsolescence, pay no more than liquidation value for it.
- *Prepaid expenses.* Buy prepaid expenses at face value. These include fire and theft insurance premiums the owner pays annually that have coverage remaining.

- *Supplies.* If supplies are usable, buy them at the price the owner paid, unless the price has changed. In that case, adjust upward or downward to reflect the change.

- *Accounts receivable.* Purchase customer obligations after first deducting those so old that they are deemed uncollectible. Additionally, if it appears that it will take 60 days, on average, to collect the rest, deduct 2 to 3 percent from the total as an expense for the investment in these receivables, unless a monthly charge is added to outstanding accounts. Remember: Time is money, and, unless the business charges the customer monthly interest, the new owner is buying accounts receivable that will not be turned into cash for 60 days. Since most retail credit cards charge 1 to 2 percent per month, the buyer should make a similar charge to the seller.

- *Goodwill.* This is the excess of the selling price over the value of the physical assets. Goodwill depends on factors such as (1) how long it would take to set up a similar business and the expense and risk associated with such a venture; (2) the amount of income to be made by purchasing an ongoing concern rather than starting a new one; (3) the price the owner of this business is asking for goodwill compared to what owners of similar businesses ask; and (4) the value associated with the seller's agreement to stay out of the same business within the competitive area.

Of these assets, goodwill is the only *intangible* one. The buyer cannot *see* goodwill; the individual can only try to assess its presence and assign a value to it. Before illustrating how this can be done, one final point merits discussion: The buyer should not pay more for goodwill than can be recovered from profits within a reasonable period. Usually this period is three to five years, although if one were purchasing a major corporation, such as Microsoft, the goodwill price might take 10 years to recover because the product is continuously innovating and may be valuable for a longer period.

ONE ACCEPTABLE FORMULA?

There is no surefire way to attach a price to the value of an ongoing operating venture. However, one formula is straightforward and may prove the most understandable for a prospective entrepreneur. The seven steps of the formula are described here and illustrated with a real-life situation. Refer to Table 2-4 as you read the steps.

> *Step 1:* Determine the value of the business by identifying the liquidation or market value of all the assets and then subtracting the debts or liabilities of the business. This has been determined to be $100,000 for this example.
>
> *Step 2:* Determine how much the buyer could earn with this money if it were invested somewhere else. If the risk in the current business is very high, this percentage should be set at 10%, or $10,000.
>
> *Step 3:* To the figure must be added a salary for the entrepreneur/manager. This figure has been set as $30,000. The sum of steps 2 and 3 represents

Table 2-4 Determining a Purchase Price	
Step	*Amount*
1. Liquidation or market value of all assets, minus liabilities	$100,000
2. Earning power of 10%	$10,000
3. Salary for the entrepreneur/manager	$30,000
4. Average annual earnings before subtracting entrepreneur/manager's salary and earning power	$30,000
5. Extra earning power of the business (step 4 minus step 3)	$5,000
6. Value of intangibles using a five-year profit figure (five times step 5)	25,000
7. Final price (step 1 plus step 6)	$125,000

Source: Adapted from "How to Buy or Sell A Business," *Small Business Reporter 8,* no. 11 (San Francisco: Bank of America National Trust and Saving Association, 1969) p. 11.

the total the prospective buyer could expect to earn if the investment were placed elsewhere and if the efforts involved in working in the business are taken into account. This total amount would be $40,000.

Step 4: Determine the average net profit before taxes and the average salary the entrepreneur/manager can obtain from this business over the next few years. This is a key calculation because it forces the buyer to answer the question, "How long will it take to recoup the investment?" This figure has been determined as $30,000.

Step 5: Subtract the earning power and the salary (steps 2 and 3) from the average net earnings figure in step 4. This represents the "extra earning power" the buyer will obtain by owning the business.

Step 6: Take this extra earning power and estimate the number of years it will exist. This, in effect, represents what the buyer is willing to pay for the firm's goodwill. In our example, a five-year profit figure has been used. This means the buyer is willing to pay $25,000 for the firm's intangible assets. If the firm is well established, 5 is a reasonable multiplier. If it is a new company, it is common to find the multiplier varying between 1 and 3. Obviously, the more established the business, the more the buyer should be willing to pay for goodwill.

Step 7: This is the final price, which equals the net market of the assets plus the value of the intangibles. In this case, the buyer has set a purchase price of $125,000 as fair and reasonable.

An advantage of this formula is that it helps the buyer arrive at a fair price for intangible assets, specifically goodwill. In our example (Table 2-4), the total of the earning power and the entrepreneur/manager's salary was less than the average annual new earnings. This can be verified easily by comparing the total amount of steps 2 and 3 with the amount in step 4: The latter is larger. However, if that latter is not larger, the seller should not assign any value to goodwill, because the earning power of the investment and the amount the buyer can earn from personal effort are greater than can be obtained from running the business. How then does the buyer decide on a final selling price?

In this case, the buyer needs to recalculate the price by determining the average annual profit and capitalizing it by the desired rate of return. For example, assume the initial data in Table 2-4 are the same except that the average annual net earnings before subtracting the earning power and entrepreneur/manager's salary are only $20,000. In this case the business has no extra earning power (step 5), so the value of the intangibles (step 6) will be zero. Additionally, since the buyer wants to obtain an earning power of 10 percent (step 2), it is necessary to take the average annual net earnings and subtract the entrepreneur/manager's salary:

$$\$20,000 - \$15,000 = \$5,000 \text{ profit}$$

After the new entrepreneur takes a salary of $15,000, only $5,000 will remain as a return on the original investment. Since the individual wants to secure a 10 percent return on the original investment, the purchase price must be 10 times the profit:

$$\$5,000 \div 0.10 = \$50,000 \text{ purchase price}$$

Since this may be difficult to grasp without practice, another example is in order. This time, still using the data in Table 2-4, assume that the average net earnings before the entrepreneur/manager's salary and earning power are subtracted is $23,000. In this case, then, the buyer's profit after salary is deducted will be $8,000:

$$\$23,000 - \$15,000 = \$8,000 \text{ profit}$$

The individual wishes to make a 10 percent profit on the investment, so the purchase price is equal to 10 times the profit:

$$\$8,000 \div 0.10 = \$80,000 \text{ purchase price}$$

Finally, consider an example in which the basic data in Table 2-4 still apply, but the average annual net earning before the entrepreneur/manager's salary and earning power is $25,000. How much should the individual now pay for the business? The answer is $100,000 because the firm will have no extra earning power. The person will just clear the desired 10 percent on investment, or $10,000 after the $15,000 salary is deducted from the $25,000 profit before taxes.

Before we close this discussion about buying an ongoing concern, a final point is in order. The formula presented here provides a reasonable estimate of what to pay for a business. However, this price must be tempered by how badly a seller wants to get rid of the business and how much the buyer wants to acquire it. Quite often the desire of either or both parties dictates the final selling price, and a mathematical formula is just the beginning. Thus, in the first example, where a final selling price of $125,000 was reached, the buyer would have to compare this price with the asking price. If the seller wants $130,000, the buyer might offer $120,000 and then negotiate up to $125,000. This does not mean, however, that the final price always will be the midpoint between the original asking price and the original bid. If the seller refuses to accept less than $130,000, the buyer should either walk away from the deal or agree to pay a premium for the business. In this case, the individual's return on investment will be reduced slightly as a result of paying more for the business. Would such a purchase be wise? This question can be answered only by the prospective entrepreneur, for, in the final analysis, "fair price" is whatever the buyer is willing to pay.[11] However, buyers must educate themselves in order to identify the fair price. Jeff Stone suggests that buyers follow a six-step process when determining the value of a business.[12] These steps include:

1. "Spending time in the trenches." Fully research the business and market and assess the viability of both.
2. "Create a sound business plan." Assess the business's potential for the future, when you will own and run the venture.
3. "Secure working capital and backup resources." It is critical that you do not handcuff the business by being underfunded after the acquisition.
4. "Invest in a strong brand/image." Be careful not to purchase a business that needs extensive reworking and image building unless you factor this work into a lower purchase price.
5. "Keep accurate and complete records." Following the acquisition, details are important. Information relating to financials, personnel, products, and/or services should be carefully tracked so that adjustments to the business plan can be made.
6. "Make a profit." Many new owners feel that it is necessary to lose money initially to get the business on track. When purchasing a business, scrutinize balance sheets, income statements, and other data so that you can determine the probability of making a profit in the future.

NEGOTIATING THE DEAL

After a proper valuation of the business is completed, the potential buyer must negotiate the final deal.[13] This negotiation process, however, involves a number of factors. Four critical elements should be recognized: information, time, pressure, and alternatives.

Information may be the most critical element during negotiations. The performance of the company, the nature of its competition, the condition of the market, and clear answers to all of the key questions presented earlier are vital components in the determination of the business's real potential. Without reliable information, the buyer is at a costly disadvantage. The seller never should be relied on as the sole information source. Although the seller may not falsify any information, he or she is likely to make available only the information that presents the business in the most favorable light. Therefore, the buyer should develop as many sources as possible. The rule should be to investigate every possible source.

Time is also a critical element. If the seller already has purchased another business and you are the only prospect to buy the existing firm, you have the power to win some important concessions from the seller. If, however, the owner has no such deadline but is simply headed to retirement, or if your financial sources wish to invest in the project quickly, you are at a serious disadvantage. In short, having more time than the other party can be very beneficial.

Pressure from others also will affect the negotiation process. If the company is owned by several partners, the individual who is selling the company may not have complete autonomy. If one of the owners is in favor of accepting an offer,

Table 2-5   Dos and Don'ts of Buying a Business

Buying an ongoing business provides many advantages for a prospective purchaser, such as a proven track record, established credit, ongoing operations, and a significantly lower chance for failure. However, without careful analysis, a person buying an ongoing business may suffer from hidden problems inherited with the business. The following list of dos and don'ts provides some practical tips to consider before signing over the check.

1. *Have a seller retain a minority interest in the business.* If a seller walks with 100 percent of the purchase money, it is highly unlikely he or she will give you any help running the business in the future. Another option would be to have the ultimate purchase price of the business dependent on the performance of the business over the next three-to-five-year period.

2. *Never rely on oral statements.* Get everything in writing; oral promises count for little after you have bought the business.

3. *Have an accountant examine the books and check the cash flow.* Your accountant must reconstruct the seller's financial statements to determine exactly how much cash is available to you.

4. *Investigate, investigate, investigate!* Find out as much as you can about the business before you fork over your hard-earned cash. Talk to vendors, suppliers, customers, and even the competition to get the real story. Go beyond the list of references the seller provides you. Also investigate the entire industry, looking for possible major shifts that could affect future business. The more time you devote to such research, the better decision you'll make.

5. *Interview the employees.* All employees have valuable information about the company they work for. If the seller is serious about selling, he or she should not be afraid to let buyers communicate with employees. Try to conduct interviews in a confidential situation; otherwise, any information you gain may be incorrect or misleading.

6. *Find out the real reason the company is for sale.* Many people want out of a successful business for legitimate reasons. Just make sure the reasons are legitimate.

Source: Adapted from Bruce J. Blechman, "Good Buy," *Entrepreneur* (February 1994): 22–25. Reprinted with permission from *Entrepreneur* magazine, February 1994.

the negotiator for the company must decide whether to accept the bid on behalf of all owners or to attempt to hold out for more money. This causes a distraction during the negotiation process.

Finally, the alternatives available to each party become important factors. The party with no other alternatives has a great deal of interest in concluding negotiations quickly. Table 2-5 outlines some additional considerations that a person should consider when purchasing a business.

For the seller, alternatives include finding another buyer in the near future or not selling at all. He or she may continue to run the business, hire a manager to do so, or sell off parts of the company. Likewise, the buyer may choose not to purchase the business or may have alternative investment opportunities available. In any event, the negotiating parties' alternatives should be recognized because they impact the ability to reach an agreement.

Once the negotiation process is complete and the price is agreed on, the new owner ought to have an action plan already outlined. This plan should have two parts. First, financing of the business should be arranged. How is the money to be raised? If some of the funds are to be borrowed, the individual already should have discussed the matter with a banker and should know how much money the bank is willing to lend. Otherwise, personal capital should be investigated.

Second, will business continue as before, or must some specific changes be made in the operation? If the new owner has decided to change some things, the plan for implementing these changes should be operational so that it can be put into effect immediately. These key action steps prepare a buyer to assume control of his or her new business.

Summary

The easiest and best way to approach a new business venture is to design a unique product or service. Sometimes this involves what is called a new-new approach—that is, the development of an entirely new idea for a product or service, as was the case with the first Polaroid camera. In most instances, however, the prospective entrepreneur/manager must be content to use a new-old approach by either expanding on what the competition is doing or offering a product or service in an area where it is not presently available.

In either event, market analysis can help a prospective entrepreneur/manager determine whether a demand for a particular good or service exists and, if so, whether this demand is sufficient to justify starting operations. Market analysis is carried out through the scientific method. The steps in this method include stating the problem or question in a clear manner, gathering all necessary facts about the problem or question, organizing and analyzing these facts, developing one or more courses of action, selecting the best alternative and implementing it, and observing the progress of this alternative and adjusting it as required. These steps can be classified into four basic groups: gathering of the facts, organization of the facts, analysis of the facts, and implementation of an action plan.

In particular, the action plan should cover three primary areas: the entrepreneur's personality, the financial picture, and other major factors vital to the action plan. To deal with the first of these, the entrepreneur needs to assess his or her strengths and work habits. On the financial side, the prospective entrepreneur/manager needs to examine the enterprise's financial picture and to determine the costs of setting up the operation and the amount of revenue that will be generated during the initial period. Finally, the prospective entrepreneur/manager must review a series of other operational considerations, ranging from the building, merchandise, and equipment needed for operations to record keeping, insurance, legal, marketing, and personal matters.

Another opportunity for entrepreneurs is the purchase of an existing successful firm. This approach has a number of advantages; three of the most important are that its successful future operation is likely, the time and effort associated with starting a new enterprise are eliminated, and a bargain price may be possible.

Before deciding whether to buy, however, the prospective entrepreneur needs to ask and answer a series of "right questions," including: Why is the business being sold? What is the physical condition of the business? What is the condition of the inventory? What is the state of the company's other assets? How many of the employees will remain? What competition does the business face? What is the firm's financial picture?

After all questions have been answered satisfactorily, the prospective buyer must determine how much he or she is willing to pay for the business. Some of the indexes used to determine an operating venture's overall value are book value, replacement value, liquidation value, past earnings, and cash flow. In the final analysis, however, the prospective entrepreneur should be concerned with buying the company's assets at *market value* and then paying something for *goodwill* if it is deemed an asset.

Review and Discussion Questions

1. What is the new-new approach to starting a new venture? How does this approach differ from a new-old approach?
2. What are the six steps in the scientific method?
3. Of the six steps in the scientific method, which is the most important for the prospective new venture entrepreneur/manager? Support your answer.
4. Market analysis can help a prospective new venture entrepreneur/manager determine whether a demand for a particular good or service exists. What does this statement mean?
5. What kinds of questions should the new venture entrepreneur be able to answer when developing an action plan? List as least five.
6. How can an individual who is thinking of going into business evaluate the financial picture of an enterprise? Use the methodology of Table 2-2 to prepare your answer.
7. In addition to personal and financial issues, what other factors should the prospective entrepreneur be concerned with? Describe at least four.
8. What are the advantages of buying an ongoing business? Explain them.
9. What "right questions" need to be answered when deciding whether to buy a business?
10. What is book value? Replacement value? Liquidation value? Past earnings? Case flow?
11. How should a prospective buyer price the assets of a company? Explain.
12. What are the seven steps involved in pricing an operating venture?
13. A prospective buyer is thinking about purchasing a business. The following facts have been gathered: The liquidation value of all assets minus liabilities is $500,000; the earning power desired is 20 percent; the prospective buyer needs a yearly salary of $40,000; the average annual earnings before subtracting the entrepreneur/manager's salary and earning power is $100,000; and any extra earning power is estimated to be of value for five years. How much should the buyer be willing to pay for the business?
14. If the price is agreed to, the buyer should be prepared to take control. What does "taking control" involve?

A Potential Business

Bob and Angie Whitney are both physical education instructors at an urban high school. Last year, Bob's grandparents died and left him an inheritance of $150,000. Not sure what to do with the money, Bob and Angie decided to put it into a savings account in which it would earn 5 percent interest. By the end of the year, they had accumulated $7,500 in interest, all of which was taxable. Their next-door neighbor, an accountant, advised they get involved with something that would shelter some of their income from taxes. "Look into a business," he suggested.

Bob and Angie do not know very much about business, and neither has taken a course in any aspect of management or finance. However, they do feel that they understand the need for physical fitness and would be comfortable with a business in this field. Last week, Bob learned about an indoor racquetball club built three years ago. The original cost for the 20 racquetball courts, dressing rooms, sauna, and lounge was $500,000. The owner told his banker he would like to sell this investment and try something else. The banker just happened to be the Whitneys' banker as well, which is how Bob and Angie learned about the venture.

The banker set up a telephone meeting with the owner, Karl Coopersmith. Karl suggested that the three of them meet at the club and tour the facilities. During the tour, the Whitneys noticed that the facilities were in good shape. They saw many people coming and going, and all of the courts were in use the entire time they were there. Karl told them that he would like to sell and was in the process of contacting a number of local bankers and accountants he knows to see if any of their clients would be interested in buying the club, either individually or in a partnership. Karl told the Whitneys that the membership dues are $175 per year, which entitles each member to use the exercise room and saunas. The cost for playing racquetball is $7 per hour, and up to four people can play at once. Due to great demand in the area, members have to call at lease five days in advance to reserve a court. Karl also told them he currently had 1211 members, and that, unless more courts were built, the club could support more than another 89 members. "As it is," he said, "it is getting difficult to get a court on the weekend or in the evening. I've got just about all the members I can handle."

Bob and Angie admitted to Karl that they do not know much about business. He encouraged them to have their accountant come by and look at his books and to advise them on the profitability of the venture. "I won't throw numbers at you," he said, "because I know you are not trained in accounting. Let's let your accountant decide if this is the right type of business for you to buy. However, let me give you the bottom line. It cost me $500,000 to build the club, and I won't sell it for less than $600,000. I have an outstanding loan at the bank for just under $450,000, so I want $150,000 cash, and the owners can assume my loan at the rate I got last year, which is 1 percent lower than loans today." Bob and Angie told Karl they would be in touch.

Your consultation: Assume you are advising Bob and Angie on whether to buy the racquetball club. What would you tell them? Be specific with your recommendations. In particular, would you suggest that they go it alone or seek other partners? Have they asked the right questions? What further questions do you feel should be asked? What stipulations should they require of Karl?

Endnotes

1. See Steve Cooper, Amanda C. Kooser, Kristin Ohlson, Karen E. Spaeder, Nichole L. Torres, and Sara Wilson, "2007 Hot List," *Entrepreneur* (December 2006): 80–93.
2. Steve Rosenbush, "Facebook's on the Block," *BusinessWeek Online*, March 28, 2006, www.businessweek.com/technology/content/mar2006/tc20060327_215976.htm (accessed October 3, 2006).
3. "Yahoo Tries to Woo Facebook With $900 Million," *Slashdot*, March 22, 2006, http://slashdot.org/article.pl?sid=06/09/22/1857219 (accessed October 3, 2006).
4. Geoff Williams, Small Business Answer Book. *Entrepreneur* 34, no. 11 (2006): 77–82.
5. Peter Mouncey and Frank Wimmer, *Market Research Best Practice: 30 Visions for the Future* (Hoboken, NJ: Wiley, 2007).
6. See Donald F. Kuratko and Richard M. Hodgetts, *Entrepreneurship: Theory, Process, & Practice*, 7th ed. (Mason, OH: Thomson/Southwestern, 2007), 653–82.
7. Fred Steingold and Emily Dostow, *The Complete Guide to Buying a Business* (Berkeley, CA: Nolo Press, 2005).
8. Entrepreneur.com, "Intangible Assets" definition, www.entrepreneur.com/encyclopedia/term/82294.html (accessed June 5, 2007).
9. Jay B. Abrams, *How to Value Your Business and Increase Its Potential* (New York: McGraw-Hill Publishing, 2005).
10. For a good discussion of buying or selling a small business, see Rene V. Richards, *How to Buy and/or Sell a Small Business for Maximum Profit* (Ocala, FL: Atlantic Publishing Group, 2006).
11. For a thorough analysis on valuation of a business, see James R. Hitchner, *Financial Valuation: Applications and Models* (Hoboken, NJ: Wiley, 2006); and Shannon P. Pratt, *Business Valuation: Body of Knowledge* (Hoboken, NJ: Wiley, 2003).
12. Jeff Stone, "Six Tips for Buying or Expanding a Business." *Financial Executive* 22, no. 5 (2006): 15.
13. See Roy J. Lewicki, David M. Saunders, and John W. Minton, *Negotiation*, 3rd ed. (New York: McGraw Hill/Irwin Publishers, 2002). This paperback gives practical examples and advice about negotiating. Also see Michael Watkins, *Negotiation: Harvard Business Essentials* (Cambridge, MA: Harvard Business School Press, 2003).

CHAPTER

FRANCHISING
THE HYBRID

INTRODUCTION

Franchising has emerged over the years as a popular form of launching into an entrepreneurial venture. A franchise is a system of distribution that enables a supplier (the *franchisor*) to arrange for a dealer (the *franchisee*) to handle a specific product or service under certain mutually agreed-upon conditions. In most cases, the franchisee is given the right to distribute and sell goods or services within a specific area. The business itself is owned by the franchisee, and the franchisor is paid a fee and/or a commission on sales. Thus, it becomes a *hybrid* form of entrepreneurial activity in that the entrepreneur has his or her own venture but it is carefully integrated back to the franchising organization. Franchising is a business model in which the primary purpose is risk minimization. In essence, the two types of franchising arrangements are the franchising of a product or service and the franchising of an entire business enterprise.

THE NATURE OF FRANCHISING

PRODUCT OR SERVICE FRANCHISE

When a *product* is franchised, the franchisee receives the goods from the franchisor and sells them through a wholesale or retail outlet. An auto dealership provides an illustration: The owner receives cars from an auto manufacturer and has an exclusive right to sell them. Retail purchasers cannot buy directly from the factory. They must go through a dealer who has a franchise. This individual receives the product from the company and, in turn, sells it to the consumer. This is also referred to as *licensing* the product. Retail firms that sell a wide variety of goods have franchise (licensing) agreements with many different manufacturers for all kinds of products: Carrier Corporation for air conditioners, Panasonic for stereo equipment, Sony for televisions, Whirlpool for washers and dryers, Dell for computers, BlackBerry for handheld devices, and so forth. In all of these cases, the control the supplier exerts over the retailer is small, and it is limited to the particular franchised product. The franchisor does not attempt to control the operation of the business itself. When a *service* is franchised, the franchisee receives a license for a trade name and the particular services to be sold. Jackson-Hewitt Tax Services, Merry Maids, and the UPS Store would all be examples of service franchises. Again, the franchisor does not attempt to control the operation of the business itself. The franchisee directs daily activities—hiring and firing of employees, operational business decisions, and budgeting concerns—whereas the franchisor maintains control over certain standardization features expected of all franchisees.

BUSINESS FRANCHISE

When the word *franchise* is used today, it often refers to the franchising of an *entire business enterprise*.[1] According to Entrepreneur.com, the top 10 franchises for 2007 are as follows:[2]

1. Subway
2. Dunkin' Donuts
3. Jackson Hewitt Tax Service
4. 7-Eleven, Inc.
5. UPS Store, The/Mail Boxes Etc.
6. Domino's Pizza LLC
7. Jiffy Lube Int'l. Inc.
8. Sonic Drive-In Restaurants
9. McDonald's
10. Papa John's Int'l., Inc.

Franchises such as these operate under a common trade name. The business operation, the establishment's appearance, the merchandise, and even the operating procedures are standardized to a high degree. In an effort to maintain this standardized image and marketing approach for the general buying public, the franchisor usually keeps a strong, formalized system of control over the business operation. In this type of a franchise arrangement, the responsibilities of both parties—the franchisor and the franchisee—are spelled out in the franchise contract and usually are considered to be of mutual advantage to both parties. The remainder of this chapter focuses on the franchising of an entire enterprise as opposed to the franchising of a particular product, product line, or service; the franchising of an entire enterprise is considered new venture activity and relates most closely to entrepreneurs.

CONVERSION FRANCHISING

Conversion franchising refers to the conversion of independent, ongoing concerns into franchise-systems members. These independents usually come from the same product or service category as the franchisor whose name they adopt. Struggling independent firms that face strong competition and adverse results may turn to a franchise's nationally known brand name, access to additional customers, marketing assistance, promise of cost savings through mass purchasing power, and improved business procedures and operations. Franchisors use a conversion strategy to achieve rapid growth and selective market entry.

Conversion franchising has been particularly successful in the highly competitive and domestically mature industries of restaurants (Starbucks), hotels (Best Western), and real estate (Century 21).[3]

HOW A FRANCHISE WORKS

Business franchise systems for goods and services generally work the same way. The franchisee, an independent entrepreneur, contracts for a complete business package. This usually requires the individual to do one or more of the following:

1. Make a financial investment in the operation
2. Obtain and maintain a standardized inventory and/or equipment package, usually purchased from the franchisor
3. Maintain a specified quality of performance
4. Pay a *franchise fee* as well as a percentage of the gross revenues
5. Engage in a continuing business relationship

In turn, the franchisor provides the following types of benefits and assistance:

1. The company name. For example, if someone buys a Burger King franchise, this provides the business with drawing power. A well-known name, such as Burger King, ensures higher sales than an unknown name, such as Ralph's Big Burgers.
2. Identifying symbols, logos, designs, and facilities. For example, all McDonald's units have the same identifying golden arches on the premises. Likewise, the facilities are similar inside.
3. Professional management training for each independent unit's staff.
4. Sale of specific merchandise necessary for the unit's operation at wholesale prices. Usually provided are all of the equipment to run the operation and the food or materials needed for the final product.
5. Financial assistance, if needed, to help the unit in any way possible.
6. Continuing aid and guidance to ensure that everything is done in accordance with the contract.[4]

THE GROWTH OF FRANCHISING

Franchising has proved to be one of the most popular vehicles for individuals seeking to pursue a career as an entrepreneur. The hybrid nature of the system, in which an entrepreneur will act independently for local matters but follow home office guidelines for major operations, has proven to be very attractive to start-up entrepreneurs. Franchised businesses currently account for almost half of all U.S. retail sales. In recent years, franchising has reacted favorably to many of the trends that have adversely affected other business segments. Franchising's ability to meet subtle but rapid shifts in consumer demands, demographic changes, and technological breakthroughs indicates that it is likely to remain a strong business segment regardless of the general state of the economy.

Franchising statistics are certainly stunning. According to a 2004 study by the International Franchising Association (IFA), more than half a million franchise businesses exist in the United State alone, employing more than 9.8 million people. Franchise businesses also provided a payroll of over $506 billion, or 5 percent of the total private sector payroll. The IFA study also found that franchise businesses created almost equal economic activity as nonfranchise businesses. Additionally, franchising has opened up opportunities for minorities and women. For example, of the 2,177 franchisors the federal government recently surveyed, 572 reported a total of 10,412 units owned by minority businesspersons. Included in this group were 3,615 African Americans; 2,808 persons with Spanish surnames; 3,616 Asian Americans; and 103 Native Americans. The greatest number of minority-owned franchises is auto products and service businesses, restaurants, food stores, and convenience stores[5] (see Table 3-1 for franchise facts). Minorities

---

TABLE 3-1 Franchise Facts

- Franchised businesses account for $803 billion in annual sales.
- Franchises represent 42 percent of all U.S. retail sales.
- Franchise sales equal 20 percent of the gross national product.
- Franchises directly employ 9.8 million people and cause residual support employment of an additional 8.3 million people. This employment results in 506.6 billion in payroll.
- One out of every 12 business establishments is a franchised business.
- A new franchise business opens every eight minutes of every business day.
- There are more than 600,000 franchised establishments in the United States.
- Seventy-five industries use franchising to distribute goods and services to consumers.
- The average initial investment level for nearly 8 out of 10 franchises, excluding real estate, is less than $250,000.
- Average royalty fees range from 3 percent to 6 percent of monthly gross sales.
- Most franchise companies have fewer than 100 units.
- The average length of a franchise contract is 10 years.
- The number of franchise units sold increased from 274,265 in 2000 to 351,459 in 2005.

Source: International Franchise Association, 2005.

TABLE 3-2 Franchising Myths

MYTH: "Franchising is fast food."

FACT: Franchising spans 75 industries, with fast food being only one industry. Examples include, but are not limited to, carpet dyeing, personnel testing, accounting, wood restoration, and interior plantscaping.

MYTH: "Franchises are expensive."

FACT: The fastest growing segment of the franchise industry is home-based business. The initial investments for quality opportunities range from $15,000 to $35,000.

MYTH: "I must invest a lot of money to own a business that will allow me to earn a lot of money."

FACT: There is no correlation between the amount of initial investment and potential earnings from a single unit. For example, annual earnings from a home-based business are often 5 to 10 times the initial investment because operating expenses are relatively low.

MYTH: "I need business experience to own a franchise."

FACT: Quality franchise systems have proven records of teaching and support their franchisees to successfully run all aspects of the business.

MYTH: "Most franchisors are big companies."

FACT: Only 6.5 percent have more than 100 franchise outlets.

MYTH: "Franchising is the same as other forms of business opportunity."

FACT: *Franchising* is a legal term. It is federally regulated, whereas multilevel marketing, distributorships, and other forms of licensing are not. Franchisors must give you their offering prospectus, which is annually registered with the Federal Trade Commission, before you invest. This explains 23 categories of information you need to know about, including a list of all franchisees.

Source: www.frannet.com.

still represent a very small portion of franchised businesses but possess a large potential for growth in the future.[6]

More important than the growth statistics are the attitude and satisfaction of franchise owners, as well as the success rate of franchise operations. Numerous studies by the franchise industry show that nearly 86 percent of all franchise operations are in business beyond the five-year mark, and only a very small percentage of franchises actually fail as a business. (See Table 3-2 for some of the common myths of franchising.)

In a study conducted for the IFA the Gallup Organization surveyed 1,011 current U.S. franchises and found that an overwhelming majority—nearly 9 out of 10 (88 percent)—said they would recommend purchasing a franchise rather than opening a nonfranchise business of their own. Nearly all—93 percent—believed that being associated with a franchise system gave them an advantage. The most important advantages, in order, were name recognition, support from the franchisor, knowledge, advertising, buying power, networking, and training.[7]

Despite the growing popularity of franchises, the potential franchisee needs to be aware that some franchise operations do fail. Table 3-3 lists the most common reasons for failure and suggests how these major pitfalls might be avoided. The boxed feature, *New Venture Perspective,* provides some interesting advice

TABLE 3-3 Reasons for Failure and Success in Franchising

Reason for Failure	Prescription for Success
Bad location	Excellent physical location
Stiff competition	Prosperous ongoing small business
Inadequate capital	Financial strength
Management "spread too thin"	Solid management team
Inappropriate business concept	A unique and protected process or marketable idea
Weak organizational structure	Simple, well-defined concept that franchisees can easily implement
Poor legal/contractual framework	Appropriate legal structure
Poor quality control	Quality control for product and services
Selling franchise outlets too quickly	Strong financial backing
Unexpected operating expenditures	Healthy gross margins
Changing consumer tastes	Long-term market prospects

NEW VENTURE PERSPECTIVE

Picking a Winner

Many businesses are turning to franchising as they seek alternative growth strategies for their companies. In fact, today more than 2,500 businesses are franchising their way to the top. The much larger pool of entrepreneurial franchisees has supplemented the growth of franchising and has taken some franchising companies to new heights. However, like with any other financial investment, risk is certainly involved. So, considering the abundance of franchise opportunities available and the risk involved, how do you pick a winning franchise? Many of the top franchisees were asked this same question.

All of the franchisees agreed that the key step in explaining a franchise opportunity is talking with other franchisees. The Federal Trade Commission concurs: "Speaking with current and former franchisees is probably the most effective way to verify the franchisor's claims." A wealth of knowledge can be gained by visiting franchise sites and talking with the owners, employees, and customers. Observing traffic and business flow also can reveal a great deal of information. Noting the quality of service and the attitude of employees, in addition to comparing sites, is important as well. *Success* magazine has developed a "Guide to Selecting a Franchise." The following are some of the steps listed in the guide:

1. *Create a customized franchisor profile.* Determine the variables that constitute your ideal franchise company based on industry, investment required, geographic preference, and so forth.

2. *Contact franchisors to request their marketing materials.* Review these materials as well as other information available on franchising.

3. *Review the offering circular.* Note the company and management background, and review the start-up/ongoing costs, level of support, provisions of the franchise agreement, and so on.

4. *Talk with franchisees.* Determine the level of franchisee satisfaction, and prepare financial projections.

5. *Visit sites.* Evaluate the day-to-day operations, and realistically determine if the business appears to be a good fit for you—especially compared with your personality, marketing ability, management skills, and level of financial and time commitment.

6. *Examine the competition.* Note how the competition rates overall and specifically in your market area. What are the strengths and weaknesses compared with the franchise you are considering?

7. *Meet with a franchise attorney and accountant.* Carefully review the franchise agreement. Prepare financial projections and, if needed, a business plan to secure financing.

8. *Complete discussions with the franchisor.* Negotiate the franchise agreement and make a commitment.

As with any business, franchise or not, the risk of ownership can be minimized through diligent research and investigation. Knowledge of every aspect of a business will increase an entrepreneur's chance of success and happiness.

Source: Katherine Callan, "Do Your Due Diligence: How to Invest in a Winning Franchise," *Success* (November 1996): 112–17; and "Ranking the Best: Survey Criteria and Methodology," *Success* (November 1996): 108–11.

for prospective entrepreneurs to examine before buying into a franchise of any type.

In addition, the global market for franchising appears to be growing rapidly. The largest market for franchising outside the United States is Europe, where approximately 4,000 franchisors operate almost 170,000 establishments. These establishments produce over $1 billion in turnover and employ nearly 1.5 million people. Within Europe, the largest country markets for franchising are France, Germany, Italy, Spain, and the United Kingdom.

Japan represents the largest and most active market for franchising in the Asia-Pacific region. In that country, 1,088 franchisors operate 225,957 establishments with sales of $157 billion.

In Australia, 850 franchisors operate 50,600 establishments, employing 507,180 full-time and part-time workers and generating $117 billion in sales, which accounts for nearly 14 percent of Australia's gross domestic product (GDP). Other promising markets in the Asia-Pacific region include Hong Kong, Singapore, Indonesia, Malaysia, and India. In Hong Kong, some 2,000 franchised establishments generate $600 million in annual sales. Mexico is the eighth leading nation worldwide in franchise development, with 780 different franchisors registered in 70 different sectors. These numbers, which are continually on the rise, indicate the global success of franchising.[8]

ADVANTAGES OF FRANCHISING

As stated previously, a number of advantages are associates with franchising.[9] Some of the most important advantages are as follows:

1. Training and guidance are provided by the franchisor.
2. The franchise offers brand-name appeal.
3. The track record of franchisees shows proof of success.
4. Financial assistance can be secured from the franchisor.

The following sections examine each of these advantages.

TRAINING AND GUIDANCE

Perhaps the greatest advantage of buying a franchise, as compared to starting a new business or buying an existing one, is that the franchisor usually will provide both training and guidance to the franchisee. As a result, the likelihood of success is much greater for national franchisees who have received this assistance than for small business owners in general. For example, it has been reported that the success rate of franchised businesses may be as high as 80 percent.

Some of the best-known training programs are these offered by McDonald's, Holiday Inn, and the UPS Store. At McDonald's, for example, the entrepreneur/franchisee is sent to "Hamburger U" before starting his or her business. There the individual learns how to make hamburgers, manage the unit, control inventory, keep records, and deal with personnel problems. Other national franchisors provide the same kind of training. For example, the Papa John's Pizza franchise requires each owner to attend a full training course that covers topics such as pizza making, merchandising, production scheduling, labor scheduling, advertising, and accounting. One of the greatest advantages of these training programs is that they provide an individual who has only a limited amount of business training the opportunity to pick up a great deal of practical information that can spell the difference between success and failure.

Another benefit is that of continuing assistance. A well-operated franchise system stays in continual contact with the franchisees, providing them with practical business tips, follow-up training, and pamphlets and manuals designed to make the overall operation more efficient.

BRAND-NAME APPEAL

An individual who buys a well-known national franchise, especially a big-name one, has a good chance to succeed. The franchisor's name is a drawing card for the establishment. Consumers often are more aware of the product or service a national franchise offers and prefer it to those offered by lesser-known outlets. One way that large franchisors accomplish this *brand-name appeal* is through advertising. Consider the television commercials you see and hear every day from Burger King, McDonald's Papa John's, KFC, Denny's, and a host of other national franchises. They all have catchy jingles that help create the all-important brand-name appeal.

A PROVEN TRACK RECORD

The third major benefit of buying a franchise is that the franchisor already has proved that the operation can be successful. Of course, if someone is the first individual to buy a franchise, this is not the case. However, if the organization has been around for 5 to 10 years and has 50 or more units, it should not be difficult to check on its success. If all of the units are still in operation and the owners report that they are doing well financially, one thing is certain: The franchisor has proved that the layout of the store, the pricing possibility, the quality of the goods and service, and the overall management system are successful. If a person buys a successful business from another individual, it may be difficult to determine how much of its success is a function of the seller's personality or drive. However, when one buys into a franchise organization that has had many successes, it is likely that the franchising concept accounts for the success rather than the managerial skills or drive of one individual.

FINANCIAL ASSISTANCE

The final main reason a franchise can be a good investment is that the franchisor may be able to help the new owner secure the financial assistance needed to run the operation. For example, many bankers will think twice about lending an owner money to open an automobile transmission-repair operation. However, if it is an AAMCO franchise, they might think differently. The banker knows that if the prospective businessperson is associated with a national chain, the chances of bankruptcy will be reduced greatly because the franchisor will stand behind the individual and try to help in every way possible. In fact, in some cases, franchisors personally have helped franchisees get started by lending them money and not requiring any repayment until the operation is up and running smoothly. In short, buying a franchise is often an ideal way to ensure assistance from the financial community.

DISADVANTAGES OF FRANCHISING

The prospective franchisee must weigh the advantages of franchising against the accompanying disadvantages. Some of the most important drawbacks are as follows:

1. Franchise fees
2. The control the franchisor exercises
3. Unfulfilled promises of some franchisors

The following sections examine each of these disadvantages.

FRANCHISE FEES

In business, no entrepreneur receives something for nothing. The larger and more successful the franchisor, the greater the franchise fee usually charged. It is not uncommon to be charged a fee of $50,000 to $500,000 for a franchise from a national chain. Smaller franchisors, or those that have not had great success, charge less. Nevertheless, deciding whether of not to take the franchise route into entrepreneurship requires weighing the return possible from putting the money into another type of business. Keep in mind that this fee covers only the benefits discussed in the previous section. The prospective franchisee also must pay for building the unit and stocking it, although the franchisor may help out by providing assistance in securing a bank loan. Additionally, a second fee is usually tied to gross sales. Typically, they must also buy their own equipment and inventory, and then pay a continuing royalty based on sales, usually between 5 percent and 12 percent. Most franchisors require buyers to pay 25 percent to 50 percent of the initial cost in cash. The rest can be borrowed—in some cases, from the franchising organization itself.[10] Table 3-4 lists the costs involved in buying a franchise.

TABLE 3-4   The Cost of Franchising

Don't let the advantages of franchising cloud the significant costs involved. Although the franchise fee may be $75,000, the actual cost of "opening your doors for business" can be more than $200,000! Depending on the type of franchise, the following expenditures are possible:

1. *The basic franchising fee.* For this, you may receive a wide range of services: personnel training, licenses, operations manuals, training materials, site selection and location preparation assistance, and more. Or you may receive none of these.
2. *Insurance.* You will need coverage for a variety of items, such as plate glass, office contents, vehicles, and more. You also should obtain what is known as *umbrella insurance;* it is inexpensive and is meant to help out in the event of crippling million (or multimillion) dollar lawsuits.
3. *Opening product inventory.* If initial inventory is not included in your franchise fee, you will have to obtain enough to open your franchise.
4. *Remodeling and leasehold improvements.* Under most commercial leases, you are responsible for these costs.
5. *Utility charges.* Deposits to cover the first month or two are usually required for electricity, gas, oil, telephone, and water.
6. *Payroll.* This should include the costs of training employees before the store opens. You should include a reasonable salary for yourself as well.
7. *Debt service.* This includes principal and interest payments.
8. *Bookkeeping and accounting fees.* In addition to the services the franchisor may supply in this area, it is always wise to use your own accountant.
9. *Legal and professional fees.* The cost of hiring an attorney to review the franchise contract, to file for and obtain any necessary zoning or planning ordinances, and to handle any unforeseen conflicts must be factored into your opening costs projections.
10. *State and local licenses, permits, and certificates.* These run the gamut from liquor licenses to building permits for renovations.

FRANCHISOR CONTROL

When people work in a large corporation, the company controls their activities. Individuals who have a personal business control their own activities. A franchise operator lies somewhere between these two extremes.[11] The franchisor generally exercises a fair degree of control over his or her operation. For example, if one were to visit a McDonald's in New York City, Chicago, and San Francisco, it would be difficult to tell them apart. The building, décor, and interior of the rooms would look identical because of the uniformity of design. The same is true for Burger King and Pizza Hut.

Likewise, operations of the various units would be the same. One can expect to eat an identically tasting hamburger regardless of which McDonald's franchise unit cooked it. In order to achieve this degree of uniformity, the franchisor keeps a very close eye on the unit's operation. If the entrepreneur does not follow franchisor directions and starts raising prices or changing the menu, the entrepreneur may not get to renew the franchise license when the contract expires. A concept called *free-riding* refers to the latitude a franchisee takes in following the policies and procedures of the franchisor. As discussed earlier, a benefit of securing a franchise is that you purchase immediate brand recognition; however, free-riding can have detrimental effects for both the franchisee and franchisor. A recent study suggest that the best control for enforcing franchisor policies and procedures is through increased formalization of policies and procedures and interaction between franchisor and franchisee. Increased centralization of decision making was found to be an ineffective way to curb free-riding and actually caused an increase in the behavior.[12]

UNFULFILLED PROMISES

In some cases, especially among lesser-known franchisors, franchisees have not received all they were promised.[13] For example, many franchisees have found themselves with trade names that have no drawing power. In other cases, the franchise system was associated with a prominent sports figure or entertainment star who had simply loaned his or her name to the organizers but had little to do with the chain's management. Most of these celebrity franchise chains have folded, after absorbing the savings of many franchisees.

Many franchisees have found that promised assistance from the franchisor has not been forthcoming. For example, instead of being able to purchase supplies more cheaply through the franchisor, many operators have found themselves paying exorbitant prices for supplies. The Select Committee on Small Business of the U.S. Congress found a large restaurant chain buying maraschino cherries for $1.59 per gallon and selling them to franchises for $4.50 per gallon. Furthermore, a pizza chain was buying spices for $3 and reselling them to franchisees for $21.50. If franchisees complain, however, they risk having their agreement with the franchisor terminated or not renewed.

The new century has brought about a greater level of concern for franchisees. Three national or international organizations now exist to assist franchisees: the

American Association of Franchisees and Dealers (AAFD), the American Franchisee Association (AFA), and the International Franchise Association (IFA). The specific purposes of these trade associations are to (1) represent franchisees in all industries in the development of franchising and its fair governmental regulation; (2) educate franchisees, potential franchisees, the government, and the general public about the needs and requirements of franchisees; (3) improve the business conditions for franchising; and (4) protect and enhance the economic investment of franchisees.

Some examples of working programs the AAFD has in place are as follows:[14]

1. Franchisee LegaLine: A national referral network of experienced franchise attorneys who provide legal services to AAFD members
2. Franchise FinancialLine and AAFD Lenders Network: A national network of experienced accountants, certified public accountants (CPAs), independent banks, and other financial services providers that provide financial services to AAFD members
3. AAFD Suppliers Network: A national network of businesses that provide a full array of goods and services and offer special AAFD members-only pricing
4. AAFD Speakers and Experts Bureau: AAFD's exclusive network of public speakers and experts representing a broad spectrum of issues of interest and concern to the franchising community
5. Council of Fair Franchising Seal Recipients: A network of franchising companies that have earned the AAFD's Fair Franchising Seal and are supporting members of the AAFD

EVALUATING THE OPPORTUNITIES

How can the potential entrepreneur evaluate a franchise operation and decide if it is a good deal? Unfortunately, no mathematical formula exists like the one for evaluating the purchase of an ongoing business in Chapter 2. Nor is it possible simply to ask a friend, because the most popular franchises, which are probably the only ones the individual is familiar with, are not giving franchises to people seeking to enter the field. This leaves only the smaller, lesser-known, and more risky franchise operations.[15]

One research study examined the relationship between the base fees and royalties paid to the franchise's overall value. The findings indicated that the age of a franchise, number of retail units, concentration in the state, and national representation are all reflected in the size of base fees and royalties. However, the key to examining the value of a prospective franchise is a proper information search.[16] In addition, in order to ensure an adequately protected investment, an evaluation of all franchise opportunities must be undertaken. Figure 3-1 illustrates a complete process model for analyzing the purchase of a franchise.

FIGURE 3-1 The Decision to Purchase a Franchise: Process Model

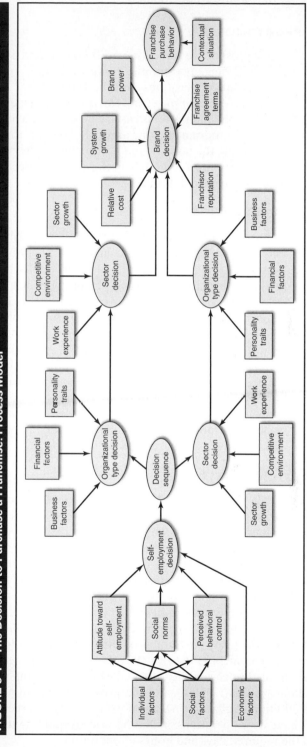

Source: Kaufmann, Patrick J. "Franchising and the Choice of Self Employment," Journal of Business Venturing, Vol. 14, No. 4, (July, 1999) p. 348.

LEARN OF OPPORTUNITIES

One of the first things a prospective franchisee must do is to find a reliable source of information about franchising opportunities. Some of the most readily available sources are newspapers, trade publications, and the Internet (see Table 3-5 for a list of useful Web sites). *Entrepreneur* magazine carries advertisements of franchise opportunities, and exhibitions and trade shows are held by franchisors from time to time in various cities. Entrepreneur.com annually lists the top franchises as well as those that are growing the fastest. Finally, franchisors themselves offer information on specific opportunities, although, in this case, one needs to beware of promises that exceed what may be delivered.

INVESTIGATE THE FRANCHISOR

The prospective investor should get as much information as possible on the franchisor. So many people have lost their life savings in franchise schemes that, except when dealing with a long-established franchisor, one is best advised to enter the investigation prepared for the worst. In particular, if the franchisor seems too eager to sell dealerships or units, it is cause for alarm. Likewise, if the franchisor does not make a vigorous effort to check out prospective investors, it is usually a sign that the seller does not think the operation will last long and probably is interested in just taking the franchise fees and absconding with them. Remember: No reputable franchisor will sell a franchise without ensuring that the buyer is capable of operating in successfully. Many of the new service franchises (Jackson-Hewitt, the UPS Store, and Jiffy-Lube, for example) have instituted policies to ensure that the applicant has the ability to handle the demands of a franchise. McDonald's, one of the most cautious of all franchisors, carefully screens all applicants, and it claims is has never had a unit go bankrupt.

SEEK PROFESSIONAL HELP

If the franchisor passes the initial investigation and offers a franchise contract, the prospective franchisee should first take it to a qualified attorney. The attorney will understand the terms of the agreement and can explain any penalties or restrictive clauses that limit what the franchisee can do.

Of major importance are contract provisions related to cancellation and renewal of the franchise. Can the franchisor take away the franchise for some minor rule infraction? More important, if the agreement is canceled, how much of the initial franchise fee will be refunded to the individual? If the franchise can be purchased back by the franchisor at 20 percent of the initial fee, the lawyer will need to examine carefully how easily the franchisor can terminate the agreement.

Other consideration include the franchise fee, the percentage of gross revenues to be paid to the franchisor, the type and extent of training to be provided, the territorial limits of the franchise, and the provisions for supplying materials to the unit. In addition, the lawyer needs to examine the degree of control the franchisor will have over operations, including price requirements, performance standards, and the required days and hours of operation.

TABLE 3-5 World Wide Web Franchise Sites

The Internet has become the foremost source of information for people of all ages, trades, and interests. Short of handing over the funds, the prospective franchisee can find everything he or she needs to ensure the successful research, selecting, and planning of a franchise business in the comfort of his or her own home.

You can search for the perfect match by location, category, investment, and actual franchise at www.betheboss.com. This site allows you to obtain pertinent information about certain franchises via showcases that provide histories, business summaries, frequently asked questions, and investment requirements. Basic franchise information, including interactive financial worksheets, ways to select the right franchise, expo information, and links to other valuable Web resources, are also available.

Multiple links from www.franchise1.com, the Franchise Handbook, offer the serious person serious answers to his or her questions. Directories, associations, a message board, and industry news are just a few of the resources available on the Web's most popular franchise site.

Franchise Works can be found at www.franchiseworks.com. There you will find different franchises listed by category as well as other business opportunities that are available. Also on the site are resources that can be used to cover all aspects of starting a business.

The International Franchise Association is a premier source for industry data. Browse www.franchise.org to stay on top of the latest government developments and hot topics that affect franchisees and franchisors worldwide.

Other Valuable Sites

American Bar Association Forum on Franchising	*www.abanet.org*
U.S. Small Business Administration	*www.sba.gov*
Statistics—USA	*www.stat-usa.gov*
Entrepreneur Magazine	*www.entrepreneurmag.com*
Minority Business Entrepreneur Magazine	*www.mbemag.com*
Franchise Times	*www.franchisetimes.com*
Franchise Update	*www.franchise-update.com*
Restaurant Business Magazine	*www.restaurantbiz.com*
Source Book Publications	*www.worldfranchising.com*
Federal Trade Commission	*www.fte.gov/bcp/franchise/netfran.htm*
Franchise.com	*http://www.franchise.com*
World Franchising	*http://www.worldfranchising.com*
Franchise Solutions	*http://www.franchisesolutions.com*
Franchise Opportunities	*http://www.franchiseopportunities.com*
Franchise Trade	*http://www.franchisetrade.com*
The Franchise Magazine	*http://www.thefranchisemagazine.net*
Franchise Info Mall	*http://www.franchiseinfomall.com*
Franchise Advantage	*http://www.franchiseadvantage.com*
U.S. Franchise News	*http://www.usfranchisenews.com*

The individual also should seek financial counsel. A good banker should be able to look over the franchisor's prospectus and give an opinion regarding its feasibility. Is the projected revenue too high for a new unit? Is the return on investment overly optimistic? Would the bank be prepared to advance to advance a loan on this type of business undertaking?

Finally, the investor should talk to a certified public accountant, who can review the date and construct a projected income statement for the first few years. Does the investment look promising? What might go wrong and jeopardize the investment? How likely are those developments? Is this the type of investment that constitutes an acceptable risk for the prospective buyer, or should the individual walk away from the deal?

Legal and financial professionals will help the prospective franchisee answer some very important questions. In particular, they will force the individual to face the risks inherent in a franchise and answer the question, "Am I willing to take this type of risk?"

THE DECISION: IT'S UP TO THE ENTREPRENEUR

After the prospective entrepreneur has gathered all of the necessary information, it is up to him or her to make the final decision on the matter. As with any form of entrepreneurial start-up, the proper research can mitigate the risks involved in the decision; however, the final decision to act is still in the hands of the entrepreneur.

TRENDS IN FRANCHISING

Trends in franchising are extending to include system-wide changes in ways of doing business. Some of the most prominent changes are as follows:

- *Internet franchising.* The franchisor Internet explosion has begun. A significant increase has occurred in the use of the Internet as a means of communication within franchise organizations, advertising by franchises, and most significantly in the rise of purchases on the Internet—many local franchises offer Internet ordering before the customer arrives. Blockbuster video stores are a good example of this service, as well as many pizza chains such as Pizza Hut.

- *Globalization of franchising.* Many franchisors overseas are expanding either vertically (growing rapidly in certain narrow industries, such as fast food or retail) or horizontally (many small U.S. franchisors entering the market).

- *Home-based franchises.* The growth in this sector is explosive because it offers people the autonomy to work at home and balance family with work aspirations. Many of these franchise opportunities exist in business-to-business services, which are usually direct-sales franchises.

- *Rural franchises.* These small markets are fertile ground if a franchisor can develop a concept that works rurally. The key to success in rural markets is the ability to provide quality services combined with low start-up construction so that the franchise can prosper even with low levels of unit volume.

In addition to these trends, the legal considerations associated with franchising continue to grow. Changes are taking place in the legal environment for both franchisers and franchisees. For example, the formerly franchisor-controlled IFA now accepts franchisees as members. This illustrates that the balance of power is shifting from franchisors to franchisees. Over the years, numerous franchise hearings have taken place in the U.S. House of Representatives. As a result, the Federal Trade Commission now provides stricter enforcement of its Franchise Disclosure Rule, as well as improved franchise laws within individual states. In the years ahead, more legislation will regulate franchising. Franchisors themselves admit that this is one of the major problems they will have to face; franchising will become more challenging as a result of legislation and court rulings, and research by the entrepreneur will be even more essential.[17]

Additionally, the retail environment throughout the United States is becoming increasingly complex. However, this merely means that today's entrepreneur/ franchisee will have to be a better businessperson than his or her predecessors. As an example, retail outlets are changing in terms of product mix, store design, and layout. Some supermarkets are fighting fast-food orders by putting in fast-food departments of their own. In short, survival in the retail environment will require creative marketing. Franchising will play an important role in this environment. The need for entrepreneurs with the ability and daring to assume the risks that will be inherent in franchise operations will be the primary challenge of the next decade.

FRANCHISING YOUR BUSINESS

The other side of franchising relates to the entrepreneur as the developer of the franchise idea and business. Fundamental changes in business and society present many opportunities for new franchisors. Among these trends are a cleaner environment, the aging baby boomer generation, niche restaurants and specialty retailing, personal and business services, and direct sales to businesses.[18]

How does one get the next franchise business off the ground? Assume that you are a successful entrepreneur considering franchising your business. First, it's important to recognize that you would be creating a business, but not the same one you already created. Second, you need to try to determine whether the idea is franchisable. Simply having a successful business does not always mean the business is a good franchise candidate. What are the growth opportunities? Is this a business with growth potential that will exceed its ability to fund its own expansion? Is this a business in which any one unit will serve only a limited, local market, as opposed to a manufacturing business that could serve a national market from a limited number of locations? How quickly could you grow on your own versus growing by selling franchises? Will a lack of rapid growth have a negative impact on your business's survival?

Before putting together a franchise plan, you must make many decisions. For every issue a prospective franchisee would consider, you must make a decision as the franchisor.[19] The shoe is on the other foot; these are very important choices. Ask yourself: What should be my franchise fee? What are the royalties I will charge? (Sections V and VI of the Uniform Franchise Offering Circular address the issues of initial and ongoing franchise fees.) What services do I give the franchisees? What rights do the franchisees have? What control do I want to retain? Who will write a franchise agreement? What training will I give them, and where, once franchisees sign on? Will I offer any financing? What sales territory rights will I provide? (Section XII covers details about how much territory the franchisee can operate within.) How will I select the franchisees themselves? The list goes on and on, and experienced legal counsel is highly recommended.

The development of a new franchise business is a complex process. For the same reasons that you would develop a business plan for any type of business, it is essential that you develop a comprehensive business plan for your new franchising firm. It also is recommended that you develop a model business plan for prospective franchisees. This step can help prospects gain financing, speed up the writing of their own business plan, and guide them in the development of their franchise. This model business plan needs to be modifies to accommodate the unique or unusual situations of individual franchises. It is important to remember that you're now in several businesses. Following are more guidelines:

1. *Developing a franchise business.* This refers to developing operating systems for your own business—that is, the headquarter business. You will need to develop functional areas such as human resources, information systems, accounting, purchasing and logistics, training for home-office employees and franchisees, and methods for franchisee evaluation.

2. *Selling franchises.* Your success depends not only on your ability to manage the business you have created but also on the expansion of your sales base by adding franchises to the firm. This is marketing of a different sort. Your firm must prospect to develop leads, market itself through appropriate channels, and screen these prospective franchises. Careful franchisee selection is key to building a strong outlet network.

3. *Servicing franchises.* Provisions of necessary business support services by the franchisor are one of the main reasons people purchase franchises. If you cannot or do not offer franchisees enough in return, such as marketing assistance and support, you'll have a revolution among the ranks. Other areas of franchisee support you need to develop include dependable suppliers, ideas, strategies for dealing with the competition, and training for the franchise owners and their employees.

4. *Learning more about running the franchised business so that you can make it worthwhile for you franchisees to stay with you.* Franchisees expect training in business methods, new product development, marketing innovation, research on the best ways to conduct the business, and the like. If you don't provide these, and do it well, the franchisees will question whether they should stick around. Remember, your success is dependent on their success.

The bottom line, the experts say, is that you must be in it for the long term. Franchising your business is not the way to quick and easy riches with all those fees and royalties rolling in. Building a successful franchise business, like building most businesses, is a slow process.

Summary

A franchise is a system of distribution that enables a supplier (the franchisor) to arrange for a dealer (the franchisee) to handle a specific product or service under certain mutually agreed-upon conditions. In essence, the two types of franchising arrangements are the franchising of a product or service and the franchising of an entire business enterprise.

Franchising has proved to be a very popular vehicle for getting into business. Franchising now accounts for $803 billion in annual sales, which equals 20 percent of the U.S. gross national product. Franchises represent 42 percent of all U.S. retail sales.

How can the average businessperson evaluate a franchise operation in order to decide if it is a good deal? One of the first things a prospective franchisee must do is find a source of information about the franchisor and the franchisee contract. Next, professionals such as a lawyer, banker, and CPA should look over the deal and offer their candid opinions. After this, the decision is up to the prospective investor. The type of checklist provided in this chapter will help the prospective investor decide.

The next part of the chapter examined future trends in franchising. Some of these are (1) Internet franchising, (2) globalization, (3) home-based franchises, (4) rural franchises, and (5) the eventual increase in regulating legislation.

The last part of the chapter reviewed the other side of franchising as it related to the entrepreneur who develops the franchise idea. The entrepreneur must remember that a business is being created that is franchisable. Therefore, developing growth opportunities for this type of business is critical. By putting together a franchise plan, potential franchisors can work through the complete process of franchising.

Review and Discussion Questions

1. What is meant by the term *franchise?*
2. In a franchising agreement, what is the franchisee often called on to do? What responsibility does the franchisor assume?
3. How fast has franchising grown during the last decade? What are the reasons for this growth?
4. What are some of the major advantages of franchising? Cite and explain three.
5. What are some of the major disadvantages of franchising? Cite and explain at least two.
6. How can a prospective franchisee evaluate a franchise opportunity? Explain.

NEW VENTURE CONSULTANT

The Franchise Opportunity

Arlene Voss has been a paralegal for 10 years and feels she knows quite a lot about business. "Every day I take depositions and research legal issues," she noted. "And I've seen lots of businesses fail because they didn't have adequate capital or proper management. Believe me, when you work in a paralegal firm, you see—and learn—plenty."

One day a franchise ad in a business magazine caught her attention. Arlene called and found out that the franchisor was selling fast-food franchises in her area. "We are in the process of moving into your section of the country," the spokesperson told her. "We have 111 franchisees throughout the nation and want to sell 26 in your state." Arlene went to a meeting that the franchisor held at a local hotel and, along with a large number of other potential investors, listened to the sales pitch. It all sounded very good. The cost of the franchise was $65,000 plus 4 percent of gross revenues. The franchisor promised assistance with site location and personnel training, and encouraged the prospective franchisees to ask questions and investigate the organization. "If you don't feel this is a good deal for you, it's not a good deal for us either; good business is a two-way street," the spokesperson pointed out. "We are going to be looking very carefully at all franchise applications, and you ought to be giving us the same degree of scrutiny."

Arlene liked what she heard but felt it would be prudent to do some checking on her own. Before leaving the meeting, she asked the spokesperson for the names and addresses of some current franchisees. "I don't have a list with me," he said, "but I can write down some that I know of, and you can get their numbers from the operator." He then scribbled four names and locations on a piece of paper and handed it to her.

Arlene called information operators for the four locations and was able to get telephone numbers for only two of the franchises. The other addresses apparently were wrong. She then placed calls to the two franchisees. The first person said she has owned her franchise for one year and felt it was too early to judge the success of the operation. When she found out Arlene was thinking about buying a franchise, she asked if Arlene would consider buying hers. The price the woman quoted was $5,000 less than what the company currently was quoting. The second person told Arlene he simply did not give out information over the phone. He seemed somewhat edgy about talking to her and continually sidestepped Arlene's requests for specific financial information. Finally, he told her, "Look, if you really want this information, I think you should talk to my attorney. If he says it's okay to tell you, I will." He then gave Arlene the attorney's number.

Before she could call the lawyer, Arlene left for lunch. When she returned, one of the partners of her firm was standing beside her desk. "Hey, Arlene, what are you doing calling this guy?" he asked, holding up the telephone number of the franchisee's attorney. "Are you planning to sue someone? That's his specialty, you know." Arlene smiled. "As a matter of fact, I am. I'm thinking of suing you guys for back wages." The attorney laughed along with her and then walked back into his office.

Your consultation: What is your appraisal of the situation? Would you recommend that Arlene buy the franchise from the woman who has offered to sell? Why or why not? What would you recommend Arlene do now?

7. In evaluating whether or not to buy a franchise operation, the potential investor should ask a series of questions. What questions should the potential investor ask about the franchisor, the franchise, the market, and the potential investor (him- or herself)?
8. Discuss the future of franchising. Explain the forecasted trends and their potential impact on investors.

Endnotes

1. Marko Grunhagen and Robert A. Mittelstaedt, "Entrepreneurs or Investors: Do Multi-Unit Franchisees Have Different Philosophical Orientations?" *Journal of Small Business Management* 43, no. 3 (2005): 207–25.
2. Entrepreneur.com. "2007 Franchise 500." www.entrepreneur.com/franchise500/index.html (accessed June 6, 2007).
3. Patrick J. Kaufman, "Franchising and the Choice of Self-Employment," *Journal of Business Venturing* (July 1999): 345–62.
4. Kirk Shivell and Kent Banning, "What Every Prospective Franchisee Should Know," *Small Business Forum* (Winter 1996/1997): 33–42; and Rupert Barkoff, *Fundamentals of Business Franchising,* 2nd ed. (Chicago: American Bar Association, 2005).
5. Entrepreneur.com. "An American Icon: Jobs and Entrepreneurship." www.entrepreneur.com/magazine/entrepreneur/2005/january/74992-2.html (accessed March 1, 2007).
6. Sara Wilson, "Pushing Forward: Is Enough Being Done in the Franchise Industry to Encourage Diversity?" *Entrepreneur* (December 2005): 122–27; and Ronald N. Langston, "Minority-Business Enterprise: The National Priority," *Franchising World* 38, no. 6 (2006): 14–16.
7. International Franchise Association Educational Foundation, Washington, DC, 2000.
8. International Franchise Association, 2000; Europeanfranchising.com, 2007; Japan Franchise Association, 2004; Franchise Council of Australia, 2004; and www.buyusa.com, 2007.
9. See Alen Peterson and Rajiv P. Dant, "Perceived Advantages of the Franchise Option form the Franchisee Perspective: Empirical Insights from a Service Franchise," *Journal of Small Business Management* (July 1990): 46–61; see also Darrell L. Williams, "Why Do Entrepreneurs Become Franchisees? An Empirical Analysis of Organizational Choice," *Journal of Business Venturing* (January 1999): 103–24.
10. Robert T. Justis and Richard J. Judd, *Franchising,* 3rd ed. (Mason, OH: Thomson Publishing, 2004); and Joe Mathews, Don DeBolt, and Deb Percival, *Street Smart Franchising* (Chicago, IL: Entrepreneur Press, 2006).
11. Robert T. Justis and Janeen E. Olsen, "Using Marketing Research to Enhance Franchisee/Franchisor Relationships," *Journal of Small Business Management* (April 1993): 121–27.
12. Roland E. Kidwell, Arne Nygaard, and Ragnhild Silkoset, "Antecedents and Effects of Free-Riding in the Franchisor–Franchisee Relationship," *Journal of Business Venturing* 22, no. 4 (2007): 522–44.
13. See Nerilee Hing, "Franchisee Satisfaction: Contributors and Consequences," *Journal of Small Business Management* (April 1995): 12–25; see also Marko Grunhagen and Robert A. Mittelstaedt, "Entrepreneurs or Investors: Do Multi-Unit Franchisees Have Different Philosophical Orientations?" *Journal of Small Business Management* 43, no. 3 (2005): 207–25.

14. For more information, see the organization's Web sites: www.aafd.org and www.franchisee.org.

15. See Timothy Bates, "Analysis of Survival Rates among Franchise and Independent Small Business Startups," *Journal of Small Business Management* (April 1995): 26–36.

16. David A. Baucus, Melissa S. Baucas, and Sherrie E. Human, "Choosing a Franchise: How Base Fees and Royalties Relate to the Value of the Franchise," *Journal of Small Business Management* (April 1993): 91–104.

17. For an excellent overview of franchises, see Rupert Barkoff, *Fundamentals of Business Franchising,* 2nd ed. (Chicago: American Bar Association, 2005), and Gaylord A. Jentz, Roger LeRoy Miller, and Frank B. Cross, *West's Business Law,* 10th ed. (Mason, OH: Thomson/Southwestern, 2007).

18. www.franchise.org, 2007; www.entrepreneur.com, 2007.

19. Thani Jambulingam and John R. Nevin, "Influence of Franchisee Selection Criteria of Outcomes Desired by the Franchisor," *Journal of Business Venturing* (July 1999): 363–96; see also Gary J. Castrogiovanni, James G. Combs, and Robert T. Justis, "Shifting Imperatives: An Integrative View of Resource Scarcity and Agency Reasons for Franchising," *Entrepreneurship Theory & Practice* 30, no. 1 (2006): 23–40.

CHAPTER 4

SUCCESSFUL BUSINESS PLANS
THE ROADMAP

INTRODUCTION

Most people who want to start a new venture need to borrow money. Banks and other financial institutions often will not loan funds without a detailed business plan that shows the planned activities of the company, its management team, its projected expenses and earnings, and its plans for repaying the loan. Even those who do not need to borrow money can profit from preparing a plan.[1]

THE NATURE OF A BUSINESS PLAN

The major advantage of a business plan is that it forces the entrepreneur to answer the following questions:

- Where am I going?
- How will I get there?
- What opportunities and problems will I run into along the way?
- How will I deal with them?

Ultimately, the business plan assesses the feasibility of an idea as a business. It is a roadmap for the would-be entrepreneur. Like all plans, much of it may not happen as expected. However, preparing the plan forces the individual to think about the conditions he or she may face. If the plan has to be changed, the person who prepared it can modify the plan to fit reality. The emphasis of the business plan should be final implementation of the venture. In other words, it is not enough just to write an effective plan; entrepreneurs also must see that the plan is executed in a way that will lead to a successful enterprise. The box feature, *New Venture Perspective,* provides an interesting look at the value of business plans.

NEW VENTURE PERSPECTIVE

Do We Really Need Business Plans?

Business schools and consultants have long believed that completing a formal business plan increases the chances of success for an entrepreneurial venture. Entrepreneurs spend long hours working on business plans that can range from 50 to 100 pages and include market research and financial projections. Recently, schools have begun to wonder whether or not business plans really do help a new venture succeed. Some scholars are suggesting that entrepreneurs who aren't looking for outside start-up financing write a *back-of-the-envelope* plan with a basic model and cash flow projections and then rework the business model after starting the business. Here is what some of the scholars had to say: "Just do it."

William Bygrave, an entrepreneurship professor at Babson College in Wellesley, Massachusetts, advocates a "just do it" mindset when entrepreneurs start businesses. He says, "What we really don't want to do is literally spend a year or more essentially writing a business plan without knowing we have actual customers." He also points out that entrepreneurs are more willing to stick with a flawed business plan after start-up because of the time invested rather than making the necessary adjustments to give the business a chance to succeed.

Critics of the traditional business plan method say that it contradicts what an entrepreneur is all about, which is the ability to learn and adapt through experience. A study completed by Babson College, which was designed to determine success among businesses that started with a business plan and those that didn't, examined 116 businesses started by alumni. The study examined characteristics such as annual revenue, number of employees, and net income, and showed that there was no statistical difference. It concluded that the only reason a person would be required to write a business plan is to raise outside capital from venture capitalists or business angels.

Additionally, Amare Bhide, an entrepreneurship professor from Columbia University, noted that 41 percent of *Inc.* magazine's 1989 list of the 500 fastest-growing private firms did not have business plans, and only 26 percent of them had basic plans. In 2002, a follow-up completed by the magazine found that the statistics were basically the same. There are competitive advantages to starting a business quickly; by the time a business plan is completed, the window of opportunity to capitalize may have already passed.

Knowing the Customer Base

Benson Honig, a professor at Wilfrid, Laurier University in Ontario, Canada, completed similar research in the late 1990s; he too found no correlation between business plan completion and profitability. His study instead suggested that the biggest factor in determining success was defining who the customers were in advance. Professor Honig has started teaching his students what he calls *contingency planning*, which involves thinking about how businesses constantly progress, change, and make decisions based on the market climate instead of using traditional business planning.

Untold Failure

Scott Shane, a professor from Case Western Reserve University, says that most evidence regarding the importance of business plans is flawed because researchers do not correct for business failure rates and only account for businesses that have survived. If researchers account for failure rates, Shane claims, they would find that a lot of businesses have failed that never had a business plan.

Still, there is general consensus that the most viable reason to write a business plan is to gain resources from venture capitalists, banks, or other outside investors such as angel investors. If outside financing is not being sought, a shorter plan with emphasis on marketing and financials seems to be preferred.

Source: Adapted from Kelly K. Spros, "Do Start-Ups Really Need Formal Business Plans?" *Wall Street Journal*, January 9, 2007, B9.

IMPORTANCE OF A BUSINESS PLAN

Business planning forces entrepreneurs to analyze all aspects of their venture and to prepare an effective strategy to deal with the uncertainties that may arise. Thus, a business plan may help an entrepreneur avoid a project doomed to failure. As one researcher states, "If your proposed venture is marginal at best, the business plan will show you why and may help you avoid paying the high tuition of business failure. It is far cheaper not to begin an ill-fated business than to learn by experience what your business plan could have taught you at a cost of several hours of concentrated work."[2] Great ideas with high potential, though they still benefit from the planning process, may not necessarily need the extensive work required by a business plan. Perhaps the value of the business plan is greatest for bad business ideas for which the process shows glaring problems that must be dealt with before the entrepreneur uses his or her own funds or investments from others.

The need to prepare a business plan extends to the entrepreneurial team as well. All of the key members should be involved in writing the plan. However, the lead entrepreneur still must understand each contribution to the team. Consultants also may be sought to help prepare a business plan, but the entrepreneur must remain the driving force behind the plan. Seeking the advice and assistance of outside professionals is always wise, but entrepreneurs need to understand every aspect because they are the people the financial sources scrutinize. Thus, the business plan stands as the entrepreneur's description and prediction for his or her venture, and it must be defended by the entrepreneur. Simply put, it is the entrepreneur's responsibility.

The business plan can provide a number of specific benefits for entrepreneurs who undertake the challenge of developing this formal document. Some of these benefits are as follows:

1. The time, effort, research, and discipline needed to create a formal business plan force entrepreneurs to view the venture critically, objectively, and holistically.

2. The competitive, economic, and financial analyses included in the business plan subject entrepreneurs to close scrutiny of their assumptions about the venture's success.

3. Because all aspects of the business venture must be addressed in the plan, entrepreneurs develop and examine operational strategies and expected results for outside evaluators.

4. The business plan quantifies goals and objectives, which provide measurable benchmarks for comparing forecasts with actual results.

5. The completed business plan provides entrepreneurs with a communication tool for outside financial sources as well as an operational tool for guiding the venture toward success.

WHAT IS A BUSINESS PLAN?

A *business plan* is the entrepreneur's roadmap for a successful enterprise. It is a written document that describes in detail a proposed venture, and its purpose is to illustrate the current status, expected needs, and projected results of a new or expanding business. Every characteristic of the project is described: marketing, research and development, manufacturing or service provision, management, risks, financing, and a timetable for accomplishing clearly identified goals. Each of these components is necessary to show a clear picture of what the venture is, where it is going, and how the entrepreneur proposes to get it there.

As highlighted by the different scholars presented in the earlier New Venture Perspective, planning is essential to the success of any undertaking. Proper planning requires that an entrepreneur formulate the objectives and directions for the future. Business plans can serve this role as an effective planning device. However, several critical factors must be addressed. The business plan must have realistic goals that are specific, measurable, and set within time parameters. A commitment to success must be supported by everyone involved in the venture. Milestones must be established for continuous and timely evaluations of progress. Finally, the business plan must be flexible to allow for the anticipation of obstacles and the formulation of alternative strategies.

New ventures and business plans go together. The reason is obvious: New ventures require capital—often substantial amounts of capital. Providers of capital, whether they are lending institutions, major investors in securities, or venture capitalists, require a great amount of information about the enterprise, and anything less than a business plan is insufficient for the task.

In summary, the business plan is the major tool for guiding the operation of the venture as well as the primary document for managing it. Its main thrust is the strategic development of the project compiled into a comprehensive document for outside investors to read and understand. It allows entrepreneurs entrance into the investment process. A subsidiary benefit is that it enables the enterprise to avoid common pitfalls that cause less-organized efforts to fail.[3]

THE COMPONENTS OF A BUSINESS PLAN

Readers of a business plan expect it to have two important qualities: It must be organized and it must be complete. The entrepreneur also should consider the intended audience when the plan is presented for funding. Mason and Stark suggest that most of the research on business plans ignores the needs of the different types of funding sources. According to their research, business plans should be customized based on the following:

- Bankers stress the financial aspects of the plan and place little emphasis on the market, entrepreneur, or other issues.

- Equity investors, capitol fund managers, venture capital fund managers, and business angels emphasize both market and financial components.[4]

With this in mind, the following list describes the 11 components that make up a complete and organized business plan.

1. *Executive summary.* A short description of the venture and its mission should be the first information the reader encounters. The executive summary should be written in an interesting way with proper emphasis on the more important aspects of the plan, such as the unique characteristics of the venture, the major mission of the venture clearly articulated, the major marketing points, and the desired end result. Its purpose is to whet the reader's appetite for more information. A good summary will guarantee that the rest of the plan will be read.

2. *Descriptions of the business.* This section contains a more comprehensive account of the venture and the mission of the proposed business model. The description of the business should include a brief history of the company where applicable and some information about the overall industry. The product or service should be described in terms of its unique value to consumers. Finally, goals and milestones should be clarified.

3. *Marketing.* The marketing section is divided into two major parts. The first is research and analysis. The target market must be identified, with emphasis on who will buy the product or service. Market size and trends must be measured, and the market share must be estimated. In addition, the competition should be studied in considerable detail. The second part is the marketing plan. This is perhaps the most important part of the business plan. It must discuss market strategy, sales and distribution, pricing, advertising, promotion,

and public relations. Some businesses make the mistake of preparing only a marketing plan; however, by itself and outside the structure of a business plan, a marketing plan will not meet the needs of a new venture.

4. *Research, design, and development.* The research, design, and development section includes developmental research leading to the product or service's design, development, or delivery. Technical research results should be evaluated, and the cost structure of the newly designed product or service should be determined.

5. *Operations segment.* This section requires an investigation focused on identifying the optimal location for the venture. Proximity to suppliers, availability of transportation, and labor supply are of prime importance. If the venture requires highly skilled or educated labor, the entrepreneur should consider areas in which the supply of talent will allow them to successfully recruit and retain employees at reasonable costs. The requirements and costs of production facilities and equipment must be determined in advance. Specific needs should be discussed in terms of the facilities required to handle the new venture (plant, warehouse storage, and offices) and the equipment that needs to be acquired (special tooling, machinery, computers, and vehicles). For Internet-based businesses, the outline of operations is essential because the customer base may be diverse and geographically dispersed. Finally, the cost data associated with any of the operation factors should be presented. The financial information used here can be applied later to the financial projections.

6. *Management.* The management team necessarily requires the presence of outstanding individuals to make the venture a success. Methods of compensation such as salaries, employment agreements, stock purchase plans, and ownership levels must be determined. The board of directors, advisers, and consultants also are part of the management team, and their selection should be based on their potential contribution to the enterprise.

7. *Critical risks.* Risks must be analyzed often to uncover potential problems before they materialize. Outside consultants often can be engaged to identify risks and recommend alternative courses of action. The important concept is that risk can be anticipated and controlled. Doing so will result in a more successful venture.

8. *Financial forecasting.* Accountants can make a major contribution to this section. Obtaining financing always has depended on fair and reasonable budgeting and forecasting. Material and labor requirements can be determined from the sales budget and projected inventory. Variable overhead can be scheduled for various capacity levels, and, when these are added to fixed overhead, the budget can be completed. A capital budget then can be prepared; when it is coupled with debt service requirements, cash flow needs can be identified. This information, thus developed, can be summarized into pro forma financial statements such as forecasted statements of earnings, financial position, and cash flows. If the work is done well, these projected statements should represent the financial achievements expected from the business. They also provide

a standard against which to measure the actual results of operating the enterprise. These financial projections will serve as valuable tools for managing and controlling the business in the first few years.

9. *Harvest strategy*. This segment projects a long-term plan for how the entrepreneur(s) will benefit from the success of the venture. Harvest strategies can include selling the business, going public and offering stock, or merging with another business.

10. *Milestone schedule*. This segment of the business plan requires the determination of objectives and the timing of their accomplishment. Milestones and deadlines should be established and then monitored while the venture is in progress. Each milestone is related to all the others, and together they constitute a network of the entire project.

11. *Appendix*. The appendix includes valuable information not contained in other sections. It may include names of references and advisers, as well as drawings, documents, agreements, or other materials that support the plan. If deemed desirable, a bibliography may be presented.

PREPARING THE BUSINESS PLAN

Constructing a business plan is a challenge because of the great amount of work required to put together the 11 components just discussed. After the requisite information is complied, the package must be assembled in good form. Remember that a business plan gives investors, suppliers, and potential employees their first impression of a company. Therefore, the plan should present a professional image. Form, as well as content, is important. The document should be free of spelling, grammatical, or typographical errors. Perfection should be the norm; anything less is unacceptable. Binding and printing should have a professional appearance. The written plan should not exceed 40 pages (20–30 is ideal). The cover page should be attractive, and it should contain the company name and address. A title page should contain the same information as the front cover, as well as the company's telephone number and the month and year the plan is presented.

The first two or three pages should contain the executive summary, which explains the company's current status, its products or services, the benefits to customers, a financial forecast summarized in paragraph form, the venture's objectives in the next few years, the amount of financing needed, and the benefits to investors. This is a lot of information for two pages, but, if it is done well, the investor will get a good impression of the venture and will be enticed to read the rest of the plan.

A table of contents should follow the executive summary. Each section of the plan should be listed, along with the page numbers on which they are found. Obviously, the remaining sections will follow the table of contents. If the last section, the appendix, is too lengthy, it may be necessary to present it is a separate binder to keep the plan within the recommended limit of 40 pages. Each of the sections should be written in a simple and straightforward manner. The purpose is to communicate, not dazzle.

An attractive appearance; proper length; executive summary; table of contents; and professionalism in grammar, spelling, and typing are important factors in a comprehensive business plan. Believe it or not, when reviewed by outside funding sources, these characteristic separate successful plans from failed ones. (See Table 4-1 for a description of Internet resources that are available for assistance when developing a business plan.)

TABLE 4-1 Internet Resources for Business Plan Development

Numerous sources are available for assistance in developing a business plan, the Internet being one of the cheapest, most easily accessible ones. The following list provides some source descriptions and current addresses.

www.gale.com
The Gale Web site has several resources that could be of use. It offers business plan examples and market research for different industries. The company maintains over 600 databases online, in print, and in e-book form.

http://fintel.us/
Fintel is a resource that can be used to help with the financial issues of putting together a business plan. It features current industry reports, financial benchmarking, customized research options, and other available resources.

www.marketresearch.com/
Marketresearch.com is the world's largest collection of market research for different industries. This Web site can provide information such as product trends and analysis of a given market.

http://factfinder.census.gov/home/saff/main.html
The FactFinder Web site is provided by the U.S. Census Bureau. This is a great resource for information regarding population, housing, economic, business, industry, and geographic data.

http://entrepreneur.com/marketingideas/lowcostideas/archive115812.html
This link to Entrepreneur.com provides a list of articles that provide low-cost ideas on how to market your business.

www.smallbiztrends.com/
Smallbiztrends.com is a site that will provide you with updates on trends that affect small and medium-sized businesses. It features traditional Web sites that contain small business data as well as a blog.

www.logoyes.com
Logoyes is a leading provider of do-it-yourself logos for small businesses. Here, one can design a logo for his or her business. To download your logo, however, it may cost some money.

www.claritas.com/MyBestSegments/Default.jsp
This site will define the market for your business. It offers information on consumer segments and defines and describes customer segmentation profiling. It can answer questions such as: What are the customers like? Where can I find them? How can I reach them?

TABLE 4-1 (*Continued*)

http://uwci.org/index.asp?p=178

This site is provided by the United Way of Central Indiana and is designed to help nonprofit organizations.

www.ibj.com

The *Indiana Business Journal* is a newspaper designed to provide information on current economic conditions and business trends in Indiana.

OTHER RESOURCES AVAILABLE THROUGH MOST LIBRARIES

Business Source Premier

This is one of the best business research databases, providing the full text for more than 2,300 journals. It includes information on the topics of marketing, management, management information systems (MIS), production operations management (POM), accounting, finance, and economics.

ReferenceUSA

ReferenceUSA is a database that provides access to information about millions of U.S. businesses and residents. It also offers information on a variety of business topics such as annual reports, Securities and Exchange (SEC) information, trade publications, and newspapers.

Standard and Poor's Net Advantage

This is a source for company, financial, and investment information. It also provides industry analysis from Standard & Poor's (S&P) analysts.

The complete business plan assessment provided in Table 4-2 offers entre-preneurs an opportunity to self-evaluate their business plan as it is developed. Each section is broken down into questions that examine the information needed in that particular segment of the business plan. Then, the columns are used to evaluate (1) whether the information is included in the plan, (2) whether the previous answer is clear, and (3) whether the answer is complete.

Finally, a well-written business plan is like a work of art: It is visually pleasing and makes a statement without saying a word. Unfortunately, the two are also alike in that they are worth money only if they're good. Following are 10 key questions to consider when writing and revising an effective business plan.

1. *Is your plan organized so that key facts leap out at the reader?* Appearances do count. Your plan is a representation of yourself, so don't expect an unor-ganized, less-than-acceptable plan to be your vehicle for obtaining funds.

2. *Is your product/service and business mission clear and simple?* Your mission should state very simply the value that you will be providing to your cus-tomers. It shouldn't take more than a paragraph.

3. *Where are you, really? Are you focused on the right things?* Determine what phase of the business you are really in, focus on the right tasks, and use your resources appropriately.

TABLE 4-2 Complete Business Plan Assessment

A COMPLETE ASSESSMENT OF THE COMPONENTS

There are 10 components of a business plan. As you develop your plan, you should assess each component. Be honest in your assessment because the main purpose is to improve your business plan and increase your chances of success.

Directions: The brief description of each component will help you write that section of your plan. After completing your plan, use the scale provided to assess each component.

5 = Outstanding—thorough and complete in all areas
4 = Very Good—most areas covered but could use improvement in detail
3 = Good—some areas covered in detail but other areas missing
2 = Fair—a few areas covered but very little detail
1 = Poor—no written parts

The 10 Components of a Business Plan

1. **Executive Summary.** This is the most important section because it has to convince the reader that the business will succeed. Using no more than three pages, you should summarize the highlights of the rest of the plan. This means that the key elements of the following components should be mentioned.

   The executive summary must be able to stand on its own. It is not simply an introduction to the rest of the business plan. This section should discuss who purchases your product or service, what makes your business unique, and how you plan to grow in the future. Because this section summarizes the plan, it is often best to write this section last.

Rate this component:	Outstanding	Very Good	Good	Fair	Poor
	5	4	3	2	1

2. **Description of the Business.** This section should provide background information about your industry, a history of your company, a general description of your product or service, and the specific mission that you are trying to achieve. Your product or service should be described in terms of its unique qualities and value to the customer. Specific short-term and long-term objectives must be defined. You should clearly state what sales, market share, and profitability objectives you want your business to achieve.

Key Elements	Have You Covered This in the Plan?	Is the Answer Clear? (yes or no)	Is the Answer Complete? (yes or no)
a. What type of business will you have?			
b. What products or services will you sell?			
c. Why does it promise to be successful?			
d. What is the growth potential?			
e. How is it unique?			

Rate this component:	Outstanding	Very Good	Good	Fair	Poor
	5	4	3	2	1

TABLE 4-2 (*Continued*)

3. Marketing.   There are two major parts to the marketing section. The first is research and analysis. Here, you should explain who buys the product or service—in other words, identify your target market. Measure your market size and trends, and estimate the market share you expect. Be sure to include support for your sales projections. For example, if your figures are based on published marketing research data, be sure to cite the source. Do your best to make realistic and credible projections. Describe your competition in considerable detail, identifying their strengths and weaknesses. Finally, explain how you will be better than your competitors.

   The second part is your marketing plan. This critical section should include your market strategy, sales and distribution, pricing, advertising, promotion, and public awareness. Demonstrate how your pricing strategy will result in a profit. Identify your advertising plans, and include cost estimates to validate your proposed strategy.

Key Elements	Have You Covered This in the Plan?	Is the Answer Clear? (yes or no)	Is the Answer Complete? (yes or no)
a. Who will be your customers? (target market)			
b. How big is the market? (number of customers)			
c. Who will be your competitors?			
d. How are their businesses prospering?			
e. How will you promote sales?			
f. What market share will you want?			
g. Do you have a pricing strategy?			
h. What advertising and promotional strategy will you use?			

Rate this component:	Outstanding	Very Good	Good	Fair	Poor
	5	4	3	2	1

4. Location.   In this segment, it is important to describe your actual location and outline its advantages. Zoning, taxes, access to transportation, and proximity to supplies should all be considered.

Key Elements	Have You Covered This in the Plan?	Is the Answer Clear? (yes or no)	Is the Answer Complete? (yes or no)
a. Have you identified a specific location?			
b. Have you outlined the advantages of this location?			

(*Continued*)

TABLE 4-2 *(Continued)*

Key Elements	Have You Covered This in the Plan?	Is the Answer Clear? (yes or no)	Is the Answer Complete? (yes or no)
c. Are there any zoning regulations or tax considerations?			
d. Will there be access to transportation?			
e. Will your suppliers be conveniently located?			

Rate this component:	Outstanding	Very Good	Good	Fair	Poor
	5	4	3	2	1

5. **Management.** Start by describing the management team, their unique qualifications, and how you compensate them (including salaries, employment agreements, stock purchase plans, levels of ownership, and other considerations). Discuss how your organization is structured and consider including a diagram illustrating who reports to whom. Also include a discussion of the potential contribution of the board of directors, advisers, or consultants.

Key Elements	Have You Covered This in the Plan?	Is the Answer Clear? (yes or no)	Is the Answer Complete? (yes or no)
a. Who will manage the business?			
b. What qualifications do you have?			
c. How many employees will you have?			
d. What will they do?			
e. How much will you pay your employees, and what type of benefits will you offer them?			
f. What consultants or specialists will you use?			
g. What regulations will affect your business?			

Rate this component:	Outstanding	Very Good	Good	Fair	Poor
	5	4	3	2	1

6. **Financial.** Three key financial statements must be presented: a balance sheet, an income statement, and a cash flow statement. These statements typically cover a one-year period. Be sure to state any assumptions and projections you made when calculating the figures.

TABLE 4-2   (Continued)

   Determine the stages at which your business will require external financing and identify the expected financing sources (both debt and equity sources). Also, clearly show what return on investment these sources will achieve by investing in your business. The final item to include is a breakeven analysis. This analysis should explain what level of sales will be required to cover all costs. If the work is done well, the financial statements should represent the actual financial achievements expected from your business plan. They also provide a standard by which to measure your results and serve as a very valuable tool to help you manage and control your business.

Key Elements	Have You Covered This in the Plan?	Is the Answer Clear? (yes or no)	Is the Answer Complete? (yes or no)
a. What is your total expected business income for the first year? Quarterly for the next two years? (forecast)			
b. What is your expected monthly cash flow during the first year?			
c. Have you included a method of paying yourself?			
d. What sales volume will you need in order to make a profit during the first three years?			
e. What will be the breakeven point?			
f. What are your projected assets, liabilities, and net worth?			
g. What are your total financial needs?			
h. What are your funding sources?			

Rate this component:	Outstanding	Very Good	Good	Fair	Poor
	5	4	3	2	1

7. **Critical Risks.**   Discuss potential risks before they happen. Examples include price cutting by competitors, potentially unfavorable industry-wide trends, design or manufacturing costs that exceed estimates, and sales projections that are not achieved. The idea is to recognize risks and identify alternative courses of action. Your main objective is to show that you can anticipate and control (to a reasonable degree) your risks.

(Continued)

TABLE 4-2   (Continued)

Key Elements	Have You Covered This in the Plan?	Is the Answer Clear? (yes or no)	Is the Answer Complete? (yes or no)
a. What potential problems have you identified?			
b. Have you calculated the risks?			
c. What alternative courses of action are there?			

Rate this component:	Outstanding	Very Good	Good	Fair	Poor
	5	4	3	2	1

8. **Harvest Strategy.**   Ensuring the survival of an internal venture is hard work. A founder's protective feelings for an idea built from scratch make it tough to grapple with such issues as management succession, organizational rivalries, and harvest strategies. With foresight, however, entrepreneurs can keep their dream alive, ensure the security of their venture, and usually strengthen their business in the process. In addition, it is important to identify the potential harvest opportunities that may be available for the venture.

Key Elements	Have You Covered This in the Plan?	Is the Answer Clear? (yes or no)	Is the Answer Complete? (yes or no)
a. Have you planned for the orderly transfer of the venture assets if ownership of the business is passed to this corporation?			
b. Is there a strategy for identifying potential harvest opportunities?			

Rate this component:	Outstanding	Very Good	Good	Fair	Poor
	5	4	3	2	1

9. **Milestone Schedule.** This is an important segment of the business plan because it requires you to determine what tasks you need to accomplish in order to achieve your objectives. Milestones and deadlines should be established and monitored on an ongoing basis. Each milestone is related to all the others, and together they constitute a timely representation of how your objective is to be accomplished.

TABLE 4-2   (*Continued*)

Key Elements	Have You Covered This in the Plan?	Is the Answer Clear? (yes or no)	Is the Answer Complete? (yes or no)
a. How have you set your objectives?			
b. Have you set deadlines for each stage of your growth?			

Rate this component:	Outstanding	Very Good	Good	Fair	Poor
	5	4	3	2	1

10. Appendix.   This section includes important background information that was not included in the other sections. This is where you would put such items as resumes of the management team, names of references and advisers, drawings, documents, licenses, agreements, and any materials that support the plan. You may also wish to add a bibliography of the sources from which you drew information.

Key Elements	Have You Covered This in the Plan?	Is the Answer Clear? (yes or no)	Is the Answer Complete? (yes or no)
a. Have you included any documents, drawings, agreements, or other materials needed to support the plan?			
b. Are there any names of references, advisers, or technical sources you should include?			
c. Are there any other supporting documents?			

Rate this component:	Outstanding	Very Good	Good	Fair	Poor
	5	4	3	2	1

Summary: Your Plan

Directions: For each of the business plan sections that you assessed, circle the assigned points on this review sheet and then total the circled points.

Components			Points		
1. Executive Summary	5	4	3	2	1
2. Description of the Business	5	4	3	2	1
3. Marketing	5	4	3	2	1
4. Location	5	4	3	2	1
5. Management	5	4	3	2	1
6. Financial	5	4	3	2	1

(Continued)

TABLE 4-2 *(Continued)*

Components		Points			
7. Critical Risks	5	4	3	2	1
8. Harvest Strategy	5	4	3	2	1
9. Milestone Schedule	5	4	3	2	1
10. Appendix	5	4	3	2	1

Total Points: _____

Scoring

50 pts.	**— Outstanding! The ideal business plan. Solid!**
45–49 pts.	**— Very Good.**
40–44 pts.	**— Good. The plan is sound with a few areas that need to be polished.**
35–39 pts.	**— Above Average. The plan has some good areas but needs improvement before presentation.**
30–34 pts.	**— Average. Some areas are covered in detail yet certain areas show weakness.**
20–29 pts.	**— Below Average. Most areas need greater detail and improvement.**
Below 20 pts.	**— Poor. Plan needs to be researched and documented much better.**

4. *Who is your customer?* Does the plan describe the business's ideal customers and how you will reach them? Is your projected share of the market identified, reasonable, and supported?

5. *Why should (or will) your customers buy? How much better is your product/ service?* Define the need for your product, and provide references and testimonial support to enhance it. Try to be detailed in explaining the ways the customer will benefit from buying your product.

6. *Do you have an unfair advantage over your competitors?* Focus on differences and any unique qualities. Proprietary processes/technology and patentable items/ideals are good things to highlight as competitive strengths.

7. *Do you have a favorable cost structure?* Proper gross margins are key. Does the breakeven analysis take into consideration the dynamics of price and variable costs? Identify, if possible, any economics of scale that would be advantageous to the business.

8. *Can the management team build a business?* Take a second look at the management team to determine whether they have relevant experience in small business and in the industry. Acknowledge the fact that the team may need to evolve with the business.

9. *How much money do you need?* Financial statements—including the income statement, cash flow statement, and balance sheet—should be provided on a monthly basis for the first year, and on a quarterly basis for the following two or three years.

10. *How does your investor get a cash return?* Whether it's through a buyout or an initial public offering, make sure your plan clearly outlines this important question regarding a harvest strategy.

This list gives entrepreneurs the benefit of self-evaluating each segment of their plan before presenting it to financial or professional sources. Following are some helpful hints for developing the business plan. Although some of these hints may seem redundant, they highlight the key points to remember.

HELPFUL HINTS:

EXECUTIVE SUMMARY

- Confine the summary to no more than three pages. This is the most crucial part of your plan because you must capture the reader's interest.
- Answer all fundamental questions. What, how, why, and where must be explained briefly.
- Complete this part after you have a finished business plan.

BUSINESS DESCRIPTION SEGMENT

- Identify your business by name.
- Provide a background of the industry along with a history of your company (if any exists).
- Clearly describe the potential of the new venture.
- Spell out any unique aspect or distinctive features of this venture.

MARKETING SEGMENT

- Convince investors that sales projections can be met and competition can be beaten.
- Use and disclose market studies.
- Identify the target market, market position, and market share.
- Evaluate all competition and specifically cover why and how you will be better that your competitors.
- Identify all market sources and assistance used for this segment.
- Demonstrate pricing strategy; your price must penetrate and maintain a market share to produce profits. (Thus, the lowest price is not necessarily the best price.)
- Identify your advertising plans and include cost estimates to validate the proposed strategy.

RESEARCH, DESIGN, AND DEVELOPMENT SEGMENT

- Cover the extent of—and costs involved in—needed research, testing, and development.
- Explain carefully what already has been accomplished (prototype, lab testing, early development).
- Mention any research or technical assistance provided for you.

OPERATIONS SEGMENT

- Describe the advantages of your location (zoning, tax laws, wage rates).
- List the production needs in terms of facilities (plant, storage, office space) and equipment (machinery, furnishings, supplies).
- Describe the access to transportation (for shipping and receiving).
- Indicate the proximity to your suppliers.
- Mention the availability of labor in your location.
- Provide estimates of manufacturing costs. (Be careful: Too many entrepreneurs underestimate their costs.)

MANAGEMENT SEGMENT

- Supply resumes of all key people in the management of your venture.
- Carefully describe the legal structure of your venture (sole proprietorship, partnership, or corporation).
- Cover the added assistance (if any) of advisers, consultants, and directors.
- Provide information on how—and how much—everyone is to be compensated.

CRITICAL RISKS SEGMENT

- Discuss potential risks before investors point them out. Examples include:
  - Price cutting by competitors
  - Any potentially unfavorable industry-wide trends
  - Design or manufacturing costs in excess of estimates
  - Sales projections not achieved
  - Product development schedule not met
  - Difficulties or long lead times encountered in the procurement of parts or raw materials
  - Greater-than-expected innovation and development costs to stay competitive
- Provide some alternative courses of action.

FINANCIAL SEGMENT

- Provide actual estimated statements. Describe the needed sources for your funds and the intended uses for the money.
- Develop and present a budget.
- Create stages of financing for purposes of allowing evaluation by investors at various points.

MILESTONE SCHEDULE SEGMENT

- Develop a timetable or chart to demonstrate when each phase of the venture is to be completed. This shows the relationship of events and provides a deadline for accomplishment.

Remember that the business plan has the following purposes:

- Leads to a sound venture structure
- Includes a marketing plan
- Clarifies and outlines financial needs
- Identifies recognized obstacles and alternative solutions
- Serves as a communication tool for all financial and professional sources

UPDATING YOUR BUSINESS PLAN

The business plan should serve as a planning tool that helps guide the start-up and execution of a new venture. Once the venture is started, the business plan is still a vital tool for planning continued growth and/or profitability. Experts at Entrepreneur.com suggest several reasons for updating the business plan:[5]

1. *The start of a new financial period.* Updating your plan on at least a yearly basis helps you project finances and plan for fiscal needs.
2. *You need additional financing.* The business plan must be up-to-date and reflect current business numbers, not the ones projected before the business was started.
3. *There's been a significant change in your market.* You must consider changes in your customer base and competition, and how these changes affect your business.
4. *Your company launches a new product or service.* It is a valuable practice to assess the feasibility of any proposed new product or service to determine its viability. Engaging the business plan process is an essential method to assess this viability.
5. *Change in management.* A new management team should develop its own plan and not rely on past information. Eventually, new management also should initiate its own strategies for growth.
6. *Your old plan doesn't seem to reflect reality.* Many business plans are written with estimated numbers and projections that may not be accurate once the business is started. Business plans should be updated to reflect the new reality as information becomes available. In addition, pre–start-up plans are often hastily written with less detail than is desired for an effective planning tool.

PRACTICAL EXAMPLE

Every new venture should have a plan, but many entrepreneurs have no idea of the details required for a complete business plan. An example of an actual business plan prepared for funding competition is included in the appendix. Each of the parts of a business plan discussed in this chapter is illustrated in this detailed example. By carefully reviewing this business plan, you will gain a much better perspective of the final appearance that an entrepreneur's plan must have.

Summary

A business plan is a roadmap for the would-be-entrepreneur. The plan contains objectives, forecasts, and a description of the business—in other words, what it will do and how it will operate. Plans may vary in length, but every plan must include detailed research that clearly illustrates the business concept, marketing element, management structure, critical risks involved, financial needs and projections, milestone objectives, and appendix material.

In each specific part of the plan, the prospective owner describes operations and addresses major issues likely to be confronted. Many entrepreneurs find it most helpful to begin their initial plan by describing how they will get into business and deal with start-up problems. Both of these areas relate to the financial side of operations. After placing dollar amounts on projected sales revenues, expenses, and profit, the new owner is in a position to develop the management and marketing parts of the plan. Those parts are easier to prepare when the financial calculations needed to support them already have been made.

No plan is complete and unchangeable; additions or deletions always are needed. Some aspects will not work out as expected, and others will have gone unnoticed in the original plan and need to be added later. In any event, the important point is that the plan provides initial direction for the owner. From there, the individual can modify material as necessary.

Review and Discussion Questions

1. What is the major advantage of a small business plan? Explain.
2. What is contained in the *executive summary* section of a small business plan? Be complete in your answer.
3. What are some of the start-up problems that should be addressed in a small business plan? Identify and describe three.
4. Of what value is a projected income statement to a small business plan? What parts of the plan does it support?
5. What kinds of issues or considerations would you address in the part of the plan that deals with purchasing and inventory control? Be complete in your answer.
6. The specific parts of a business plan will vary depending on the goods or services the firm is selling. Explain this statement.
7. Overall, what does a business plan look like? What are the main parts of such a plan? How would a plan for a small business manufacturing firm differ from one for a small retailing firm? Compare and contrast them.

A Failure to Plan?

Dick Raskobb has been in business for nine months. When he first opened his lawn care business, he had $33,000 in initial capital. Many of his friends thought he was crazy.

Dick listened politely but went ahead and opened his store. He had five years of experience in selling lawn care products. He knew that many people around town spent a great deal of time and money on their lawns, particularly in the upper-middle-income sections of town. Dick's store is located in a small shopping center in just such a section.

The store officially opened on May 1. For the first couple of weeks, business was moderately slow. By the end of the month, however, Dick was doing a booming business. His projected monthly sales were $18,000. In June, he did $27,000 of business. July and August brought in $30,000 and $36,000, respectively. However, in September, operations began to slow down dramatically. Sales fell to $18,000. During the next three months, they plummeted to $16,000, $15,000, and $14,000. Dick's total monthly expenses, including rent, store maintenance, and finance charges on credit purchases of equipment, total $8,000. His gross margin on sales is 40 percent; therefore, on the $156,000 of revenue for June through December, he made $62,400. However, his monthly expenses claimed $48,000 of this, meaning that his profits were a mere $14,400 for seven months of work. Dick is extremely upset with sales over the past four months. He also is concerned that his initial $33,000 of capital is almost all gone because of the $2,500 salary he has drawn each month.

Yesterday, Dick dropped by to see a friend at a nearby bank. The friend listened quietly as Dick told his tale of woe. When Dick was finished, the banker asked him, "Do you have a business plan I can see?" Dick admitted to her that he did not: "When things started off so well, I didn't see any real need to draw one up." The banker nodded her head and said, "That's typical, although you should have put one together before you started the business. Did it ever occur to you that you were opening your store just as the lawn care business was entering its big season? You were starting off with your best months and should have planned for the downturn. If you had done a business plan, you would have picked this up. In any event, if you want a loan, I need from you a business plan with clear financial projections. In particular, I'd like a projected income statement for the next 12 to 18 months."

Dick agreed with everything the banker told him. He also promised to draw up a plan. "I don't know how much money I'll need, but I hope to know when I've done the plan," he told her. "I'll be back to see you a week from today."

Your consultation: Assume that you are advising Dick on how to draw up his business plan. Given the information in the case, be as comprehensive as possible in describing what it should include. Whenever feasible, make suggestions regarding financial requirements, paying particular attention to the seasonal nature of the business.

Endnotes

1. Fred L. Fry and Charles R. Stoner, "Business Plans: Two Major Types," *Journal of Small Business Management* (January 1985): 1–6. For additional information on writing effective plans, see Jeffrey A. Timmons, Andrew Zacharakis, and Stephen Spinelli, *Business Plans that Work* (New York: McGraw-Hill, 2004).
2. Joseph R. Mancuso, *How to Write a Winning Business Plan* (New York: Simon & Schuster, 1992), 44. See also Bruce R. Barringer, *Effective Business Plans* (Upper Saddle River, NJ: Prentice Hall, 2008).
3. See Donald F. Kuratko, "Demystifying the Business Plan Process: An Introductory Guide," *Small Business Forum* (Winter 1991): 33–40.
4. Colin Mason and Matthew Stark, "What do Investors Look for in a Business Plan? A Comparison of the Investment Criteria of Bankers, Venture Capitalists, and Business Angels," *International Small Business Journal* 22(6): 227–48.
5. Entrepreneur.com. "An Introduction to Business Plans." www.entrepreneur.com/startingabusiness/businessplans/article38290-3.html (accessed June 6, 2007).

CHAPTER 5

LEGAL FORMS OF VENTURES
The Structure

INTRODUCTION

Entrepreneurs are often perplexed by the issues involved in selecting the correct form of business to operate, and the various tax implications only add to their confusion. Owners of new ventures often select the sole proprietorship business form by default, but, as the business grows, they begin to consider a change. Instead of selection by default, each form of business organization should be examined carefully, and the entrepreneur should weigh the advantages and disadvantages of each against his or her own (and the venture's) needs. Whether an entrepreneur is starting a venture that is manufacturing, service, or Internet based, the legal aspects surrounding the forms of organization are the same. A change in the legal form of business can be made at different points in the life of the business if the original selection becomes inappropriate. However, careful consideration should be given to current and future needs as well as to the cost of formation.[1]

FORMS OF BUSINESS ORGANIZATION

This chapter examines the advantages and disadvantages of the different forms of business organization:

1. Sole proprietorships
2. Partnerships
3. Corporations

When examining these legal forms of organizations, entrepreneurs need to consider a few important factors:

- How easily the form of business organization can be implemented
- The amount of capital required to implement the form of business organization
- Legal considerations that might limit the options available to the entrepreneur
- The tax effects of the form of organization selected
- The potential liability to the owner of the form of organization selected[2]

SOLE PROPRIETORSHIP

A sole proprietorship is a business that is owned and controlled by only one person. This is by far the most common form of ownership in the United States (see Table 5-1).[3] Why is this form of ownership so popular? The answer is found in the many advantages it offers.

ADVANTAGES OF PROPRIETORSHIPS

Numerous advantages are associated with proprietorships, but four are particularly important:

1. Financial advantages
2. Lack of restrictions
3. Secrecy
4. Personal satisfaction

FINANCIAL ADVANTAGES

Perhaps the major advantage of a proprietorship is that the owner/manager owns the entire business, and all of the profits belong to him or her. Of course, it is necessary to pay taxes on these earnings, but these are just regular income taxes (except for a self-employment tax that must be paid). For example, if the proprietor earns $40,500 this year and has deductions of $14,500—leaving a net

TABLE 5-1 Business Ownership in the United States		
Form of Ownership	*2003[1]*	*2006e[2]*
Proprietorship	19,710,000	20,163,635
Corporation	5,401,000	5,681,797
Partnership	2,375,000	2,780,928

Sources: 1. U.S. Census Bureau, Statistical Abstract of the United States: 2007.
2. 2006e is the estimated number of business entities in the United States according to annual growth from 2003.

of $30,000—she will pay the same amount of taxes as an office worker who earns the same amount of money and has identical deductions. Additionally, proprietors sometimes have higher credit ratings than owners of partnerships or corporations, because their personal assets as well as their business assets stand behind them.

LACK OF RESTRICTIONS

Another advantage of proprietorships is the lack of restrictions. The individual has a great deal of freedom in deciding how the firm will be run. No partners or stockholders must be consulted. Additionally, because the operation is usually much smaller than that of other forms of business, a proprietorship is often much easier to manage. It has fewer people and fewer complicated business dealings. Finally, although in some cases a license must be obtained from the state (such as in the operation of a bar or a barbershop), proprietorships have no serious restrictions on either starting or terminating operations. Thus, an individual can form a proprietorship and then close the business without having to get permission from a state or federal agency.

SECRECY

A third advantage of proprietorships is secrecy. Sometimes the less the competition knows about one's business, the better. A sole proprietor needs to reveal very few things about his or her operation. Of course, the owner must file federal and state income tax returns. For the most part, however, the proprietor can keep operations secret, and the competition can only make estimate the proprietorship's sales, profit margins, and overall financial strength.

PERSONAL SATISFACTION

Many proprietors report that the best aspect of owning their own business is the personal satisfaction they derive from it. The individual can work as many, or as few, hours a week as he or she wants. Additionally, the goals pursued are the proprietor's own. If the business is a success, the owner knows it is because of his or her own contributions.

DISADVANTAGES OF PROPRIETORSHIPS

Despite the advantages just described, proprietorships also feature drawbacks. In determining whether this type of operation will be best for the business, the owner needs to consider factors such as:

1. Unlimited liability
2. Limited size
3. Limited life

UNLIMITED LIABILITY

Perhaps the greatest drawback of the sole proprietorship is unlimited liability; the individual is responsible for all debts incurred. Creditors have a claim for these debts and can exercise it against both the business assets and the personal

assets of the proprietor. As a result, if the owner's operation is worth $80,000 and the individual has debts of $125,000, creditors can sue the proprietor and force him or her to liquidate personal assets to pay the financial obligations. This explains why a sole proprietor may have a higher credit rating than other business owners. For example, the president of a corporation may find that the bank will lend the corporation up to 75 percent of the firm's value. If the company suffers a financial setback, the only property the bank has a claim against is the assets of the corporation. However, if a proprietor suffers the same setback, the bank also can claim the owner's personal assets. When a bank determines a fair line of credit for a business, it adds together the owner's business and personal assets.

LIMITED SIZE

Because a proprietorship has only one owner, the amount of capital that can be raised for operations is limited. For example, assume a bank has a policy of lending up to 50 percent of the value of a business, and a sole proprietorship has personal and business assets worth $150,000. The bank will lend the company up to $75,000. However, this is as far as the bank is willing to go. If the owner needs an additional $25,000 to take advantage of a business opportunity, one of the few ways to get the money is to take in another partner who has personal assets of $50,000, with the bank lending 50 percent of that value. This may, of course, vary by industry type or the degree of the entrepreneur's experience.

To a large degree, the growth of a proprietorship is dependent on reinvested profits. Financially speaking, the business's growth is limited. In particular, sole proprietorships are virtually excluded from entering areas in which large capital expenditures are required, such as mass-production operations and large manufacturing plants.

An additional problem arises from the business having only one owner. That individual is responsible for doing everything: buying, selling, extending credit, advertising, hiring, firing, and handling all other business-related matters. This amount of work can be quite a burden; as the business increases in size, the owner may find that he or she is weighed down by all of the responsibility. One way to deal with these duties is to delegate authority to subordinates, but the owner still must make the major decisions. When all of these tasks are considered, it is evident that the proprietorship is indeed limited by size. Any attempt to grow beyond a particular limit will result in uncontrollable operations.

LIMITED LIFE

The life of the proprietorship depends entirely on the proprietor. If the individual dies, is imprisoned, goes bankrupt, or simply chooses to cease operations, the business dies. This presents a risk both to the people who work for the firm and to the creditors. In order to offset some of these risks, it is common for creditors to require the proprietor to carry life insurance sufficient to cover all financial obligations. In this way, should the owner die unexpectedly, the face value of the policy can be used to pay all of the firm's debts. If the policy size is sufficiently large, it may even be possible for someone else to continue operating the business,

but this is unlikely because a proprietor usually leaves the estate to his or her spouse. In most cases, the spouse does not know enough about the business to keep it going, or does not care to.

THE PARTNERSHIP

A partnership, as defined by the Revised Uniform Partnership Act (RUPA), is "an association of two or more persons to carry on as co-owners of a business for profit."[4] In recent years, the partnership has declined in popularity. At present, only about 10 percent of all business firms in the United States are partnerships. Nevertheless, millions of them exist, and they account for billions of dollars in sales (see Figure 5-1).

In most cases, partnerships consist of two owners, although they can involve any number of partners. For example, advertising agencies, stock brokerages, and public accounting firms often have five or more partners. In addition, master limited partnerships have evolved; these blend the interests of several private partnerships into one larger "master" partnership (see Table 5-2 for characteristics).

A partnership can be formed by people simply getting together and agreeing to operate a business. However, such an informal arrangement is unlikely. If only to protect themselves in case one of the partners dies, most partners prefer to have a formal partnership contract drawn up. An example of a simple partnership contract is provided in Figure 5-2. More specific terms usually are spelled out after item 5. These typically cover the following areas:

1. The division of profits and losses
2. The method to be followed if original partners withdraw from the firm or new ones enter the business
3. The division of assets in case the partnership is dissolved
4. The duties of the partners
5. The manner in which any controversies that arise from the contract will be settled (a typical approach is arbitration)

At the bottom of the agreement, after all of the provisions are listed, the partners sign their names. The document is then a legally binding contract for all of the parties involved.

TYPES OF PARTNERSHIPS

A partnership can involve various types of partners. Members of the general public tend to think of all partners as equally responsible for the debts of the business and equally entitled to the profits. However, this is a simplistic view. In actuality, the rights, duties, and obligations of the partners usually are determined by factors such as how much money each has invested in the partnership, how much liability each is willing to assume, and whether each partner wants his or her membership known to the general public. In all, the three categories of partners are general partners, limited partners, and other types of partners.

FIGURE 5-1 **Revenues and Profits of Various Types of Legal Business Structures**

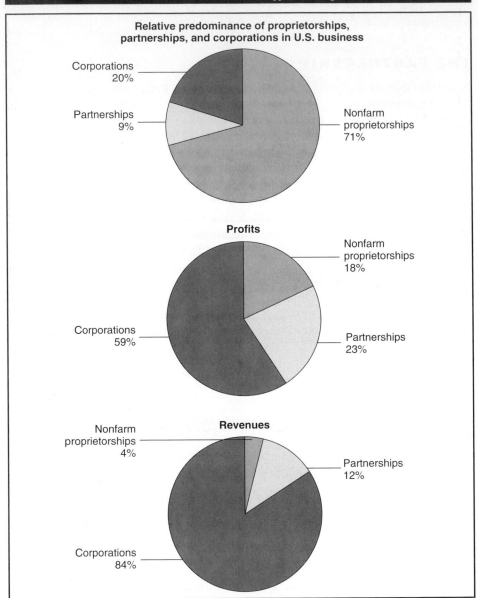

Source: Statistical Abstract of the United States: 2007, Section 15.

GENERAL PARTNERS

General partners have unlimited liability and are usually very active in the operation of the business. Each partnership must have at least one general partner. In this way, someone assumes ultimate responsibility for all of the firm's obligations

TABLE 5-2   Principal Characteristics of Partnerships Under the RUPA

1. A partnership may be created with no formalities. Two or more people merely need to agree to own and conduct a business together in order to create a partnership.
2. Partners have unlimited liability for the obligations of the business.
3. Each partner, merely by being an owner of the business, has a right to manage the business of the partnership. Because partners are liable for all obligations of the partnership, in effect each partner is an agent of the other partners.
4. Partners are fiduciaries of the partnership. They must act in the best interests of the partnership, not in their individual best interests.
5. The profits or losses of the business are shared by the partners, who report their shares of the profits or losses on their individual federal income tax returns because the partnership does not pay federal income taxes.
6. A partnership may own property in its own name.
7. A partnership may sue or be sued in its own name. The partners may also be sued over a partnership obligation.
8. A partner may sue his or her partners during the operation of the partnership.
9. A partner's ownership interest in a partnership is not freely transferable. A purchaser of a partner's interest does not become a partner but is entitled to receive only the partner's share of the partnership's profits.
10. Generally, a partnership has a life apart from its owners. If a partner dies, the partnership usually continues.

Source: Adapted from: Jane P. Mallor, A. James Barnes, Thomas Bowers, and Arlen W. Langvardt, *Business Law: The Ethical, Global, and E-Commerce Environment,* 12th ed. (New York: McGraw-Hill Irwin, 2004), 825.

FIGURE 5-2   Example of Partnership Contract

This agreement is executed on this _____ day of _____ 20 _____ between _____ and _____, all of _____.

1. The name of the partnership will be _____.
2. The principal place of business of the partnership will be at _____.
3. The partnership will engage in the business of _____ and in such other related business as agreed upon by the partners.
4. The partnership will begin operations _____, 20 _____, and will continue until terminated as herein provided.
5. The initial capital of the partnership shall be $_____. Each person agrees to contribute cash or property as agreed upon valuation as follows:

PARTNER	AMOUNT	PERCENT
_____	$_____	_____
_____	_____	_____
_____	_____	_____
_____	_____	_____

and is authorized to enter into contracts for the firm. If all of the partners fall into this category, the organization is commonly known as a *general partnership*.

LIMITED PARTNERS

Under the provisions of the Revised Uniform Limited Partnership Act (RULPA), which has been enacted by most states, individuals who want to invest in a partnership but do not want to risk all of their assets can do so as limited partners. Their liability is limited to the amount of money they have invested in the company. For example, if Bob puts $5,000 into his uncle's firm and is a limited partner, the most Bob can lose in case of bankruptcy is $5,000. However, his uncle (assuming that he is the general partner) can lose all of his business and personal assets.

OTHER TYPES OF PARTNERS

Although the most common types of partners are general and limited, other categories include silent, secret, dormant, and nominal. A *silent partner* is one who is known as a partner by the general public but who does not play an active role in the operation of the business. A *secret partner* is just the opposite; he or she is not known as a partner by the general public but does play an active role in the operation of the business. A *dormant partner* is not known as a partner by the general public and does not play an active role in the operation of the business. A *nominal partner* is a partner in name only—this typically occurs when a well-known person allows his or her name to be used by a partnership. The individual invests no money in the firm and plays no role in its management.

Before we continue, it is important to know that some people may have limited liability according to the partnership contract but may end up with unlimited liability because of some action they take. For example, a limited partner is not empowered to act in the name of the firm; he or she plays no active role in the operation. However, if a limited partner enters into a contract for the partnership by passing him- or herself off as a general partner, the individual can become liable for any losses resulting from this action.

Likewise, a nominal partner can get into the same bind. For example, Anita Gomez, an investor, has been asked for a loan by the general partner, David Smith. Gomez would not ordinarily lend money to a partnership, but in this case she is willing to do so because she knows that Ben Arturo, a local millionaire, is a partner; if the business gets into trouble, she believes Arturo will bail it out. Smith has told her that, although Arturo is a general partner, some of his funds are tied up in a big European deal, and thus he is unable to come up with the money right now. Unbeknownst to Gomez, she is being told a lie. Arturo is Smith's cousin; in an effort to help Smith's business, he has allowed the Arturo name to be used. The business is called Arturo Hardware, but Arturo does not have a financial interest in the store—he is a nominal partner. Given this information, can Arturo be held responsible if Gomez lends Smith the money and the store goes bankrupt? Without getting into the legal ramifications of the problem, let us introduce one final fact. Arturo knows that Smith has passed him off as a general partner.

Because of this, Arturo *can* be held liable for the firm's obligations. If a nominal partner knows that he (or she) is being passed off as a general partner and does not step forward to reveal himself to be a nominal partner, he loses his liability protection.

In short, if a nominal or limited partner passes her- or himself off as a general partner, the courts will rule that the nominal or limited partner is now a general partner and can be held responsible for any debts that arise because of the misrepresentation.

The *limited liability partnership (LLP)* is a form of partnership that allows professionals to enjoy the tax benefits of a partnership while avoiding personal liability for the malpractice of other partners. If a professional group organizes as an LLP, innocent partners are not personally liable for the wrongdoing of the other partners. The LLP is similar to a limited liability company (LLC; discussed later in the chapter). The difference is that LLPs are designed more for professionals who normally do business as partners in a partnership. Like limited liability companies, LLPs must be formed and operated in compliance with state statutes, which vary from state to state. Generally, a state statute limits in some way the normal individual collective liability of partners. One of the reasons LLPs are becoming so popular among professionals is that most statutes make it relatively easy to establish them. This is particularly true for an existing partnership. Converting from a partnership to an LLP is easy because the firm's basic organizational structure remains the same. Additionally, all of the statutory and common-law rules that govern partnerships still apply (apart from those modified by the LLP statute). Normally, LLP statutes are simply amendments to a state's already existing partnership law.[5]

The *limited liability limited partnership (LLLP)* is a relatively new variant of the limited partnership. An LLLP provides elected limited liability status for all of its partners, including general partners. Except for this liability status of general partners, limited partnerships and LLLPs are identical (see Table 5-3 for characteristics of limited partnerships and LLLPs).

ADVANTAGES OF PARTNERSHIPS

Numerous advantages are associated with partnerships.[6] The most important ones are as follows:

1. Increased sources of capital and credit
2. Improved decision-making potential
3. Improved chances for expansion and growth
4. Definite legal status

INCREASED SOURCES OF CAPITAL AND CREDIT

The proprietor relies on his or her own personal funds to provide the capital that the business needs. This capital also backs any credit that others extend to the firm. However, because only one person owns the proprietorship, the individual's

TABLE 5-3 Principal Characteristics of Limited Partnerships and LLLPs

1. A limited partnership or LLLP may be created only in accordance with a statute.
2. A limited partnership or LLLP has two types of partners: general partners and limited partners. It must have one or more of each type.
3. All partners, limited and general, share the profits of the business.
4. Each limited partner has liability limited to his capital contribution to the business. Each general partner of a limited partnership has unlimited liability for the obligations of the business. A general partner in an LLLP, however, has liability limited to his capital contribution.
5. Each general partner has a right to manage the business, and he or she is an agent of the limited partnership or LLLP. A limited partner has no right to manage the business or to act as its agent, but he or she does have the right to vote on fundamental matters. A limited partner may manage the business yet retain limited liability for partnership obligations.
6. General partners, as agents, are fiduciaries of the business. Limited partners are not fiduciaries.
7. A partner's rights in a limited partnership or LLLP are not freely transferable. A transferee of a general or limited partnership interest is not a partner but is entitled only to the transferring partner's share of capital and profits.
8. The death or other withdrawal of a partner does not dissolve a limited partnership or LLLP unless there is no surviving general partner.
9. Usually, a limited partnership or LLLP is taxed like a partnership.

Source: Adapted from: Jane P. Mallor, A. James Barnes, Thomas Bowers, and Arlen W. Langvardt, *Business Law: The Ethical, Global, and E-Commerce Environment,* 12th ed. (New York: McGraw-Hill Irwin, 2004), 877.

capital and credit are limited. A partnership can overcome this problem, at least partially, by bringing in more people with capital to invest and personal assets that can be used as collateral for bank loans and credit. Banks and creditors often feel that less risk is involved in lending to a partnership than to a proprietorship because more people can pay the outstanding debts should the business suffer a financial setback.

IMPROVED DECISION-MAKING POTENTIAL

The saying "two heads are better than one" has particular application to partnerships. Three or four partners increase the chances of making better decisions collectively than one proprietor operating alone. This is particularly true if each partner is a specialist in some area. For example, if one is a salesperson, another is an accountant, and a third is the idea person, the partnership may be able to outperform any competitive proprietorship.

IMPROVED CHANCES FOR EXPANSION AND GROWTH

Thanks to the increased sources of capital and credit and the improved decision-making potential, the partnership is usually in a much better position to expand and grow than is the proprietorship. In particular, the partnership has the money and managerial expertise to supervise more employees and manage larger facilities. Therefore, as the operations increase in size, the owners are able to maintain control of operations.

DEFINITE LEGAL STATUS

Because partnerships have been in existence for centuries, many court decisions have been rendered in regard to all sorts of legal problems. Thus, a good lawyer can answer virtually any question that might arise about partner ownership, liability, or continuity of operations.

DISADVANTAGES OF PARTNERSHIPS

Although partnerships have many advantages, they also have some disadvantages. A few are very similar to the sole proprietorship disadvantages. Following are four significant disadvantages:

1. Unlimited liability
2. Problem of continuity
3. Managerial problems
4. Size limitations

UNLIMITED LIABILITY

As noted earlier, some partners are limited partners; as long as they do nothing to jeopardize this status, they can lose only their investment should the business suffer a financial setback. The other partners are general partners, and they must assume unlimited liability for all obligations. However, it is important to remember that profits and losses are not always shared equally. It is common to share everything in relation to capital contribution. For example, the individual who puts up half the money gets half of the profits and, of course, must take responsibility for half of the losses. Yet, this is not always the way that profits and losses are divided, because the general partners are considered *both individually and collectively liable* for the partnership debts. This means that if one of the general partners cannot contribute his or her share of the losses, the others must make it up. The other partners, of course, can sue the delinquent partner, but, for the moment, it is they who must pay. With this in mind, it should be obvious why wealthy persons do not like to be general partners in businesses in which everyone else has only moderate wealth. They can end up carrying their poorer partners.

PROBLEM OF CONTINUITY

If one of the partners dies, goes to jail, is judged insane, or simply wants to withdraw from the business, the partnership is terminated. As the number of partners increases, so does the likelihood that one of these events will occur. For example, consider the case of five partners, one of whom dies. In order to reorganize the partnership, the remaining partners must buy out the deceased individual's share, the value of which may be difficult to determine. In addition, if the partners do not have the necessary assets, such action is impossible. In this case, the only alternative may be to bring in a partner with the money to buy out the share of the deceased. However, it is often difficult to find a person who is acceptable to all of the partners—a requirement for any new partner. Such problems affect the continuity of partnerships.

MANAGERIAL PROBLEMS

Although all of the general partners have the right to contract in the name of the business, the firm may find that "too many cooks spoil the broth." One way to overcome this problem is to have each partner restrict his or her activities to one area of operations. For example, one partner works exclusively in purchasing, another handles the bookkeeping, and a third sells. However, even when these agreements are spelled out in writing, problems are common and partners may interfere in one another's areas of responsibility.

SIZE LIMITATIONS

Although a partnership usually can raise more money than a proprietorship, the amount of capital and credit that bankers and suppliers will provide is limited. Sooner or later, the firm reaches its limit. Thus, a partnership can grow larger than a proprietorship, but it cannot reach the size of large corporations because its financial assets will not permit it to do so. See Table 5-4 for a comparison of partnership types.

TABLE 5-4 A Basic Comparison of Partnership Types		
Characteristic	*General Partnership (UPA)*	*Limited Partnership (RULPA)*
Creation	By agreement of two or more persons to carry on a business as co-owners for profit	By agreement of two or more persons to carry on a business as co-owners for profit. Must include one or more general partners and one or more limited partners. Filing of a certificate with the secretary of state is required.
Sharing of profits and losses	By agreement; or, in the absence of agreement, profits are shared equally by the partners, and losses are shared in the same ration as profits	Profits are shared as required in the certificate agreement, and losses are shared likewise, up to the amount of limited partners' capital contributions. In the absence of a provision in the certificate agreement, profits and losses are shared on the basis of percentages of capital contributions.
Liability	Unlimited personal liability of all partners	Unlimited personal liability of all general partners; limited partners liable only to the extent of their capital contributions.
Capital contributions	No minimum or mandatory amount; set by agreement	Set by agreement.

TABLE 5-4   (Continued)

Characteristic	General Partnership (UPA)	Limited Partnership (RULPA)
Management	By agreement, or in the absence of agreement, all partners have an equal voice	General partners by agreement, or else each has an equal voice. Limited partners have no voice or else are subject to liability as general partners (but *only* if a third party has reason to believe that the limited partner is a general partner). A limited partner may act as an agent or employee of the partnership and vote on amending the certificate or on the sale or dissolution of the partnership.
Duration	By agreement, or can be dissolved by action of the partners (withdrawal), operation of law (death or bankruptcy), or court decree	By agreement in the certificate or by withdrawal, death, or mental incompetence of a general partner in the absence of the right of the other general partners to continue the partnership. Death of a limited partner, unless he or she is the only remaining limited partner, does not terminate the partnership.
Distribution of assets or liquidation—order of priorities	1. Outside creditors 2. Partner creditors 3. Partners, according to capital contributions 4. Partners, according to profits	1. Outside creditors and partner creditors 2. Partners and former partners entitled to distributions before withdrawal under the agreement or the RULPA 3. Partners, according to capital contributions 4. Partners, according to profits

Source: Gaylord A. Jentz, Roger LeRoy Miller, and Frank B. Cross, *West's Business Law,* 10th ed. (Mason, OH: Thomson/Southwestern, 2007), 677.

THE CORPORATION

Most large businesses in the United States today are corporations (e.g., Google, eBay, Yahoo!, Microsoft, Intel, etc.). Although they constitute only about 20 percent of all businesses, corporations account for more than 90 percent of all business receipts and the largest percentage of wages paid.

What makes the corporation such a popular form of organization? One reason is that, legally, a corporation is an artificial being that has the right to conduct business affairs in its own name, to sue and to be sued, and to exist indefinitely.

ORGANIZING THE CORPORATION

In contrast to proprietorships and partnerships, permission must be obtained from the state to create a corporation. The first step in this process is usually to file the necessary application form with the appropriate state official. Most states require at least three incorporators, each of whom must be an adult, and the payment of the necessary fees at filing time. Aside from this, usually little other paperwork has to be done.

Figure 5-3 shows the basic form of an application for incorporation. Generally the form is written so that the firm's activities and objectives are not very limited.

FIGURE 5-3 Application for Incorporation

ARTICLES OF INCORPORATION OF
_____

We, the undersigned natural persons of the age of 21 years or more, acting as incorporators of a corporation under the _____ Business Corporation Act, adopt the following Articles of Incorporation for such corporation:

FIRST: The name of the corporation is _____

SECOND: The period of its duration is _____

THIRD: The purpose or purposes for which the corporation is organized are _____
_____

FOURTH: The total number of shares that the corporation shall have authority to issue is _____

FIFTH: The corporation will not commence business until at least one thousand dollars has been received by it as consideration for the issuance of the shares.

SIXTH: Provisions limiting or denying to shareholders the preemptive right to acquire additional or treasury shares of the corporation are _____

SEVENTH: Provisions for the regulation of the internal affairs of the corporation are ___
_____

EIGHTH: The address of the initial registered office of the corporation is _____
_____ and the name of its initial registered agent as such address is _____
_____

NINTH: The number of directors constituting the initial board of directors of the corporation is _____ and the names and addresses of the persons who are to serve as directors until the first annual meeting of shareholders or until their successors are elected and shall qualify are

Name   Address
_____   _____
_____   _____
_____   _____
_____   _____
_____   _____

TENTH: The name and address of each incorporator is
_____   _____
_____   _____

Date _____, 20 _____   Incorporators

In addition, because the incorporators often want to minimize taxes, they will investigate the incorporation fees and taxes that the various states levy. As a result of their tax rates, Delaware, Maryland, and New Jersey are very popular states in which to incorporate; however, the corporation does not have to operate in those states.

Once the filing is complete and the approval to incorporate has been given, the secretary of the state will issue a corporate charter. This charter relates facts such as the type of business the firm is in and the number of shares of stock it intends to issue. The business must operate within the confines of this charter, and any changes have to come from either the stockholders or new governmental regulations.

THE CORPORATE STRUCTURE

The corporate charter provides the basis for the corporate structure. According to the charter, the stockholders own the firm and have the right to elect the board of directors. These individuals, in turn, choose the president, who appoints the top corporate officers. This process continues down the line, all the way to the workers' level.

The people who own the stock, the stockholders, are permitted to elect the members of the board of directors. For example, if a total of 10,000 shares are issued for the Jones Corporation, and Alice owns 10 shares of the stock, she is the owner of 1/1,000th of the firm and can cast her 10 votes for any director she wants. The same is true for those who hold the other 9,990 shares of stock. Under this procedure, the largest stockholders have the greatest amount to say about the management of the corporation.

The board of directors, meanwhile, is responsible for ensuring that the business is managed properly. In this capacity, they are charged with formulating long-range direction, approving plans of top management, and seeing that overall policy is carried out. If some problem with the management occurs and the company is not doing well, the board of directors may decide to hire a new president. Thus, the board of directors, voted into office by the stockholders, is ultimately responsible for the overall management of the business (see Table 5-5 for characteristics of corporations).[7]

ADVANTAGES OF CORPORATIONS

The corporate form of ownership offers five important advantages:

1. Limited liability
2. Indefinite life
3. Growth potential
4. Managerial efficiency
5. Transfer of ownership

TABLE 5-5 Principal Characteristics of Corporations

1. *Legal status.* A corporation is a legal person and a legal entity independent of its owners (*shareholders*) and its managers (officers and the *board of directors*). Its life is unaffected by the retirement or death of its shareholders, officers, and directors. A corporation is a person under the Constitution of the United States.

2. *Powers.* A corporation may *acquire, hold,* and *convey property* in its own name. A corporation may *sue* and *be sued* in its own name.

3. *Management.* Shareholders elect a board of directors, which manages the corporation. The board of directors may delegate management duties to officers. A shareholder has *no right or duty to manage* the business of a corporation, unless he is elected to the board of directors or is appointed an officer.

4. *Owners' liability.* The shareholders have *limited liability.* With few exceptions, they are not liable for the debts of a corporation after they have paid their promised capital contributions to the corporation.

5. *Transferability of owner's interest.* Generally, the ownership interest in a corporation is *freely transferable.* A shareholder may sell her shares to whomever she wants whenever she wants. The purchaser becomes a shareholder with the same rights that the seller had.

6. *Taxation.* A corporation pays *federal income taxes* on its income. Shareholders have personal income from the corporation only when the corporation makes a distribution of its income to them. This creates a *double-taxation* possibility: The corporation pays income tax on its profits, and, when the corporation distributes the after-tax profits as dividends, the shareholders pay tax on the dividends.

Source: Adapted from Jane P. Mallor, A. James Barnes, Thomas Bowers, and Arlen W. Langvardt, *Business Law: The Ethical, Global, and E-Commerce Environment,* 12th ed. (New York: McGraw-Hill Irwin, 2004), 893.

LIMITED LIABILITY

Stockholders in a corporation are like limited partners in that they can lose no more than they have invested in the business. For example, assume that Andy and Sue buy 100 shares of stock in their cousin Bob's corporation for $1,000. A year later, the business goes bankrupt. How much do Andy and Sue lose as a result? Only $1,000. Keep in mind, however, that *Bob* may lose a lot more, because he may be personally responsible for the corporation's debts. Earlier, we noted that some people in a partnership may be limited partners while others are general partners. Lenders are aware that the liability of the investors in a small corporation is limited. Therefore, in order to secure a large loan, banks or other lending institutions will require the owner to sign both personally *and* in the name of the business. This individual does not have limited liability. However, this is only reasonable — no bank would be foolish enough to lend a small corporation a great deal of money and then find, in the case of financial failure, that its ability to collect is restricted to the business's assets. Lenders want to ensure that the owner is as careful as possible with the money. What better way to do this than to make the person personally liable for the obligation?

INDEFINITE LIFE

Unlike proprietorships or partnerships, corporations can exist indefinitely. If a major stockholder dies, the ownership is simply transferred to his or her heirs. If these people do not want the stock, they can sell it. In short, as long as a market for the stock exists (and it should if the corporation is doing well), the business ownership may change hands, but the corporation remains in existence. A look at some of the major corporations in the United States—including Standard Oil of Indiana (1889), General Electric (1892), IBM (1911), General Motors (1916), and Ford Motor Company (1919)—bears this out.

GROWTH POTENTIAL

In contrast to proprietorships or partnerships, corporations generally have greater growth potential because they can raise more capital. By selling shares of stock, the company often can raise large amounts of money. Each stockholder may buy only 10 or 20 shares, but if enough people are willing to invest, a corporation can raise enough capital to expand.

MANAGERIAL EFFICIENCY

As a business grows in size, it requires greater managerial expertise. The proprietorship is heavily dependent on the skills and abilities of the proprietor; the partnership relies greatly on the capabilities of the general partners. However, the corporation often separates ownership from management so that the people who own the company do not manage it. Even when they do, they still tend to bring in specialists, such as sales managers, accountants, and lawyers. In short, as the size of the firm increases, so does the reliance on professional management.

TRANSFER OF OWNERSHIP

An individual who buys stock in a corporation is given a stock certificate. This certificate can be sold if the individual is not happy with the investment, as long as a market for the stock exists. Small corporations have limited markets; as a result, it may be difficult for them to sell stock immediately. Large firms have ready markets for their stock and usually have no problem making immediate sales. The financial section of any newspaper provides the latest prices of many corporations' stock, from AT&T to General Motors to Home Depot. Regardless of the corporation's size, if the company is in good financial shape, the investor generally is able to sell the stock easily.

DISADVANTAGES OF CORPORATIONS

Some of the disadvantages associated with the corporate form of ownership are as follows:

1. Heavy taxation
2. High organizing expenses
3. Government restrictions
4. Lack of secrecy

HEAVY TAXATION

Corporations are subject to heavier taxes on their earnings than either proprietorships or partnerships. In recent years, this rate has gone as high as 39 percent on income over $100,000 up to $335,000, and 34 percent on everything above this amount. Then, corporations are subject to a tax collected by the state in which they are incorporated. Finally, if the company gives a dividend to stockholders, these individuals must pay a personal income tax on the dividend—thus subjecting corporate earnings to double taxation.[7]

HIGH ORGANIZING EXPENSES

In order to incorporate, a business must pay certain fees. These include a charter fee to the state in which the business incorporates and corporate fees to all of the states in which it operates. (These fees are sometimes in the form of a tax for the right to conduct business in the particular state.) Additionally, because of all the legal procedures and red tape, the company usually has to have an attorney. All of this can add up to a sizable incorporation bill.

GOVERNMENT RESTRICTIONS

Relative to proprietorships and partnerships, corporations face many more governmental restrictions. Their stock sales are regulated by federal and state governments, and the organization must maintain records and reports for examination by government agencies. Additionally, if it tries to merge or consolidate with another organization, the corporation is required to comply with certain laws.

LACK OF SECRECY

Because the corporation has to make various records available to the government, its operations are much less confidential than those of other organizational forms. Additionally, the corporation must provide an annual report to each stockholder so that, as the firm gets bigger, the degree of secrecy declines. Everyone, including the competition, can obtain the firm's sales revenues, gross profit, total assets, net profit, and other financial data. Virtually nothing is secret. Table 5-6 provides a complete comparison of the three legal forms of organization discussed so far.

TABLE 5-6 Comparison of the Legal Forms of Organization			
Characteristic	*Sole Proprietorship*	*Partnership*	*Corporation*
Method of creation	Created at will by the owner	Created by agreement of the parties	Charter issued by the state; created by statutory authorization
Legal position	Not a separate entity; the owner is the business	Not a separate legal entity in some states	Always a legal entity separate and distinct from its owners; a legal fiction for the purposes of owning property and being a party to litigation

TABLE 5-6   (Continued)

Characteristic	Sole Proprietorship	Partnership	Corporation
Liability	Unlimited liability	Unlimited liability	Limited liability of shareholders; shareholders are not liable for the debts of the corporation
Duration	Determined by the owner; automatically dissolved on the owner's death	Terminated by agreement of the partners, by the death of one or more of the partners, by withdrawal of a partner, by bankruptcy, and so on	Can have perpetual existence
Transferability of interest	Interest can be transferred, but the individual's proprietorship then ends	Although a partnership interest can be assigned, the assignee normally does not have the full rights of a partner	Shares of stock can be transferred
Management	Completely at the owner's discretion	Each general partner has a direct and equal voice in management unless expressly agreed otherwise in the partnership agreement	Shareholders elect directors, who set policy and appoint officers
Taxation	The owner pays personal taxes on business income	Each partner pays income taxes based on a pro rata share of net profits, whether or not they are distributed	Double taxation; the corporation pays income tax on net profits, with no dedication for dividends, and shareholders pay income tax on disbursed dividends they received
Organizational fees, annual license fees, and annual reports	None	None	All required
Transaction of business in other states	Generally no limitation	Generally no limitation	Normally must qualify to do business and obtain a certificate of authority

Source: Gaylord A. Jentz, Roger LeRoy Miller, and Frank B. Cross, *West's Business Law,* 10th ed. (Mason, OH: Thomson/Southwestern, 2007), 741.

THE S CORPORATION

In an effort to help small businesses, Congress has provided for Subchapter S corporations, named after the subchapter of the Internal Revenue Code that permits their existence. These corporations now are called S corporations. The tax code allows earnings of these small corporations to be taxed as partnership income to stockholders. In this way, the double taxation on dividends is avoided.

In order to exercise this tax option, the S corporation must meet a number of conditions. Two of the most important, based on the latest legislative changes, are that it can have no more than 75 stockholders and that no more than 25 percent of the corporate income can come from such passive investments as dividends, rent, and capital gains.

An S corporation has other advantages. The full explanation of the impact and value of this option for a small corporation is best left to the firm's accountant or an outside certified public accountant. The option is available, and it should be considered. However, it is neither a tax dodge nor a remedy for tax problems. This is obvious in that only 20 percent of small business corporations have chosen the S corporation option. Its specific advantages are simply not of value to every small corporation.[8]

The legal system has developed the S corporation as a legal *person,* separate from its owners, to encourage risk taking and faster economic development. Incorporation remains one of the linchpins of liability protection, and, for business owners, it remains the necessary first step in minimizing their exposure to personal liability.

However, incorporation is no panacea. There are at least 10 categories of circumstance or conduct that can lead to a business owner's personal liability, as follows.[9]

1. Failure to actually operate as a legal corporation
2. Business assets owned outside the corporation
3. Personal guarantees of corporate obligations
4. Receipt of excessive corporate distributions
5. Personal faith (responsibility) for negligence
6. Piercing the "corporate veil"
7. Payment of past unpaid wages
8. Pension and profit-sharing plans, and other ERISA plans
9. Shareholder liability for taxes
10. Environmental laws

THE LIMITED LIABILITY COMPANY

An increasing number of states have authorized a new form of business organization called the *limited liability company (LLC).* The LLC is a hybrid form of business enterprise that offers the limited liability of the corporation with the tax advantages of a partnership.

By 1997, all states had enacted LLC statutes; they are far from uniform, however, with variations based on the corporate and partnership laws of whatever state is enacting the LLC statute. A major advantage of the LLC is that, like the partnership and the S corporation, the LLC does not pay taxes as an entity; rather, profits are passed through the LLC and paid personally by the company members. Another advantage is that the liability of members is limited to the amount of their investments. In an LLC, members are allowed to participate fully in management activities, and, under at least one state's statute, the firm's managers need not even be members of the LLC. Yet another advantage is that corporations and partnerships, as well as foreign investors, can be LLC members, whereas these entities cannot be shareholders in S corporations. Also in contrast to S corporations, no limit is placed on the number of shareholder members of the LLC.

The disadvantages of the LLC are relatively few. Perhaps the greatest disadvantage is that LLC statutes differ from state to state, and thus any firm engaged in multistate operations may face difficulties. In an attempt to promote some uniformity among the states in respect to LLC statutes, the National Conference of Commissioners on Uniform State Laws drafted a uniform limited liability company statute for submission to the states to consider for adoption. Until all of the states have adopted the uniform law, however, an LLC in one state will have to check the rules in the other states in which the firm does business to ensure that it retains its limited liability.[10]

Table 5-7 provides a complete comparison chart of the legal forms of organization.

Summary

A proprietorship is owned and controlled by one person. It is currently the most common form of business ownership in the United States. Some of the advantages it offers are certain financial advantages, lack of restrictions, secrecy, and personal satisfaction. Its disadvantages include unlimited liability, limited size, and limited life.

A partnership is an association of two or more persons who serve as co-owners of a business for profit. The two major types of partners are general and limited, and several less common types exist. General partners have unlimited liability; limited partners' financial responsibility is restricted to their investment. Other partners tend to have limited liability. However, this can change if they represent themselves to the public as general partners and, as a result of their action, cause the partnership some financial loss. The advantages of the partnership include greater capital and credit, improved decision-making potential, improved chances for expansion and growth, and definite legal status. The drawbacks include unlimited liability, continuity problems, management problems, and size limitations.

Most large businesses in the United States are corporations. As an entrepreneurial venture increases in size, its legal form of organization warrants attention. Although permission from the state is necessary for a corporation to start up, this structure provides some very important advantages, including limited liability,

TABLE 5-7 General Characteristics of Forms of Business

	Sole Proprietorship	Partnership	Limited Liability Partnership	Limited Partnership	Limited Liability Limited Partnership	Corporation	S Corporation	Limited Liability Company
Formation	When one person owns a business without forming a corporation or LLC	By agreement of owners or by default when two or more owners conduct business together without forming a limited partnership, an LLC, or a corporation	By agreement of owners; must comply with limited liability partnership statute	By agreement of owners; must comply with limited partnership statute	By agreement of owners; must comply with limited liability limited partnership statute	By agreement of owners; must comply with corporation statute	By agreement of owners; must comply with corporation state; must elect S Corporation status under Subchapter S of Internal Revenue Code	By agreement of owners; must comply with limited liability company statute
Duration	Terminates on death or withdrawal of sole proprietor	Usually unaffected by death or withdrawal of partner	Unaffected by death or withdrawal of partner	Unaffected by death or withdrawal of partner, unless sole general partner dissociates	Unaffected by death or withdrawal of partner, unless sole general partner dissociates	Unaffected by death or withdrawal of shareholder	Unaffected by death or withdrawal of shareholder	Usually unaffected by death or withdrawal of member
Management	By sole proprietor	By partners	By partners	By general partners	By general partners	By board of directors	By board of directors	By managers or members

TABLE 5-7 (*Continued*)

	Sole Proprietorship	Partnership	Limited Liability Partnership	Limited Partnership	Limited Liability Limited Partnership	Corporation	S Corporation	Limited Liability Company
Owner Liability	Unlimited	Unlimited	Mostly limited to capital contribution	Unlimited for general partners; limited to capital contribution for limited partners	Limited to capital contribution	Limited to capital contribution	Limited to capital contribution	Limited to capital contribution
Transferability of Owners' Interest	None	None	None	None, unless agreed otherwise	None, unless agreed otherwise	Freely transferable, although shareholders may agree otherwise	Freely transferable, although shareholders usually agree otherwise	None, unless agreed otherwise
Federal Income Taxation	Only sole proprietor taxed	Only partners taxed	Usually only partners taxed; may elect to be taxed like a corporation	Usually only partners taxed; may elect to be taxed like a corporation	Usually only partners taxed; may elect to be taxed like a corporation	Corporation taxed; shareholders taxed on dividends (double tax)	Only shareholders taxed	Usually only members taxed; may elect to be taxed like a corporation

Source: Jane P. Mallor, A. James Barnes, Thomas Bowers, and Arlen W. Langvardt, *Business Law: The Ethical, Global, and E-Commerce Environment,* 12th ed. (New York: McGraw-Hill Irwin, 2004), 823.

indefinite life, growth potential, managerial efficiency, and transfer of ownership. The disadvantages associated with the corporate form of ownership include heavy taxation, high organizing expenses, government restrictions, and lack of secrecy. Additionally, the owner should have a certified public accountant examine the company's books and help it decide whether or not to convert to an S corporation or a limited liability company.

Review and Discussion Questions

1. What is a proprietorship?
2. What are some of the advantages and disadvantages of a proprietorship? List and describe three of each.
3. In contrast to proprietorships, how popular are partnerships? Explain.
4. How does a general partner differ from a limited partner?
5. Briefly describe the role of each of the following in an organization: silent partner, secret partner, dormant partner, and nominal partner.
6. What is a limited liability partnership (LLP)?
7. What are some of the advantages and disadvantages of a partnership? List and describe three of each.
8. Explain how a business incorporates.
9. What are some of the advantages and disadvantages of incorporating? Discuss four of each.
10. Why would a small business choose to become an S corporation or a limited liability company? Explain.

NEW VENTURE CONSULTANT

GOING PUBLIC?

When Blake, Adam, and Gavin Barker started their retail electronics store ten years ago, they formed a partnership. "All for one and one for all" is the way Blake put it. "We each put $50,000 into the business and agreed to share all profits and losses equally." When it came to expanding the operation, they used the same approach: Each put up one third of the necessary capital.

The business grew slowly for the first five years. Sales were $1,495,000 by the end of that period. The past five years, however, have shown rapid growth, and sales now have hit the $6 million mark. The brothers would like to expand the operation again, but it appears it will cost approximately $2,500,000 to carry out their plan to increase inventory, add more floor space, and open a second store across town. "We just don't have the $2,500,000," Harvey explained, "and we are reluctant to borrow that much money. After all, we started as a small partnership. We never thought we'd get this big, and we don't have the internal funds to support big expansion."

The firm's accountant has suggested they consider incorporating and selling stock to raise the money. This idea sounds good to the brothers, but they are concerned about losing control. The accountant explained they could keep half of the stock for themselves, so they would never have to worry about being forced out. This was welcome news, but it has not dispelled all of their fears. In particular, the brothers are concerned about three facts: (1) Their tax rate would be higher as a corporation than it is as a partnership; (2) they would have large organizing expenses; and (3) they would experience more governmental restrictions. Of the three, the tax rate is the most important to them. Nevertheless, they realize that unless they incorporate, they will be unable to finance their expansion.

Your Consultation: Assume you are advising the Barker brothers on their situation. What are the benefits of their incorporating? Briefly identify and describe three of the most important. How serious are the drawbacks about which the partners are concerned? Explain. Is incorporation a wise decision for the Barker brothers? Why or why not?

Endnotes

1. See Constance E. Bagley and Craig E. Dauchy, *The Entrepreneur's Guide to Business Law* (Mason, OH: Thomson/Southwestern, 2003).
2. David S. Hulse and Thomas R. Pope, "The Effect of Income Taxes on the Preference of Organizational Form for Small Businesses in the United States," *Journal of Small Business Management* 34, no. 1 (1996): 24–35. See also Sandra Malach, Peter Robinson, and Tannis Radcliffe, "Differentiating Legal Issues by Business Type," *Journal of Small Business Management* 44, no. 4 (2006): 563–76.
3. For further discussion on the legal aspects of proprietorships, see Gaylord A. Jentz, Roger LeRoy Miller, and Frank B. Cross, *West's Business Law,* 10th ed. (Mason, OH: Thomson/Southwestern, 2007), 652.
4. For the complete Revised Uniform Partnership Act, see Gaylord A. Jentz, Roger LeRoy Miller, and Frank B. Cross, *West's Business Law,* 10th ed. (Mason, OH: Thomson/Southwestern, 2007), A203–A212.
5. For further discussion on the legal aspects of LLPs, see Gaylord A. Jentz, Roger LeRoy Miller, and Frank B. Cross, *West's Business Law,* 10th ed. (Mason, OH: Thomson/Southwestern, 2007), 675.
6. For an excellent overview of partnerships, see Gaylord A. Jentz, Roger LeRoy Miller, and Frank B. Cross, *West's Business Law,* 10th ed. (Mason, OH: Thomson/Southwestern, 2007), 663–83.
7. See David S. Hulse and Thomas R. Pope, "The Effect of Income Taxes on the Preference of Organizational Form for Small Businesses in the United States," *Journal of Small Business Management* (January 1996): 24–35.
8. See Gaylord A. Jentz, Roger LeRoy Miller, and Frank B. Cross, *West's Business Law,* 10th ed. (Mason, OH: Thomson/Southwestern, 2007), 699–700; and Constance E. Bagley and Craig E. Dauchy, *The Entrepreneur's Guide to Business Law* (Mason, OH: Thomson/Southwestern, 2003), 53–55.
9. Kenneth P. Brier, "A Dirty Dozen of Liability," *Family Business* (Winter 1994): 45–48.
10. See Gaylord A. Jentz, Roger LeRoy Miller, and Frank B. Cross, *West's Business Law,* 10th ed. (Mason, OH: Thomson/Southwestern, 2007); and Constance E. Bagley and Craig E. Dauchy, *The Entrepreneur's Guide to Business Law,* (Mason, OH: Thomson/Southwestern, 2003).

CHAPTER

MARKET RESEARCH
THE NICHE

INTRODUCTION

Marketing is a key component that must be understood by any entrepreneur who hopes to succeed.[1] A *market* is a group of consumers who behave in a similar way. For example, after Christmas, many stores have sales to clear out merchandise left over from the holiday shopping season. In particular, they offer holiday cards and wrapping paper at large discounts. Some people start shopping for the next year's holidays on December 26. Those people constitute a market. So do those who buy suits that cost between $200 and $300, those who purchase only Nissans, and those who camp out in front of electronics stores to get the latest video game system. In each instance, a classification or market niche exists into which these people can be categorized.[2]

DETERMINING MARKET NICHES

People buy all sorts of products and services. Thus, they fall into *many* market niches. For example, using only price as the determinant of demand, consider the following individuals and the price ranges within which they buy goods:

	Mr. A	Ms. B	Mr. C
Suits	$200–300	$125–225	$70–150
Books	5–50	3–20	3–10
Automobiles	9,000–22,000	7,000–14,000	4,000–10,000
Homes	125,000–195,000	80,000–120,000	45,000–85,000
Restaurant meals	20–35	15–25	12–20
Watches	124–3000	50–150	30–60

Mr. A appears to be the most affluent. Certainly, he is willing to spend more money for the goods and services he buys. Mr. C appears to be the least affluent. He buys much less expensive products than Mr. A and is more likely than Mr. A to be a bargain shopper. Ms. B falls somewhere in between. In all, three different market niches for goods are described in this example: high price, medium price, and low price.[3]

RELEVANT PRICE RANGE

When analyzing market niches, the entrepreneur launching a new venture needs to be concerned with both relevant price range and competition. This price range is important because current customers will not buy *above* certain levels nor will they buy *below* certain levels. Additionally, the entrepreneur cannot sell at a profit below a specific level. These three factors help determine the *relevant price range*.[4] If the current price is above the minimum level for customer acceptance and owner's profit and below the level considered too high, the price is within the relevant range. How high or low can the owner set a price? It depends on the customers in the market niche. For example, using the graph in Figure 6-1 as an illustration, any price higher than A is too high; current customers will not buy the suits for that much money. Meanwhile, any price below point B is too low; customers will consider the suits to be of inferior quality. Note in the graph that point B is above the acceptable profit level. In this example, customers are willing to pay high prices; unless the owner wants to lose this market niche, prices should remain within the relevant range. Other stores can cater to those who want to pay more and less than this range.

Note that the relevant price range in the graph is between $275 and $350. Although this price is relatively high, a strong demand exists for suits in this range; that is, the high price does not scare away customers. The reason is undoubtedly the high quality of the suits. They are regarded by these buyers as

FIGURE 6-1 Suit Purchases

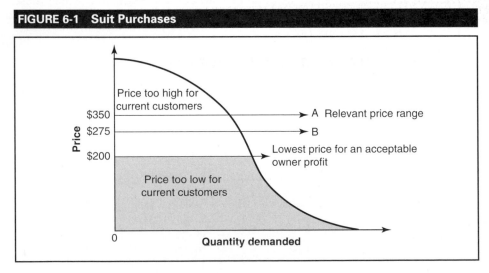

an oligopoly do not have a unique good or service for sale, they know that the strategies of each will affect the others. As a result, they tend to have a philosophy of "live and let live." They often do not compete on the basis of price but use advertising and personal selling to draw customers to their establishments.

MONOPOLISTIC COMPETITION

Monopolistic competition exists when an industry has many firms, each producing only a small share of the output demand. In order to capture as large a share of this market as possible, each firm attempts to distinguish its goods and services from those of the competition. Advertising, credit, personal selling, and reputation all are used to draw people away from other products and businesses. Competition is vigorous. Common illustrations of monopolistic competition include restaurants, cleaning establishments, service stations, shoe stores, and grocery stores. Most new ventures fall into this category.

PURE COMPETITION

Pure competition exists when many independent sellers offer products in the same basic way. The products are standardized—almost identical—and buyers are indifferent to which one they purchase. In addition, no firm can exercise significant control over the product's price because none supplies more than a small fraction of the total output demand. The most common example of this is in agriculture. Farmers who sell corn, wheat, or barley find that sellers buy their produce on the basis of weight (bushels) because very little difference exists, if any, between corn grown in one field and corn grown in the next.

These market models are contrasted in Table 6-1. As noted earlier, the market model into which most new ventures fall is monopolistic competition. A business survives in this type of market by examining the current needs of the customers, determining which goods and services appeal to them, and giving them what they want. This is done by examining the firm's market niche and continually conducting marketing research.

TABLE 6-1 Comparison of Market Models

	Monopoly	*Oligopoly*	*Monopolistic Competition*	*Pure Competition*
Number of Firms	One	A few	Many	Very many
Control over Price	Much	Depends on what the others do	Some	None
Type of Product	Unique	Unique or standardized	Unique or standardized	Standardized
Access to the Industry	Impossible	Difficult	Fairly easy	Very easy
Use of Nonprice Competition	Public relations advertising	Much	Much	None

EXAMINING THE CURRENT MARKET NICHE

Once the new venture owner/manager understands a market and the ways in which it is affected by both price and competition, he or she is in a position to examine the venture's current *market niche*.[8] Who are the customers? Do they pay for their purchases with cash or credit? Who are the bargain shoppers? What do they buy? How often do they buy? Answers to questions such as these provide a customer profile. Based on the results, the owner/manager can determine what to stock, how to price, where to advertise, and what service to provide.[9]

MARKET NICHE ANALYSIS: AN EXAMPLE

One of the first ways to examine a business's market niche is to break down the types of customers and their shopping habits. For example, consider the case of a pharmacy store owner who gathered age data on customers who frequented the store during a two-week period. A breakdown of customers' ages revealed the following information:

Adolescents and children	960
Males, age 20–40	1,140
Males, age 41–60	940
Males, age 60+	830
Females, age 20–40	1,250
Females, age 41–60	1,440
Females, age 60+	1,600

A breakdown of their buying habits, based on information gathered by store employees and the owner, reveals the profile shown in Table 6-2.

Using this information, the owner knows that many of the customers like to charge purchases and that traffic is much heavier on weekends than during the week. Additionally, whereas everyone buys some product lines (staples and cosmetics), only about one-third of the customers eat at the lunch counter.

Data like these are useful for examining customer purchasing habits. By collecting similar data at a later time, the owner can obtain even more information—in particular, changes in customer buying habits that indicate *trends*. For instance, the pharmacy store in our example has a lunch counter. However, most pharmacies today do not have lunch counters because the return on investment is too low, and people tend to prefer to eat at restaurants and fast food chains. As a result, many pharmacy store owners have taken out lunch counters and put in music, books, and other fast-moving merchandise. Will this trend affect the drugstore in our example?

This is difficult to say, but one thing is certain: It is a development the owner should monitor by periodically comparing the cost of running the lunch counter with the revenue it generates. Is the return on this investment as high as it is in other areas of the store? This is referred to as *return-on-investment (ROI) control,* and it is one of the most effective control procedures. In essence, it tells

TABLE 6-2 Breakdown of Drugstore Customers' Buying Habits				
Type of Customer	*Cash Purchases*	*Charge Purchases*	*Bargain Shoppers*	*Daytime Shoppers*
Adolescents and Children	X			X
Males, 20–40		X		
Males, 41–60		X		
Males, 60+	X			X
Females, 20–40		X	X	X
Females, 41–60	X	X	X	
Females 60+	X		X	X

Evening Shoppers	*Weekend Shoppers*	*Buy Fad Items*	*Buy Staples (Newspapers, Gum, Candy, etc.)*	*Eat at Lunch Counter*	*Buy Health and Cosmetic Products*
	X	X	X	X	X
X	X		X		X
X	X		X		X
	X		X		X
X	X	X	X		X
X	X		X		X
		X	X	X	X

the owner/manager to keep only those product lines that provide at least a minimum return on investment. The owner must establish what this minimum is, but let us assume the drugstore offers 10 major product lines and wants a return of at least 12 percent from each. At the end of the year, the accountant closes the books and makes the calculations, which reveal the following:

Major Line	Return on Investment (%)
1	17
2	13
3	21
4	29
5	11
6	14
7	28
8	6
9	12
10	2

From the data, it is obvious that items 5, 8, and 10 are not producing a desirable return. Using this information, the owner must decide whether to drop them. If the lines are not new and do not hold some promise for the future, they should be dropped. The only exception to this is if they are *complementary products*—products bought by people who come into the store to buy something else. If that is the case, it may be wise for the store to carry both lines, because customers may go elsewhere if they cannot obtain both kinds of products at this location.

MARKET NICHE DANGER SIGNALS

In addition to the marketing analysis, the owner should use some qualitative criteria to judge whether the store is meeting the needs of its customers. This often can be determined by observing the behavior of customers and employees. Examples of danger signals are as follows:

1. Many customers leave the store without buying anything.
2. Many former customers no longer shop in the store.
3. Customers do not buy additional items or trade up to more expensive items.
4. Traffic (pedestrian and vehicular) in front of the store has fallen off.
5. Customers are returning more merchandise than they used to.
6. This month's sales are down from the previous year, as are sales for the year to date.
7. Employees are slow in greeting customers.
8. Employees appear indifferent and make customers wait unnecessarily.
9. Employees' personal appearance is not neat.
10. Salespeople lack knowledge of the store's merchandise.
11. The number of employee errors is increasing.
12. Because of high prices, the store has a reputation for greediness.
13. The better-qualified employees are leaving for jobs with competitors.

Although knowledge of the current market niche and customer buying habits is very important, a more vital consideration is the changes that will occur in the next three to five years. How will the market change? Remember: Today's successful products eventually will become marginal winners and then losers. New goods and services must be in the wings, ready to replace the current ones. These can be identified and cultivated through marketing research. The "New Venture Perspective" box provides an interesting look at how smaller ventures compete with today's "big box" stores.

MARKETING RESEARCH

Marketing research is the systematic study of the factors that affect a venture's sales in its particular market niche. If the entrepreneur operating the new venture is astute, he or she has been conducting some kind of marketing research from the first day the business opened, if not earlier during the business planning

---

NEW VENTURE PERSPECTIVE

Competing with Giants

How can a small retail venture compete against the power, size, prices, and selection offered by giant mass merchandisers? Wal-Mart, for example, generated more than $312.4 billion in global revenue for 2006; employed over 1.6 million people; and managed 6,700 stores in 14 countries, serving more than 176 million customers each week.

Although a new Wal-Mart can expect sales in excess of $20 million annually, specialty stores located close by will lose an estimated 9.9 percent in sales, building materials stores will lose 10.4 percent, apparel stores will lose 11.5 percent, and home-furnishings stores will lose 18.9 percent.

In order to survive such competition and remain distinctive in the eyes of customers, new ventures need to apply the following strategies:

1. Offer products unavailable in larger stores.
2. Develop a reputation for better product knowledge.
3. Offer personalized service/delivery, repair, installation, and so on.
4. Emphasize high-grade products (counter to the low-end goods sometimes sold by the "giants").
5. Stock different product lines than larger stores carry.
6. Help promote the community to attract new customers from surrounding areas.
7. Constantly stress the "family" part of the family business by using expressions such as "locally owned" when promoting or advertising the company.

Source: Adapted from David Diamond, "When Wal-Mart Comes to Town," *Family Business* (December 1990): 36–41; and Wal-Mart information, www.walmartfacts.com, 2007.

---

process.[10] Location, customer needs, competition, and product lines long have been recognized as areas of concern. The problem with most businesses, however, is that conditions change over time, and owners may not be aware of them. In general, marketing research can confirm hunches, reveal additional information, identify opportunities, and clarify advertising targets and the types of media necessary to reach them.

In particular, *marketing habits* change. For example, many people in metropolitan areas used to take public transportation to shop downtown. However, the massive movement of people to the suburbs and increasing automobile ownership have led to the emergence of the suburban shopping center as the dominant retail outlet in most parts of the country. This same mobility, in conjunction with the advent of larger and better refrigerators and freezers, has changed the food-buying habits of many people. Instead of making a few purchases at the neighborhood grocery each day, most people now do large-scale food shopping at a supermarket, at lower prices, once or twice a week.

Likewise, trends toward shorter working hours, online shopping, and greater interest in convenience products, do-it-yourself foods, and sports equipment have been noted. In addition, rising purchasing power in the world's developed countries has increased the demand for luxury products and services. All of these changes have a tremendous effect on buying habits and increase the need for a business to remain flexible. This is where marketing research enters the picture.[11]

HOW TO CONDUCT MARKETING RESEARCH

The data collected through market research efforts should be decision oriented rather than background oriented. Specifically, the data gathered are used to solve specific problems or make a particular decision.[12] How can the new venture owner obtain the necessary marketing research? Three broad sources should be considered. First, trade associations, regular business advisors, business agencies, and, to a limited extent, suppliers can offer factual information. Second, the entrepreneur can acquire the services of an independent marketing research service. Third, the entrepreneur can organize a marketing research effort within the firm itself. The best method for a particular business depends on its resources, the availability of the needed information, the complexity and size of the problem, and, most important, the cost involved.[13]

SECONDARY SOURCES

Regardless of who conducts the research, a good place to begin is with data from currently available secondary sources. These documents present statistics compiled about the industry, the competition, and the local area, as well as information gleaned from business publications. Secondary sources are fundamental for marketing research and often yield great value for the investment. However, they should *never* be the only sources tapped, because they seldom provide all of the information the owner/manager needs. Two of the most important secondary sources are local statistics and sales analysis.

LOCAL STATISTICS

One way to begin a marketing research effort is to obtain statistics on the local community. These often can be procured from the chamber of commerce (local and state), the city government, and census data. Analyzing these data can help the owner compile a profile of the local population by age distribution, average income, family size, automobile ownership, home ownership, and number of school-age children. (See Chapter 4 for some useful Web sites that provide several sources of statistics and secondary data.)

Another important area of consideration is the changing population. Currently, more than half the population of the United States is younger than 45 years of age. These people have different buying habits than older people. The geographic breakdown of this population can tell the new venture owner/manager where people are moving to and from. For example, in recent years, Arizona, Florida, California, and Colorado have increased in population. States that either have lost population or grown very slowly are North Dakota, South Dakota, Virginia, and Wyoming. By studying population changes, the business owner can determine whether the firm is located in a growing area or one that is likely to become economically stagnant in the next 5 to 10 years.

Another way to get local statistics without expending a lot of time and effort is to read the local newspaper and subscribe to trade journals and business publications. The local newspaper often carries reports of income levels for the community and the region, and its financial section is another ready source of important statistical information. Additionally, publications such as *Business Week,* the *Wall Street Journal,* and *Fortune* offer a wealth of information that can prove useful for making marketing decision. The astute business owner/manager will cut out and save statistics that directly affect his or her business. In this way, the individual can compile a *market fact file* for marketing research.

SALES ANALYSIS

Sales analysis is a type of marketing research that can be conducted within the place of business. By analyzing sales data, the owner/manager can answer many questions, such as the following: How many dishwashers did we sell last year? How many freezers did we sell? What is our most profitable product line? What is our biggest seller? Did most people pay cash or charge it? Do most of our customers live close by or more than 10 miles away? These questions are answered easily by examining sales slips that include the customer's name and address, the date, the item sold, and the amount paid for the item recorded.

PRIMARY SOURCES

Statistics and sales analysis can provide important information, but the data gathered are limited in that they are historical. No new facts are considered—only old information is studied. Additionally, data are not specific to the target market in which the entrepreneur plans to do business. Collecting current data requires some form of survey research. This can be done by the new venture itself, or an outside survey research firm can be hired. In either case, the steps in the research are the same.

SURVEY RESEARCH

Conducting marketing survey research involves six steps:

1. *Analyze the situation.* What are the conditions in the industry and in the local area? For example, assume the new venture owner provides rug-cleaning services. The first task of the owner/manager or the marketing survey organization is to gather background information. This could be done by asking the trade association or national industry group to which the business owners belong if any national or area surveys have been conducted. Then, the chamber of commerce and other local sources of data can be consulted. During this background research, investigators should obtain information that will help complete the second step.

2. *Formulate a statement of the problem or goal.* Obviously, the entrepreneur is having the research conducted with a purpose in mind. Sometimes this is nothing more than a desire to know whether to expand services by moving into another geographic area.

3. *Design the research.* How will further information be collected so that the situation can be analyzed in sufficient depth?

4. *Carry out the survey.* Numerous methods can be used; among the most common are interviews and questionnaires. Regardless of who carries them out, however, the issue of bias must be addressed. Sometimes, the way a person asks a question generates a particular response. The same is true for the way a question is written in a questionnaire. For example, if the owner of the rug-cleaning firm decides to interview 100 people in the local area to ask them questions about rug cleaning, the owner will get different answers depending on how the questions are phrased. If the owner asks, "Would you consider using my firm to clean your rugs?" the respondent would probably yes. However, the person is not saying that he or she *will* do so, merely that he or she will *consider* it. A better way to gather marketing research data is to ask open-ended questions such as "How do you clean your rugs?" The answer will tell the owner how many people hire professionals (or do it themselves). This answer will indicate something about how area homeowners value their time and who can afford such services. These data, in turn, will provide some bases for distinguishing potential rug-cleaning customers from people who will do it themselves.

5. *Tabulate, analyze, and report the information.* At this stage, the information is put into some meaningful form. Sometimes, the person collecting the information will believe that the answers point to one overall conclusion because he or she remembers several of the interviewees very well, and those people all said the same thing. However, analyzing all of the responses may show that more people gave the opposite answer.

6. *Apply the data to the purpose.* What percentage of interviewees said that they hire professionals for rug-cleaning services? How many potential homes will use this service every year? How many competing firms offer rug cleaning? What percentage of this market can the firm capture? By answering these questions, for example, the new venture owner is in a position to determine whether it is a good idea to expand the business into another geographic area.

FOCUS GROUPS

Focus groups are small groups (usually 7 to 10 participants) that are selected from a broader population and interviewed through facilitator-led discussions for opinions and attitudes about a particular issue. Focus groups are a common market research tool that yields qualitative data in a condensed amount of time. Conducting effective focus groups requires attention to five steps:

Step 1: **Prepare for Session**
  1. Identify the major objective(s) of the meeting.
  2. Develop four to six questions.

3. Invite potential participants to the meeting.
4. Approximately three days before the session, call each participant who initially agreed to participate to remind him or her to attend.

Step 2: **Develop Questions**
1. Develop four to six questions. Sessions should last up to 2.5 hours—in this amount of time, one can ask a maximum of six questions.
2. Allow time for follow-up and probing of answers to the four to six questions.
3. Ask yourself what problem or need will be addressed by the information gathered during the session.

Step 3: **Plan the Session**
1. Scheduling: Plan meetings to be between 1 and 2.5 hours long. Avoid lunch meetings, during which participants may be distracted. If you provide food, serve it before, during a break, or after the meeting.
2. Setting and refreshments: Hold sessions in a conference room or another setting with adequate lighting, comfortable chairs, and space for a facilitator to work the crowd. Configure chairs so that all participants face one another, and provide name tags or name cards.
3. Set the ground rules: It is important that all participants participate as much as possible; keep the meeting moving to cover all questions. A few important rules include: a) stay focused, b) maintain a timeline, and c) get closure upon and summarize each of the questions.
4. Agenda: Use an agenda that includes a welcome, review of agenda, review of the purpose of the meeting, review of focus group rules of engagement, introductions, questions, and wrap up.
5. Number of participants: Focus groups are usually conducted with 6–10 participants who have a similar characteristic (e.g., age group, status, income, target market, etc.).
6. Record the session with either a note taker or some type of audio or video recorder. Also use flip charts, postcards, or other tools that provide a record of what was said.

Step 4: **Facilitate and Manage the Session**
1. Stick to the agenda and goals of the meeting.
2. Introduce yourself and others who are helping you.
3. Explain how you will record the information and protect confidentiality as needed.
4. When you are finished with each focus group question, summarize your findings for the group (the notetaker may do this).
5. Ensure participation: If one or two people are dominating the meeting, call on others. Consider using a round-table approach in which a question is asked of everyone, and—moving in one direction around the table—each person is given a minute to answer.
6. Close the session: Tell participants that they will receive a copy of the report generated from their answers (if necessary), thank them for coming, and adjourn the meeting.

Step 5: **Follow Up Immediately After the Session**
   1. Transcribe all responses into a report. Do not delay, because some of the nuances of the meeting may be forgotten.
   2. Have a few participants review your report to check for accuracy.
   3. Take action on suggestions, if possible.

If conducted properly, focus groups yield a great deal of information in a very short period of time. However, the data are qualitative in nature and cannot be statistically analyzed.

OTHER DATA COLLECTION METHODS

One of the most common methods of data collection is the home interview. Another method of gathering data, and probably the simplest method of all, is the *store interview* or questionnaire. Retail stores, in particular, can use this approach with very little trouble. A common technique is to have a personable, pleasant interviewer approach customers and ask them to answer a few simple questions. Usually, these questions are limited in number and take only a few moments to answer. The information is recorded on an easily marked interview card so that a permanent record of the comments exists. Typical questions include: "How often do you visit this store?" "Where do you live?" "How many times a week do you shop?" "What kind of products do you come to this store to buy?" "Why do you like shopping at this store?" If the owner experiences some resistance from interviewed shoppers, other methods can be used. For example, instead of asking shoppers a series of questions, the business can use point-of-sale survey cards that shoppers fill out and drop in a box. Included on the survey card is room for the person's name and answers to a few questions. Then the owner can draw a predetermined number of responses from the box, with these respondents receiving a prize. In this case, the survey instrument is used both to gather information and as a contest entry form.

Another method that new ventures often use is the *mail survey*. This type of questionnaire is sent to the respondent with a request to fill it out and return it in a prepaid or postage-guaranteed envelope. Such surveys usually are cheaper than personal interviews and easier to tabulate. Many people, indeed, do respond to mail questionnaires depending on the purpose of the survey and the party that is inquiring. In fact, some companies have found them to be more reliable than interviews. For example, one large consumer-goods firm discovered that the results obtained from interview surveys were different from those obtained from a mail survey. After it analyzed the eventual buying habits of the consumers, the firm found the mail survey to be more accurate.

A third common form of survey is the *telephone interview*. Using this method, the owner/manager should first ensure that respondents know they are being asked to participate in a survey. Prepared questions are asked, and the answers are recorded. The obvious advantages of telephone interviews are that a single interviewer can handle a large number of respondents, and the overall cost is relatively low. Of course, the person carrying out the interview must have a pleasant voice, and the questionnaire the person reads should be simple, direct, and brief. If the call takes too long, the respondent is likely to terminate it. In addition, many states have implemented no-call legislation that may regulate if and how phone surveys can be conducted.

Finally, owners should not overlook *specialized surveys* for collecting consumer data, some of which lend themselves to *demonstration approaches*. New products or product prototypes often are researched this way. A place is created where consumers can examine the products and ask questions about them. Supermarkets often set up demonstration tables where new food items are cooked and shoppers are urged to sample products. Department stores also do this when a salesperson demonstrates how a new product works and encourages the shopper to buy one before leaving the store.[14]

USING RESEARCH DATA

Once the data are collected, the business owner must decide how to use the information. Until now, all the owner has done is collect a mass of facts and figures. First, the data must be tabulated and arranged in some useful form. For example, if a new venture owner believes most shoppers in his toy store are children or young parents, he might be interested in the number of people in this section of town who are in the age ranges of 0 to 9 (children) and 20 to 39 (the most common ages for parents), and whether the numbers are increasing or decreasing. Assume that the owner has collected census data for the metropolitan area for both 10 years ago and today, and finds the data presented in Table 6-3.

Note that the percentage breakdowns are nearly the same today as they were 10 years ago. Approximately 26 percent of the group is children below the age of 10, and almost 30 percent of the group is between the ages of 20 and 39. Thus, no significant population shifts have occurred. Additionally, to the owner's advantage, the number of people in the local area has increased by 45 percent.

TABLE 6-3   Age Distribution in the Local Area

	10 Years Ago		Today	
Age (Years)	*Number*	*Percentage of Population*	*Number*	*Percentage of Population*
0–9	88,617	26.4	125,768	25.8
10–19	76,212	22.6	112,386	23.0
20–29	51,007	15.2	82,087	16.8
30–39	42,839	12.7	55,320	11.5
40–49	36,793	11.0	42,107	8.6
50–59	25,107	7.5	40,567	8.2
60+	15,361	4.6	29,138	6.1
Total	335,936	100.00	487,373	100.00

The foregoing leads to the next important step in using research data: The owner must *interpret the statistics*. What do the statistics tell the owner that can help in making decisions? This is often the most difficult part of the research. The owner must evaluate the data objectively and not twist or distort their meaning.

INTERNET MARKETING

Marketing a Web site is not unlike marketing a bricks-and-mortar business in that a budget should be set, a plan should be laid out, and the work remains never-ending. The difference is that the Internet is a direct-sales distribution channel. With Internet marketing, the seller–buyer relationship can be established immediately, and the waiting period following a traditional marketing campaign is almost eliminated. This environment therefore requires a top-notch marketing plan. Established Web sites are able to pursue traditional marketing by spending a significant amount of money to run commercial ads. Experts, however, recommend that start-ups keep their marketing budget at 10 percent of revenues or less; budget constraints call for creative and cost-effective marketing. Three steps to help lure customers to a site once it is up and running are described below.

STEP 1: CO-MARKETING DEALS AND BANNER ADS

Using co-marketing, two or more related sites swap links with each other—the amount of money exchanged depends on the situation. One of the more popular deals is between 1800 Flowers and American Online (AOL): 1800 Flowers paid AOL $25 million to maintain a four-year status as the AOL florist. Banner ads obtained through co-marketing deals are the cheapest and most efficient way for a new site to start down the path toward brand identity and loyalty. Banner ads work because they reach the target audience. According to industry gurus, vertical-community sites that enhance the distribution channel are the most favored posting sites, and they yield strong results.

STEP 2: BECOME A POPULAR LINK

The most common approach to marketing a Web site is to get it linked up to one of the major search engines: Yahoo!, Google, Excite, MSN, and so forth. It is, however, one thing to be linked, and another to make it so the business name pops up more often and under any related search. Keywords are the key! Meta tags give the name and description of the storefront and are part of the Web site's software code. The more keywords in the company's meta tags, the greater the chance that the Web site address will pop up when someone is searching for the products or services that the company has to offer.

STEP 3: SPONSOR CONTESTS, SPECIALS, AND OTHER INTERACTIVE FEATURES

Contests and specials are the hottest ways to grab Internet users. Successful companies aren't settling for the hits—they're vying for the relationship. The goal is to formulate a site that keeps the product, service, or Web page on the customers' minds after they leave. This goal can be accomplished by interacting with the potential customer, providing an incentive for him or her to return by allowing the visitor to play a fun game, win a prize, and, in the best case, volunteer information for a database. Interactive features that provide the feeling of a demonstration allow the potential buyer to better appreciate the product. An e-mail channel for company and product questions can also aid in establishing a connection with Web surfers.

Summary

A market is a group of consumers who behave in a similar way. Because people buy all sorts of goods and services, many market niches exist. When analyzing market niches, an owner/manager needs to consider the relevant price range and competition. The relevant price range is the minimum-to-maximum price that customers will pay. Competition represents the threat to this niche, and the degree of competitiveness determines whether a range of prices exists or similar goods can be substituted for particular product. Thus, of four types of markets—monopoly, oligopoly, monopolistic competition, and pure competition—monopolistic competition and its high degree of competitiveness most concerns the new venture owner/manager. In addition to understanding price and competition, the new venture owner needs to understand the firm's current market niche. The development of a customer profile is one of the best ways to do this.

Marketing research is the systematic study of factors that affect a business's sales. Analyzing these factors is important because customer-buying habits continually change. Secondary sources, such a local statistics and sales analyses, are good places to begin marketing research. These can be supplemented with primary sources, such as market survey research, in which previously unavailable data are gathered. After these new data are obtained, the owner/manager must know how to objectively arrange, analyze, and interpret them to draw valuable conclusions. The individual must not allow personal biases or opinions to alter an objective evaluation of the data. If the owner/manager can do this correctly, maximum value may be derived from the survey.

Review and Discussion Questions

1. What do the terms *markets* and *market niche* mean?
2. Explain what a new venture owner/manager needs to know about relevant price range.
3. How does each of the following market types differ from the others: monopoly, oligopoly, monopolistic competition, and pure competition?

4. Explain how a customer profile can be useful to an owner/manager who is interested in examining a market niche.
5. What is meant by the term *marketing research*?
6. How can local statistics and sales analyses help an owner/manager gather research data?
7. How is market survey research carried out? Explain the six steps.
8. What are the most common data collection methods that new ventures use for marketing research? Describe at least two.
9. Specifically, what should a new venture owner know about using research data? How can the information be useful? Explain.
10. Explain some of the key steps to remember when marketing on the Internet.

NEW VENTURE CONSULTANT

An Inquisitive Nephew

The Grant Building, located in a large metropolitan area, is a 55-story office building. On the ground floor and the floor immediately below it are shops, including a luggage store owned and managed by Margie and Hank Brandon. Suitcases and attaché cases are their specialty, although they sell supplemental merchandise as well.

A few weeks ago, Margie's nephew, Gerald, dropped by. He works for a marketing research firm across town and came by to take the couple out to lunch. During the visit, the three of them began talking about the store's business. Margie said that they felt very lucky to be located in the Grant Building because "our customers are located in the same building. Every time one of the big executives needs a new attaché case or has his suitcase damaged during a business trip, we can expect a visit from him."

The statement intrigued Gerald. "How do you know that all of your customers are located in the Grant Building?" he asked. Hank explained that the store did not advertise and that "most of the people who come into the store are people I see coming into the building every day."

Gerald then asked them how they generated sales to people who did not work in their building. "Don't you do *any* type of advertising at *all?*" Gerald learned that Margie and Hank had moved into the Grant Building six years earlier, when they heard about a shop vacancy. They had been selling suitcases and other leather goods in a small store across town. The business was doing all right, but they were convinced that they could do much better by catering to businesspeople.

Gerald was very impressed, especially because Margie and Hank had been able to survive in business through common sense and, perhaps, some luck. Nevertheless, he suggested that they conduct some marketing research to see what they could learn about their customers and, in the process, to increase their sales and profits.

Margie and Hank said they would be happy to have him come by and design a marketing research study for them, especially after Gerald told them that he would not charge them for it. "I just want to see if I can help you do even better," he said.

Gerald is scheduled to visit them tomorrow. In the interim, he has asked them to have their records for the past two years available and to be prepared to give him approximately two hours of their time. "I think I can design a program that will collect all of the information you need without taking too much of your time. All I'll need from you will be some initial assistance and the promise that you will ask each customer to fill out the form I have made up for you, since this will give us some background on who shops at your store and why."

Your consultation: What is marketing research? How can it help owner/managers like Hank and Margie? What kind of marketing research survey do you think Gerald will put together for them? Explain. How can a survey of this kind be of any value to the owners?

Endnotes

1. Jeffrey G. Covin, Kimberly M. Green, and Dennis P. Slevin, "Strategic Process Effects on the Entrepreneurial Orientation-Sales Growth Rate Performance," *Entrepreneurship Theory & Practice* 30, no. 1 (2006): 57–82.
2. See Philip Kotler and Gary Armstrong, *Principles of Marketin*g (Upper Saddle River, NJ: Pearson/Prentice Hall, 2008); and O. C. Ferrell and Michael Hartline, *Marketing Strategy*, 4th ed. (Mason, OH: Thomson/Southwestern Publishing, 2008).
3. See David L. Kurtz, *Contemporary Marketing* (Mason, OH: Thomson/Southwestern, 2008).
4. Timothy Matanovich, Gary L. Lilien, and Arvind Rangaswamy, "Engineering the Price–Value Relationship," *Marketing Management* (Spring 1999): 48–53.
5. Philip Kotler and Gary Armstrong, *Principles of Marketing.* (Upper Saddle River, NJ: Pearson/Prentice Hall, 2008).
6. See Stephanie Prause, "The True Value of Market Research" *NZ Business* 20, no. 9 (2006): 21.
7. R. Chaganti, R. Chagnti, and V. Mahajan, "Profitable Small Business Strategies Under Different Types of Competition," *Entrepreneurship Theory and Practice* (Spring 1989): 21–35.
8. William G. Zikmund and Barry J. Babin, *Exploring Marketing Research*, 9th ed. (Mason, OH: Thomson/Southwestern, 2007); see also Boyd Cohen and Monika I. Winn, "Market Imperfections, Opportunity, and Sustainable Entrepreneurship," *Journal of Business Venturing* 22, no. 1 (2007): 29–49.
9. See Jack Harms, "Are You a Marketing-Oriented Company?" *Small Business Reports* (March 1990): 20–24.
10. Stephen W. McDaniel and A. Parasuraman, "Practical Guidelines for Small Business Marketing Research," *Journal of Small Business Management* (January 1986): 1–8.
11. See Robin T. Peterson, "Small Business Adoption of the Marketing Concept vs. Other Business Strategies," *Journal of Small Business Management* (January 1989): 38–46; see also Bret Golann, "Achieving Growth and Responsiveness: Process Management and Market Orientation in Small Firms," *Journal of Small Business Management* 44, no. 3 (2006): 369–85.
12. R. Deshpande and G. Zaltman, "Factors Affecting the Use of Market Research Information: A Path Analysis," *Journal of Marketing Research* 24 (1982): 32–38. See also R. Ganeshasundaram and N. Henley, "The Prevalence and Usefulness of Market Research: An Empirical Investigation into 'Background' versus 'Decision' Research." *International Journal of Market Research* 48, no. 5 (2006): 525–50.

13. For a detailed discussion of marketing research, see John A. Pearce II and Steven C. Michael, "Marketing Strategies That Make Entrepreneurial Firms Recession-Resistant," *Journal of Business Ventures* (July 1997): 301–14.
14. For examples of various approaches, see Robert F. Hurley and G. Thomas M. Hult, "Innovation Market Orientation and Organizational Learning: An Integration and Empirical Examination," *Journal of Marketing* (July 1998): 42–54; Fareena Sultan and Gloria Barczak, "Turning Marketing Research High Tech," *Marketing Management* (Winter 1999): 25–30; and Andy Lockett, "Conducting Market Research Using the Internet: The Case of Xenon Laboratories," *Journal of Business & Industrial Marketing* 19, no. 3 (2004): 178–87.

CHAPTER 7

STRATEGIC PRICING
THE HOOK

INTRODUCTION

The pricing challenge is a major challenge for entrepreneurial ventures. Entrepreneurs must understand a number of basic considerations when they are developing a pricing strategy. The new venture's primary consideration when pricing must be cost. No one can afford to sell below the cost level—at least not for very long. However, since this point is obvious, we won't spend much time on it here. Rather, let us turn to other pricing considerations. These include the following:

1. The nature of the product
2. The competition
3. The marketing strategy
4. The customer and value perception
5. General business conditions

PRICING CONSIDERATIONS

THE NATURE OF THE PRODUCT

The demand for some products seems to be little affected by a change in price. For example, whether the price of salt is raised or lowered has little effect on the quantity sold. However, the demand for many products *does* respond to price, and this demand can be stimulated by price changes in two ways. First, some goods will sell better if the price is *lowered*—that is, if demand increases. However, the opposite approach is to *raise* the price and manage to maintain approximately the same demand as before. If this occurs, it must be because buyers believe the product or service is still a good value at the higher price.

THE COMPETITION

A second pricing consideration is the competition. The way competing firms price similar goods affects what the new venture owner/manager can charge. This is particularly so when customers cannot distinguish the product that one store sells from what another sells. For example, for most people, milk is milk, so it really does not matter where a person buys it as long as the store is located conveniently. As a result, if two stores are across the street from each other and the price of milk is 5 cents a gallon less at one of them, customers will flock to that store. The same is true for bread, shoelaces, socks, and gasoline.

Few products are bought *solely* on the basis of price; however, often people will pay more money for a particular good because it has a quality image. Television sets are an example. If a set has problems, the average consumer will not know how to repair it. Therefore, when a person buys a television set, quality will be a major criterion, and price will rank further down the list. Of course, the new venture owner/manager cannot guarantee quality in televisions, appliances, or similar goods, but the person can try to secure franchise agreements from well-known major manufacturers so that he or she can carry their products. This will provide a competitive edge over other stores.

Finally, regardless of quality, most goods eventually wear out or break down. Sooner or later, a car needs an engine repair or a computer has a hard drive that crashes, requiring replacement. This is where service comes in. Few new ventures can compete with large companies on a head-to-head price basis. However, they can distinguish their goods and services from those of the competition through personal service. For example, many people who go to a service station for car maintenance will return if the service is satisfactory. They may also buy their gasoline and other auto-related products there. Similarly, services such as haircuts, dental work, and health care are influenced greatly by their quality. Thus, price in and of itself will not always determine demand. In fact, businesses that offer high quality often can raise their prices without suffering any decline in demand.

THE MARKETING STRATEGY

A third pricing consideration is marketing strategy. Some new ventures prefer to be price leaders even if this means lower overall volume. Others prefer simply to meet the competition and price their merchandise between the highest and lowest prices of other sellers. Still others like to price low and make their money through increased volume.

The owner must decide whether he or she wants to make a lot of profit in the short run or aim for long-run profit in the form of repeat business. If the owner sells fad items, prices probably will be high because the store has little chance of repeat business for any particular line. Additionally, if the fad suddenly fades, the owner may wind up with a lot of unsalable inventory. To prevent this, the owner will want to recover the investment as soon as possible. In contrast, many new ventures sell the same types of goods and services all the time. If they are high quality, the owner may have high prices and develop a reputation for being "expensive but good." Conversely, owners who sell items of average quality usually price them competitively and work on securing repeat business.

Marketing strategy helps the public identify a firm. When people want to buy something at the lowest possible price, they go to companies they have come to know as discounters. But when they want to buy something of high quality that, if not satisfactory, can be returned, they go to stores that have a reputation for handling these kinds of transactions. In short, marketing strategy helps the business establish an *image*.

THE CUSTOMER AND VALUE PERCEPTIONS

There is no question that in today's environment a new venture entrepreneur must consider the targeted customer in the pricing strategy decision. In this vein, the customer's perception of value in the product or service is the ultimate judge of a fair price. Thus, entrepreneurs must be conscious of the value perception being created by their product or service. In addition, entrepreneurs must be willing to enhance their venture's image of value because that eventually will impact the price that customers are willing to pay.

GENERAL CONDITIONS

Most ventures are affected by general business conditions; this is particularly true for newer enterprises. When economic conditions are poor, it is common for newer enterprises to keep inventories at a minimum and price goods to move fast. The impact of the economic environment is most noticeable at the wholesale level, because wholesalers tend to sell large quantities of goods on a very narrow profit margin. Changes in their cost of doing business often must be passed along immediately to protect this narrow margin. At the retail level, price changes are slower in coming because most stores price their goods high enough to absorb minor variations in the cost of doing business. Nevertheless, all costs eventually are passed along to the consumer.[1]

Remember, price is not just *what* the entrepreneur charges but *how* he or she charges. For example, eBay could charge by the auction, it could sell memberships and allow members to engage in as many auctions as they want for one price, or it could charge only the seller or the buyer a commission based on the dollar value of the transaction. Let's begin by examining some of the key factors in pricing.

KEY PRICING FACTORS

All pricing methods begin with understanding costs and what kind of price is necessary to break even on an item. New venture owner/managers may reduce the price and try to cut losses on a particular line; however, that should only happen as a result of careful analysis of certain key factors. Three basic factors to consider when setting a price are as follows:

1. The cost of goods
2. Competitive prices
3. Market demand

THE COST OF GOODS

The primary objective of pricing for profit is to set a price that is high enough to cover the cost of the goods and the expenses incurred in selling them to generate some profit. A simple formula for this follows:

$$\text{Selling Price} = \text{Purchase Price} + \text{Operating Expenses} + \text{Profit}$$

Note that, in this formula, operating expenses fall into two categories: production costs (materials and labor) and overhead (rent for the building, utility bills, and other general costs not covered directly when production costs are determined). Profit is then a percentage of the total.

COMPETITIVE PRICES

We already have discussed competitive prices in some depth. Most new venture owner/managers keep an eye on what their competitors are charging for similar goods and services. Unless new ventures have some good reason not to, most price with the competition.

MARKET DEMAND

Although demand has been examined in some detail already, we need to consider profit versus volume. Research reveals that many sellers try to hold the line on price to maintain market share. Sometimes, however, demand is so strong that the owner will raise the price as high as market conditions allow. This usually can be done only when a new product or service is in short supply, coupled with a strong market demand. Additionally, it is important to remember that an *ideal* price may exist. This can be illustrated by a demand schedule, a graph that plots varying prices against anticipated demand for each price (see Figure 7-1). Note that four points are designated on this schedule. Computing the total revenue at each point, we get the following:

$$2,500 \text{ unit @ } \$45 \text{ each} = \$112,500$$
$$5,000 \text{ unit @ } \$35 \text{ each} = \$175,000$$
$$7,500 \text{ unit @ } \$25 \text{ each} = \$187,500$$
$$10,000 \text{ unit @ } \$15 \text{ each} = \$150,000$$

In this case, the owner should price at $25, because revenue would be maximized at that point. Anything higher or lower than $25 will result in less revenue. According to the schedule, if the owner is willing to give up $37,500, he or she

FIGURE 7-1   Price and Demand

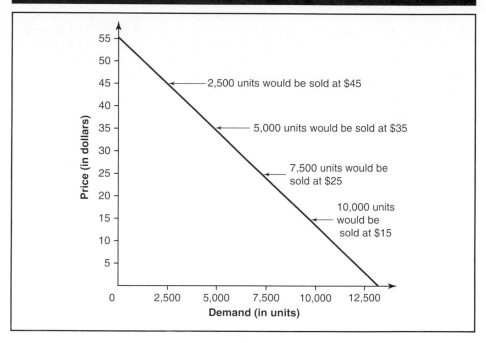

could sell another 2,500 units by pricing at $15. Typically, however, the owner prices for profit, so the $25 price would be preferred over the $15 price.[2]

PRICING STRATEGIES

New ventures employ a wide variety of pricing strategies. However, they all have two common objectives: (1) to earn a profit for the firm and (2) to garner and maintain market demand for the product.

The specific pricing strategy is dictated by a number of considerations. For example, some companies tie their pricing to the product life cycle of the good (see Table 7-1). When the product is first introduced, they use one type of pricing strategy. When the product begins to mature, they employ another pricing strategy. As the good begins moving into the declining phase, they implement a third strategy. Regardless of whether this strategy is used, a host of pricing techniques typically serves as the basis for pricing decisions.[3] The following section examines some of the most common.

Skimming pricing is the technique of selling at a high price to skim off of the strongest demand in the marketplace. This strategy particularly helps a new venture generate high profit per unit. However, the strategy is often maintained for only a short time because the conditions that allow for skimming usually do not last very long. A common example is a new venture that has a product that is in strong demand, such as a clothing store with the latest and hottest clothing lines.

TABLE 7-1 Pricing for the Product Life Cycle

Customer demand and sales volume will vary with the development of a product. Thus, pricing for products needs to be adjusted at each stage of their life cycle. The following outline provides some suggested pricing methods that relate to the different stages in the product life cycle.

Product Life-Cycle Stage	Pricing Strategy	Reasons/Effects
Introductory Stage • Unique product	Skimming: deliberately setting a high price to maximize short-term profits	Initial price set high to establish a quality image, to provide capital to offset development costs, and to allow for future price reductions to handle competition
• Nonunique Product	Penetration: setting prices at such a low level that products are sold at a loss	Allows quick gains in market share by setting a price below competitors' prices
Growth Stage	Consumer pricing: combining penetration and competitive pricing in order to gain market share; depends on consumer's perceived value of the product	Demands on number of potential competitors, size of total market, and distribution of that market
Maturity Stage	Demand-oriented pricing: a flexible strategy that bases pricing decisions on the demand level for the product	Sales growth declines; customers very price-sensitive
Decline Stage	Loss leader pricing: pricing the product below cost in an attempt to attract customers to other products	Product possesses little or no attraction to customers; idea is to have low prices bring customers to newer product lines

The store often will price this product at a high markup because the owner knows that anyone who wants to buy the latest fashions will pay a premium to get them early. When other clothing stores begin carrying similar lines of clothing, the owner then will drop the price down to the usual level because customers will no longer pay a premium price for a product they can obtain more cheaply elsewhere.

In some cases, skimming is an ongoing strategy because market conditions support this approach. A good example is high-end electronics stores in which customers expect to pay high prices and often equate price with quality. A beauty salon that charges $50 for a haircut may not attract many customers, but if it is located in a fashionable part of town and appeals to upscale clientele, the business is likely to do quite well with a skimming strategy. Moreover, if the salon decides to lower its prices in order to increase the number of customers, the owner would likely find that the new strategy hurts the company's reputation and results in a substantial decline of both revenue and profits. Skimming also is used when customers are willing to pay a premium for services they cannot, or will not, perform themselves. Lawn sprinkler installation companies often find that they can charge high prices because homeowners do not know how to put in a sprinkler system and are willing to pay a premium price for this service. Although some competitors will try to capture the market share by offering lower installations prices, this strategy is often unsuccessful because the customer equates price with quality. As a result, the individual is afraid that a low-priced sprinkler system will continually break down or need an inordinate amount of periodic maintenance. The psychological effect helps installation companies maintain their skimming strategy.

Skimming also is used profitably when customers perceive a major difference between the high-priced good or service and lower-priced ones. For example, many patients prefer to stay with their current dentist rather than go to a university dental clinic or a large dental facility located in a shopping center despite the fact their current dentist often charges higher prices. These patients are convinced that the dental care they receive from their dentist is superior to what they would get in a shopping center. Whether or not this is true, it helps explain why dentists in small offices are able to attract and maintain clientele in the face of lower-priced competition.

Penetration pricing is the strategy of employing a low price that is competitive and designed both to stimulate demand and to discourage competition. Penetration pricing most typically is used for low-priced goods where the firm's objective is to trade profit per unit for gross sales. Many new ventures, for example, have found that when charging a high price for an item—$2.99, for example—they will sell 100 units a month, but at $2.49 they will sell 500 units a month. If the cost of the unit is $2, the business will make a total profit of $99 at the high price and $245 at the lower price.

Another benefit of penetration pricing is that it discourages new competitors because the profit per item is low, and these firms often are unwilling to compete vigorously for the necessary market share. (This is in contrast to a skimming strategy, which often attracts competitors who see the opportunity for large profit per unit.) Penetration pricing also helps a new venture build an image as a place where merchandise can be purchased at reasonable prices.

Another term used here is *parity pricing*, which means that the entrepreneur will charge at or near what the competitors are charging. Marketing researchers Kotler and Armstrong[4] claim that the choice of strategy affects the competition that entrepreneurs might face. A strategy with high margins may draw in others who would like to take advantage; however, a low margin strategy may drive competitors out. To decide what to do, ask the following questions:

- How does the company's product or service compare to the competition?
- How strong are current competitors?
- How does the competitive landscape influence customer price sensitivity?

Many new ventures use penetration or parity pricing because they are better able to control their costs than larger competitors. Thus, they can afford to earn lower profit per unit and still remain viable. However, penetration pricing must be closely coordinated with inventory ordering to ensure that the business neither runs out of merchandise nor overstocks. Many companies feel this is a small price to pay for the potentially large profit they can generate using penetration pricing.

A *sliding price strategy* is a method of moving prices in relation to demand. This strategy involves a combination of skimming and penetration pricing. In most cases, goods are priced high and demand at this level is skimmed off. Then, as demand weakens, the firm will lower its price and continue to generate demand. The move into penetration pricing will continue until the company drops the product line or freezes the price at the lowest level it can go.

In some cases, a sliding price strategy involves fluctuations both up and down. For example, when auto dealers receive a shipment of new cars, they try to sell the cars for as close to sticker price as possible. The dealers know that customers who want a new car will pay a premium price during the early months of the year. So, when new cars reach the market in September or October, it is common to find auto dealers using a skimming strategy. As the sales year wears on, however, demand will slacken; during January and February, it is common to find dealers more willing to bargain and take lower prices. Some customers prefer to buy new cars at the tail end of the sales year (July, August, and September) because they know the dealer wants to clear out the current year's models to make way for new models. This scenario shows how dealers use skimming strategy followed by penetration pricing. However, this is not the only sales strategy pattern that they employ.

If a new car is selling very well, the dealer will not resort to penetration pricing; instead, he or she will employ a skimming strategy throughout the entire year. Conversely, if the dealer knows that a monthly demand exists for 15 to 17 of this year's new trucks and the company received 24 trucks last month, the dealership will turn to penetration pricing to entice sales. However, if the business received only 9 of these vehicles from the manufacturer this month, the car dealer will use a skimming strategy because he or she knows that the demand is greater than the supply on hand. Therefore, using a sliding price strategy, prices can slide down *or* up, depending on the business's reading of customer demand. This means that companies that sell a number of different products or product lines will use a sliding price strategy that results in a variety of price changes.

In most cases, however, a sliding price strategy follows a skimming and then penetration pattern with progressively lower prices. One of the main reasons for this pattern is competition from new product offerings. For example, the price of microcomputers has continued to fall—machines that cost $2,200 ten years ago are now being purchased, with more advanced systems, for less than half that price. As technology causes old products to become outmoded, sellers must lower their prices to maintain demand. New venture owners who sell these units know that the longer they have these units on hand, the greater the likelihood that they will have to lower prices in order to create the necessary demand. At this point, the pricing emphasis is more on penetration than skimming.

Odd pricing is the setting of a price just below a round number. Examples include pricing a good at $1.99 rather than $2.00, or $299 rather than $300.[5] This strategy is based on the belief that customers perceive the odd price as much lower than the round number price. Obviously, the price is not significantly lower, as perceived, but the phenomenon helps account for why odd pricing often is referred to as *psychological pricing.* The major question for new venture owners is, how much of an impact on sales will an odd price generate? The answer depends on the price. For example, razor blades that sell at $2.99 are often more attractive than similar offerings at $3.00, but few people would be influenced to buy a refrigerator for $999.99 rather than $1,000 because the penny difference is not regarded as a sufficient savings. Recent research shows that odd pricing tactics can be helpful to new venture owners, but the approach has to vary depending on price level. Following are four guidelines that have been recommended:

1. *Product selling for under $1:* Prices for these goods should end in 9 because this is psychologically attractive and generates higher profits for the firm. For example, a product selling at 59 cents will sell just as well as one priced at 54 cents. Thus, it is advisable to round the price up to 9 and maximize profits.

2. *Product selling for $1 to $10:* The two best numbers in this price category are 9 and 5. Therefore, if a new venture feels that it must price a product below $5, a selling price of $4.99 is often an attractive one. If the company feels that too many of its products are priced one cent below the dollar, then $4.95 is a good alternative. If we compare the market appeal of prices for a good in the mid-$8 range, for example, $7.49 is preferable to $7.50, and $7.45 is better than $7.44. Additionally, in the $1 to $10 range, prices such as $6.41 or $9.52, a penny or two above a round number, are no better at attracting sales than are $6.49 or $9.55. By sticking to the 9 and 5 options, new venture owners can generate more sales and profits in the $1 to $10 range.

3. *Products selling above $10 and up to $100:* At these higher levels, the effect of prices ending in 9 diminishes significantly. People cannot perceive the difference between $10.99 and $11.00 as important. Instead, new venture owners should use prices ending in 25 cents, 50 cents, or 75 cents. For example, $10.75 is more attractive than $10.99, and $99.50 is more attractive than $99.99. At higher-level prices, the 25-cent difference is easier to evaluate.

4. *Products selling above $100:* At this level, only whole-dollar prices should be used. A television set selling for $699.99 will not generate any more demand than one selling for $700, so cents should be dropped from the price label. Additionally, it is important not to use decimal points after the dollar price. For example $700 is preferable to $700.00 because the zeros after the decimal point make the price look higher. Working with these basic guidelines, a new venture owner can revert back to the use of 9 and 5. For example, a refrigerator selling for $999 will be more attractive than one selling for $1,000. If the owner wants to nudge the price a little lower, $995 is another good choice. However, $992 or $991 will be no more effective than $995 in generating demand.

Odd pricing works only when it has a psychological benefit. The objective of the strategy is to make the price more attractive without giving away very much profit. One recent research study found that people perceive odd prices as being much lower than even prices. Participants in the study reported that they would buy significantly fewer items if even pricing were utilized, even though the price was .3 percent different. This result was found for pricing at four different pricing levels.[6] For this reason, odd pricing tends to be used with competitive products and is more likely to supplement penetration pricing than a skimming strategy.

Leader pricing is the marking down of a popular product to attract more customers. The objective of this pricing strategy is to build customer traffic. One of the most popular forms of leader pricing has been the use of *loss leaders*, which are products sold below cost in an effort to generate increased overall sales for all products in a store. In many states, loss leaders have been outlawed because they are viewed as unfair competition. However, the basic idea of attracting customers through lower-than-usual prices continues to be a mainstay of most new venture pricing strategies. The logic behind leader pricing is that customers may come to buy one extremely low-priced product but end up buying normally priced products as well. The objective of the strategy is to increase the number of people coming into the business.

A store often uses leader pricing on an in-demand product to attract business. At other times, this strategy is employed to help cut large inventory levels. A good example is a St. Louis office-supply store that accidentally ordered 1,000 calculators rather than the 100 they planned to stock. To promote sales, the store advertised the machines at a very low price with the intention of attracting students who were getting ready to return to school. Within nine days, the store sold all of the units, as well as a large number of school-related supplies. The retailer has run a special back-to-school sale ever since and has attracted more than twice the usual number of customers during the 10-day sales period.

Price lining is the process of offering merchandise in several different price ranges. Some experts call this *price flexibility* and relate it to the decision to apply the same price to all segments or to differentiate based on different customers or regions.[7] One-price policies work best in mass-selling markets, and variable pricing is usually applied when individual bargaining is involved.

Price lining often takes the form of three price ranges: low, medium, and high. A good example of this strategy is a pizzeria that offers three different types of pies: regular, additional, and grand. A regular pizza costs $8.95; a pizza with two additional toppings costs $11.95; and a grand pizza, which contains a wide assortment of toppings, costs $14.95. When customers place their orders, the individual who totals the bill knows that only three prices exist, regardless of what the individual wants on the pizza. As result, price lining makes it easy to keep track of prices.

Businesses that use price lining try to cater to a variety of consumer tastes. The pizza example involves three price market niches. Some firms will cater to as few as two prices, whereas others will have four or more price ranges. As the number of product lines increases, however, it is common to find only two or three ranges per line because of the desire to simplify the buying, pricing, and stocking of merchandise.

Price lining most commonly is used when it is possible to distinguish among grades or levels of goods and services. Car washes, for example, often have a variety of service levels, ranging from a basic car wash (the least expensive service) to a deluxe wash and wax (the most expensive service). Beauty salons, coffee shops, auto parts stores, and many other new ventures use price-lining strategies. The most important benefits of this technique are that it allows the company to offer a variety of prices for its goods and services and helps it cater to a series of different market niches.

Price bundling is a type of pricing in which customers acquire a "host of goods or services" along with the products they purchase.[8] A good example of bundled pricing is the purchase of a cell phone and a calling plan. In order to get the special price on a desired cell phone, you must also sign up for a calling plan that bundles minutes, weekend calling, e-mail, text messaging, insurance, and so forth, all at one cost.

Geographic pricing is the technique of charging customers based on where they live. Simply stated, this pricing strategy passes on the cost of transporting goods to buyers. In some cases, this is handled merely by charging customers the cost of the products "plus shipping." If the company is located in New Jersey, the product's final cost will be greater for customers in San Francisco than for those in Philadelphia.

New ventures that sell locally seldom charge for transportation, unless it is a standard practice in the industry or the cost of delivering goods or services is a large percentage of the overall bill. For example, if a dry cleaner charges $1.50 per shirt, the store will not deliver two shirts to a customer who lives 20 miles away without adding a delivery charge. At a cost of 25 cents per mile for the company vehicle, it would cost $10 round trip. The business would lose money on free delivery to the customer. To overcome resistance to geographic pricing, some companies divide the local area into zones and let customers know the additional charge for delivery to their zone. Other businesses simply have a fixed delivery charge, such as $5 per order. Then they can group the orders and make a series of deliveries to customers, thus reducing the out-of-pocket expense per order and in many cases making a profit. This technique often is accepted without question by customers, even though, on close analysis, some people are paying more than they should for the service. For example, a person who lives only a few miles away will be charged the same transportation fee as someone who lives a great distance from the company.

In determining a geographic pricing strategy, companies also take into account hourly employee costs. Many firms resolve this situation by using part-time help to handle delivery and paying these people the minimum wage. If a number of deliveries are to be made per hour, employees will take this job because they are counting on tips from clients. In this way, a person paid minimum wage who makes three deliveries in this period may end up earning a total of $11 or more per hour. As a result, the firm never has to worry about hiring delivery people, and the transportation charge per order more than covers the hourly wage and cost of operating the vehicle.

A *discount* is a reduction in the list price. Many new ventures find that they can boost sales profitably by deviating from a fixed-price strategy. In some cases, this is a result of selling experience; in other cases, it is mandated by competitive practices, and the business has no alternative but to grant discounts. A recent article in the *Harvard Business Review* by Jim Geisman and John Maruskin suggests that a firm ask itself several questions when deciding to offer a discount:

- Are discount dollars being invested in the market segment that offers the best strategic value for the company?
- Do discount levels vary widely, and, if so, what is the basis for this variation?
- Are discounts consistent over time, or do they increase at the end of a quarter?
- Is widespread discounting a uniform problem across the company?

Some experts suggest that a company monitor its discount practices to ensure that pricing fits the firm's competitive place in the market and overall marketing strategy.[9]

New ventures commonly use a number of different types of discounts. These types of discounts are discussed as follows.

A *seasonal discount* is a price reduction given during particular times of the year. These typically occur before or after peak buying periods. For example, swimsuit manufacturers offer discounts to retailers in the Midwest who buy before peak summer months. Because most bathing suits are sold between May and August, these discounts are given in March and April. Manufacturers use discounting to help increase sales as well as to minimize their cost of warehousing inventory. Retailers, in turn, offer seasonal discounts in the late summer and early fall in an effort to sell merchandise that soon will have no market demand and have to be warehoused.

Another good example of new venture discounting involves post-holiday products, such as Valentine's Day candy, which is marked down on February 15, and Yuletide decorations, cards, and wrapping paper, which are heavily discounted during the last week of December. In an effort to generate even higher sales, some retailers have begun changing these holiday sales periods and now offer discounts *before* the holiday. For example, Christmas sales on the Friday and Saturday after Thanksgiving are now quite common. One of the primary reasons for the change in this price strategy is that new ventures are learning that they must discount their products before large competitors do because the latter typically win these head-to-head price wars.

Another common strategy is *special group discounting,* such as 25 percent off of list price for all senior citizens. This strategy has been very helpful in recent years in building and maintaining a loyal customer base among seniors, who are often retired and are careful about how they spend their money. Other groups often targeted include educators, students, police, and firefighters.

A third type of discount is the *quantity discount,* which offers a lower cost per unit as the volume of the order increases. For example, a store may charge $35 for one shirt, $60 for two shirts, $75 for three shirts, and $20 for each additional shirt. Another variation of the strategy is to offer shirts for $35 each, or three for $90. In this case, the company encourages people to buy three shirts rather than trying to entice them up the sales ladder one shirt at a time.

A fourth variation of this strategy is a *cash discount.* Although this can take a variety of forms, one of the most important among new ventures is to offer a price reduction of 3 to 5 percent on purchases if the individual will pay with cash or check rather than a credit card. Simply stated, the store owner offers to pass the fee that the credit-card company charges the store back to the customer as an added inducement to buy. This discount tactic is legal and is gaining popularity because of current competitive retailing practices that emphasize discount buying. In the past, store owners simply assumed credit-card fee costs as part of the expense of doing business. If someone paid in cash, this constituted 3 to 5 percent more profit for the owner. If someone used a credit card, the owner took satisfaction in the fact that the credit-card company would guarantee the sale.

COMBINATION STRATEGIES

The pricing strategies outlined so far are common among new ventures. Some are relied on more than others, but in most cases firms employ a combination of strategies. For example, whether the business is using a skimming or a penetration strategy, the owner often will consider a cash discount in lieu of a credit card purchase. In addition, regardless of pricing techniques, the company is likely to select target markets and offer special deals to these groups. Simply put, pricing strategies are often package deals that answer the question "What do we have to do to get this person (or group's) business?"

Of course, this does not mean that new venture owners always are willing to discount heavily, to absorb all transportation charges, or to make other types of special deals. New venture owners should be aware of the consequences of a "low price war."[10] If they find that their prices are continuously being discounted, this may be a dangerous strategy to follow. Prices that are discounted to the extreme could lead to complete failure of the new venture due to lack of any profit margin.

Two other areas that must be considered to understand pricing strategies are market conditions and image. If market conditions are favorable because the company has a unique product or service, the new venture owner does not have to accommodate every buyer. The firm can be selective and sell to those willing to pay the premium price. Automobile companies such as BMW utilize this strategy: BMW limits supply and holds its dealers to a strict price level. Conversely, if demand is weak, the new venture owner is likely to make very attractive offers in order to generate demand. At the same time, it is important to remember that new ventures must maintain their image. If a store has a reputation for attracting upscale clientele, pricing strategies will focus on supporting and sustaining high prices because this is the firm's target market. In contrast, if the company has created an image as a low-price competitor, it continually will try to maintain this reputation by keeping down costs and passing these savings along to the customer.

Both types of firms will go out of their way to reinforce their price image through advertising and other forms of promotion. A good example is Wal-Mart when it was still a small, but rapidly growing, retailer in the South. The firm advertised itself as having everyday low prices and standing behind its merchandise. One day, a man drove to a Wal-Mart store and told the manager that he did not like the tires he had purchased at the store; the tires did not give him the ride he wanted. The manager told the customer to go to a tire dealer, buy another set of tires, and bring the first ones back for a full refund. The man did this and was pleased with Wal-Mart's approach. What the store manager did not tell the man was that he could not have bought the original tires at Wal-Mart because, at the time, the company did not sell tires. However, the manager took them and issued the refund because he wanted to make the buyer a customer for life. This story has been told and retold at Wal-Mart in an effort to get personnel to understand the company's philosophy of retailing. In the process, the story has helped build the Wal-Mart image, a critical factor in every pricing strategy.

HOW NEW VENTURES SET PRICES

We now examine how prices are set by new ventures in each of the following categories: wholesalers, retailers, service, and manufacturing establishments.

WHOLESALERS

Wholesale prices generally are based on an established markup or gross profit for each line. At the wholesale level, price is very important because most retailers base their purchase decisions very heavily on it. If the wholesaler is not competitive, retailers will buy from a different wholesaler. Additionally, because wholesalers purchase in large quantities and cannot always pass along price increases immediately, they can lose money if prices fluctuate greatly. In particular, the wholesaler can get squeezed between the manufacturer and the retailer. If the manufacturer raises prices and the retailer resists increased costs, the wholesaler may have to absorb a large reduction in profit or even a loss. Because wholesalers have small profit margins, they monitor price movements carefully.

One way they do this is by keeping abreast of competitors' prices; a second way is by charging different retailers different prices for the same merchandise. This price differentiation is determined by factors such as the size of the order (larger orders get lower prices per unit), the individual retailer's bargaining ability, and the services—such as credit and delivery—extended to a retailer. Wholesalers commonly use a discount or price schedule for each group of goods or services, with maximum and minimum prices for different quantities.

Retailers

Retailers provide the most interesting example of new venture pricing.[11] Except when the store uses manufacturers' suggested prices, the owner needs to be concerned with many of the concepts we already have discussed, including the nature of the product, competition, and general business conditions. Of these, the nature of the product is usually the most significant, because different types of products are priced in different ways.

Staple convenience goods — such as candy bars, chewing gum, newspapers, or magazines — that are standardized tend to carry customary prices or the going market price. These goods usually have low prices, and any price cutting will be met quickly by the competition.

Fashion goods tend to be priced high and, if they do not sell, then marked down. Novelty or specialty goods also carry a high markup; once the novelty wears off or the selling season is over, the price is lowered.

Groceries, on average, tend to be purchased in terms of the best buys. Many supermarkets have adopted unit pricing to help with this process. In fact, many states require it by law. *Unit pricing* calls for the listing of the product's price in terms of some unit of measurement, such as an ounce, pint, or yard. For example, if the price per ounce for sugar is listed, consumers are able to comparison shop and determine which product offers the most for the money. Competitive pressures likely will force the small, independent grocer to do the same eventually.

A recent study on pricing strategy suggests that the retailer should focus on six issues when developing a price strategy. These issues include:

- Identify key determinants of local store pricing. These key determinants include competitors, brand, customer, and so forth.
- Set segment pricing based on store format and the cluster of competitors.
- Neutralize price as a competitive factor. It is suggested that the retailer set competitive pricing on *known value items* and feature them so that pricing on all other items is not emphasized.
- Manage promotion intensity and avoid head-to-head competition on non-value items.
- Create distinctive categories and coordinate pricing based on category. Identify those items with high price promotion intensity and price them differently than other categories.
- Tailor prices based on market, category, brand, competition, and customer. Some products and brands are more price consistent.[12]

How do retailers, in particular, determine prices? Except when this decision is made for them, as with manufacturers' suggested retail prices, they tend to use systems of *markup* and *markon.*

Markup

Markup is the difference between the selling price of a good and its cost to the business. Sometimes the term used is *gross margin,* which means the same thing. Some business owners mark up each item individually, but an average markup for various lines of goods carried is more common. For example, watches may be marked up 100 percent, television sets 35 percent, and dairy products 16 percent. Using this approach, the time devoted to marking up goods can be reduced greatly.

Retailers have two basic ways of marking up goods: 1) use a *percentage of the retail selling price* and 2) use a *percentage of the cost of the good*. For example, if a pair of socks costs $2 and is sold for $3, the markup ($1) on retail selling price is 33 percent ($1/$3), and the markup on cost is 50 percent ($1/$2). The markup on the selling price is always a smaller percentage because the denominator in the calculation is larger. Today, most businesses base their markup percentage on the retail price, because this tells them how much of their sales dollar can be used to pay bills and how much will be left over for profit.

The computation of markups is not difficult, especially if the owner has a markup table such as the one show in Table 7-2. A *markup table* allows the businessperson to determine the retail price quickly. The following examples illustrate how this is done.

TABLE 7-2   A Markup Table

Markup as Percentage of Retail Price	Markup as Percentage of Cost	Markup as Percentage of Retail Price	Markup as Percentage of Cost
10	11.11	31	44.93
11	12.36	32	47.06
12	13.64	33	49.25
13	14.94	34	51.52
14	16.28	35	53.85
15	17.65	36	56.25
16	19.05	37	58.73
17	20.48	38	61.29
18	21.95	39	63.93
19	23.46	40	66.67
20	25.00	41	69.49
21	26.58	42	72.41
22	28.21	43	75.44
23	29.87	44	78.57
24	31.58	45	81.82
25	33.33	46	85.19
26	35.14	47	88.68
27	36.99	48	92.31
28	38.89	49	96.08
29	40.85	50	100.00
30	42.86		

Example 1:
A retailer who sells electronics uses a standard 50 percent markup on retail on all flat-screen TVs. How much should a retailer charge for a TV that costs $500? To answer this question, the following five steps should be taken:

1. Determine the cost of the good, which, in this case, is $500.
2. Find the required gross profit figure (50 percent) in the "Markup as Percentage Retail Price" column in Table 7-2
3. Find the corresponding figure opposite 50 percent in the "Markup as Percentage of Cost" column in the table, which is 100 percent.
4. Multiply the cost of the good ($500) by that figure to get the dollars-and-cents markup on cost. In this case: $500 × 1.00 = $500.
5. Add the markup-on-cost result ($500) to the cost of the good ($500) to arrive at the selling price: $500 + $500 = $1,000 selling price.

The solution can be checked by determining the results of selling 100 TVs.

Sales revenue (100 TVs × $1,000)	$100,000
Less: Cost of goods (100 TVs × $500)	50,000
Gross profit	$50,000

Gross profit as a percent of sales:

$$\frac{50.000}{100,000} \times 100\% = 50\%$$

Thus, a markup of 100 percent on the cost of goods will produce a 50 percent gross profit (markup on retail).

Example 2:
A college bookstore is about to receive the books it has ordered for the fall semester. A quick scan of the sales reports shows that many of the hardcover business texts cost the store $80. The markup on retail is 25 percent. How much does the owner need to charge in order to attain this markup? To answer this question, the same five steps are used.

1. Determine the cost of the good, which, in this case, is $80.
2. Find the required gross profit figure (25 percent) in the "Markup as Percentage Retail Price" column in Table 7-2.
3. Find the corresponding figure opposite 25 percent in the "Markup as Percentage of Cost" column in the table, which is 33.33 percent.
4. Multiply the cost of the good ($80) by that figure to get the dollars-and-cents markup on cost. In this case: $80 × .33 = $26.40.
5. Add the markup-on-cost result ($26.40) to the cost of the good ($80) to arrive at the selling price: $80 + $26.40 = $106.40 selling price.

The solution can be checked by determining the results of selling 100 books.

Sales revenue (100 texts × $106.4)	$10,640
Less: Cost of goods (100 texts × $80)	8,000
Gross profit	$2,640

Gross profit as a percent of sales:

$$\frac{2,640}{10,640} = 25\%$$

Thus, a markup of 33.33 percent on the cost of goods will produce a 25 percent gross profit (markup on retail).

In these two examples, the selling prices after markup were $1,000 and $106.40, respectively. However, the selling price usually is adjusted up or down to make the price more appealing—especially for electronics, which the consumer does not *have* to buy. The student, of course, may feel that he or she cannot get through the course without the textbook. In any event, instead of charging $1,000 for the TV, the retailer may price it at $999.00 or $995.00. The bookstore may do the same, opting for a final price of $105.75. This *psychological pricing* attracts people better than would a price rounded to the nearest dollar. Additionally, the business should compare its proposed price to the competition to make sure that it is competing appropriately.

MARKON

In addition to the initial markup, many retailers compute a *markon*. Simply stated, a *markon* is an increase in the initial markup on goods that will be reduced in price later, or on goods that can be damaged or stolen easily. For example, high-fashion goods tend to have a limited market. Therefore, although a shirt may be priced at $29.75 initially, if it does not sell, it may be marked down to $24.75 and then to $19.75. With the unpredictability of the market in mind, the retailer will add a sufficient markon to ensure that, after markdowns, the desired gross margin is maintained.

As an example, consider a retailer that estimates that, of the 300 shirts purchased last week, it will be possible to sell 100 at $29.75, another 100 at $24.75, and the last 100 at $19.75. Additionally, assume that the owner wants a gross margin on sales of 40 percent and that the cost of each shirt is $15. From Table 7-2, it is obvious that a 40 percent markup on retail price requires the owner to add 66.67 percent to the cost. This results in a retail price of $25 ($15 × .667 − $10 markup plus the original cost of $15). Thus, the retailer must sell each shirt at an *average* price of $25. The retailer must add a markon to this price so that it can be reduced later on. Without our showing the specific mathematical computations, the owner will average (approximately) $25 if the three prices—$29.75, $24.75, and $19.75—are used and 100 shirts are sold at each price level. This is illustrated in the following table:

Price	Shirts Sold	Total
$29.75	100	$2,975.00
24.75	100	2,475.00
19.75	100	1,975.00
		$7,425.00

Dividing $7,425 by 300 gives an average selling price of $24.75.

SERVICE ENTERPRISES

The many types of service enterprises vary widely in their pricing methods. In most cases, however, these firms employ one of two strategies: (1) they charge what everyone else is charging, or (2) they set their own prices and try to justify the decision by differentiating the service and presenting it in a unique or creative way. Each of these approaches has benefits and drawbacks.

CHARGING COMPETITIVELY

When a service enterprise charges the same as its competition, this implies a number of assumptions. One is that the competition knows its own costs and is pricing for profit. If this is not the case, many firms that price at this level will lose money. A second assumption is that each firm's service cannot be distinguished from that of the competition, so a common price is justified for this generic offering. A third assumption is that oligopolistic market conditions exist so that any firms that raise their price will lose substantial market share, and any that lower their price will find all of the competition following suit. Thus, the only logical strategy is to price at the same level as everyone else.

The primary benefit of pricing with the competition is that no market resistance occurs with regard to this price. Customers do not complain by noting, "We can get this same service cheaper from other companies." Another benefit is that it saves the new venture time and money because a cost analysis is not needed to arrive at a price. The firm simply follows the competition.

The primary drawback to this pricing strategy is that the company does not analyze its costs, so the owner has no way of knowing for sure whether the firm is pricing for profit. The company actually may be losing money at this price level. A second drawback is that the firm is a market follower. It does nothing different from the competition. As a result, the company's profit is limited sharply, and strategy typically is directed at providing more and more service, rather than better service, because quantity (giving as much service as possible at this predetermined rate) is given precedence over quality (giving distinctive service at rates determined by market conditions).

Despite the drawbacks to a strategy of following the leader when setting price, many small service enterprises use this approach. As long as they understand their cost structure and know that they are making an acceptable profit at this price, this strategy is viable. However, if they are able to differentiate themselves, they often can increase profit by raising their price and maintaining (and often increasing) market share.

DIFFERENTIATING THE SERVICE

As noted, the problem with a follow-the-leader pricing strategy is that it fails to address the unique service offerings of a company. To the extent that a new venture provides better service than its competition, more profitable strategies exist. However, these strategies are all based on the assumption that the customer will pay more for better service. In determining whether this is true, new ventures can alter their prices and evaluate the elasticity of demand.

Elasticity of demand determines the effect of price increases on sales revenue. If demand is elastic, price *decreases* will result in greater revenue and profit. Conversely, if demand is inelastic, price *increases* will create more revenue and profit. Of course, some customers may refuse to pay the higher price, but a sufficient number of them will and, thus, the price increase will generate higher revenue. Following is a table that shows how one service company raised its price by 20 percent and lost only 10 percent of its customers:

	Before Price Raise	*After Price Raise*
Number of customers	700	630
Revenues per customer	$ 1,000	$ 1,200
Total revenue	$700,000	$756,000
Profit (20% of revenue)	$140,000	$151,000
Benefit of raising price:	$ 11,200	

This simple illustration shows the effect of a price increase under inelastic market-demand conditions. Of course, if the demand were elastic, the company would have lost money because the increase in price would have been more than offset by the decline in demand. However, this is why it is necessary to test market demand by tinkering with price and seeing what happens. If the market does not respond to increased service at a higher price, the firm will maintain its current pricing levels. However, the key to the success of price increases is differentiated service.

Service firms attempt to differentiate themselves from the competition in a number of ways.[13] It is important to remember that effective differentiation is often a matter of perception. If a beauty salon purchases new high-tech computer software that helps clients visualize a new hairstyle, does this result in a better haircut? Probably not, but the client may feel that this new software is worth the additional $3 for a haircut. All of the other ways that businesses differentiate themselves have one aspect in common: They provide increased value for which the buyer is prepared to pay.

An example of this concept is home delivery. Many people buy pizza only from outlets that deliver. Is the quality of this pizza better than that of the competition? The answer is that the taste and quality are acceptable to the buyers, but it is delivery service that ensures the order. The cost of this service is often minimal because, as noted earlier, drivers typically work for minimum wage and tips, which can add up to a substantial hourly rate.

Another example of differentiation is payment convenience. Many new ventures grant credit to their customers and settle the bill at the end of the month. Although this strategy can result in a loss of some profits (e.g., people do not pay or pay late, and the company has to carry the debt on its books), it helps boost sales and the profit accompanying these revenues.

Lower prices also help to differentiate one service from another. Many new ventures cannot afford to offer a variety of supplemental services, so they focus on cutting their costs to the bone and passing on these savings to the customer. A number of strategies are employed in this process, but they all have one aspect in common: Services that have little value to the customer are eliminated, and those that are important are given priority. A good example is provided by home-improvement stores, where people buy residential materials and fixtures. These stores buy large quantities so that they can obtain substantial discounts, but they do not provide delivery, and they do not use their salespeople to market the products vigorously. Instead, the stores train their people to provide assistance to customers by listening to what the buyer needs, showing the individual where these materials are located in the store, and, in some cases, helping the person choose a specific fixture or appliance for the job. As a result of this service, these stores now are riding the crest of the home-improvement craze sweeping the nation.

When differentiating service, new venture owners must answer three questions: 1) What can be done to attract more business? 2) How much is the cost of adding these services? and 3) What effect will this decision have on profit? Based on the answers, the owner can formulate a plan of action.

NEW VENTURE PERSPECTIVE

Power Retailing for New and Smaller Ventures?

Joel Evans and Barry Berman from Hofstra University suggest that a power retailing strategy can be used by firms of all sizes, not just the big chain stores. The power retailing concept centers on applying consistent, direct, and responsive marketing and pricing strategies. Power retailers such as Wal-Mart and Toys "R" Us stay in touch with customer needs and wants, place orders in quantity, and utilize modern inventory and logistics systems.

Evans and Berman identify three key principles that retailers, regardless of size or type of business, can learn from the concept of power retailing:

1. There must always be a *game plan* for the firm that is outlined in advance.

2. The retailer's focus must always be on consumers and how to best satisfy them.

3. A firm needs to be dominant in at least one aspect of its strategy. A smaller, newer venture can be a power retailer by serving an unfulfilled consumer need.

Any retail should identify customers' minimum expectations for each element of its strategy (e.g., pricing strategy, store hours, product selection, and customer services). Evans and Berman suggest that, even if a firm dominates in other areas of its strategy, it must still satisfy the minimum standards set by consumers.

Six different strategies are suggested for a firm to act as a power retailer.

1. Be price oriented and cost efficient to appeal to price-sensitive shoppers.
2. Be upscale to appeal to full-service, status-conscious consumers.
3. Be convenience oriented to appeal to consumers interested in shopping ease, nearby locations, or long store hours.
4. Offer a dominant assortment with an extensive selection of the product lines carried to appeal to consumers interested in variety and in-store shopping comparisons.
5. Be customer-service oriented to appeal to people who are frustrated by the decline in retail service (as they perceive it).
6. Be innovative or exclusive and provide a unique method of operations (such as kiosks at shopping centers) or carry products/brands/services not stocked by other stores to appeal to customers who are innovators, bored, or looking for items not in the *me too* mold.

These methods can be utilized separately or in combination; however, the business must excel in at least one of the areas. Competition should dictate the strategies your business employs.

Source: Adapted from Joel R. Evans and Barry Berman, "Power Retailing: Not Just for Large Firms," *About.com,* http://retailindustry.about.com/library/uc/be/uc_be_power.htm (accessed February 12, 2007).

PRICING TECHNIQUES

Many service enterprises set their price based on the going rate or what they feel the market will bear. However, more analytical ways of determining price exist. One is to keep careful cost records so that the company knows the expenses associated with each job. For example, assume that Neal is in the computer-repair business. The average engineer working for Neal is paid $44 per hour, including benefits. To this price Neal must add a markup for operating expenses (electricity, telephone, depreciation of machinery, insurance, and other expenses), as well as profit. Assuming Neal has set a figure of 30 percent to cover expenses, the computation for service is as follows:

$$\text{Price per hour} = \$44/\text{hour} \times \frac{1.00}{1.0 - 3.0}$$

$$= \$44 \times 1.428$$

$$= \$62.83 \text{ per hour}$$

In all likelihood, Neal will round this number to $65 per hour. In addition, the buyer will have to pay for the cost of materials and supplies through a markup.

Therefore, even if Neal's estimate of expenses is low, he has enough room to ensure profit. This is particularly true given that many small operations set minimum charges for service. A job billed at one hour may be completed in 45 minutes, thus allowing the employee to move on to another task.

Although this method of pricing the work is fairly simple, it is indicative of most small service firms. They do not employ sophisticated analysis in their profit pricing strategy. Instead, they use a system that is easily understandable and can be modified without much effort. This process is similar to that used by small manufacturers.

MANUFACTURERS

The primary basis for pricing by small manufacturers is usually some form of *cost plus,* wherein the company charges a markup over its own expenses. As with service enterprises, however, this pricing strategy often requires a great deal more thought than simply adding a predetermined percentage to overall cost. In most cases, small manufacturers will use a combination of competitive rates and differentiation techniques.

CHARGING COMPETITIVELY

The simplest approach to pricing for manufacturers is to charge the going rate. However, manufacturers try to improve this strategy by working to contain and, where possible, drive down costs. They do this in a number of ways. One way is to negotiate carefully with vendors, thus ensuring the lowest possible cost of raw materials and supplies. In turn, these savings can be passed on to buyers; doing so will generate increased demand for the company's output. A second way to drive down costs is to reduce production bottlenecks and inefficiencies. One of the best techniques is process mapping, in which the steps used to accomplish the job are reduced or combined in some way. The result is time saving, which cuts the cost of the job and helps make the company more price competitive. A third way is to purchase new equipment that increases productivity and allows the firm to both lower prices and provide an increased number of products. Most small manufacturers focus heavily on price competitiveness, and, in markets where it is difficult to differentiate between one product and another, this is often the best pricing strategy to employ.

DIFFERENTIATING THE PRODUCT

Depending on the type of manufactured good, it often is possible to differentiate a product and charge a premium price. This can be done on a number of bases: Before deciding which one (or more) of these is important, the small manufacturer needs to have a solid understanding of retail buyers' needs. For example, complex products that are difficult to repair tend to carry higher markups. The customer is willing to pay for high-quality original parts because he or she wants the assurance that the product will not break down or need continuous servicing. In contrast, when the product (or its parts) is easy to replace and can be purchased from many different suppliers, it is difficult to differentiate the product, and the manufacturer will compete most heavily on the basis of price.

Three of the most common ways to differentiate manufactured goods are on the bases of quality, delivery, and reliability. Where quality is concerned, technological advances are extremely important. A small manufacturer that remains on the cutting edge of technology and either develops or purchases these advances for use in the company's products will find some customers willing to pay extra for these benefits.

Delivery is a second way that manufacturers try to differentiate themselves. Today, many companies do not want to carry a great deal of inventory; they want inventory delivered on an as-needed basis. This just-in-time inventory strategy means that manufacturers must align their production plans with the purchase plans of buyers. New ventures willing to deliver what is needed, when it is needed, and in desired quantities find that they are better able to secure and hold customers.

A third differentiation strategy is reliability encompassed in effective service. If something goes wrong with the product, the buyer wants the manufacturer to stand behind the sale, replace the unit, or repair it as quickly as possible. Firms willing to do this can differentiate themselves from the competition and garner buyer loyalty.

PRICING TECHNIQUES

Small manufacturers rely most heavily on three pricing techniques. The most common is to sell at the going rate. For example, small manufacturers that produce units according to specifications the buyer provides typically will charge a price similar to that of other firms. Moreover, the buyer tends to shop for the contract by asking for bids from a number of small manufacturers; if the price is too high, the company either will not get the job or will be told the prices competitors have bid and be asked to bring its price into line or to drop out of the bidding.

A second common pricing technique involves a multiplier applied to the direct costs of a job. For example, if a job has direct costs of $300 and the multiplier is 1.7, the company will price the job at $510 ($300 × 1.7). The 70 percent differential covers all nondirect costs as well as profit. Although this technique is simple to apply, the biggest shortcoming is that the price differential may be too high—thus driving away business—or too low—resulting in little, if any, profitability. The key to using a multiplier effectively is to know the relationship between direct and indirect costs and profitability.

A third common pricing technique is cost plus, which is the same approach that service industries use. The benefit of this approach is that a company that knows its costs cannot lose money on a job because it also has an add-on for profit. The drawback to this approach is that it can result in uncontrolled costs and a manufacturer pricing itself out of the market. For example, if a new motor costs $400 to manufacture and a company uses a multiple of 2, the buyer will pay $800. The competition may be selling for the same price. However, if the manufacturer applies cost-saving techniques to its operation and drives down the cost to $345 per unit, the company may drop its price to $690 and force everyone else to take lower profits or drop out of this particular market. Therefore, a cost-plus system is effective only when coupled with a vigorous cost-containment program.

Summary

This chapter examined pricing techniques and strategies. The venture owner's primary consideration when pricing must be cost; the individual cannot afford to sell below the cost level. In addition, the owner must consider the nature of the product, the competition, marketing strategy, and general business conditions. Pricing for profit also requires an understanding of the cost of goods, competitive prices, and market demand. Drawing on such considerations, new venture owners apply a variety of pricing techniques.

One of the most common techniques is skimming pricing, a strategy characterized by a high price designed to satisfy the market niche that is willing to pay a premium price. Another common technique is penetration pricing, which is characterized by a low competitive price designed both to stimulate demand and to discourage competition. A third common approach is a sliding price strategy, characterized by prices that move in relation to demand. Other typical pricing techniques include odd pricing, leader pricing, price lining, geographic pricing, and discounting. In most cases, the new venture will use two or more of these techniques, employing what is commonly called a combination pricing strategy.

Competition is often keen among wholesalers, and retailers will buy elsewhere if prices are too high. As a result, the wholesaler sometimes cannot readily pass along manufacturers' price increases to the retailer. For this reason, the owner/manager spends a good deal of time watching wholesale prices to ensure that the business is not caught in a price squeeze.

Retailers often price on the basis of a predetermined markup. For example, on certain goods it is typical to add on 50 percent. The markups provided in Table 7-2 illustrate how these price additions can be computed, as a percentage of both cost and retail price. In addition to the initial markup, many retailers compute a markon.

Service enterprises sometimes charge competitively, but they often try to differentiate their offerings to increase their overall profit. Some of the bases for a differentiation strategy include home delivery, convenience, and lower price. Common pricing techniques include following the competition and adding a markup to operating expenses.

Manufacturers set their prices in accordance with the cost of production. If they produce more than one product, they will use a particular method for allocating costs. Next, a margin of profit is determined and a final selling price is set. Common pricing techniques for small manufacturers include following the competition, using a multiplier, and calculating cost plus.

Review and Discussion Questions

1. What should an owner/manager know about the following price considerations: nature of the product, competition, marketing strategy, and general business conditions?
2. Explain how the following factors influence the owner/manager's objective of pricing for profit: cost of goods, competitive prices, and market demand.
3. How do the following pricing techniques work: skimming, penetration, sliding price, odd pricing, leader pricing, price lining, geographic pricing, discounts, and combination pricing strategy?
4. Why do most new ventures use a combination pricing strategy?
5. How do wholesalers set their prices? Do they charge these prices frequently? Explain.
6. One of the most important retail pricing concepts is markup. How does a markup work? Incorporate these terms in your answer: *cost, markup as a percentage of retail selling price, markup as a percentage of cost,* and *selling price.*
7. When would a retailer use a *markon?* Give an example, being sure to define the term *markon.*
8. How do service organizations set prices? Use two examples in your answer.
9. Explain how manufacturers set their prices. Use an example in your answer.

NEW VENTURE CONSULTANT

Games for Sale

The Toy Store is a retail outlet that caters to people of all ages. The store carries the types of items found in most other toy stores plus unique games that appeal to teenagers and adults. Included in the latter category are the ever-popular computer games of skill. The Toy Store has an agreement with a large manufacturer wherein it serves as the only retail outlet for the manufacturer's games within a 50-mile radius. Because of patent rights, the manufacturer is the only firm currently producing these games.

The store's typical toys are priced in line with the competition. The unique games, however, are not. In fact, the owner of the store, who has total control over the pricing of games, is determined to charge what the market will bear. Unfortunately, he does not know how to set the best price because he does not have any guidelines to follow. He has looked for similar games in some of the large department stores in the hope that he could charge 20 percent over this amount. However, he has found nothing.

One pricing method he has been considering is to put a 50 percent markup on games, in contrast to the 33 percent he gets on toys. When he puts a 33 percent markup on games, he is unable to keep enough in stock—demand is so high that he continually runs out. However, he is concerned about pricing too high and losing customers.

One of his friends has told him that a number of factors must be taken into consideration when pricing. Some of these are the nature of the product, the type of competition, the marketing strategy the business typically has used, and the state of the economy. However, the owner is unsure of how these particular factors affect a pricing decision.

Ultimately, what the owner wants to do is determine an ideal markup for the goods, price them at this level, and be done with the matter. He wishes he knew more about pricing. Not having had any real training in setting prices, however, he believes that the best thing he can do is price games extremely high and, if they do not sell, start reducing the price downward to the point where supply and demand balance out. He realizes that this is a trial-and-error approach, but it is the best option he can think of under the circumstances.

Additionally, the owner does not know very much about advertising. He tends to run the same basic newspaper ad week after week. It shows a picture of a couple of the store's toys and one of the games, and provides the price of each. The purpose of the ad is to attract people to the store. Although the store is doing quite well, the owner believes that his ads could be improved. The problem is that he lacks the inspiration for improving them. He simply writes the ads on the basis of instinct.

Your consultation: Assume that the owner is a personal friend of yours and has related this information to you. As best you can, give him your recommendations regarding the pricing of the unique computer games. Also explain to him how he can charge prices in order to maximize his profits without losing customers. Be as specific as possible.

Endnotes

1. Timothy Matanovich, Gary L. Lilien, and Arvind Rangaswamy, "Engineering the Price–Value Relationship," *Marketing Management* (Spring 1999): 48–53.
2. See Eric Mitchell, "How Not to Raise Prices," *Small Business Reports* (November 1990): 64–67.
3. Hermann Simon and Robert J. Dolan, "Price Customization," *Marketing Management* (Fall 1998): 11–18.
4. Philip Kotler and Gary Armstrong, *Principles of Marketing* (Upper Saddle River, NJ: Pearson/Prentice Hall, 2008).
5. Fred Luthans and Richard M. Hodgetts, *Business,* 2nd ed. (Fort Worth, TX: The Dryden Press, 1993), 407.
6. George Y. Bizer and Richard E. Petty, "An Implicit Measure of Price Perception: Exploring the Odd-Pricing Effect," *Advances in Consumer Research* 29 (2002): 220–21.
7. David L. Kurtz, *Contemporary Marketing* (Mason, OH: Thomson/Southwestern, 2008).
8. David L. Kurtz, *Contemporary Marketing* (Mason, OH: Thomson/Southwestern, 2008).
9. Jim Geisman and John Maruskin, "A Case for Discount Discipline," *Harvard Business Review* (November 2006): 84.
10. Akshay R. Rao, Mark E. Bergen, and Scott Davis, "How to Fight a Price Way," *Harvard Business Review* (March/April 2000): 107–16.
11. Candida G. Brush and Radha Chaganti, "Business Without Glamour? An Analysis of Resources on Performance by Size and Age in Small Services and Retail Firms," *Journal of Business Venturing* (May 1999): 233–58.
12. Ruth N. Bolton, Detra Y. Montoya, and Venkatesh Shankar, "Beyond EDLP and HiLo: A New Customized Approach to Retail Pricing," *European Retail Digest* 49 (Spring 2006): 7–10.
13. For more on this topic, see Michael E. Porter, *Competitive Advantage* (New York: The Free Press, 1985): 119–63.

CHAPTER

START-UP CAPITAL
THE INJECTION

INTRODUCTION

Generally new ventures are started by *bootstrapping*[1]—in other words, entrepreneurs try to initiate the venture with marginal financial resources from personal savings, family, and friends. Studies have investigated the various sources of capital preferred by entrepreneurs. These sources range from debt (banks, credit cards, finance companies) to equity (angel investors, venture capital) depending on the type of financing that is arranged. Entrepreneurs may have a number of sources of capital as their venture develops. Remember that the level of risk and the stage of the firm's development impact the appropriate source financing for entrepreneurial ventures.

BASIC TYPES OF CAPITAL

Keep in mind that venture financing comes from two basic sources: debt and ownership equity. *Debt* is borrowed money that must be repaid at some predetermined date in the future. Ownership equity, however, represents the owners' investment in the company—money they have personally put into the firm without any specific date for repayment. As owners, they recover their investment by withdrawing money from the company or by selling part or all of their interest in the firm. (See Table 8-1 for a new venture owner's financial glossary.

Debt capital is divided into three categories: (1) current or short term, (2) intermediate term, and (3) long term. Short-term liabilities (debt) include borrowed money that must be repaid within the next 12 months; intermediate term refers to loan-payback periods from 1 to 10 years; and long-term debt is payable sometime beyond 10 years, depending on the loan terms.

TABLE 8-1 A Financial Glossary for New Venture Owners

Accrual system of accounting A method of recording and allocating income and costs for the period in which each is involved, regardless of the date of payment or collection. For example, if you are paid $100 in April for goods sold in March, the $100 would be considered income for March under an accrual system. (Accrual is the opposite of the cash system of accounting.)

Asset Anything of value that is owned by you or your business.

Balance sheet An itemized statement listing the total assets and liabilities of your business at a given moment. It is also called a *statement of condition*.

Capital (1) The amount invested in a business by the proprietor(s) or stockholders. (2) The money available for investment or money invested.

Cash flow The schedule of your cash receipts and disbursements.

Cash system of accounting A method of accounting whereby revenue and expenses are recorded when received and paid, respectively, without regard for the period to which they apply.

Collateral Property you own that you pledge to the lender as security on a loan until the loan is repaid. Collateral can be a car, home, stocks, bonds, or equipment.

Cost of goods sold This is determined by subtracting the value of the ending inventory from the sum of the beginning inventory and purchases made during the period. Gross sales less costs of goods sold gives you gross profit.

Current assets Cash and assets that can be easily converted to cash, such as accounts receivable and inventory. Current assets should exceed current liabilities.

Current liabilities Debts you must pay within a year (also called *short-term liabilities*).

Depreciation Lost usefulness or expired utility; the diminution of service yield from a fixed asset or fixed asset group that cannot or will not be restored by repairs or replacement of parts.

Equity An interest in property or a business, subject to prior creditors. An owner's equity in his or her business is the difference between the value of the company's assets and the debt owed by the company. For example, if you borrow $30,000 to purchase assets for which you pay a total of $50,000, your equity is $20,000.

Expense An expired cost; any item or class of costs of (or loss from) carrying on an activity; a present or past expenditure defraying a present operating cost or representing an irrecoverable cost or loss; an item of capital expenditures written down or off; or a term often used with some qualifying expression denoting function, organization, or time, such as selling expense, factory expense, or monthly expense.

Financial statement A report summarizing the financial condition of a business. It normally includes a balance sheet and an income statement.

Gross profit Sales less the cost of goods sold. For example, if you sell $100,000 worth of merchandise for which you paid $80,000, your gross profit is $20,000. To get net profit, however, you would have to deduct other expenses incurred during the period in which the sales were made, such as rent, insurance, and sales staff salaries.

Income statement Also called *profit and loss statement;* a statement summarizing the income of a business during a specific period.

Interest The cost of borrowing money. Interest is paid to the lender and usually expressed as an annual percentage of the loan. That is, if you borrow $100 at 12 percent interest, you pay 1 percent ($.01 \times \$100 = \$1$) interest per month. Interest is an expense of doing business.

Liability Money you owe to your creditors. Liabilities can be in the form of a bank loan, accounts payable, and so on. They represent a claim against your assets.

TABLE 8-1   (Continued)

Loss When a business's total expenses for the period are greater than the income.

Net profit Total income for the period less total expenses for the period (see *gross profit*).

Net worth See *equity*.

Personal financial statement A report that summarizes your personal financial condition. Normally this includes a listing of your assets, liabilities, large monthly expenses, and sources of income.

Profit Usually refers to net profit; see *net profit* and *gross profit*.

Profit and loss statement See *income statement*.

Variable cost Costs that vary with the level of production on sales, such as direct labor, material, and sales commissions.

Working capital The excess of current assets over current liabilities.

Source: Donald F. Kuratko and Richard M. Hodgetts, *Entrepreneurship: Theory, Process, & Practice,* 7th ed. (Mason, OH: Thomson/Southwestern, 2007), 312–13.

DEBT CAPITAL

SHORT-TERM LOANS

A *short-term loan* is one that is scheduled to be repaid within a period of one year. The most common forms of short-term loans are trade credit-created—in which the seller allows the buyer to take the merchandise immediately and pay for it later—and short-term bank loans. Short-term loans are particularly helpful when a temporary need for more capital exists, such as when retailers build up a seasonal inventory and pay for it once it is sold. For example, it is typical to find businesses that sell swimwear increasing their inventory during the late spring, whereas those that sell skiwear will begin building up their inventory in the early fall. Without trade credit or a short-term bank loan, the owner would have to have a large amount of capital on hand to handle peak buying periods. Most trade credit and short-term bank loans are *self-liquidating;* that is, the money obtained from the sale of the inventory is used to pay off the loan. Most bank-financed loans are unsecured, which means that they are not backed by collateral. However, if the business does not have a good credit rating or if a lot of money is involved, the bank will insist that the loan be secured by some of the business's assets.[2]

INTERMEDIATE-TERM LOANS

Intermediate-term loans provide capital for periods from 1 to 10 years. Such loans are usually paid back in a series of installments. Intermediate-term loans fill the gap in the financial requirements of many small and moderate-sized businesses. They make capital available for reasons beyond temporary needs, helping the owner who needs funds to expand the operation but lacks the capital resources. Thanks to this type of loan, owners are able to purchase machinery, equipment, and other fixed assets immediately and pay for them over the life of the loan.

In return, most banks and other lenders impose certain conditions. Primary among these are usually the right of the lender to control major expenditures

TABLE 8-2 Entrepreneurs' Ratings of Reasons for Loan Rejection[a]			
Reason for Rejection	*Mean Rating*	*Males*	*Females*
Bad timing	4.22	3.89	4.52
Insufficient collateral	4.14	4.23	4.13
Inability to develop good chemistry	3.96	4.00	4.05
Excessive loan request	3.88	3.77	3.89
Lack of demonstration of critical management skills	3.82	3.97	3.65
Insufficient market research	3.69	3.69	3.70
Incomplete business plan	3.68	3.77	3.59
Loan officer failed to appreciate the entrepreneur's business experience	3.59	3.83	3.39
Lack of demonstration of critical entrepreneurial skills	3.38	3.71	3.05
Gender bias	2.96	2.78	3.14

[a.] Rating scale: 1 = not at all important; 6 = very important.

Source: E. Holly Buttner and Benson Rosen, "Rejection in the Loan Application Process: Male and Female Entrepreneurs' Perceptions and Subsequent Intentions," *Journal of Small Business Management* (January 1992): 62.

during the life of the loan and the requirement that the borrower furnish the lender with annual financial statements. In this way, the business is prevented from doing anything that might seriously endanger its chances of repaying the loan. Furthermore, it is common for the loan to be backed by collateral, such as the plant and equipment that the business has purchased with the loan proceeds.

LONG-TERM LOANS

Long-term loans have duration of 10 or more years. Only businesses that have been in existence for an extended period can get loans for this length of time. Thus, they are usually reserved for large, stable corporations. Additionally, it is common for the lender to insist on collateral. When collateral is given in the form of a mortgage, however, long-term loans also can be secured by small and intermediate-sized businesses. After all, if the business goes bankrupt, the bank can always step in, take the property, and sell it, thereby recovering at least part of the loan. Aside from this method of securing long-term funds, however, the new venture must often turn to equity capital to meet its needs. (See Table 8-2 for reasons entrepreneurs have their loan rejected.)

EQUITY CAPITAL

Equity capital is an investment in the business and requires no promise from the borrowing firm to repay. The investment, which usually comes about through the sale of common stock, is a permanent part of the firm's capital structure. This structure can be increased either by investing profits back into the business or by selling additional stock to investors.[3]

In many cases, equity capital is the only way a new venture can increase its capital base; banks and other financial institutions may not be willing to assume the risk associated with lending the firm money, or the company may have borrowed so much already that the bank is unwilling to go any further. In financial terms, the company is *overextended*—it has nothing more to borrow against. When this happens, the business must sell stock, reinvest earnings, or pass up growth opportunities because no additional sources of capital exist for taking advantage of these opportunities.

SOURCES OF CAPITAL

Choosing a source of capital is not an easy decision. Numerous alternatives exist depending on the business, how much funding is needed, the firm's credit rating, prior sales records, and the economy in general.[4] The following sections examine some of the major capital sources available to the new venture firm and their relative merits and drawbacks.[5]

PERSONAL SAVINGS

It is important that a new venture owner have some personal assets in the business. Indeed, a main source of ownership equity for a beginning business typically comes from personal savings.

A study conducted by the National Federation of Independent Business found that *personal savings* are most frequently used for financing. Figure 8-1

FIGURE 8-1   Sources of Small Business Start-Up Capital

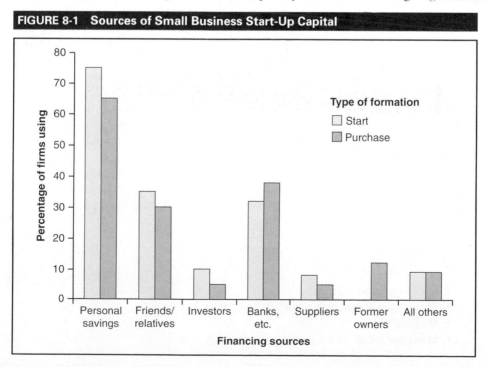

illustrates that 74 percent of the entrepreneurs in this study used personal savings when they purchased or started a business from scratch.

Personal savings invested in the business eliminate the requirement of fixed interest charges and a definite repayment date. If profits fail to materialize exactly as expected, the business is not strapped with an immediate drain on capital.

FRIENDS AND RELATIVES

At times, loans from friends or relatives may be the only available source of new venture financing. In this way, friends and relatives often can be a shortcut to financing. However, friends and relatives who provide business loans sometimes feel they have the right to interfere in the management of the business. Be careful: Financial troubles also may strain the bonds of friendship and family relationships.

VENTURE CAPITALISTS

A growing source of equity for high-growth new ventures is through experienced professional firms that provide a full range of financial services. New venture owners should recognize that these professional firms are specialized in particular industries and are looking for a large investment payback. Even though there is more venture capital available today, the trend is toward concentration of the funds under the control of larger venture capital firms.[6]

Keep in mind that it takes a long time to raise venture capital; on average, it may take six to eight weeks from the initial contact. If the entrepreneur has a well-prepared business plan, the investor will be able to raise money in that time frame. A venture capitalist will see between 50 and 100 proposals a month. Of that number, 10 will be of some interest. Of those 10, 2 or 3 will receive a fair amount of analysis, negotiation, and investigation. Of the 2 or 3, one may be funded. This funneling process of selecting one out of 100 takes a great deal of time. Once the venture capitalist has found that one, he or she will spend a significant amount of time investigating possible outcomes before funding it.

De Clercq, Fried, Lehtonen, and Sapienza outline several suggestions for maximizing the value of the entrepreneur–venture capitalist relationship during the preinvestment, postinvestment, and exit phases. A summarized list of these suggestions is provided as follows:[7]

Preinvestment
- Get venture capital
  - Secure a good referral
  - Have a good business plan
  - Be honest
  - Have patience

- Get the right venture capitalists
  - Identify complementary skills
  - Look for commitment
  - Establish trusting relationships
- Obtain the right amount of money
- Obtain a fair deal

Postinvestment

- Respect the venture capitalists
  - Legal authority
  - Power of money
- Respect yourself
- Communicate with the venture capitalists
- Be trustworthy
- Remain objective

Exit Phase

- Avoid a premature exit
- Exit harmoniously

INFORMAL INVESTORS

Many private individuals invest in entrepreneurial ventures, including persons who have moderate to significant business experience as well as affluent professionals. This source of financing has come to be known as *informal capital,* in that no formal marketplace exists in which these individuals invest in companies. Appropriately, these investors have acquired the name *business angels.*[8]

The traditional path to locating angels is through contact with business associates, accountants, and lawyers. A more recent approach involves formal angel networks or clubs. One example is the Venture Club in Indianapolis, Indiana. This group meets once a month, and entrepreneurs give presentations concerning their financial needs. The idea is to bring potential informal investors together as a network for entrepreneurs. These networks can increase the odds of finding an investor. Other entrepreneurs continue to be the best source of help in identifying prospective informal or private investors. Table 8-3 illustrates the five key questions that every financing source asks.

INTERNAL FUNDS

One of the most basic sources of capital, and one often overlooked by new ventures, is internal funds. These are monies kept in the firm in the form of retained earnings. Of course, few businesspeople forget what they have earned in profits the previous year and have reinvested in the business, but many of them fail to consider that what they will make this year can be invested in the business to help

TABLE 8-3 Five Key Questions Every Financing Source Asks

1. How much money do you need? (Provide exact amount)
2. What do you plan to use it for? (Working capital or specific assets?)
3. How will this money improve the business? (Provide actual projections)
4. How are you going to pay it back or provide a return on the money? (Demonstrate cash-flow projections)
5. Do you have an alternate plan in case of a critical problem? (Provide a contingency plan)

meet expansion needs. Instead, they rush outside of the business to look for bank loans. *The first place to look for funding is within the business itself.* With careful budgeting, many small firms can raise part or all of the money they need.

TRADE CREDIT

Another commonly overlooked capital source is *trade credit,* by which suppliers, in effect, help finance operations. For example, most credit transactions have terms of 30, 60, or 90 days. The most common trade-credit terms are *2/10, net 30* ("two ten, net thirty"); if the buyer pays the bill within 10 days, the seller gives a 2 percent discount, and, regardless of the buyer's position on payment schedules, the entire bill must be paid within 30 days.

Consider, for example, the effects of this approach on a business that buys $10,000 of merchandise on the first day of every month. If the merchandise is paid for on delivery, instead of within 10 days, the owner needs to have $10,000 available. Like most owners of new ventures, however, this one does not have that much on hand, so the owner arranges for a bank loan. Borrowing the money on the 1st of every month and repaying it by the 30th, for all practical purposes, results in the business having a $10,000 outstanding loan at all times. Assuming a 10 percent interest rate, the annual loan cost is $1,000.

Instead, trade credit can be used to finance the inventory. By taking delivery on the 1st of the month and not paying until the 10th, the new venture owner will need a loan for only 20 days per month, so the interest paid for the year will be only $667 ($10,000 × 0.1 × 20/30). Furthermore, the owner gets the 2 percent discount, or $200 per month, taken off of the bill. In a year's time, the use of trade credit saves the business $2,400. After subtracting the loan cost of $667, the owner is ahead $1,733. Thus, trade discounts can be very profitable.

Another way of using trade credit is to get the supplier to provide the goods on consignment. Using this type of arrangement, the buyer does not pay for the goods until they are sold. Auto dealers, large-appliance retailers, and farm-equipment dealers, for example, often pay for goods only after they are sold.

BANKS

Banks offer many types of loan services. Some of the most common are lines of credit, straight commercial loans, term loans, accounts-receivable loans, warehouse-receipt loans, and collateral loans. The following sections examine each of these types.

LINE OF CREDIT

A *line of credit* is an informal agreement or understanding between the borrower and the bank with regard to the maximum amount of credit the bank will provide the borrower at any one time. However, with this type of agreement, the bank has no legal obligation to provide the stated capital. A similar arrangement that does legally commit the bank is a *revolving credit agreement.* The entrepreneur should arrange for a line of credit in advance of the actual need because banks extend credit only in situations about which they are well informed.

STRAIGHT COMMERCIAL LOANS

Straight commercial loans usually are made for a period of 30 to 90 days. They generally are based on the financial statements of the borrower and are self-liquidating. It is common to use these loans for seasonal financing and building up inventories.

TERM LOANS

Term loans have a maturity of between 1 and 10 years. Most have shorter terms (one to four years) and are unsecured. Longer-term loans, however, generally are backed by some of the firm's assets. In either event, small loan repayments are made throughout the life of the loan—monthly, quarterly, biannually, or annually. Depending on the specific terms of the agreement, it is not uncommon to make a large payment at the end of the loan. This is referred to as a *balloon loan,* in which the periodic repayments are rather small and the bulk of the loan is paid off at the end of the term. This, of course, can be very beneficial to a new venture because it means that on a loan of $25,000 for five years, perhaps as much as $20,000 can be paid at the end. This gives the company time to build up its business before having to make the large final payment. Furthermore, today's dollars will be inflated in five years, so the business is able to borrow *hard* dollars now and repay the loan with *soft* dollars later on.

ACCOUNTS-RECEIVABLE LOANS

Accounts-receivable loans are made by many large banks. In this case, the loan is made against the company's outstanding receivables; when they are collected, the bank is repaid. In some instances, the bank becomes actively involved by notifying the business's customers to make payments on its accounts directly to the bank. These collections then are credited to the borrower's account—after service and interest charges are deducted, of course. In other instances, the bank does not get involved directly, and the new venture simply collects the receivables and sends the proceeds to the bank to repay the loan. The disadvantages of this type of loan arrangement are that the cost is high and considerable record keeping is required. As a result, a business must have a large amount of accounts receivable to make this method of raising capital feasible.

WAREHOUSE-RECEIPT LOANS

With *warehouse-receipt loans,* inventory is stored in warehouses, and a receipt for the inventory is given to the bank as security for a loan to pay off the supplier. As the business sells the merchandise, the business owner buys back portions of the loan. This kind of borrowing enables the business to operate with a small investment in working capital. However, warehouse-receipt loans are used only for nonperishable items that are readily marketable. Thus, if the business owner cannot sell the goods, the bank can assume ownership and seek a buyer of its own. Such an approach ensures that the bank will, at worst, suffer only a partial loss of the loan.

COLLATERAL LOANS

Banks make *collateral loans* on the basis of such security as real estate mortgages, life insurance policies (the cash surrender value), stocks, and bonds. The borrower puts up the collateral, and the bank advances the money. As the loan is repaid, the collateral is returned to the borrower.

NEW VENTURE PERSPECTIVE

Credit Unions to the Rescue

Amid all of the Wall Street talk of initial public offerings (IPOs), venture capital, and mezzanine financing, a new breed of financing has emerged for smaller firms and entrepreneurial start-ups: credit unions. Credit unions are expanding their loan activities to small and medium-sized businesses. Minnesota had the highest percentage increase in loans (9.1 percent), but Maine, New Hampshire, Florida, Oklahoma, Kansas, and Montana all report increases above 8 percent. Nationally, 21 percent of credit unions are engaged in loans to small firms (excluding agriculture loans), representing an 18.4 percent increase over 2004.

This increase in lending by credit unions is explained by the decline in traditional bank loans due to consolidation. Small local banks have been merged into larger banks that are less responsive to the local needs of entrepreneurs and small firms.

Credit unions can fill the gap left by the small bank because they are generally local, member-driven institutions. Since they have nonprofit status, they can often offer lower interest rates than banks. Consequently, more credit unions are participating in Small Business Administration loan programs. Most of these loans are less than $150,000.

In general, a credit union's mission centers on returning profit to the community in the form of lower interest rates and fees. The mission also includes an emphasis on customer/member relations. Credit unions may be more flexible with regard to structure deals than the larger, nonlocal banks.

A new phenomenon that has occurred with credit unions is the formation of credit union service organizations (CUSOs). Over 50 of these cooperatives have been formed across the United States to share the expense of expanding the number of loan products a credit union can offer. These cooperatives offer a great advantage to the venture owner looking for start-up or expansion financing.

Source: Scott Sutherland, "Credit Unions to the Rescue," *Restaurant Business* 105 (October 2006): 11–14.

OTHER PRIVATE SOURCES OF CAPITAL

In addition to the capital sources discussed in the preceding sections, other private sources of capital exist. The following sections examine some of them.

INSURANCE COMPANIES

Insurance companies collect billions of dollars every year. Some of these funds are used to pay claims, but a large portion is invested. This is particularly true for life insurance. Few people who buy a life insurance policy will die this year; however, the insurance company has to invest the monies paid for premiums to pay the face value of the policy when the policyholder does die. One of the primary ways the company accrues money is by investing in real-estate loans or mortgages, particularly in new construction. Therefore, insurance companies may be interested in lending money to the new venture owner, especially one who has a construction firm. Additionally, if the owner has an insurance policy that has built up some cash surrender value, he or she can borrow that money at a relatively low interest rate. For example, although most banks today charge 10 percent annual interest for loans, the typical insurance policy allows the policyholder to borrow the cash surrender value at 5 to 6 percent.

FINANCE COMPANIES

Some finance companies specialize in lending money to businesses. These firms are not to be confused with personal finance companies, which loan small sums to individual consumers. The finance companies of interest here deal mostly in secured loans, usually with interest rates much higher than those banks charge. Such companies often provide loans after a bank has reviewed the situation and decided against granting the business a loan. Because the potential risk to the finance company is higher, the interest charge and origination fees are also higher.

FACTORS

Another source of capital, especially short-term funds, is *accounts-receivable factoring. Factors* (which are similar to brokers) advance companies money on the basis of accounts receivable. They differ from other financial sources in that they *buy* the accounts receivable. This means that they purchase them without recourse; if a person who owes an account receivable does not pay, the factor is the one who loses money. By contrast, when a bank finances accounts receivable, the business that borrowed the funds must make good on a failure to pay. Because the factor takes a greater risk, the cost of factoring is much higher than for accounts-receivable financing. Additionally, the factor is unlikely to buy all of a business's accounts receivable. Rather, it will determine which ones offer the best chance for payment and buy those accounts. The remainder will be left for the business to collect. Some businesspeople object to the high cost of factoring and to the factor dealing directly with their customers. However, when a new venture needs money, factoring may be the only possible way to raise the necessary capital.

SMALL BUSINESS ADMINISTRATION

The Small Business Administration (SBA) is an independent agency of the federal government. It was established by Congress for the purpose of advising and assisting the nation's small businesses. One of the primary areas in which it helps small firms is guaranteeing loans.

In past years, the SBA had monies for direct loans. However, these funds have all but dried up. The only two groups that currently can obtain direct SBA loans are Vietnam veterans and disabled individuals. All others who qualify for assistance must settle for SBA guaranteed loans. These loans are negotiated by the new venture owner and the bank, with repayment guaranteed by the SBA. Direct SBA loans currently have a maximum of $150,000, whereas the loan-guarantee program allows the SBA to offer a maximum of $750,000. New ventures that negotiate the best rate they can with their local banker pay approximately 2¼ percent over the prime rate for loans of seven years or less, and 2¾ percent over the prime rate for loans that last longer than seven years.[9]

In order to qualify for a direct or guaranteed SBA loan, a company must qualify as a small business and meet the agency's credit requirements. In order to be a small business, the company must fit the following conditions:

- Is independently owned and operated
- Is a for-profit firm
- Is not dominant in its field
- Has two-year average net profit after taxes of less than $2.5 million

In order to meet SBA credit requirements, the applicant must qualify in these ways:[10]

- Be of good character
- Show the ability to operate a business successfully
- Have enough capital in an existing firm so that, with an SBA loan, the business can operate on a sound financial basis
- Create at least one job for every $50,000 in SBA financing provided
- Show that the past earnings record and future prospects of the firm indicate an ability to repay the loan and other fixed debts, if any, out of profits
- Be able to provide, from personal resources, sufficient funds to have a reasonable amount at hand to withstand possible losses, particularly during the early stages of a new venture

An individual or business that meets these requirements can then formally apply for a loan. The SBA recommends that those already in business follow seven steps:

1. Prepare a current financial statement (balance sheet) listing all assets and all liabilities of the business.

2. Prepare an earnings (profit and loss) statement for the current period to the date of the balance sheet.

3. Prepare a current personal financial statement for the owner or for each partner or stockholder who owns 20 percent or more of the corporate stock.

4. List the collateral to be offered as security for the loan, and estimate the present market value of each item.

5. State the amount of the loan request and the exact purposes it will be used for.

6. Take all of this material to your banker and ask for a direct bank loan. If you are turned down, ask the bank to make the loan under the SBA's Loan Guarantee Plan or Immediate Participation Plan. If the bank is interested in an SBA-guaranteed or participation loan, ask the banker to contact the SBA and discuss the application. In most such cases, the SBA deals directly with the bank.

7. If a guaranteed loan or a participation loan is not available, write or visit the nearest SBA office.

Individuals who need a loan to start a business should follow these eight steps:

1. Describe the type of business to be established.

2. Describe your experience and management capabilities.

3. Prepare an estimate of how much you or others have to invest in the business and how much you will need to borrow.

4. Prepare a current financial statement, listing all personal assets and liabilities.

5. Prepare a detailed projection of earnings for the first year that the business will operate.

6. List the collateral to be offered as security for the loan, and estimate the present market value of each item.

7. Take all of this material to your banker and ask for a direct bank loan. If you are turned down, ask the bank to make the loan under the SBA's Loan Guarantee Plan or Immediate Participation Plan. If the bank is interested in an SEA-guaranteed or participation loan, ask the banker to contact the SBA and discuss the application. In most such cases, the SBA deals directly with the bank.

8. If a guaranteed loan or a participation loan is not available, write or visit the nearest SBA office.[11] Table 8-4 provides an outline of the SBA's 7(a) programs.

STATE AND LOCAL DEVELOPMENT COMPANIES

The SBA is also authorized to guarantee some state and local development company funds to finance specific new ventures. An increasing number of states and local communities are organizing development corporations, or industrial

TABLE 8-4 Small Business Administration Specialized Loan Programs

7(a) Loan Guaranty: One of SBA's primary lending programs. It provides loans to small businesses that are unable to secure financing on reasonable terms through normal lending channels. The program operates through private-sector lenders that provide loans that are, in turn, guaranteed by the SBA; the agency has no funds for direct lending or grants. The maximum amount the SBA can guarantee is generally $750,000.

LowDoc: Designed to increase the availability of loans of less than $150,000 and to streamline/expedite the loan review process.

SBA Express (formerly Fastrak): Makes it easier and faster for lenders to provide small business loans of $150,000 or less. Allows lenders to use their own forms and processes to approve loans guaranteed by the SBA. Provides a rapid response from the SBA (within 36 hours of receiving a complete application). Lets lenders take advantage of electronic loan processing.

Community Express: A pilot SBA loan program that was developed in collaboration with the National Community Reinvestment Coalition (NCRC) and its member organizations. Under the pilot, which will initially be limited to selected NCRA lenders, an SBA Express-like program will be offered to predesignated geographic areas that serve mostly new markets and small businesses. The maximum loan amount is $250,000. The program will also include technical and management assistance designed to help increase the loan applicator's chance for success.

CAIP Loan Program: The U.S. Community Adjustment and Investment Program (CAIP) was created to help communities that suffered job losses because of changing trade patterns with Mexico and Canada following the North American Free Trade Agreement (NAFTA). The CAIP promotes economic implementation of the adjustment by increasing the availability and flow of credit and encourages business development and expansion in affected areas. Through CAIP, an SBA-guaranteed loan of as much as $750,000 is available to businesses in eligible communities to create new, sustainable jobs or to preserve existing jobs.

CAPLines: An umbrella program to help small businesses meet their short-term and cyclical working-capital needs with five separate programs.

International Trade: Designed for businesses preparing to engage in or already engaged in international trade, or adversely affected by competition from imports. The SBA can guarantee as much as $1.25 million for a combination of fixed-asset (facilities and equipment) financing and Export Working Capital Program (EWCP) assistance.

Export Working Capital Program: Designed to provide short-term working capital to exporters through a combination effort of the SBA and the Export-Import Bank. Loan requests of $833,000 or less are processed by the SBA; loan requests of more than $833,000 may be processed through the Export-Import Bank. When a EWCP plan is combined with an international trade loan, the SBA's exposure can reach as much as $1.25 million.

Pollution Control: Designed to provide loan guarantees to eligible small businesses for the financing of the planning, design, or installation of a pollution control facility. The SBA maximum loan is $1 million.

DELTA: Defense Loan and Technical Assistance (DELTA) is a joint SBA and Department of Defense effort to provide financial and technical assistance to defense-dependent small firms that are adversely affected by cutbacks in defense.

TABLE 8-4   (*Continued*)

Minority and Women's Prequal: A pilot program that uses intermediaries to assist prospective minority and women borrowers in developing viable loan application packages and securing loans.

Disabled Assistance: The SBA has not been provided funding for direct disabled assistance loans, but such individuals are eligible for all SBA loan guaranty programs.

Qualified Employee Trust: Designed to provide financial assistance to employee stock ownership plans.

Veteran's Loans: The SBA has not been provided funds for direct loans to veterans, although veterans are eligible for special consideration under SBA's guaranty loan programs.

SBA Microloan Program: This program works through intermediaries to provide small loans that range from as little as $100 to as much as $25,000.

SBA Certified Development Company (504) Program: The 504 program makes long-term loans available for purchasing land, buildings, machinery, and equipment, and for building, modernizing, or renovating existing facilities and sites.

Source: "Financing Your Business-Loan Programs," *U.S. Small Business Administration*, 2006, www.sba.gov/financing (accessed June 15, 2007).

foundations, to promote the establishment or expansion of business in their areas. Some of the services these organizations offer are as follows:

- *Buying, developing, and selling industrial sites.* This usually results in less delay and more reasonable prices for the small manufacturer seeking a site than do negotiations through regular business channels.

- *Buying and building plants for lease or sale.* Here, too, a purchase price may be lower than would have been available otherwise. If the plant is leased, less investment in fixed assets by the new venture will be necessary, and more money can be available for working capital.

- *Providing funds by direct intermediate- or long-term loans or by purchase of stock in the business.* In some cases, development companies will lend larger amounts in proportion to the value of the security for longer periods than are customary for banks.

- *Giving management, engineering, and other counseling services to new ventures.* By pooling the knowledge of the businesspeople of the community, an industrial foundation often is able to provide expert advice.

The SBA's role in this area has diminished in recent years. During the 1970s, it participated directly and actually loaned some of the funds to development companies. Today its role is to guarantee part of the monies raised. In a typical arrangement, the state or local development company will put up 10 percent of the total funds, borrow 50 percent from the bank, and float *debentures* (unsecured bonds) for the remainder. The SBA guarantees the debentures. As an example, Table 8-5 provides the description of the Certified Development Company Program (504).

TABLE 8-5   Small Business Administration Certified Development Company Program (504)

General Program Description

The Certified Development Company (CDC) program was started to alleviate a perceived shortage of long-term credit for existing, healthy small businesses needing to expand operations. CDCs work with financial institutions to package long-term loans for small businesses. Loan proceeds may be used for fixed-asset acquisition, including land acquisition/construction of business buildings, land improvements, purchase of an existing business building, purchase of long-life equipment, and leasehold improvements under certain conditions. In addition, loan proceeds may be used for certain costs associated with a project, such as surveying, engineering, and architectural fees. CDCs may not provide working capital.

In a typical loan package, 50 percent of the funds come from a private lender, 40 percent come from the issue of a 100 percent SBA-guaranteed debenture, and 10 percent come from the borrowing firm.

The maximum SBA debenture/loan amount per small business is $1 million. The interest rate on the portion of the loan derived from the debenture issue is fixed and will equal approximately ¾ percent over the interest on Treasury bonds of a comparable maturity. The financial institution will determine the interest rate charged on its portion of the loan, and this rate may be either fixed or variable.

Eligibility Criteria

CDCs can package loans for new-business start-ups and for existing businesses seeking to expand. However, most CDC assistance goes to existing businesses. In order to qualify for assistance, a firm must be independently owned and operated, be for profit, have been turned down by at least one financial institution for financing of the entire project, and have a net income not exceeding $2 million over the past two years. Other requirements may also apply.

Some types of businesses are explicitly excluded from eligibility under this program. These include lending institutions, passive investment companies, real-estate investment companies, and unregulated media firms.

Application Procedure

Preliminary information can be obtained directly from the appropriate CDC. If your project meets eligibility criteria, you will have to work with a financial institution to prepare an application. Several pieces of information will be required during the application. Among these are a description of the business; current and past financial statements; a description of the project to be financed; personal history and financial statements from all officers, directors, and owners of 20 percent or more of the firm's stock; resumes of the principals; a projected operating statement for two years; and a statement from a bank explaining why it will not finance the entire project.

Source: U.S. Small Business Administration, *Certified Development Company Program (504)* (Washington, DC: U.S. Government Printing Office, 2000).

SMALL BUSINESS INVESTMENT COMPANIES

Another avenue for securing funding is through small business investment companies (SBICs), which are licensed by and operate under the responsibility of the SBA. The purpose of SBICs is to provide venture capital to new ventures. This capital can take various forms, ranging from secured to unsecured loans, debt security with equity characteristics, or pure equity represented by common and preferred stock.

Venture capital is characterized as high risk and tends to be responsive to the needs of the new venture rather than to the requirements of those who are investing the funds. More important, a very active and continuing relationship tends to exist between the new venture and the venture capitalist. Although some SBICs will consider start-ups, most look for companies that are already running but need additional capital to expand or otherwise maximize their potential. Some SBICs are indistinguishable from conventional venture capital firms, with one important difference: The SBA won't let SBICs take more than a 49 percent interest in a company, so the entrepreneur retains control. As far as debt financing is concerned, SBICs typically loan between $100,000 and $5 million at an interest rate that can be quite high—as much as 17 or 18 percent.

Over the years, SBICs have provided venture capital to qualifying new ventures in start-up and growth phases. To date, SBICs have invested more than $13 billion in more than 78,000 new ventures.[12]

In the past, many SBICs preferred to lend money to firms already in business. During the 1990s, however, SBICs invested in start-ups, especially firms in high-tech fields. Because of the gains some of these firms made with their technological breakthroughs, SBICs realized that they were passing up a very high potential profit by excluding them from investment consideration. Today, most SBICs look for a modest but steady return on their investments.

Minority Enterprise SBICs (MESBICs) have been formed for the purpose of providing venture capital and equity financing to new ventures owned by people who are economically or socially disadvantaged, including African Americans, Puerto Ricans, Mexican Americans, Native Americans, and Eskimos. The MESBICs have an organizational structure similar to SBICs except that the nature of the SBA leverage is different. Certain rules and regulations have been liberalized to enable the MESBICs to overcome financing problems unique to businesses owned by members of minority groups. It is common to find MESBICs investing in tandem with commercial banks, with funds 90 percent guaranteed under other SBA programs.

SMALL BUSINESS INNOVATION RESEARCH PROGRAM

The Small Business Innovation Research (SBIR) program was established in 1982 under the Small Business Innovation Development Act. Although the SBIR solicitation process and award authority were assigned to participating federal agencies, the legislation authorizes SBA to do the following:

- Implement the program government-wide
- Set the governing program policy
- Monitor the performance of the federal agencies participating in the program

- Analyze the annual reports of each of these agencies on the progress of the SBIR program
- Report SBA findings to Congress

The functions required of the SBA under the act are implemented through the Office of Innovation, Research, and Technology. Specifically, the act requires each federal agency with an extramural research and development (R&D) budget in excess of $100 million per fiscal year to establish an SBIR program. The agency funds the program by setting aside a graduated percentage of R&D dollars specified by the legislation.

The SBIR program has three phases:

1. The majority of Phase I awards are $100,000 for a six-month period or less and are designed to evaluate the scientific and technical merit and feasibility of an idea.
2. In Phase II, projects from Phase I with the most potential are funded for two years to proceed with product development. The majority of these awards are funded for $750,000 or less.
3. Phase III involves private investment aimed at bringing an innovation to the marketplace. This phase also may include production contracts with a federal agency for the federal government's future use. No SBIR funds may be used during Phase III.[13]

MINORITY BUSINESS DEVELOPMENT AGENCY

The Minority Business Development Agency (MBDA) was started with SBA seed money and operates under SBA guidelines. The MBDA provides special assistance to minority individuals, partnerships, and corporations. It helps them to acquire and control medium- and large-sized firms, divisions, and established product lines. The qualification of a minority business owner as disadvantaged is the same as that for MESBIC-assisted businesses.

The MBDA also makes grants to professional consulting firms to assist minority buyers in the entire process—from analyzing and negotiating for a business to actually acquiring it. These consulting firms also help identify the best source of financing and prepare the applications, documentation (other than legal), and other information that lenders and investors require.

Minorities interested in obtaining MBDA help must demonstrate (1) financial ability by providing at least 5 percent of the total cost to purchase the business in cash or tangible assets, and (2) a sound knowledge of the particular business and industry. The business to be acquired must show a sound potential for profits based on products and markets; demonstrate a high growth rate in sales, earnings, and similar measures; and exhibit technological and capital requirements consistent with the capability of the new owners. Finally, the business should have net assets in excess of $1 million or gross revenues in excess of

$3 million during the preceding 12 months. If all of these requirements are met, the MBDA will assist in identifying sources of capital for purchasing the company.

Summary

One of the first questions a prospective new venture owner must be able to answer is, "What kind of capital do I need, and where can it be obtained?" Basically, four types of capital exist: short-term loans, intermediate-term loans, long-term loans, and equity capital. Each was discussed in this chapter.

After determining the type of capital needed, the prospective entrepreneur must follow through and determine the source of this type of capital. Of the large number of capital sources, those discussed in this chapter included internal funds, trade credit, equity sources, banks, other private sources of capital, the Small Business Administration, state and local development companies, small business investment companies, and the Minority Business Development Agency. In each instance, we examined the types of capital and services typically provided. Some of these capital sources are more valuable to one kind of business than another — factoring, for example, would be used by a business that has a large amount of accounts receivable but not by a business that deals basically for cash.

In the latter part of the chapter, we examined the role of the SBA in helping the new venture owner obtain capital despite being turned down by his or her local bank. Regardless of the type of business, capital sources exist that can help the owner raise the all-important initial funding. Despite the potential risk to the investor, the business may find a venture capitalist who feels that the firm is promising and will return a large profit. The most important task for the new venture is to investigate these capital sources before plunging headlong into the venture.

Review and Discussion Questions

1. What are the two most common forms of short-term loans? Explain them.
2. What are intermediate-term loans, and when do new ventures use them? What about long-term loans?
3. What is equity capital?
4. Explain how new ventures use the following capital sources: internal funds, trade credit, and equity sources.
5. What kinds of loan services do banks provide for new ventures? Describe four of them.
6. Discuss how the following can be of value to new ventures that want to raise capital: insurance companies, finance companies, and factors.
7. In what way(s) does the SBA help new ventures raise capital? Be specific.
8. Explain how each of the following helps new ventures meet their capital needs: state and local development companies, small business investment companies, and the Minority Business Development Agency.

┌───┐

NEW VENTURE CONSULTANT

The Charter Business

Joe Miller wants to go into business for himself. He has skippered his own small private yacht for more than 10 years, and he knows that many tourists come to Florida every year between October and March. Some of them like to travel to the Bahamas or down toward South America by renting a boat, a skipper, and a crew. Naturally, not too many people can afford the high fees associated with this type of vacationing, but Joe believes there are enough visits to justify his going into this charter business.

After shopping around for six months, Joe has found a new large sailboat that can sleep 10 people. It retails for $400,000 and, according to a friend who owns one, is very popular with people who want to rent a boat and go sailing for a couple of weeks. Joe has saved $75,000 in the past five years and believes that, with a loan from a bank, he can buy the boat and go into the charter business.

During the past month, however, Joe has been very disappointed. He has applied for a loan at five banks, and they have all told him the same thing: "We think your idea has a great deal of merit. Undoubtedly, many people want to charter sailboats and spend their vacation on the high seas. However, we are not set up for that type of business. We prefer to lend money for houses or automobiles, and sailboats are really out of our bailiwick. Perhaps another bank would be interested in such a loan, but, at least for the time being, we do not feel qualified to get into this line."

Joe is disappointed because he was counting on using the sailboat as collateral for the loan. Since the boat costs $400,000 and is expected to increase in value each year (because of inflation) by 3 to 4 percent, the bank's loan would be very safe. Furthermore, Joe cannot understand the logic of the banks. Not one of them told him the business venture was a bad idea. In fact, after he explained his anticipated costs and revenues to one of the bankers, the banker told him his presentation was well thought out and made good business sense. Nevertheless, no one is willing to lend him the money.

However, Joe has not given up. He has learned that sometimes the Small Business Administration will guarantee loans that banks have turned down. He has decided to go down to the nearby SBA field office to talk to someone there. If it looks feasible, he intends to fill out the papers and submit his application immediately.

Your Consultation: Help Joe by providing him advice and assistance. What types of loans does the SBA guarantee? What are some of the prerequisites for borrowing with SBA assistance? How should Joe prepare for his visit? Should he take any materials with him? What are his chances for success? Explain.

└───┘

Endnotes

1. Jay Ebben and Alec Johnson, "Bootstrapping in Small Firms: An Empirical Analysis of Change over Time," *Journal of Business Venturing,* November, 2006, 21 (6): 851–865.

2. Allen N. Berger & W. Scott Frame, "Small Business Credit Scoring and Credit Availability," *Journal of Small Business Management,* 45 (1), 2007. pp 5–22. See also, Brian T. Gregory, Matthew W. Rutherford, Sharon Oswald, & Lorraine Gardiner, "An Empirical Investigation of the Growth Cycle Theory of Small Firm Financing," *Journal of Small Business Management,* 43 (4), 2005. pp. 382–392.
3. Larry D. Wall, "On Investing in the Equity of Small Firms," *Journal of Small Business Management,* 45 (1), 2007. pp. 89–93.
4. Allen N. Berger & W. Scott Frame, "Small Business Credit Scoring and Credit Availability," *Journal of Small Business Management* 45 (1), 2007. pp. 5–22.
5. For a complete analysis of sources of finance for small businesses, see "Financing Patterns of Small Business," *The State of Small Business: A Report to the President* (Washington, DC: U.S. Government Printing Office, 1995), 276–296; see also, Elijah Brewer III, "On Lending to Small Firms" *Journal of Small Business Management,* 45 (1), 2007. pp. 42–46.
6. Jonathan D. Arthurs and Lowell W. Busenitz, "Dynamic Capabilities and Venture Performance: The Effects of Venture capitalists," *Journal of Business Venturing,* March, 2006, 21 (2):195–216; Dirk De Lercq & Harry J. Sapienza, "Effects of Relational Capital and Commitment on Venture Capitalists' Perception of Portfolio Company Performance," *Journal of Business Venturing,* 21 (3), May, 2006. pp. 326–347. See also, Charles Baden-Fuller, Alison Dean, Peter McNamara, and Bill Hilliard, "Raising the Returns to Venture Finance," *Journal of Business Venturing,* 21 (3), May, 2006. pp. 265–285.
7. De Clercq, Dirk, Fried, Vance H., Lehtonen, Oskari, and Sapienza, Harry J. "An Entrepreneur's Guide to the Venture Capital Galaxy," *Academy of Management Perspectives,* Aug. 2006, Vol. 20, p. 90–112.
8. John Freear, Jeffrey E. Sohl, and William E. Wetzel, Jr., "Angels and Non-angels: Are There Differences?" *Journal of Business Venturing* (March 1994): 109 123. Jeffrey Sohl, "The Angel Investor Market in 2004" Center for Venture Research, University of New Hampshire, May 2005.
9. Boyce D. Watkins, "On Governance Programs that Increase Small Firms' Access to Capital," *Journal of Small Business Management,* 45 (1), 2007. pp. 133–136.
10. "SBA 504 and 7(a) Loan Programs Fact Sheet" Council of Development Finance Agencies. Retrieved February 13, 2007 from http://www.cdfa.net/cdfa/cdfaweb.nsf/pages/5047afactsheet. html.
11. See: Ben R. Craig, William E. Jackson & James B. Thomson, "Small Firm Finance, Credit Rationing, and the Impact of SBA-Guaranteed Lending on Local Economic Growth, *Journal of Small Business Management,* 45 (1), 2007. pp. 116–132.
12. *Financing Your Business* (Washington, DC: U.S. Small Business Administration, www.sba.gov, 2006).
13. Kathleen C. Brannen and Joel C. Gard, "Grantsmanship and Entrepreneurship: A Partnership Opportunity under the Small Business Innovation Development Act," *Journal of Small Business Management* (July' 1985): 44–49.

CHAPTER 9

FINANCIAL STATEMENTS
THE SCORECARD

INTRODUCTION

Financial statements are powerful tools that owners can use to manage their ventures.[1] The basic financial statements with which an owner/manager needs to be familiar are the balance sheet and the income statement. The following sections examine each of these in depth and provide a foundation for understanding the financial records that are needed.

FINANCIAL STATEMENTS

THE BALANCE SHEET

A balance sheet is a financial statement that reports a business's financial position at a specific time. Many accountants like to think of it as a picture taken at the close of business on a particular day. The closing date is usually the one that marks the end of the business year for the organization (e.g., December 31).

The balance sheet is divided into two parts: the financial resources owned by the firm and the claims against these resources. Traditionally, these claims against the resources come from two groups: the creditors who have a claim to the firm's assets and can sue the company if these obligations are not paid, and owners who have rights to anything left over after the creditors' claims have been paid.

The financial resources that the firm owns are called *assets*. The claims that creditors have against the company are called *liabilities*. The residual interest of the firm's owners is known as *owners' equity*. When all three are placed on the balance sheet, the assets are listed on the left, and the liabilities and owners' equity are listed on the right.

Assets	Liabilities and Owners' Equity

An asset is something of value the business owns. In order to determine the value of an asset, the owner/manager must do the following:

1. Identify the resource.
2. Provide a monetary measurement value of that resource's value.
3. Establish the degree of ownership in the resource.

Most assets can be identified easily because they are tangible, such as cash, land, and equipment. However, *intangible assets* also exist. These are assets that cannot be seen; examples include copyrights and patents.

Liabilities are the debts of the business. These may be incurred either through normal operations or through the process of obtaining funds to finance operations. A common liability is a short-term account payable that occurs when the business orders merchandise, receives it, and has not yet paid for it. For example, assume that a company receives merchandise during the third week of the month but does not pay for it until it pays all of its bills on the first day of the following month. Were the balance sheet constructed at the end of the month, the account still would be payable at that time.

Liabilities are divided into two categories: short term and long term. *Short-term liabilities* are those that must be paid during the coming 12 months. *Long-term liabilities* are those that are not due and payable within the next 12 months, such as a mortgage on a building or a five-year bank loan.

Owners' equity is what remains after the firm's liabilities are subtracted from its assets—it is the claim the owners have against the firm's assets. If the business loses money, its owners' equity will decline. This will become clearer when we explain why a balance sheet always balances.[2]

UNDERSTANDING THE BALANCE SHEET

In order to fully explain the balance sheet, it is necessary to examine a typical one and determine what each entry means. Table 9-1 provides an illustration; note that it includes three sections: assets, liabilities, and owners' equity. Within each of these classifications are various types of accounts. The sections that follow examine each type of account presented in the table.

CURRENT ASSETS

Current assets consist of cash and other assets that are reasonably expected to be turned into cash, sold, or used up during a normal operating cycle. The most common types of current assets are those listed in Table 9-1.

Cash refers to coins, currency, and checks on hand. It also includes money the business has in its checking and savings accounts.

TABLE 9-1   EntreX Corporation Balance Sheet for the Year Ended December 31, 2009

Assets

Current Assets

Cash		$ 200,000
Accounts receivable	$375,000	
Less: Allowance for uncollectible accounts	$ 25,000	350,000
Inventory		150,000
Prepaid expenses		35,000
Total current assets		$ 735,000

Fixed Assets

Land		$ 330,000
Building	$315,000	
Less: Accumulated depreciation of building	80,000	
Equipment	410,000	
Less: Accumulated depreciation of equipment	60,000	
Total fixed assets		915,000
Total assets		$1,650,000

Liabilities

Current Liabilities

Accounts payable	$150,000	
Notes payable	25,000	
Taxes payable	75,000	
Loan payable	50,000	
Total current liabilities		$300,000
Bank loan		200,000
Total liabilities		$500,000

Owners' Equity

Contributed Capital

Common stock, $10 par, 40,000 shares	$400,000	
Preferred stock, $100 par, 500 shares		
Authorized, none sold	----------	
Retained Earnings	750,000	
Total owners' equity		1,150,000
Total liabilities and owners' equity		$1,650,000

Accounts receivable are claims of the business against its customers for unpaid balances from the sale of merchandise or the performance of services. For example, many firms sell on credit and expect their customers to pay by the end of the month. Or, in many of these cases, they send customers a bill at the end of the month and ask for payment within 10 days.

The *allowance for uncollectible accounts* refers to accounts receivable that are judged to be uncollectible. How does a business know when receivables are not collectible? Unfortunately, there is no simple answer to this question. However, assume the business asks all of its customers to pay within the first 10 days of the month following the purchase. An aging of the accounts receivable shows that the following amounts are due the firm:

Number of Days Outstanding	2009 Amount of Receivables
1–10	$325,000
11–20	25,000
21–30	20,000
31–60	5,000
61–90	7,500
97+	17,500

In this case, the firm might believe that anything more than 60 days old will not be paid and will write it off as uncollectible. Note that in Table 9-1 the allowance for uncollectible accounts is $25,000, the amount that has been outstanding more than 60 days.

Inventory is merchandise held by the company for resale to customers. Current inventory in our example is $150,000, but this is not the entire inventory that the firm had on hand all year. Naturally, the company started the year with some inventory and purchased more as sales were made. This balance sheet figure is what was left at the end of the fiscal year.

Prepaid expenses are expenses the firm already has paid but that have not yet been used. For example, insurance paid on the company car every six months is a prepaid-expense entry because it will be six months before the entire premium has been used. As a result, the accountant would reduce this prepaid amount by one-sixth each month. Sometimes supplies, services, and rent are also prepaid, in which case the same approach is followed.

FIXED ASSETS

Fixed assets consist of land, building, equipment, and other assets expected to remain with the firm for an extended period; they are not totally used up in the production of the firm's goods and services. Some of the most common types are listed in Table 9-1.

Land is property used in the operation of the firm. This is not land that has been purchased for expansion or speculation; that would be listed as an investment rather than a fixed asset. Land is listed on the balance sheet at cost, and its value usually is changed only periodically. For example, every five years, the value of the land might be recalculated so that its value on the balance sheet and its resale value are the same.

Building consists of the structures that house the business. If the firm has more than one building, the total cost of all the structures is listed.

Accumulated depreciation of building refers to the amount of the building that has been written off the books due to wear and tear. For example, referring to

Table 9-1, the original cost of the building was $315,000, but accumulated depreciation is $80,000, leaving a net value of $235,000. The amount of depreciation charged each year is determined by the company accountant after he or she checks the Internal Revenue Service rules. However, a standard depreciation is 5 percent per year for new buildings, although an accelerated method sometimes is used. In any event, the amount written off is a tax-deductible expense. Depreciation therefore reduces the amount of taxable income to the firm and helps lower the tax liability. In this way, the business gets the opportunity to recover part of its investment.

Equipment is the machinery the business uses to produce goods. This is placed on the books at cost and then is depreciated and listed as the *accumulated depreciation of equipment*. In our example, this amount is $60,000. The logic behind equipment depreciation and its effect on the firm's income taxes is the same as that for accumulated depreciation on the building.

CURRENT LIABILITIES

Current liabilities are obligations that will become due and payable during the next year or within the operating cycle. The most common current liabilities are listed in Table 9-1.

Accounts payable are liabilities that are incurred when goods or supplies are purchased on credit. For example, if the business buys on a basis of net 30 days, during those 30 days the bill for the goods will constitute an account payable.

A *note payable* is a promissory note that is given as tangible recognition of a supplier's claim or a note given in connection with an acquisition of funds, such as for a bank loan. Some suppliers require that a note be given when a company buys merchandise and is unable to pay for it immediately.

Taxes payable are liabilities that are owed to the government—federal, state, and local. Most businesses pay their federal and state income taxes on a quarterly basis. Typically, payments are made on April 15, June 15, and September 15 of the current year, and January 15 of the following year. Then the business closes its books, determines whether it still owes any taxes, and makes the required payments by April 15. Other taxes payable are sales taxes. For example, most states and some cities levy a sales tax; each merchant must collect the taxes and remit them to the appropriate agency.

A *loan payable* is the installment on a long-term debt that must be paid during the current year. As a result, it becomes a part of the current liabilities. The remainder is carried as a long-term debt. Note in the table that $50,000 of this debt was paid in 2009 by the EntreX Corporation.

LONG-TERM LIABILITIES

As previously mentioned, long-term liabilities consist of obligations that will not become due or payable for at least one year or within the current operating cycle. The most common long-term liabilities are bank loans.

A *bank loan* is a long-term liability due to a loan from a lending institution. Although it is unclear from the balance sheet in the table how large the bank loan originally was, it is being paid down at the rate of $50,000 annually. Thus, it will take four more years to pay off the loan.

CONTRIBUTED CAPITAL

The EntreX Corporation is owned by individuals who have purchased stock in the business. Various kinds of stock can be sold by a corporation, the most typical being common stock and preferred stock. Only common stock has been sold by this company.

Common stock is the most basic form of corporate ownership. This ownership gives the individual the right to vote for the board of directors. Usually, for every share of common stock held, an individual is entitled to one vote. As shown in Table 9-1, the corporation has issued 40,000 shares of $10 *par* common stock, raising $400,000. Although the term *par value* may have little meaning to most stockholders, it has legal implications; it determines the legal capital of the corporation. This legal capital constitutes an amount that total stockholders' equity cannot fall below except under certain circumstances (the most common is a series of net losses). For legal reasons, the total par value of the stock is maintained in the accounting records. However, it has no effect on the *market value* of the stock.

Preferred stock differs from common stock in that its holders have preference to the assets of the firm in case of dissolution. This means that, after the creditors are paid, preferred stockholders have the next claim on whatever assets are left. The common stockholders' claims come last. The table shows that 500 shares of preferred stock were issued, each worth a par value of $100, but none has been sold.

RETAINED EARNINGS

Retained earnings are the accumulated net income over the life of the corporation to date. In the table, the retained earnings are shown as $750,000. Every year this amount increases by the profit the firm makes and keeps within the company. If dividends are declared on the stock, they, of course, are paid from the total net earnings. Retained earnings are what remain after that.

WHY THE BALANCE SHEET ALWAYS BALANCES

By definition, the balance sheet *always* balances.[3] If something happens on one side of the balance sheet, it is offset by something on the other side. Hence, the balance sheet remains in balance. Before examining some illustrations, let us restate the balance sheet equation:

$$Assets = Liabilities + Owners' Equity$$

Following are some typical examples of business transactions and their effect on the balance sheet.

A CREDIT TRANSACTION

The EntreX Corporation calls one of its suppliers and asks for delivery of $10,000 of materials. The materials arrive the next day, and the company takes possession of them. The bill is to be paid within 30 days. How is the balance sheet affected? *Inventory* goes up by $10,000, and *Accounts payable* rise by $10,000. The increase in current assets is offset by an increase in current liabilities. Continuing this illustration, what happens when the bill is paid? The company issues a check for $10,000, and the *Cash* account declines by this amount. At the same time, *Accounts payable* decrease by $10,000. Again, these are offsetting transactions, and the balance sheet remains in balance.

A BANK LOAN

Table 9-1 shows that the EntreX Corporation had an outstanding bank loan of $200,000 in 2009. Assume that the company increases this loan by $100,000 in 2010. How is the balance sheet affected? *Cash* goes up by $100,000, and *Bank loan* increases by the same amount; again, balance is achieved. However, what if the firm uses this $100,000 to buy new machinery? In this case, *Cash* decreases by $100,000 and *Equipment* increases by a like amount. Again, a balance exists. Finally, what if EntreX decides to pay off its bank loan? In this case, the first situation is reversed; *Cash* and *Bank loan* (long-term liabilities) decrease in equal amounts.

COMPANY SELLS STOCK

Suppose that the company issues and sells another 40,000 shares of $10 par common stock. How does this action affect the balance sheet? This answer is rather simple: *Common stock* increases by $400,000, and so does *Cash*. Once more, a balance exists.

With these examples in mind, it should be obvious why the balance sheet *always* balances. Every entry has an equal and offsetting entry to maintain the balance sheet equation:

$$Assets = Liabilities + Owners' Equity$$

Keep in mind that, in accounting language, the terms *debit* and *credit* denote increases and decreases in assets, liabilities, and owners' equity. The following table relates debits and credits to increases and decreases.

Category	A Transaction Increasing the Amount	A Transaction Decreasing the Amount
Asset	Debit	Credit
Liability	Credit	Debit
Owners'equity	Credit	Debit

Applying this idea to the preceding examples results in the following:

	Debit	Credit
Credit Transaction		
Inventory	$ 10,000	
Accounts payable		$ 10,000
Bank Loan		
Cash	100,000	
Bank loan		100,000
		(*Continued*)

	Debit	Credit
Stock Sale		
Cash	400,000	
Common stock		400,000
	$510,000	$510,000

THE INCOME STATEMENT

The *income statement* is a financial statement that shows the change that has occurred in a firm's position as a result of its operations over a specific period. This contrasts with the balance sheet, which reflects the company's position at a particular point in time.

The income statement reports the success (or failure) of the business during a particular period. In essence, it shows whether revenues were greater than or less than expenses. These *revenues* are the monies the venture has received from the sale of its goods and services. The *expenses* are the costs of the resources used to obtain the revenues. These costs range from the price of materials used in the products the firm makes to the salaries it pays its employees.

Most income statements cover a one-year interval, but it is not uncommon to find monthly, quarterly, or semiannual income statements. All of the revenues and expenses accumulated during this time are determined, and the net income for the period is identified. Many firms prepare quarterly income statements but construct a balance sheet only once a year. This is because they are interested far more in their profits and losses than in examining their asset, liability, and owners' equity positions. However, it should be noted that the income statement drawn up at the end of the year will coincide with the firm's fiscal year, just as the balance sheet does. As a result, at the end of the business year, the organization will have both a balance sheet and an income statement. In this way, they can be considered together and the interrelationship between them can be studied. We will consider this in greater depth in Chapter 10, when we look at some of the financial ratios that simultaneously analyze balance sheet and income statement data.

A number of different types of income and expenses are reported on the income statement. However, for purposes of simplicity, the income statement can be reduced to three primary categories:

1. Revenues
2. Expenses
3. Net income

Revenues are the gross sales the business makes during the particular period under review. Revenue often consists of the money actually received from sales, but this need not be the case. For example, sales made on account still are recognized as revenue, as when a furniture store sells $500 of furniture today, delivers it tomorrow, and receives payment two weeks from now. From the moment the goods are delivered, the company can claim an increase in revenue.

Expenses are the costs associated with producing goods or services. For the furniture store situation just cited, the expenses associated with the sale would include the costs of acquiring, selling, and delivering the merchandise. Sometimes these are expenses that will be paid later. For example, the people who deliver the furniture may be paid every two weeks, so the actual outflow of expense money in the form of salaries will not occur at the same time the work is performed. Nevertheless, it is treated as an expense.

Net income is the excess of revenue over expenses during the particular period under discussion. If revenues exceed expenses, the result is a *net profit*. If the reverse is true, the firm suffers a *net loss*. At the end of the accounting period, all of the revenues and expenses associated with all of the sales of goods and services are added together, and then the expenses are subtracted from the revenues. In this way, the firm knows whether it made an overall profit or suffered an overall loss.[4]

UNDERSTANDING THE INCOME STATEMENT

In order to explain the income statement fully, it is necessary to examine one and determine what each account is. Table 9-2 illustrates a typical income statement. It has five major sections:

1. Sales revenue
2. Cost of goods sold
3. Operating expenses

TABLE 9-2   EntreX Corporation Income Statement for the Year Ended December 31, 2009

Sales Revenue	$ 1,750,000	
Less: Sales returns and allowances	50,000	
Net sales		$1,700,000
Cost of Goods Sold		
Inventory, January 2009	$ 150,000	
Purchases	1,050,000	
Goods available for sale	$1,200,000	
Less: Inventory, December 2009	200,000	
Cost of goods sold		1,000,000
Gross margin		$ 700,000
Operating Expenses		
Selling expenses	$ 150,000	
Administrative expenses	100,000	
Total operating expenses		250,000
Operating income		$ 450,000
Financial Expenses		$20,000
Income before income taxes		$ 430,000
Estimated income taxes		172,000
Net profit		$ 258,000

4. Financial expense

5. Income taxes estimated

REVENUE

Every time a business sells a product or performs a service, it obtains revenue. This often is referred to as *gross revenue* or *sales revenue*. However, it is usually an overstated figure because the company finds that some of its goods are returned or some customers take advantage of prompt-payment discounts.

Sales revenue in Table 9-2 is $1.75 million. However, the firm also has returns and allowances of $50,000. These returns are common for companies that operate on a "satisfaction or your money back" policy. In any event, a new venture should keep tabs on these returns and allowances to see if the total is high in relation to the total sales revenue. If so, the firm will know something is wrong with what it is selling and can take action to correct the situation.

Deducting the sales returns and allowances from the sales revenue, the company finds its *net sales*. This amount must be great enough to offset the accompanying expenses in order to ensure a profit.

COST OF GOODS SOLD

As the term implies, the *Cost of goods sold* section reports the cost of merchandise sold during the accounting period. Simply put, the cost of goods for a given period equals the beginning inventory plus any purchases the firm makes, minus the inventory on hand at the end of the period. Note that in Table 9-2 the beginning inventory was $150,000 and the purchases totaled $1.05 million. This gave EntreX goods available for sale totaling $1.2 million. The ending inventory for the period was $200,000, so the cost of goods sold was $1 million. This is what it cost the company to buy the inventory it sold. When this cost of goods sold is subtracted from net sales, the result is the *gross margin*. The gross margin is the amount available to meet expenses and to provide some net income for the firm's owners.

OPERATING EXPENSES

The major expenses, exclusive of costs of goods sold, are classified as *operating expenses*. These represent the resources expended, except for inventory purchases, in generating the revenue for the period. Expenses often are divided into two broad subclassifications: selling expenses and administrative expenses.

Selling expenses result from activities such as displaying, selling, delivering, and installing a product or performing a service. Expenses for displaying a product include rent for storage space, depreciation on fixtures and furniture, property insurance, and utility and tax expenses. Sales expenses, salaries, commissions, and advertising also fall into this category. Costs associated with getting the product from the store to the customer also are considered selling expenses. Finally, if the firm installs the product for the customer, all costs, including the parts used in the job, are considered in this total. Taken as a whole, these are the selling expenses.

Administrative expenses is a catchall term for operating expenses not directly related to selling or borrowing. In broad terms, these expenses include the costs associated with running the firm. They include salaries of the managers, expenses associated with operating the office, general expenses that cannot be related directly to buying or selling activities, and expenses that arise from delinquent or uncollectible accounts.

When these selling and administrative expenses are added together, the result is *total operating expenses.* Subtracting the total operating expenses from the gross margin gives the firm its *operating income.* Note in Table 9-2 that selling expenses are $150,000, administrative expenses are $100,000, and total operating expenses are $250,000. When subtracted from the gross margin of $700,000, the operating income is $450,000.

FINANCIAL EXPENSE

The *financial expense* is the interest expense on long-term loans. In Table 9-2, this expense equals $20,000. Many companies include their interest expense on short-term obligations as part of their financial expense.

ESTIMATED INCOME TAXES

As noted earlier, corporations pay estimated income taxes; then, at some predetermined time (for example, December 31), the books are closed, actual taxes are determined, and any additional payments are made (or refunds claimed). When these taxes are subtracted from the income before income taxes, the result is the *net profit.* In our example, the EntreX Corporation made $258,000.

KEEPING PROPER RECORDS

The balance sheet and income statement are important financial statements. However, the new venture also needs to keep adequate accounting records for control purposes.[5] The two most basic books of record are the Sales and Cash Receipts Journal and the Cash Disbursement, Purchases, and Expense Journal.

SALES AND CASH RECEIPTS JOURNAL

The Sales and Cash Receipts Journal records the business's daily income (Table 9-3 provides an example). Note that total sales on March 15 amounted to $520; this was credited to the account. Of this amount, $210 was charged, resulting in $310 in cash taken in. Additionally, $150 in accounts receivable was collected. However, $10 was lost due to change errors made by the employee running the cash register. The business deposited $450 in the bank.

Note that Table 9-3 distinguishes debits (DR) and credits (CR). In *income accounts,* a credit is an increase to the account and a debit is a decrease. In *expense accounts,* a debit is an increase and a credit is a decrease. The total of debits and credits should be equal. When they are not, an error exists in the entries. Meanwhile, the sum of the total sales column tells the firm how much has been sold during the period; this is the total used in the income statement.

CASH DISBURSEMENT, PURCHASES, AND EXPENSE JOURNAL

The Cash Disbursement, Purchases, and Expense Journal is a record of expenditures of funds by the new venture. Table 9-4 illustrates a page from this journal.

TABLE 9-3 Sales and Cash Receipts Journal

Date	Description and/or Account	Total Sales (DR)	Credit Sales (DR)	Collected on Accounts (CR)	Misc. Income and Expenses Income (CR)	Misc. Income and Expenses Expense (DR)	Bank Deposit (DR)
3/15	Daily summary	$520.00	$210.00	$150.00			$450.00
	Cash short					$10.00	
3/16	Daily summary	$635.00	$300.00	$210.00			$550.00
	Cash over				$5.00		
3/17	Daily summary	$410.00	$225.00	$175.00			$345.00
	Cash short					$15.00	

TABLE 9-4 Cash Disbursement, Purchases, and Expense Journal

Date	Payee and/or Account	Check Number	Amount of Check (CR)	Merchandise Purchased (DR)	Gross Salaries (DR)	Payroll Deductions Income Tax (CR)	Payroll Deductions Social Security (CR)	Misc. Income and Expenses Income (CR)	Misc. Income and Expenses Expenses (DR)
3/15	Acme Office Supplies	511	$ 75.00	$ 75.00					
3/15	Jackson Properties (rent)	512	$ 425.00						$425.00
3/16	Judson Materials, Inc.	513	$ 175.00	$175.00					
3/16	Anderson Materials Company	514	$ 100.00	$100.00					
3/17	Complete Furniture Rental	515	$ 90.00						$ 90.00
3/17	Payroll	516	$1,100.00		$814.00	$220.00	$66.00		

Note that the debits and credits balance; if they do not, an error exists, and the bookkeeper needs to check the figures to find it. Using this journal and the Sales and Cash Receipts Journal, revenues, expenses, and changes in balance sheet accounts can be determined and financial statements can be drawn up.

MANAGING THE BOOKS

A number of options for maintaining the books are available to the new venture owner/manager.[6] One option is to turn the job over to an accountant who will come in once a month and take care of everything. However, because this is often expensive, it is the least popular method.

Another option is to have a full- or part-time employee keep the books. For example, many businesses hire a retired person or have one of their employees learn how to keep the books. Still others use a freelance bookkeeper who also keeps books for a number of other firms. Working on a contract basis, the person spends a few hours each week maintaining each company's books. This arrangement is often no more expensive than hiring a part-time employee bookkeeper.

Finally, the owner/manager can maintain the books personally. The advantage of this approach is that the individual constantly is aware of his or her firm's financial situation. On the negative side, this takes time away from other management duties. As a result, most new ventures use part-time or freelance bookkeepers.

COMPUTERS, SOFTWARE, AND FINANCIAL PREPARATION

In recent years, a variety of computer programs have been developed to handle such needs as bookkeeping, billing, and financial control.[7] Prices vary for the software, but most programs start around $150.00. Most modern software programs require a reasonably new computer with adequate memory storage and speed.

Many new ventures find that they cannot afford the luxury of a major accounting firm—a bookkeeper is all they need. Their accountant periodically reviews the books and brings them up to date. At the end of the year, the accountant closes the books, prepares the income tax forms, and gets everything in order for the owner to send to the IRS. However, more and more entrepreneurs are finding that computerized software packages are a good investment. The level of technology and functionality has increased tremendously, along with ease of use.[8]

NEW VENTURE PERSPECTIVE

Financial Software for Your Business?

When a person decides to go into business, he or she is faced with a large group of possibilities when it comes to financial management. An entrepreneur could spend anywhere from hundreds to thousands and even tens of thousands of dollars on accounting and business management software. Some of the popular options include Microsoft Small Business Financials, Microsoft Office Professional Accounting, QuickBooks, and Peachtree. The key aspects of each software package are as follows.

The primary concern of many start-ups is cash flow; the expenses related to financial software can be a little deceiving because of licensing agreements and rights of purchasing businesses. Microsoft Office Professional Accounting 2007 retails for around $175, the lowest of the software bundles. Trailing extremely close is Peachtree at around $180. Third is QuickBooks, which costs close to $300. The heavyweight in this category is Microsoft Small Business Financials, which costs almost $1,000; however, the license includes accessibility by two users, whereas the other three are limited to one user per license.

The setup is relatively the same for both QuickBooks and Peachtree: there are several (approximately 15–20) preset charts of accounts from which to choose, with variations based on organization size and industry. The Microsoft packages have a smaller number of presets. All of the packages include the ability to alter charts of accounts after the initial setup.

Another key to the setup process is the setup interview. Peachtree and Quick-Books include a well-defined set of questions and instructions with appropriate field masks. The Microsoft setup questionnaire leaves a lot to be desired; it lacks defined questions, includes answer boxes that do not reflect the information needed, and offers poor instruction.

The general accounting entries are similar across all of the packages; all provide double-entry accounting inputs that will not allow the entries to be out of balance. There is a little variation with regard to the ability to customize reports; however, QuickBooks and Peachtree do not have a report limit. Microsoft Office Professional Accountant limits the user to 60 customizable reports.

One key asset for Microsoft Small Business Financials is its interactivity with Internet payment companies. The process of accepting orders from vendors online is an advantage compared to the other two companies.

QuickBooks and Peachtree accounting software packages possess the greatest share of the market because of the amount of time and development invested in their respective market segments. QuickBooks is more refined, whereas Intuit—the producer of QuickBooks—seems to be better at targeting professional accountants via marketing and at providing support when needed. When QuickBooks users encounter problems (other than those that tech support can handle), they can search for a professional in the region who can be of assistance. QuickBooks has truly dominated this feature. Each year, Intuit charges firms approximately $400 to stay listed on their Web site as professional support, which in turn provides the firms with new clientele while providing Intuit professional support in the field. Peachtree has not developed this ability to the extent that Intuit has. Microsoft's accounting software is still fairly new, having only hit the market two years ago. Thus, they have few certified professionals in the field.

Microsoft Office Professional Accounting, QuickBooks, and Peachtree all provide the basic accounting functions. The higher-end Microsoft Small Business Financials (SBF) offers a step up from the basics. SBF includes modules to track inventories, depreciate fixed assets, print shipping and receiving reports, view reports from varying periods, manage customer relationships, and much more. This software serves as Microsoft's middle ground between the lower-end accounting software and Microsoft's Dynamics GP (formerly Great Plains ERP software). Microsoft even offers its customers a deal, in which the amount invested in SBF will be deducted from the cost of upgrading to the ERP software, should the customer decide to do so.

The choice of software package is based on the needs of the venture. With minimum investment, the venture owner can maintain an accurate account of financial information. All of the popular packages reviewed here have proven capacities and acceptable levels of user satisfaction. If the firm can afford it, it may be advisable to purchase the higher-end software by Microsoft that integrates more financial management functions. As the venture grows, this software will be able to handle the increased financial documentation necessary to manage the business.

One other advantage to having the financials prepared in house by the venture owner is that he or she learns to understand the numbers and gains a good understanding of how the business is performing.

EARLY WARNING SIGNS OF FINANCIAL TROUBLE

The importance of financial statements for new ventures cannot be overemphasized. To keep careful track of a new firm's health, the manager must understand the balance sheet, income statement, and cash flow statement, as well as sales journals and purchasing journals. If these statements are understood, managers can learn to recognize the signs of financial problems before those problems ruin the business. The following list illustrates many of the early warning signs of financial trouble that new venture owner/managers need to be aware of:

- Declining profits despite increased sales
- Decreasing gross margin
- Dwindling cash flow
- Shrinking market share
- Receding sales volume
- Increasing interest expenses in relation to sales
- Swelling overhead expenses
- Irregular, inaccurate, or untimely internally prepared financial reports
- Repeated failure to meet overly optimistic sales forecasts
- Continual stretching of accounts receivable
- Growing write-offs of uncollectible receivables
- Increasing payables in relation to revenues
- Credit limits nearing exhaustion
- Increased pressure from creditors to pay
- A continual need to float checks as a result of bank overdraft
- Declining debt-to-worth ratio
- Lack of control over purchasing and personnel
- Slow-turning or out-of-balance inventories

Summary

The new venture owner/manager needs to be familiar with two basic financial statements: the balance sheet and the income statement. The balance sheet reports a business's financial position at a specific time. This statement is divided into two parts: the firm's financial resources and claims against these resources. Resources, which consist of assets, are equal to creditor claims and owners' equity combined. This results in the accounting equation:

$$Assets = Liabilities + Owners' Equity$$

A complete description of the balance sheet was presented, and accounts commonly found in each of the three sections of this financial statement were described. A balance sheet always balances, because any change in assets is offset by an equal change in either liabilities or owners' equity or by an equal and opposite change in assets.

The income statement is a financial statement that shows the changes that have occurred in a firm's position as a result of its operations over a specific period. The five sections of the income statement are sales revenue, cost of goods sold, operating expenses, financial expense, and tax expense.

The two most basic books of record are the Sales and Cash Receipts Journal and the Cash Disbursement, Purchases, and Expense Journal. The first records daily income to the business, and the second records the firm's disbursement of funds.

The new venture owner/manager has a number of options for managing the books. The most common approach is to use an in-house or freelance bookkeeper (in conjunction with an accountant) who periodically balances the books, sees that the books are closed properly at the end of the fiscal year, prepares tax forms, and verifies that everything is in order for the new year. For keeping books, billing, and maintaining financial control, new ventures today need a microcomputer. Before investing in a computer and related peripherals, the owner/manager should compare the various financial management software packages to ensure that the expenditure will be used effectively. (See the "New Venture Perspective" box for more information on software packages.)

Review and Discussion Questions

1. What is a balance sheet?
2. Define the following terms: *assets, liabilities,* and *owners' equity.*
3. Describe the major sections of the balance sheet. What are the major accounts in each section? Be specific.
4. Why does the balance sheet always balance?
5. What is an income statement?
6. Describe in detail the five major sections of the income statement.
7. How does the Sales and Cash Receipts Journal work? What types of information does it contain?
8. How does the Cash Disbursement, Purchases, and Expense Journal work? What types of information does it contain?
9. Explain why the two journals mentioned in questions 7 and 8 are the most basic record books for an owner of a new venture.
10. List the owner/manager's options for managing the company's books. Which option do you favor? Why?
11. When using a microcomputer to handle a business's financial control needs, what software packages are the most beneficial? Use the "New Venture Perspective" story in the chapter to assist your explanation.

Fashion or Financial Savvy?

Sheri Delanor owns a boutique in a fashionable shopping district. She opened the store 12 months ago and has done very well. A primary reason for her success is that she knows fashion. Everything she buys is snapped up by her customers immediately. Two other fashion boutiques are located on her street, and neither of them does as well as Sheri's boutique.

Two weeks ago, Sheri visited with her accountant, Manuel Ortega, who is a certified public accountant (CPA). Talking about the financial side of her enterprise, Sheri told Manuel, "I sell things for more than they cost me, so I know I make a profit. Outside of that, I'm in the dark."

Manuel had prepared the income statement accompanying this case for Sheri. Sheri looked at the statement and asked Manuel what it meant. He explained that the statement showed that she is doing quite well. "I see," Sheri said, "but I think you should tell me more. What are all these things, and what do I need to know about this information? Remember, I'm a fashion expert, not a financial expert."

Your consultation: What do the *Sales Revenue* and *Cost of Goods Sold* sections indicate about Sheri's business? What does the *Operating Expenses* section indicate about the operation? Explain your answers. Overall, how well is Sheri's business doing?

Sheri's Boutique
Income Statement for the Year Ended December 31, 2009

Sales Revenue	$450,000	
Less: Sales returns and allowances	25,000	
Net sales		$425,000
Cost of Goods Sold		
Inventory, January 1, 2009	$ 25,000	
Purchases	200,000	
Goods available for sale	225,000	
Less: Inventory, December 31, 2009	30,000	
Cost of goods sold		195,000
Gross margin		230,000
Operating Expenses		
Selling expenses	$ 20,000	
Administrative expenses	60,000	
Total operating expenses		80,000
Operating income		$150,000
Financial Expense		5,000
Income before income taxes		145,000
Estimated Income Taxes		45,000
Net profit		$100,000

Endnotes

1. Kenneth M. Macur and Lyal Gustafson, "Financial Statements as a Management Tool," *Small Business Forum* (Fall 1992): 23–34. See also Robert Dove, "Financial Statements," *Accountancy* (January 2000): 7.

2. See W. Steve Albrecht, James D. Stice, Earl K. Stice, and Monte Swain, *Accounting: Concepts and Applications,* 10th ed. (Mason, OH: Thomson/Southwestern, 2008).

3. See Jacqueline Emigh, "Balance Sheet," *ComputerWorld* (November 15, 1999): 86.

4. See "Financial Reporting Standard for Smaller Entities," *Accountancy* (January 1998): 81–109; and Carl S. Warren and James M. Reeve, *Financial and Managerial Accounting,* 9th ed. (Mason, OH: Thomson/Southwestern, 2007).

5. See David B. Byrd and Sandra D. Byrd, "Using the Statement of Change in Financial Position," *Journal of Small Business Management* (April 1986): 31–38; and John Capel, "Balancing the Books," *Supply Management* (November 4, 1999): 94.

6. Jennifer Francis, "Have Financial Statements Lost Their Relevance?" *Journal of Accounting Research* (Autumn 1999): 319–53.

7. Fritz G. Grupe, "Financial and Strategic Planning Software," *Small Business Forum* (Winter 1992): 70–80.

8. J. Collins, "Small Business Software Grows Up," *Journal of Accountancy* (March 2006): 50–60.

CHAPTER 10

FINANCIAL ANALYSIS
THE GAUGES

INTRODUCTION

Analysis of financial statements involves the comparison of a business's performance with that of other businesses in the same industry.[1] This assists the new venture owner in identifying deficiencies and taking appropriate actions to improve performance. Financial statement analysis is useful both as a way to anticipate future conditions and, more important, as a starting point for planning actions that will influence the future course of events. The goal of any business is to correct its weaknesses and capitalize on its strengths. Financial statement analysis is a tool for accomplishing that goal from a financial perspective.[2]

The most effective way to examine financial statements is by *ratio analysis*. A ratio expresses a mathematical relationship between one item and another. In financial statement analysis, ratios are computed among various financial items. These ratios are merely indicators; any judgment regarding whether they are good or bad must be based on an understanding of what other firms in the industry are doing and how they are performing.[3] We will examine key ratios derived from the balance sheet and the income statement.

BALANCE SHEET ANALYSIS

In Chapter 9, we examined the component parts of the balance sheet. In this chapter, we undertake an analysis of this financial statement. To do so, it is necessary to compare a company's balance sheets for at least two periods. We will use the EntreX Company's balance sheets for 2008 and 2009; their data are placed side by side in Table 10-1.

TABLE 10-1 EntreX Corporation Balance Sheet for the Years Ending December 31, 2008 and December 31, 2009

Assets	2008		2009	
Current Assets				
Cash		$125,000		$200,000
Accounts receivable	$400,000		$375,000	
Less: Allowance for uncollectible accounts	40,000	360,000	25,000	350,000
Inventory		135,000		150,000
Paid expenses		50,000		35,000
Total current assets		$670,000		$735,000
Fixed Assets				
Land		$315,000		$330,000
Building	$315,000		$315,000	
Less: Accumulated depreciation, building	65,000	250,000	80,000	235,000
Equipment	$420,000		$410,000	
Less: Accumulated depreciation, equipment	30,000	390,000	60,000	350,000
Total fixed assets		955,000		915,000
Total assets		$1,625,000		$1,650,000

Liabilities	2008		2009	
Current Liabilities				
Accounts payable	$245,000		$150,000	
Notes payable	50,000		25,000	
Taxes payable	100,000		75,000	
Loan payable	50,000		50,000	
Total current liabilities		$445,000		$300,000
Long-Term Liabilities				
Bank Loan		250,000		200,000
Total liabilities		$695,000		$500,000
Owners' Equity				
Contributed Capital				
Common stock, $10 par, 40,000 shares	$400,000		$400,000	
Preferred stock, $100 par, 500 shares authorized, none sold	----------		----------	
Retained Earnings	530,000		750,000	
Total owners' equity		930,000		1,150,000
Total liabilities and owners' equity		$1,625,000		$1,650,000

Many comparative methods are used to analyze balance sheets. However, because new venture owner/managers seldom need to use sophisticated techniques, we concentrate on two types of ratios that are useful for analyzing the balance sheet: those reflecting the firm's current position and those reflecting its long-run position.

CURRENT-POSITION RATIOS

A liquidity ratio indicates how easily an asset can be turned into cash (or is already in the form of cash). A business with a high liquidity ratio is referred to as *highly liquid*. However, high or low liquidity is not by itself good or bad. Before judging how good a ratio is, we must look at the industry and see what is considered good for the particular type of business.

The company's current position is most commonly measured by three liquidity ratios:

1. Working capital
2. Current ratio
3. Acid-test ratio

WORKING CAPITAL

A company's working capital actually is not a ratio, but it is a very important measure of current financial position. The calculation of working capital is as follows:

Current Assest − Current Liabilities

For the EntreX Corporation (Table 10-1), here is the calculation:

	2008	2009
Total current assets	$ 670,000	$ 735,000
Total current liabilities	− 445,000	− 300,000
Working capital	**$ 225,000**	**$ 435,000**

The company had $225,000 in working capital last year and $435,000 this year. This calculation shows that the firm has more than adequate capital to pay its short-term obligations. As a result, the business should have no trouble paying its bills as they come due.

Computing working capital is useful especially for determining a firm's short-term financial strength. Obviously, the company must have sufficient working capital to do business on a day-to-day basis. Inadequate working capital is often the first sign of financial difficulty for a firm.[4]

CURRENT RATIO

The *current ratio* is simply the relationship between current assets and current liabilities. It is one of the best-known and most commonly employed financial ratios. For the EntreX Corporation, the ratio is computed as follows:

	2008	2009
Total current assets	$670,000	$735,000
Total current liabilities	$445,000	$300,000
Current ratio	**1.51**	**2.45**

The computation shows a substantial increase in the current ratio from 1.51:1 to 2.45:1. Is this good or bad? No hard and fast rules exist. However, a rule of thumb in recent years is that anything above 1.0:1 is satisfactory. (Note that 2.0:1 or higher is generally considered satisfactory for a manufacturing firm.) For the EntreX Corporation, the ratio has risen above the 2.0:1 level; this ratio is much better than before. Keep in mind, however, that a current ratio can be too high. For example, if comparisons show that most firms in the EntreX Corporation's industry have current ratios in the neighborhood of 2.2:1, then a 5:1 ratio would be excessive.

ACID-TEST RATIO

The acid-test ratio, often referred to as the *quick ratio,* is a measure of the firm's ability to convert its current assets quickly to cash for the purpose of meeting its current liabilities. To calculate the acid-test ratio, it is first necessary to determine which assets are most rapidly convertible to cash. Aside from cash itself, accounts receivable (after allowing for uncollectible accounts) are included, because they usually can be sold quickly to banks and finance companies. Noticeably absent, however, are inventory and prepaid expenses; neither of these is convertible to cash in the short run. The quick ratio for EntreX (Table 10-1) is calculated as follows:

	2008	2009
Current assets (less inventory and prepaid expenses)	$485,000	$550,000
Current liabilities	$445,000	$300,000
Acid-test ratio	**1.09**	**1.83**

The trend from 2008 to 2009 is favorable. In fact, an acid-test ratio of 1.0 is considered satisfactory because it indicates that a company easily can pay all current liabilities within a short period.

LONG-RUN–POSITION RATIOS

Although owner/managers always are interested in their firms' short-run position, it is important to consider long-run stability.[5] Three balance sheet ratios reflect a company's long-run position:

1. Debt/asset ratio
2. Equity/asset ratio
3. Debt/equity ratio

DEBT/ASSET RATIO

The debt/asset ratio expresses the relationship between a company's total debt (liabilities) and total assets. This ratio tells the owner/manager how much of the firm's assets have been financed by debt and provides creditors with an indication of how much protection they have. If the ratio is very high, the firm does not have much equity; most of the company's assets are provided by debt. In such a case, creditors might be wise to refuse the company any more credit. When a firm goes out of business, it usually cannot sell its assets for the dollar amount shown on the balance sheet. As a result, the total amount the creditors and owners receive is less than the amount of their claims on the balance sheet. However, the creditors have first claim to the assets, and sometimes nothing is left for the stockholders. The creditors' question is, "Does the firm have enough equity to prevent our having to settle for less than what is truly owed us?" The lower the debt/equity ratio, the more likely the creditors will get their money back. For the EntreX Corporation, the debt/equity ratio is as follows:

	2008	**2009**
Total liabilities	$ 695,000	$ 500,000
Total assets	$1,625,000	$1,625,000
Debt/asset ratio	**42.8%**	**30.3%**

As shown, the ratio is reduced from 42.8 to 30.3 percent between 2008 and 2009. The creditors of the corporation have a greater degree of protection than before.

EQUITY/ASSET RATIO

The equity/asset ratio is computed by dividing the owners' equity by the total assets. It is the complement of the debt/asset ratio; that is, if the debt/asset ratio were 45 percent, the equity/asset ratio would be 55 percent.

The equity/asset ratio is of particular interest to investors because it indicates the percentage of total assets the owners can claim. A very low equity/asset ratio is an indication that in the event of financial difficulties, the owners may receive little, if any, of their original investment. For example, if an equity/asset ratio is 10 percent, it means that 10 percent of the assets are owners' equity and 90 percent are due to debt. In case of dissolution, creditors would be entitled to so much of the firm's assets that nothing would be left for the owners after the debt is paid. Theoretically, then, the higher the equity/asset ratio, the more advantageous it is for the owners (and for the creditors).

The equity/asset ratio for the EntreX Corporation follows:

	2008	**2009**
Total owners' equity	$ 930,000	$1,150,000
Total assets	$1,615,000	$1,650,000
Equity/asset ratio	**57.2%**	**69.7%**

Before we continue, one point merits attention. It is *not* always advantageous to the firm to have the highest equity/asset ratio. Many times, it is good business for the firm to borrow some money. This is particularly true when the rate of interest is less than the return that the owners can generate with the funds. For example, if it costs 15 percent to borrow money from the bank but the business can make 28 percent on this money, then borrowing is indeed wise. The important notion is not to borrow *too much.* If the business does make 28 percent, it can put some of the profits back into the firm. The natural inclination is to make money on someone else's funds and not tie up one's own funds. However, sooner or later the business may grow large and accumulate so much debt that a slowdown in the economy could drastically affect its ability to meet debt obligations. For this reason, debts must be undertaken prudently. Too little debt may deny the firm a source of funds for increasing profits. Too much debt can be overburdening. By consulting industry statistics, the company can get an idea of a desirable ballpark equity/asset ratio.

Debt/Equity Ratio

This ratio expresses the relationship between liabilities and owners' equity. A very high debt/equity ratio indicates to creditors that they are financing most of the business's operations. It also indicates to the owners their claim in the business is small.

For the EntreX Corporation, the debt/equity ratio is calculated as follows:

	2008	**2009**
Total liabilities	$695,000	$ 500,000
Total owners' equity	$930,000	$1,150,000
Debt/equity ratio	**74.7%**	**43.5%**

This comparison indicates that debt, as a percentage of equity, is declining. The firm's operations are increasingly financed through owners' equity. This, of course, is a direct result of plowing net profits back into retained earnings. In 2009, the net profit was $258,000, as noted in Table 10-2. As shown in the preceding calculation, owners' equity increased by this amount while total liabilities decreased. This trend should be viewed positively by both the owners of EntreX and its creditors.

INCOME STATEMENT ANALYSIS

As with the balance sheet, financial ratios can be used to analyze the income statement. Some ratios use data from the income statement exclusively. Others, known as combination ratios, draw on data from both the balance sheet and the income statement. Both types of ratio analyses are useful for evaluating a new venture's income and profitability performance. To best interpret financial ratios, it is

Table 10-2   EntreX Corporation Income Statement for the Years Ending December 31, 2008 and December 31, 2009

	2008	*2009*
Sales Revenue	$1,565.000	$1,750,000
Less: Sales returns and allowances	65,000	50,000
Net sales	$1,500,000	$1,700,000
Cost of Goods Sold		
Inventory, January 1	$ 135,000	$ 150,000
Purchases	1,000,000	1,050,000
Goods available for sale	$1,135,000	$1,200,000
Less: Inventory Dec. 31	150,000	200,000
Cost of goods sold	985,000	1,000,000
Gross margin	$ 515,000	$ 700,000
Operating Expenses		
Selling expenses	$ 125,000	$ 150,000
Administrative expenses	95,000	100,000
Total operating expenses	220,000	250,000
Operating income	$ 295,000	$ 450,000
Financial Expense	20,000	20,000
Income before income taxes	$ 275,000	$ 430,000
Estimated Income Taxes	125,000	172,000
Net profit	$ 150,000	$ 258,000

helpful to research the industry standards for your type of business. In general, research has shown that there are no significant differences in liquidity ratios between large and small firms.[6] We will use the EntreX Corporation's income statements for 2008 and 2009 in our analysis (see Table 10-2).

INCOME STATEMENT RATIOS

Balance sheet ratios provide indicators of short-run and long-run financial stability. Income statement ratios provide information on current operating performance and efficiency. Two of the most important are the operating-expense ratio and the number of times interest is earned.

OPERATING-EXPENSE RATIO

Operating expenses are expenses that are incurred in the normal day-to-day running of the business. These include selling and administrative expenses but not interest or income tax expenses. The operating-expense ratio is calculated by dividing total operating expenses by net sales.

For 2008 and 2009, the EntreX Corporation operating-expense ratio is calculated as follows:

	2008	**2009**
Total operating expenses	$ 220,000	$ 250,000
Net sales	$1,500,000	$1,700,000
Operating-expense ratio	**14.7%**	**14.7%**

The ratio is the same for both years. Selling and administrative expenses are up almost 14 percent, but so are net sales. This is a good sign; it shows that the firm is keeping operating expenses under control.

NUMBER OF TIMES INTEREST IS EARNED

A second indicator of financial stability is the number of times interest is earned on long-term debt. This appears on the income statement as the financial expense. If a firm barely can meet this expense, it may be in financial trouble. Conversely, a business that can meet this expense easily is probably in sound financial condition. The number-of-times-interest-earned ratio is computed by dividing *operating income* (income before financial expense and income taxes) by annual financial expense.

For the EntreX Corporation, that calculation is as follows:

	2008	**2009**
Operating income	$295,000	$450,000
Annual financial expense	$ 20,000	$ 20,000
Number of times interest is earned	**14.7**	**22.5**

The ratio is very high for both 2008 and 2009. Therefore, firm should have no trouble paying its interest on the bank loan.

If the EntreX Corporation wanted to be more conservative, as some owner/managers do, it could deduct income tax from operating income before dividing by annual financial expense. In this case, the calculations would be as follows:

	2008	**2009**
Operating income	$170,000	$278,000
Annual financial expense	$ 20,000	$ 20,000
Number of times interest is earned	**8.5**	**13.9**

The number of times interest is earned is now lower, but it is still more than adequate. What really counts, however, is the trend from year to year. In the preceding calculations, the trend is upward. As long as the ratio does not drop drastically, EntreX should be able to more than meet its interest payments.

COMBINATION RATIOS

As previously mentioned, some ratios show the relationship between items on the income statement and the balance sheet. Four of the most common are:

1. Inventory turnover
2. Accounts-receivable turnover
3. Rate of return on total assets
4. Rate of return on equity

INVENTORY TURNOVER

Inventory turnover is the average number of times that inventory is replaced during the year. A low inventory turnover indicates that goods are not selling very well; they are remaining on the shelf in the warehouse for extended periods. If already paid for, inventory represents tied-up money that is not providing any return to the business. If inventory was obtained on consignment, the firm can send back whatever it does not sell, but it must pay the storage bill as long as the goods are on hand. Of course, a very high turnover may not be good, for it can indicate that the firm continually is running out of items and having to turn customers away. As a result, most companies want a turnover that is neither too low nor too high.

To compute turnover, cost of goods sold is divided by the average inventory. Ideally, average inventory is computed by adding the beginning inventory for each month, from January of one year through January of the following year, and dividing by 13. This assures that no bias occurs as a result of the traditionally lower inventory figures at the end of the calendar year. However, it is much easier to take the beginning inventory for the year, add it to the ending inventory, and divide by two. This provides an average that is satisfactory for most purposes. In addition, once the turnover is determined, it is possible to calculate the average number of days to turn over, thereby providing the manager with a detailed view of the inventory picture.

For the EntreX Corporation, the place to start is with a computation of the average inventory for both 2008 and 2009 (see Table 10-2). The calculations are as follows:

$$\text{Average inventory} = \frac{\text{Beginning inventory} + \text{Ending inventory}}{2}$$

$$\text{For 2008:} \quad \frac{\$135,000 + \$150,000}{2} = \$142,500$$

$$\text{For 2009:} \quad \frac{\$150,000 + \$200,000}{2} = \$175,000$$

Next, the number of times the inventory turned over is calculated using these values. Finally, the average number of days to turn over is obtained by dividing the number of days in a year by inventory turnover. These calculations are as follows:

	2008	2009
Cost of goods sold	$985,000	$1,000,000
Average inventory	$142,000	$ 175,000
Inventory turnover	**6.91**	**5.71**
Days in a year	365	365
Inventory turnover	6.91	5.71
Average number of days to turnover	**53 days**	**64 days**

These calculations indicate an unfavorable trend. In 2008, EntreX's inventory turnover was 6.91, whereas in 2009, it dropped to 5.71. Additionally, in 2008 it took 53 days to turn over the inventory, and in 2009 it took 64 days. The time needed to turn over the inventory is lengthening.

What accounts for this increase? The calculations do not, in and of themselves, provide the answer. Perhaps, in order to increase its sales, the firm has been forced to carry more slow-moving items. That would increase inventory and result in a lower turnover. In such an instance, the decrease in turnover would not be a very negative factor. However, if the firm simply has been buying more goods in anticipation of higher sales, it now should reduce purchases and maintain lower inventories.

ACCOUNTS-RECEIVABLE TURNOVER

The analysis of accounts receivable is similar to that of inventory turnover—it is a measure of how rapidly accounts receivable are collected. In general terms, the higher this turnover, the better. A low turnover usually is regarded as unfavorable for two reasons: The interest expense in maintaining receivables is increasing, and an abnormally high number of these receivables may become uncollectible.

The accounts-receivable turnover is computed by dividing net sales by average accounts receivable. Since we have no data for the EntreX Corporation for 2007, we will use the accounts receivable for 2008 (from Table 10-1) and assume that the beginning and ending receivables were the same. This gives us an average of $360,000. Meanwhile, for 2009 (also from Table 10-1), the average receivables are figured as follows:

$$\frac{\$360,000 + \$350,000}{2} = \$355,000$$

The remaining calculations are as follows:

	2008	2009
Net sales	$1,500,000	$1,700,000
Average accounts receivable	$ 360,000	$ 355,000
Accounts receivable turnover	**4.2**	**4.8**

Days in a year	365 days	365 days
Accounts receivable turnover	4.2	4.8
Average age of accounts receivable	**86.9 days**	**76.0 days**

Overall, the trend for the EntreX Corporation is favorable. Turnover has risen from 4.2 to 4.8 times, and the average number of days from sale to collection has declined from 86.9 to 76 days.

Many times, as a company's sales increase, its accounts receivable also increase but the turnover of the receivables declines. This often is occasioned by a lenient credit policy that allows poor-risk customers to buy on credit. Such customers tend to purchase up to their credit limit and then fall behind in their payments. As a result, although sales are up, so are receivables, and the chance of collecting on all of these accounts is very small. More and more must be written off as uncollectible. At EntreX Corporation, this has not happened.

RATE OF RETURN ON TOTAL ASSETS

In addition to knowing the net income of the company, the owner/manager needs to know the rate of return that the business is earning on its assets. The greater the amount of assets, the more income the firm should earn. In short, by comparing operating income and average assets, owner/managers can determine how well the firm has performed with its available resources. This ratio is known as the *rate of return on total assets* and is computed by dividing operating income by average assets.

Using Table 10-1, we can determine EntreX's average assets for 2009 as follows:

$$\frac{(\$1,625,000 + \$1,650,000)}{2} = \$1,637,500$$

We do not know the company's average assets for 2008 because we do not have 2007 figures. However, assume that the assets between 2007 and 2008 remained the same, giving an average of $1,625,000. The rate of return on total assets can be computed as follows:

	2008	**2009**
Operating income	$ 295,000	$ 450,000
Average assets	$1,625,000	$1,650,000
Rate of return on total assets	**18.2%**	**27.3%**

This return is very good: 18.2 percent is far higher than what could have been obtained if the money had been invested in a bank note or simply left in a savings account. It is also a higher return than the 10 percent the firm currently is paying on its bank loan. In short, the company is making a fine return. In 2009, this return was 50 percent higher than in 2008, which indicates even better performance.

RATE OF RETURN ON EQUITY

Although the rate of return on total assets discloses how well management is performing with the resources available, the new venture owner also is interested in how this translates in terms of his or her own investment. This can be determined by a simple calculation of the rate of return on (common stockholders) equity, in which the net income is divided by the owners' equity.

This computation for the EntreX Corporation is as follows:

	2008	**2009**
Net income	$150,000	$258,000
Common stockholders' equity	$400,000	$400,000
Rate of return on equity	**37%**	**64.5%**

EntreX's rate of return on equity is extremely high. The owners earned a return of 37.5 percent in 2008 and 64.5 percent in 2009. Of course, it is important to analyze why EntreX has performed so remarkably. If everyone else in the industry did as well, the conclusion would have to be tempered accordingly. If everyone else did poorly, the owner/manager would want to investigate what makes EntreX so successful. In either event, an industry comparison would be very helpful.

NEW VENTURE PERSPECTIVE

The Z-Score

Edward I. Altman, author and professor at New York University, was the first to suggest using statistics as indicators for business failure. Almost 30 years ago, Altman developed Z-score analysis as a technique to help determine the likelihood of a company going bankrupt. The tool was devised and refined after studying 66 companies: 33 control firms and 33 experiment firms. The test can be used internally to assess financial health and externally by investors to judge the stability of on investment.

Plugging numbers from the financial statements into the five formulas and then multiplying by the predetermined weight factor will result in a ratio. When the five ratios are added, a number between −4 and +8 will indicate the company's *fiscal fitness.*

Ratio	Formula	Weight Factor	Weighted Ratio
Return on total assets	Earnings before interest and taxes/total assets	×	3.3
Sales to total assets	Net sales/total assets	×	0.999
Equity to debt	Market value of equity/total liabilities	×	0.6

Ratio	Formula	Weight Factor	Weighted Ratio
Working capital to total assets	Working capital/total assets	×	1.2
Retained earnings to total assets	Retained earnings/total assets	×	1.4
		Z-Score:	

Z-Score above 2.99: You're in good shape

Z-Score between 2.99 and 1.81: Warning sign

Z-Score below 1.81: You could be heading toward bankruptcy

Source: Adapted from "Check Your Z-Score: How's your Fiscal Fitness?" www.inc.com, 2000.

LIMITATIONS OF FINANCIAL STATEMENT ANALYSIS

Until now, we have been concerned with the various ways to analyze financial statements. However, we need to moderate our remarks with some comments on the limitations of financial statement analysis for comparing companies.[7] Accounting experts have stated such limitations as follows:

1. Companies may have differing year-ends, which could result in a different composition of assets, particularly current assets. For example, one company may choose to operate on a fiscal year that comes at a low point in its production. This causes its inventory to be at an exceptionally low level, whereas its cash, marketable securities, and accounts receivable are unusually high. Another company, selecting a point for its fiscal year when accounts receivable are low, finds its inventory and cash positions at a high point. Of course, these problems—although they complicate comparisons among companies—are of no importance when the ratios for a company are compared against themselves over a certain period; the firm will always be at either a low inventory level or a low receivable level at a particular time of year.

2. Companies may have acquired their property, plant, and equipment in differing years. Because the accountant follows a stable dollar approach to financial reporting, periods of inflation between the times that two companies acquire assets may result in vast dollar differences between the amounts shown for two assets that serve the same purpose. Again, comparisons of one company's results over time are affected only mildly by this condition.

3. Companies may account for the same items using alternative accounting methods.

4. Finally, industry patterns cause significant differences among companies in terms of the amount and the relationship of a particular item to the total. For example, a company that takes more than a year to manufacture a particular machine,

such as a printing press, tends to have a large inventory balance when compared to a company that is merely selling purchased items, such as a grocery store selling produce.

These limitations illustrate that, whereas the owner/manager can compare his or her own firm's financial statements from one year to the next to determine improvements or problems, care must be exercised when making comparisons with other firms. It is necessary to ensure that the firms chosen for comparison are indeed similar; that is, they should sell the same types of goods and services, be about the same financial size, and operate under similar economic conditions.[8]

FINANCIAL BUDGETING

Budgets are plans as well as control tools. As plans, they pinpoint objectives that the new venture wants to attain in areas such as sales, product line growth, number of personnel, expenses, and so forth. In each case the owner/manager sets a target, such as sales of $230,000, 11 percent growth of product line A, or increasing the number of personnel by two employees. The individual then can incorporate these objectives into the financial budgeting process by asking what the firm must do to attain them. One answer might be that it must increase sales by 25 percent. If the business can do that, the other objectives will be attained in the process.

However, without covering a long list of the objectives that a new venture might have, let us look at the two most valuable types of financial budgeting: sales budgets and cash budgets. Then we will examine other budgetary considerations.

SALES BUDGET

The sales budget is the primary budget for the new venture; once it is worked out, all of the other budgets flow from it. For example, if the owner/manager believes that sales for the following year will equal $400,000, the business will want to stock inventory, hire personnel, and put together a marketing strategy based on this objective. Of course, the owner/manager needs more information than just the total sales figure. It is necessary to break down the dollar amount by month or quarter so that all of the other budgets can be tied to a particular time of year. For example, if half of the sales are expected during the first three months of the year, half of the production should be finished and ready for shipping during (or soon after) that period. Likewise, greater cash and personnel demands on the business will occur during that quarter of the year than any other.

By linking the other budgets to sales, the owner/manager can adjust expenditures up or down depending on the status of operations. If sales are greater than expected, production can be raised and the number of personnel can be increased. Conversely, if sales are slower, production can be halted temporarily and some employees can be released.

How closely everything should be tied to sales depends on the size of the business. If the organization has sufficient capital to ride out a sluggish six months, the owner/manager need not be as concerned as he or she would need to be if the firm were living hand to mouth. Depending on how closely operations must be monitored, the firm can control them on a weekly or biweekly basis or let them go as long as three to six months.

CASH BUDGET

Cash budgeting is vital to new venture survival.[9] At the heart of the cash budgeting process is *cash planning*. Cash planning requirements for a new venture are of two types: the daily and weekly cash needs for the normal operation of the business, and the maintenance expenses of the organization during this period. The first type relates to cash on hand for day-to-day operations. Usually, the business estimates its needs for a 30- to 60-day period and then determines how much money it is likely to collect during this time. If a cash shortage is anticipated after comparing the inflows and outflows, a line of credit or a short-term loan can be arranged.

The maintenance part of this budget takes into account expenses such as insurance, rent, payroll, purchases, services, and taxes. This long-run view of operations provides the firm the opportunity to balance its annual cash needs. Figure 10-1 provides a sample cash budget form that can be used to accomplish both the operational and maintenance objectives.

The first four lines in Figure 10-1 help determine the amount of cash that will be collected over the next three months. The *collection on accounts receivable* (line 2) is especially important and warrants discussion. Remember that many new ventures sell on credit; although these obligations may be due within 30 days, some people wait 60 to 90 days—and others never pay. How much will be collected each month? To answer this question, the owner/manager needs to examine past collections. For the sake of discussion, however, assume that the business's records show that half of all sales are made for cash and the other half are paid within 90 days. Of this latter amount, 70 percent are collected the first month, 20 percent the second, 8 percent the third, and the remaining 2 percent are written off as uncollectible. Additionally, assume sales were $8,000 in October, $10,000 in November, and $16,000 in December, so 50 percent of these sales will be estimated as cash sales for January through March. Using these data, the owner/manager can determine both cash and accounts-receivable collections. Table 10-3 shows these calculations.

Lines 5 through 12 in Figure 10-1 take into account items for which the firm pays cash. Some of these outflows, such as administrative expense and repayment of the loan, will remain basically the same; others will rise or fall depending on the activity level. For example, as production goes up, payroll and raw materials expenses will go up; the reverse is also true.

Lines 14 through 19 of Figure 10-1 involve balancing the cash account, along with a determination of any short-term loans that will be needed and the amount

FIGURE 10-1   Cash Budget Form

CASH BUDGET
(for three months ending March 31, 2009)

	January		February		March	
	Budget	*Actual*	*Budget*	*Actual*	*Budget*	*Actual*
EXPECTED CASH RECEIPTS						
1. Cash sales						
2. Collection on accounts receivable						
3. Other income						
4. Total cash receipts						
EXPECTED CASH PAYMENTS						
5. Raw materials						
6. Payroll						
7. Other factory expenses (including maintenance)						
8. Advertising						
9. Selling expense						
10. Administration expense (including salary of owner/ management)						
11. New plant and equipment						
12. Other payments (taxes, including estimated income tax; repayment of loans; interest, etc.)						
13. Total cash payments						
14. Expected cash balance at beginning of the month						
15. Cash increase or decrease (item 4 minus item 13)						
16. Expected cash balance at end of month (item 14 plus item 15)						
17. Desired working cash balance						
18. Short-term loans needed (item 17 minus item16, if item 17 is larger than item 16)						
19. Cash available for dividends, capital cash expenditures, and/or short-term investments (item 16 minus item 17, if item 16 is larger than item 17)						
CAPITAL CASH						
20. Cash available (item 19 after deducting dividends, etc.)						
21. Desired capital cash (item 11, new plant and equipment)						
22. Long-term loans needed (item 21 less item 20, if item 21 is larger than item 20)						

Source: J. H. Feller, Jr., *Is Your Cash Supply Adequate?* Small Business Administration, Management Aids, No. 174 (Washington, DC: U.S. Government Printing Office, 1990).

TABLE 10-3 Cash and Accounts-Receivable Collection Calculations					
Month	*Cash Sales*	*70% of Receivables 30 Days Old +*	*20% of Receivables 60 Days Old +*	*8% of Receivables 90 Days Old =*	*Total Collected on Accounts Receivable*
January	$4,000	$5,600	$1,000	$320	$6,920
February	$5,000	2,600	1,600	400	$4,800
March	$6,000	2,800	800	640	$4,940

Note: The accounts-receivable collection constitutes a flow of cash into the firm. By tracking its flow on a monthly basis, the owner can determine the amount of cash the business will have for operations.

of cash, if any, that will be available for dividends and short-term investments. Lines 21 and 22 help the firm compare desired cash with actual cash to see how much is available for capital investment.

OTHER BUDGETARY CONSIDERATIONS

Sales and cash budgets are not the only ones that a new venture needs to control its operations. Others are spin-offs of items on the cash budget form (Figure 10-1), including payroll, advertising, selling expense, and new plant and equipment budgets.[10] Depending on the size of the firm, these budgetary categories will be handled through the cash budget or broken out and given special consideration. For example, a manufacturing operation may have a manufacturing and purchasing budget, whereas a sales business may have a selling expense budget. However, because the new venture will not want to overburden itself with budgets, it should have as few as possible.

As a result, the astute owner/manager uses the exception principle of control to handle budgetary problems. This principle holds that the owner/manager should be concerned with results that are extremely good or extremely bad, not with operations that go as expected. If sales for January are forecasted at $8,000 and instead total $8,200, the firm has little need for concern. However, if sales total $15,000, the owner/manager should be concerned about filling the orders (if it is a manufacturing firm) or purchasing more materials or products (if it is a retail or wholesale operation). Likewise, sales of only $4,000 would be a sufficient deviation to warrant making changes in the next month's budget by curtailing purchases, laying off some people, or taking other actions.

The most important fact to remember is that budgetary controls must be kept in proper perspective—they are tools that help the business set goals and evaluate performance. If problems occur, budgets should help the owner/manager pinpoint where and why they arose. For this reason, every budget should possess two characteristics: economy and timeliness. If the budget is too cumbersome or detailed, it may take $1 of effort to pinpoint a 50-cent problem. The budget must be worth its cost. In addition, the budget should be timely; it should allow the owner/manager to collect, analyze, and interpret information in time to take required action. If the company runs on a fixed three-month budget but is subject to widely varying sales fluctuations, it may be out of cash before the budget period is over. In this case, the firm needs to budget for shorter periods—that is, a month at a time. Finally, remember that, in most cases, the owner/manager can rely on one or two budgets, such as the sales and cash budgets, and can assume that if these are in line, everything else is okay. Generally, the owner/manager will be right.

Summary

One of the most effective control techniques for new ventures is financial analysis. The balance sheet provides the owner/manager with the opportunity to examine the current state of the firm's assets and liabilities as well as the owners' equity. Some of the most useful ratios in this examination are working capital, current ratio, acid-test ratio, debt/asset ratio, equity/asset ratio, and debt/equity ratio.

The income statement also can be examined using ratio analysis. Two of the most common metrics are the operating-expense ratio and the number-of-times-interest-earned ratio.

Some useful combination ratios draw on data from both the balance sheet and the income statement. Four of the most common ratios are inventory turnover, accounts-receivable turnover, rate of return on total assets, and rate of return on equity.

The budget is another useful financial analysis tool. New ventures must be careful not to have too many budgets, because the paperwork is time consuming. By relying on a couple—such as the sales budget and cash budget—the new venture can maintain effective budgetary control. To handle budgetary problems, the astute owner/manager uses the exception principle of control. In this way, he or she concentrates on major developments and not on minor problems.

Review and Discussion Questions

1. How does a business compute its working capital? Provide an example.
2. What does the current ratio tell the owner/manager? What is a *good* current ratio?
3. Explain how the acid-test ratio differs from the current ratio.
4. Why would the owner/manager be interested in the debt/asset ratio? In the equity/asset ratio? Be sure to explain in your answer what each ratio tells the owner/manager.
5. Which ratio is of greater interest to the owner/manager: the operating expense or the number of times interest is earned? Support your answer.

6. How is inventory turnover computed? What does it tell the owner/manager?
7. How is accounts-receivable turnover computed? What does this calculation tell the owner/manager?
8. Which ratio is of greater interest to the owner/manager: the rate of return on total assets or the rate of return on equity? Support your answer.
9. List and explain three of the limitations of financial analysis.
10. How does a sales budget work?
11. How does the cash budget help the owner/manager control operations? Include a description of this budget in your answer.
12. Explain the value of the exception principle of control to the owner/manager.

NEW VENTURE CONSULTANT

A Case of Liquidity

The Compton Company's accountant put together the comparative balance sheet for 2008 and 2009 and gave it to Ed Compton, the company president. (See the balance sheet that accompanies this case study.)

After looking at the statement for a few minutes, Ed told the accountant that he was very pleased with the company's performance during the past two years. The accountant agreed with his analysis, and they began talking about various balance sheet items. As they were engaged in their conversation, Rose Compton entered Ed's office. She has been working for the company for almost six months, and Ed is familiarizing her with the business.

Ed introduced Rose to the accountant and told the accountant he had been explaining the balance sheet format to Rose just a few weeks earlier. "However, now that we have a comparative balance sheet, we can calculate a few financial ratios and really see if our performance has improved this year."

Ed could see that Rose did not understand this particular remark. He then turned to the accountant and said, "Why don't you and Rose have a cup of coffee, and maybe you can explain some financial ratios to her. I really think she should learn something about financial analysis, and who could teach her better than an accountant?"

The accountant agreed, adding that he had to be back to his office in an hour. "That's okay," Ed said. "Just give her a brief introduction to liquidity, and show her a couple of liquidity ratios." The accountant promised to do so.

Your consultation: What is meant by the term *liquidity?* Explain. What types of ratios should the accountant compute when analyzing the corporation's liquidity? List them, and calculate these ratios. What do they tell you about the firm? Be specific in your evaluation.

Compton Company Balance Sheet for the Years Ending December 31, 2008 and December 31, 2009

Assets	2008		2009	
Current Assets				
Cash		$30,000		$40,000
Accounts receivable	$100,000		$140,000	
Less: Allowance for uncollectible accounts	5,000	95,000	7,000	133,000
Inventory		50,000		40,000
Prepaid expenses		2,000		2,000
Total current assets		$177,000		$215,000
Fixed Assets				
Land		$40,000		$40,000
Building	$100,000		$100,000	
Less: Accumulated depreciation, building	25,000	75,000	30,000	70,000
Equipment	70,000		70,000	
Less: Accumulated depreciation, equipment	30,000	40,000	40,000	30,000
Total fixed assets		$155,000		$140,000
Total assets		$332,000		$355,000

Liabilities	2008	2009
Current Liabilities		
Accounts payable	$33,000	$16,000
Notes payable	10,000	—
Taxes payable	4,000	5,500
Loan payable	10,000	10,000
Total current liabilities	$57,000	$31,500
Long-Term Liabilities		
Bank loan	100,000	90,000
Total Liabilities	$157,000	$121,000

Owners' Equity		
Contributed Capital		
Common stock, $2 par, 25,000 shares	$50,000	$50,000
Preferred stock, $100 par, 1,000 shares authorized, none sold	—	—
Retained Earnings	125,000	183,500
Total owners' equity	175,000	233,500
Total liabilities and owners' equity	$332,000	$355,000

Endnotes

1. Clyde Stickney, Paul Brown, and James M. Whalen, *Financial Reporting, Financial Statement Analysis, and Valuation: A Strategic Perspective,* 6th ed. (Mason, OH: Thomson/South-Western, 2007).

2. Christine Post-Duncan, "The Manager's Guide to Financial Statement Analysis," *The National Public Accountant* (November 1999): 30.

3. See Jerome Osteryoung, Richard L. Constand, and Donald Nast, "Financial Ratios in Large Public and Small Private Firms," *Journal of Small Business Management* (July 1992): 35–46.

4. See Jerome Osteryoung, Richard L. Constand, and Donald Nast, "Financial Ratios in Large Public and Small Private Firms," *Journal of Small Business Management* (July 1992): 35–46; and Patricia Lee Huff, "Are There Differences in Liquidity and Solvency Measures Based on Company Size?" *American Business Review* (June 1999): 96–107. See also Ram Mudambi and Monica Zimmerman Treichel, "Cash Crisis in Newly Public Internet-Based Firms: An Empirical Analysis," *Journal of Business Venturing* 20 (July 2005): 543–71.

5. See Robert Hitchings, "Ratio Analysis as a Tool in Credit Assessment," *Commercial Lending Review* (Summer 1999): 45–49.

6. Jerome Osteryoung, Richard L. Constand, and Donald Nast, "Financial Ratios in Large Public and Small Private Firms," *Journal of Small Business Management* (July 1992): 35–46.

7. For example, see Eugene E. Comiskey, "Analyzing Small Company Financial Statements: Some Guidance for Lenders," *Commercial Lending Review* (Summer 1998): 30–43.

8. For an interesting discussion, see Patricia Lee Huff, "Should You Consider Company Size When Making Ratio Comparisons?" *National Public Accountant* (February/March 2000): 8–12.

9. See Krishna G. Palepu and Paul M. Healy, *Business Analysis and Valuation: Using Financial Statements, Text, and Cases*, 4th ed. (Mason, OH: Thomson/South-Western, 2008).

10. See, for example, Christine Post-Duncan, "The Manager's Guide to Financial Statement Analysis," *National Public Accountant* (November 1999): 30; and Robert Dove, "Financial Statements," *Accountancy* (January 2000): 78.

CHAPTER

HUMAN RESOURCES
THE PEOPLE

INTRODUCTION

Diversity, globalization, deregulation, and technology are changing the nature of jobs and work. For instance, a pronounced shift from manufacturing jobs to service jobs has occurred in both North America and Western Europe. Today, more than two-thirds of the U.S. workforce is employed in producing and delivering services, not products. In fact, of the 21 million new jobs added to the U.S. economy since the late 1990s, virtually all have been in the services industry. These service jobs, in turn, required new types of *knowledge* workers, new human resource (HR) management methods to manage them, and a new focus on human resources.[1]

THE CHALLENGE OF MANAGING HUMAN RESOURCES

Approximately 99.7 percent of all businesses in the United States have fewer than 500 employees, and less than 80 percent have fewer than 10 employees.[2] Smaller firms pay more than 45 percent of the U.S. payroll and generate up to 80 percent of jobs annually. Smaller firms also employ 41 percent of high-tech workers. However, most of the research and literature in human resource management has tended to focus on larger, more established companies. Most human resource management books assume that a firm has at least one human resource professional in place with the expertise and competence to understand and carry out the practices described in their publications. Although most new firms and smaller ventures aim to grow into larger firms, focus is needed to provide guidance on effectively dealing with human resource issues as these businesses face the challenges presented by larger employee groups. In support of this argument, a study of young entrepreneurs found that HR topics ranked highest among areas that required learning.[3] Another research study of 323 smaller firms showed that superior human resource decisions based on a family-like work environment lead to better organizational performance.[4]

These rapid changes in the work environment have major implications for human resource management, including a need for more awareness and appreciation of differing cultural backgrounds in recruitment, selection, and promotion. The low supply of skilled and experienced labor also can have a direct effect on small-business survival. Small-business owners must rise to this challenge. Employees in smaller firms are sometimes the difference between success and failure. Responsibilities for smaller businesses are just as great as they are for larger firms, but duties are not delegated as easily. Table 11-1 illustrates the positions and responsibilities for human resource management in smaller firms versus larger corporations.

INCREASING REGULATORY CONCERNS

Governmental regulations targeted toward the workplace are clearly focused on human resources. Generally, these regulations apply to all categories of employees—including supervisors, professionals, and executives—who work for employers that have 15 or more employees. However, similar state laws and regulations may affect even smaller organizations. Table 11-2 describes the various key laws that affect human resource management.

As shown in the table, numerous regulations affect business owners; although it is not our intent to cover the specific details of these regulations, three acts and a Supreme Court decision have profound effects on small firms and therefore warrant particular attention.[5] First is the 1964 Civil Rights Act (CRA). This is one of the major laws that regulates employers on the selection of employees. Title VII of the 1964 CRA prohibits employers, unions, and employment agencies that have 15 or more employees or members from discriminating with regard to any employment decision (e.g., selection, compensation, firing, and other benefits of employment) against an employee on the basis of gender, race, color, religion, or national origin. In addition, this act created the Equal Employment Opportunity Commission (EEOC). The EEOC was given the power to investigate and challenge any person or company allegedly participating in unlawful employment procedures identified in Title VII. The EEOC was originally established to investigate discrimination based on race, color, religion, gender, or national origin. Now, however, they also investigate charges of pay, age, and handicap discrimination.

The Americans with Disabilities Act (ADA) was passed on July 26, 1990, and covers all employers that have 15 or more employees. The general premise of the ADA is that employers may not discriminate against a qualified person with regard to hiring, advancement, discharging, compensation, training, and other terms, conditions, and privileges of employment because of a disability. A qualified individual

TABLE 11-1   Responsibilities for Human Resource Management in a Small Company Versus a Large Corporation

Small Company		Large Corporation	
Position	*Responsibilities*	*Position*	*Responsibilities*
Human Resources Director	Grievances Human resource planning Labor relations Managerial/ professional compensation	Vice President, Human Resources	Executive committee Human resource planning Organization planning Policy development
Assistant Human Resources Director	Recruiting Interviewing Orientation Reassignments Recruiting Safety and health Special programs Terminations Training Wage and salary administration	Director, Recruitment and Employment Director Compensation and Benefits	Interviewing Placement Recruiting Terminations Testing Bonus, profit-sharing plans Compensation administration Employee benefits Job analyses and evaluation Performance appraisal Surveys
Personnel Assistant	Employee benefits Employee services Interviewing Job descriptions Job evaluation Suggestion plan Testing Training	Director, Labor Relations	Arbitration Cafeteria Contract administration Grievance procedure Health and safety Medical plans Negotiations
Administrative Assistant	Interviewing Records Secretary to staff Word processing	Director, Training and Development Director, Employee Relations	Career planning and development Exit interviews Management development Orientation Quality circles Training Contract compliance Employee counseling Equal Employment Opportunity (EEO) relations Outplacement Staff assistance program

Source: Wendell L. French, *Human Resources Management,* 6th ed. (Boston: Houghton Mifflin, 2007), 15. Copyright © 2007 by Houghton Mifflin Co. Adapted with permission.

TABLE 11-2 Major Governmental Laws That Affect Human Resource Management

Equal Pay Act, 1963

Prohibits discrimination on the basis of sex in wage payments for jobs that require equal skill, effort, and responsibilities under similar working conditions in the same establishment.

Civil Rights Act, 1964

Title VII prohibits employment or membership discrimination by employers, employment agencies, and unions based on race, color, religion, sex, or national origin; the act created the Equal Employment Opportunity Commission (EEOC).

Age Discrimination in Employment Act (ADEA), 1967

Prohibits discrimination against persons aged 40–65 in such matters as hiring, job retention, compensation, and other terms, conditions, and privileges of employment.

Occupational Safety and Health Act (OSHA), 1970

Authorizes the secretary of labor to establish mandatory safety and health standards

Equal Employment Opportunity Act, 1972

Amendments to the Civil Rights Act permit the EEOC to bring enforcement actions in the federal courts.

Vocational Rehabilitation Act, 1973

Requires federal contractors to take affirmative action to employ and promote qualified persons with disabilities.

Employee Retirement Income Security Act (ERISA), 1974

Prescribes eligibility rules, vesting standards, and an insurance program for private pension plans.

Vietnam Era Veterans' Readjustment Assistance Act, 1974

Protects the employment rights of all disabled veterans and sets forth obligations of employers to military reservists and National Guard members called to activity duty.

Amendments to Age Discrimination in Employment Act, 1978

Extend protection until age 70 for most workers and without an upper limit for federal employment.

Pregnancy Discrimination Act, 1978

Requires employers to give pregnant workers the same group health insurance or disability benefits given to other workers, and makes it illegal to fire or refuse to employ a woman because of pregnancy.

Immigration Reform and Control Act, 1986

Makes it illegal for employers to hire illegal immigrants; requires proof of legal authorization to work from all employees hired after November 6, 1986; imposes record-keeping requirements on employers; and provides stiff fines for hiring undocumented workers and for paperwork violations.

Amendments to Age Discrimination in Employment Act, 1986

Bars most mandatory retirement programs.

Employee Polygraph Protection Act, 1988

Bars most private employers from using polygraph tests when screening applicants and from testing current employees unless they have a reasonable suspicion of theft.

TABLE 11-2　(Continued)

Drug-Free Workplace Act, 1988

Requires employers with federal contracts to establish policies and procedures to create and make a good-faith effort to maintain a drug-free workplace.

Older Workers Benefit Protection Act, 1990

Requires that waivers of ADEA rights be "knowing and voluntary" and codifies the "equal benefit or equal cost" principle.

Americans with Disabilities Act (ADA), 1990

Makes it illegal to discriminate in human resource procedures against individuals with known physical or mental limitations who can perform the essential functions of the job; requires employers to make "reasonable accommodation" for applicants and employees with disabilities.

Family and Medical Leave Act (FMLA), 1993

Protects health insurance coverage for workers and their families when an employee changes or loses a job.

Health Insurance Portability and Accountability Act (HIPPA)

Requires large employers to give workers unpaid leave for up to 12 weeks for family or medical emergencies.

Source: Adapted from Jeffrey S. Hornsby and Donald F. Kuratko, *Frontline HR* (Mason, OH: Thomson South-Western, 2005), 21–41.

with a disability is defined as "an individual who, with or without reasonable accommodation, can perform the essential functions of the position that he desires or holds." "Essential functions" are job tasks that are fundamental and not marginal. The ADA requires employers to provide reasonable accommodation to persons with disabilities unless doing so would result in an "undue hardship" on the operation of the business. The ADA defines "reasonable accommodation" as making existing facilities that employees use readily accessible to and usable by persons with disabilities; restructuring jobs; creating part-time or modified work schedules; reassigning qualified personnel with disabilities to vacant positions; acquiring or modifying equipment or devices; adjusting or modifying examinations, training materials, or policies; and providing qualified readers or interpreters.

The third act that affects human resource management is the Family and Medical Leave Act (FMLA), which took effect on August 5, 1993, and entitles eligible employees to take up to 12 weeks of unpaid, job-protected leave each year (or 12-month period) for specified family-related and medical reasons. The FMLA applies to all public agencies, including state, local, and federal employers; local educational agencies (schools); and private-sector employers that employ 50 or more employees in 20 or more workweeks of the current or preceding calendar year. The FMLA and the related regulations issued by the U.S. Department of Labor on June 4, 1993, are extremely complex and impose a variety of requirements on employers. Covered employers must display the FMLA poster in conspicuous places in their work sites, develop a company policy on FMLA to be included in the employee handbook, prepare a notice describing both the employee's and employer's obligations to be given to all employees who request FMLA leave, and set up the required FMLA record-keeping system.

In addition to the laws passed in the 1990s, the U.S. Supreme Court recently increased the burden on businesses by requiring them to prevent sexual harassment in the workplace. Sexual harassment is viewed by the courts as a form of sexual discrimination protected by Title VII of the 1964 Civil Rights Act. Specifically, unwanted, unwelcome, and repeated behavior of a sex-based nature is prohibited. In 1998, the Supreme Court ruled that a business must have a policy defining the firm's stance on sexual harassment, a training program on what behavior is prohibited, a procedure for making a complaint, and an appeals procedure if an employee is unhappy with a decision. The employer must take immediate corrective action when a complaint is filed. This responsibility includes separating the parties, confidentially investigating the issues, and taking the appropriate steps to prevent future incidents. Supervisors should be instructed to stop any sexual harassment when they observe it, even if the victim does not file a complaint. In addition, there must be a "tangible job detriment" for the person doing the harassing. In other words, the punishment must fit the offense.[6]

As these three laws and court decision demonstrate, new venture owners need to perform human resource management functions carefully in order to attract, train, develop, and retain a quality workforce. In the following sections, we examine many of the critical functions involved with human resource management, with a focus on the areas of staffing and performance management.

STAFFING

One of the most important parts of the human resource management process is staffing. The identification of employees who have the necessary knowledge, skills, and abilities to perform a job is critical at all stages of company development. However, the need to find good employees who function well in new fast-paced, growth-oriented firms increases the need to carry out the staffing function in a systematic fashion.[7] We will examine each of these areas and present some staffing principles for small-business owners.

ASSESSING STAFFING NEEDS

The first step in staffing is to determine how many new employees will be needed during the next 6–12 months. The owner/manager begins this task by examining current operations and foreseeable work requirements, and by predicting the probable turnover rate. The individual should be able to answer the following key questions:

- Will any additional workers be needed, or can the present workforce do all of the work?
- Can any jobs be eliminated, thereby freeing people for other work?

- If more people are needed, should they be full-time or part-time?
- Can I hire temporary help to assist with seasonal demands?

On the basis of the answers to these questions, the owner/manager can begin recruiting the necessary human resources.

HUMAN RESOURCE RECRUITING

When recruiting human resources, owners should take the following four steps:

1. Assess short-run and long-run needs.
2. Write a job description and specifications for each vacancy.
3. Organize a recruiting campaign.
4. Learn governmental regulations regarding discrimination in employment.

With these steps in mind, the owner/manager can begin formal recruiting. Several personnel sources are available for recruiting in smaller ventures. These sources are described as follows.

PRESENT EMPLOYEES
Is a new person really needed, or would a current employee fit the bill? If the latter is the case, recruit this person; promotion is good for employee morale.

FORMER EMPLOYEES
Sometimes past employees who left of their own accord can be rehired. In addition, these people may refer applicants. If someone is rehired, the owner/manager should look at why the person left in the first place. Regardless of how well the individual performed in the past, the owner should be wary of hiring someone who tends to move from job to job. The owner should look for workers who are likely to stay with the business for the indefinite future.

COMMERCIAL EMPLOYMENT AGENCIES
A reliable employment agency can be very helpful in locating applicants. These agencies, if used properly, will do the initial screening of candidates and send over only those who appear to have the qualifications set forth by the owner/manager. These agencies are also very good for assistance with hiring seasonal help or replacements for employees on various types of leave. Such agencies charge fees for their services.

CLASSIFIED ADVERTISEMENTS
Classified newspaper ads are one of the most common ways a business attracts recruits. Many people who are out of work look in the *help wanted* section of the newspaper. In the ad, the owner/manager can give a short description of the job, needed qualifications, and starting salary. In some cases, however, it is preferable to give a salary range or simply to say that salary is competitive. This practice would apply to certain managerial or technical positions.

THE INTERNET

The Internet is close to becoming the most common method to recruit employees. Several Web sites—such as Monster.com and Careerbuilder.com—offer services that enable applicants to post their resumes for employers to see. Applicants can also identify companies that have paid to have their job openings posted, and have their resume forwarded directly to those organizations. Many companies utilize their own Web sites to attract recruits. They list current job openings and provide a direct link for applicants to e-mail their resumes to the company.

SCHOOLS AND PROFESSORS

Many trade schools, business schools, and universities offer employment or career services for their students and alumni. By spending an afternoon interviewing at one of these locations, a business may be able to recruit some highly qualified applicants.

As the business taps the available labor supply, it may find that more applicants are available than positions. At this point, the owner must decide whom to select.

SCREENING POTENTIAL EMPLOYEES

When screening job applicants, the place to start is with an employment *application form.* This provides information on the person's background and training. Is the business looking for a salesperson? If so, someone with selling experience may be preferable to someone without it. Is a mechanic being sought? If so, the person should have some training and experience in this area. The application form helps screen out those who are least likely to be successful in the job.

In addition, the applicant should be *interviewed.* Much can be learned about a person during the interview. Does the individual have the right temperament and personality for the job? Has the person written anything on the application form that warrants discussion? Do any questions that were not on the application form need to be answered?

In general, most firms—especially newer, smaller firms—do not understand the problems related to using an interview for selection. When employees who conduct interviews are not trained, issues such as sexual discrimination and harassment can arise. In addition, without sufficient practice and planning, the interview is an unreliable method for obtaining information about applicants.

The solution to most of these problems is to develop and conduct a *structured interview:* a set of job-related interview questions, based on a job analysis, that are consistently asked of each applicant for a specific job.[8] In addition, interviewers should have a predetermined set of criteria on which to base their judgments regarding each candidate's performance so that they refrain from comparing job applicants with one another and committing the contrast effect (i.e., judging candidates on the basis of prior candidates). For example, if the individuals interviewed before one candidate were excellent, that candidate may not be rated as highly by the interviewer as his or her performance would objectively indicate. Conversely, if the individuals interviewed before one candidate

Outsourcing

Being a small-business owner or entrepreneur is not a full-time job—it's three or four full-time jobs. The roles that the person must play are numerous and, of course, require extensive knowledge of all aspects of running a growing, profitable, and compliant business. Corporations regularly outsource the tasks they choose not to handle in-house. Small businesses, however, are not always so financially fortunate. Instead, entrepreneurs are usually stuck with mastering a task themselves or hiring a high-salary employee to do so. Duties that can be outsourced include accounting, payroll, health care planning, and other various human resource functions that require time-consuming paperwork and legal compliance hassles.

The professional employer organization (PEO) industry, which dates back to the early 1980s, is growing at an amazing 25 to 30 percent annually. This trend is attributed not only to the growing number of business owners, but also to the fact that current owners are realizing the true value of using PEOs. Spending money on the *co-employer* is justified by the time that the owner/entrepreneur is able to save and instead focus on operations and generating revenue. In addition, given the competition among start-ups to find the best employees, PEOs offer another plus. By taking advantage of their large member numbers, PEOs are able to leverage for discounts on human resource benefit rates and pass them on to the customers.

PEOs were established to offer basic services such as payroll processing, tax payments, and health insurance. Because of the rising demand in the outsourcing market, many started offering retirement plans, workers' compensation insurance, and regulatory compliance monitoring as well. (Larger organizations offer an even broader menu of services, but they usually service corporations that can afford the high price tag.) The $22 billion industry includes approximately 1,700 operating PEOs that provide services for 2 to 3 million Americans. PEOs make their profits by charging 4 to 8 percent of payroll dollars; hence, high-cost-of-living areas are prime targets for their services.

Some businesses remain skeptical about using PEOs because their legal status is not uniform across the country. Furthermore, federal legislation has not defined to what extent PEOs are liable for wage and tax mistakes, workers' compensation, or unemployment insurance. PEO accreditation comes only from industry groups, and little guidance is available for handling the co-employment situation, justifying the contracts used when entering into business, and drawing the line between the two entities. It is still unclear as to where PEOs fall under FSLA and EEOC guidelines and regulations. Facing the uncertainties, though, is worth the risk to some. "There are 1,001 things to do," says one Internet start-up owner. "It seemed to me a PEO would have some advantages. Number one is time savings."

Experts predict that the PEO industry will continue to grow as legislation is written for them and their legal status is clarified. Growth, however, won't result from new entrants but from mergers and acquisitions. This consolidation will allow cheaper and understandably clearer service to emerge and will ultimately ease the government burden for small-business owners.

Source: Carolyn Hirschman, "For PEOs, Business Is Booming," *HR Magazine* (February 2000): 42–48.

were unacceptable, that candidate would more likely be rated higher than his or her objective performance level.

In some cases, a *test* is in order. For example, if the person will be required to carry heavy material as part of the job, the individual should be asked to demonstrate this ability. If the employer has some question about the applicant's physical health in regard to the job's tasks, a medical exam should be required. Meanwhile, if the person will be typing or operating a machine, these skills should be checked as well. Is the individual sufficiently fast and accurate? Keep in mind, however, that the test must measure skills that are actually used on the job. If a company gives a math test but the job requires no math, the business can be accused of discrimination or of using an improper testing instrument. In short, tie the test to the job; if this is not possible, do not use tests to screen applicants. Many states have passed legislation to protect employers when they are conducting good-faith reference checks.[9]

SELECTING AND ORIENTING EMPLOYEES

If the screening process is carried out properly, the owner/manager should be in a position to select applicants who are most fit for the job. When making the final cut, the owner/manager should direct attention toward applicants' references; they should be checked for both accuracy and input. Has the individual actually worked as an engineer for this other company? Why did the person leave the job? Does the applicant have any shortcomings that have not yet been identified but could be determined in a phone call to the previous employer?[10] Would the previous employer rehire this person if he or she were available?

If the individual checks out and is hired, the next step is indoctrination, or job orientation. The person should be made to feel at home in the organization. Many new employees feel lost or nervous during their first few days on the job. To help them overcome this, managers should show them around, introduce them to people they will be working with, and show them how their job fits into the overall mission of the enterprise.

PRINCIPLES OF EFFECTIVE STAFFING

Owner/managers should be aware of a number of staffing principles. Among the most important are the following:

- *Staffing objective.* Owner/managers should fill all positions with personnel who are both willing and able to occupy them.
- *Staffing.* The more adequately that owner/managers define the jobs to be done, the personnel requirements for these jobs, and the kinds of training and development required, the more likely workers are to be competent in their jobs.
- *Job definition.* The more clearly each job is defined, the more likely personnel are to know what is expected of them.

- *Open competition.* Owner/managers who fill job openings on the basis of the best-available candidate are more likely to hire effective people than those who recruit on the basis of friendship or expediency.
- *Employee appraisal.* If job requirements are spelled out clearly and used as a basis for evaluating personnel, motivation will remain high, and tardiness, absenteeism, and turnover will be minimized.
- *Employee training.* The more effectively personnel are trained, the better job they will do.
- *Owner/manager training.* If owner/managers obtain on-the-job training and attend outside workshops and clinics designed to improve their performance, overall company efficiency and profit should increase.

PERFORMANCE MANAGEMENT

Planned programs for employee improvement are critical if an organization wants to survive and compete in a global marketplace. In addition, newer firms with growth-oriented strategies must continuously assess the strengths and weaknesses of the current workforce so that weaknesses can be eliminated through additional training or by replacing workers with individuals who have the requisite skills and abilities. This section focuses on the key performance management activities that assist in developing employees: training, performance appraisal, compensation, and employee discipline and counseling.

TRAINING

To obtain the greatest efficiency from employees, it is helpful to develop a training program. Such a program should be based on careful planning that includes the following:

1. Establishing training needs and goals
2. Choosing the most practical training methods
3. Evaluating the results[11]

In a very small business operation, the owner/manager usually does the training. In a slightly larger operation, it is possible to have a supervisor train production and maintenance people, an office manager train clerical workers, and a sales manager perform this function with salespeople.

The method of training will depend greatly on the type of job and its skill requirements. However, in broad terms, four training methods are available:

- *Conference or structured discussion.* This is a guided discussion of important ideas. It usually involves a leader and is an excellent method for training supervisors. Human relations training is typically handled this way.
- *Lecture.* This is ideal for providing basic policy and procedural information to trainees.

- *Role playing.* This consists of acting out particular scenarios. It is particularly useful to teach salespeople how to sell or supervisors how to discipline subordinates. It involves learning by seeing and doing.

- *Programmed instruction.* This consists of a *canned* presentation in which the individual learns at his or her own pace. These programs can be used to support the training effort and do not cost very much.

- *On-the-job training.* This is the most practical method in small business. It is used for specific job training, such as showing someone how to run a machine.

On-the-job training is the most common training method for small businesses. The first step is to break down the job into its various parts. This can be accomplished by writing a job breakdown sheet (which may be kept for future reference as a training aid). It is not advisable to try to create a job breakdown off the top of one's head; even the most skilled trainers fail to remember each step in carrying out a job. When working out the various job steps that need to be explained to the trainee, many trainers actually like to do the job and write down each step as they complete it. By doing so, they know that they have a complete list for instructional purposes.

ON-THE-JOB TRAINING STEPS

Although the preceding discussion provides some general information and guidelines for training people, the owner/manager also should know a number of specific facts about training.[12] For example, on-the-job training, which may vary in length from a few hours to several full days, depending on the complexity of the work, has four distinct steps that should be followed:

1. Preparation
2. Demonstration
3. Application
4. Inspection

In the *preparation* step, the trainer should find out what the trainee already knows about the job. The trainer then can proceed to cover what the individual still needs to learn. In the *demonstration* step, the trainee should be shown how the job is done. As each step in this process is completed, the trainer should encourage the trainee to ask questions. If the trainee asks none, the trainer should take the initiative and ask some (e.g., "What have I just told you about how to do that step?" "What would you do if this particular problem developed?" "How would you handle the situation?"). If questions alone are insufficient, the trainer can also ask the trainee to carry out the step (e.g., Show me how you would do it").

Next, the trainer should allow the trainee to perform the entire process for him- or herself. In this *application* step, the trainer should not oversee the operation too closely because this may make the trainee nervous. The trainer should stand off to one side and watch. When the trainee does something right, the trainer should offer praise. If the trainee runs into trouble, the trainer should step in and demonstrate how to correct the situation. Finally, in the *inspection* step the trainer looks over what has been done and evaluates it. The evaluation should be a positive one: If the trainee has done the job wrong, this should be pointed out and advice should be given with regard to how the error can be avoided. The trainer also should close on a positive note, indicating support and confidence in the trainee.

PERFORMANCE APPRAISAL

Performance appraisal is the formal, systematic assessment of how well employees are performing their jobs in relation to established standards and the communication of that assessment to employees. The purpose of performance appraisal is to provide both managers and employees with feedback on how well the latter are doing. These appraisals help determine actions such as merit pay increases, promotions, training, transfer, and discharge. In large measure, performance appraisal is the primary process for evaluating and developing organizational personnel.[13]

A well-designed appraisal system has five basic characteristics:

1. It is tied directly to the job and measures the individual's ability to carry out successfully the requirements of the position.
2. It is comprehensive, measuring all of the important aspects of the job rather than just one or two.
3. It is objective, measuring task performance rather than the interpersonal relationship of the rater and the ratee.
4. It is based on standards of desired performance that were explained to the employee in advance.
5. It is designed to pinpoint the strong points and shortcomings of a person and to provide a basis to explain why these shortcomings exist and what can be done about them.[14]

Managers can design and implement a performance appraisal system in many ways so that it will have these characteristics. One of the most useful approaches is to tie the appraisal closely to the objectives of the position. In addition, the business owner or manager must take into account two key issues. The first is organizational considerations such as leadership style, culture/climate, and availability of appraisal training. The second issue is appropriateness for the job; the performance appraisal process and instrument must match the types and levels of the jobs in the company.[15]

Although a number of different techniques can be used to conduct performance appraisals, and most organizations design their own techniques, the most popular one is *graphic rating scales*. These are easy to fill out; regardless of how the scales are constructed, the category or factor generally is listed on the left, and varying degrees of the category or factor are listed along a continuum to the right. The form often contains a description of each category. Quality of work, for example, may be defined as "the caliber of work produced or accomplished in comparison to accepted quality standards." If the evaluation results are to be used to compare people within the same unit or department, some sort of weight usually is given to each factor, such as 1 for a marginal rating, 2 for below average, 3 for average, 4 for above average, and 5 for outstanding. Figure 11-1 is an example

FIGURE 11-1   Illustration of a Performance Appraisal Instrument

PART I: IDENTIFICATION

Name _____   Position _____

Rating Period From _____   To _____

Rater Name _____   Title _____

Number of months rater has directly observed job performance _____

PART II: RATING SCALES

Please identify the important job duties performed by this employee and rate his or her performance using the following scale: 1 = very poor, 2 = below average, 3 = average, 4 = above average, and 5 = excellent.

Job Duties	Rating	Comments
1.	1 2 3 4 5	
2.	1 2 3 4 5	
3.	1 2 3 4 5	
4.	1 2 3 4 5	
5.	1 2 3 4 5	
6.	1 2 3 4 5	
7.	1 2 3 4 5	
8.	1 2 3 4 5	
9.	1 2 3 4 5	
10.	1 2 3 4 5	

PART III: GOAL ACCOMPLISHMENT

Please review the goals set for this appraisal period in terms of their accomplishment.

Organizational Goals

Goal #1:   1 2 3 4 5   Measure:

Performance Assessment
Goal #2:   1 2 3 4 5   Measure:

Performance Assessment
Goal #3:   1 2 3 4 5   Measure:

Performance Assessment
Goal #4:   1 2 3 4 5   Measure:

PART IV: DEVELOPMENTAL APPRAISAL SUMMARY

Please summarize the employee's strengths and weaknesses, and your recommendations for improvement.

_____

_____

_____

_____

_____

_____

_____

FIGURE 11-1   (*Continued*)

PART V: GOAL SETTING
(for the next review period)

During the performance appraisal feedback session, set new goals for the next appraisal period. Make sure that there is agreement on how each goal will be measured for accomplishment.

Organizational Goals

Goal #1	Measure:
Goal #2	Measure:
Goal #3	Measure:
Goal #4	Measure:

PART VI: SIGNATURES

This report is based on my observation and knowledge. My signature indicates that I have reviewed this appraisal of both the employee and the job. It does not mean that I agree with the results.

_____   _____

Supervisor   Date   Employee   Date

of an integrative performance appraisal instrument that utilizes graphic rating scales and management by objective goal setting.

Recently, many employers have turned to 360-degree feedback. In addition to supervisor feedback, information is obtained from coworkers, clients, vendors, and other parties. The goal of this process is to provide developmental feedback relevant to how the employee can change real job behaviors. One company, UPS, utilizes 360-degree feedback at its airline operations headquarters in Louisville, Kentucky. Its *quality performance review* measures critical skills such as customer focus, financial and internal business knowledge, people skills, business values, and leadership.[16]

VALUE OF PERFORMANCE APPRAISALS

Formal performance appraisals are valued in several ways. Effective managers believe that appraisal systems can be a beneficial tool for improving employee performance, attendance behavior, and job satisfaction. More specifically, effective appraisal systems can serve the following purposes:

- Personal development
- Reward
- Motivation
- Personnel planning
- Communication[17]

MANAGEMENT BY OBJECTIVES

How can a smaller business systematically assess employee performance? One way is through an integrative system like management by objectives (MBO).

FIGURE 11-2 The Basic Management by Objectives (MBO) Cycle

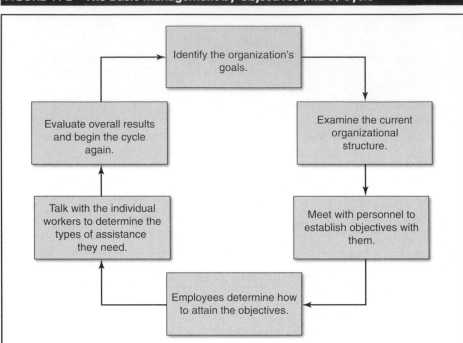

An applied form of goal setting, the MBO process is a simple one that consists of six steps. These steps are illustrated in Figure 11-2.

First, the owner/manager identifies the business's goals. What are the sales and profit objectives? What would the owner like to accomplish? Second, the owner/manager needs to look over the current organizational structure to see what everyone is doing. This helps the individual determine whether personnel activities are supporting achievement of the goals. Can the goals be attained if everyone keeps doing what they currently do? Or should work assignments be changed so that a better blending occurs between goals and activities? Third, the owner/manager needs to sit down with each employee and review his or her objectives for the year, limiting them to a manageable four or five. This need not be a highly formal process. However, the worker should know exactly what job(s) he or she is to perform. For a salesperson, this is usually quite simple. For example, the owner/manager and employee may agree that the latter will "sell $75,000 worth of merchandise this year." For the office worker, purchasing manager, or sales clerk, it is more difficult to set specific, measurable performance objectives. Nevertheless, some attempt should be made, for only in this way can the owner/manager help to ensure that the biggest rewards go to the most productive workers. In any event, the employee and the owner/manager must agree on what the employee is to do. In this way, work assignments are made clear, and the worker has input in the decision.

Fourth, the employee decides how the assigned objectives can be attained efficiently. What shortcuts can be used to improve productivity? How can sales be increased? What steps can be taken to become more efficient? During this stage of the process, the worker answers such key questions as "What must be done?" "How will it be done?" and "How will I know when I've done a good job?" Fifth, during the year, the owner/manager maintains a basis for evaluating each worker's performance. Additionally, he or she can identify and help workers who are having problems. Finally, results are measured against objectives. This is the last stage of the controlling process, and for many owner/managers it is an arbitrary evaluation in which he or she concludes that the employee has done a poor, average, or good job. A better way to carry out this evaluation, however, is to use a rating form that is simple and to the point.

Benefits of MBO

MBO is very popular because it is both comprehensive and easy to understand. In particular, managers like it because it helps them identify important business objectives and the people who are responsible for attaining them. A second benefit is that, whenever possible, these objectives are quantified and a time dimension is applied. Thus, the worker knows what is expected and when particular objectives are to be attained. Third, MBO helps the manager identify the organization's key objectives. The business can pursue many goals, but some are more important than others—these are the ones that merit consideration. In addition, minor objectives are often accomplished in the attainment of major ones. Finally, MBO frees owner/managers for more important activities. It encourages them to delegate time-consuming jobs and to devote their energies to major planning and control matters so that they are not inundated with busywork to the overall detriment of the business.

Compensation

Another important aspect of staffing is compensation, which takes two forms: wages/salaries and benefits. The former is the money people are paid on a weekly, biweekly, or monthly basis, and the latter consists of retirement benefits, insurance programs, sick leave, and paid vacations.

Wage and Salary Systems

Most smaller, growing firms have essentially two choices when it comes to wage and salary compensation: Employees can be paid either on the basis of *time* (by the hour, day, week, or month) or on the basis of *output* (an incentive piece-rate plan). In either case, compensation must be within the guidelines of the Equal Employment Opportunity regulations to avoid discriminatory inequalities. This means that equal pay must be given for substantially equal work. Therefore, once a job has been established and a pay rate set, anyone who performs this job should be paid the same rate. The only exception is if the person has been doing the job for a number of years and has received annual pay increases. In such a case, any new, incoming employee need be paid only the current *starting* wage.

Straight salary is a fairly clear-cut compensation method, so let us concentrate on *incentive compensation systems.* Using these systems, an individual's pay is based on how much work is done. For example, in some instances, the worker is paid a straight piece rate; he or she receives money for each item produced or processed, such as 25 cents per widget. In other cases, the person is given a guaranteed day rate, such as $25 per day, regardless of how much work is done, as well as an incentive per item, such as 10 cents per piece.

Experts do not universally agree as to which method of wage payment is best.[18] However, generally speaking, incentive wages are both practical and effective *only* under the following conditions:

1. The units of output are measurable and readily distinguishable. In this way, it is possible to tell how much work the individual actually has done.
2. A clear relationship exists between output and the worker's effort. The individual should be rewarded directly for what he or she does.
3. Quality is less important than quantity (if the work is highly technical, the output achieved with incentive wages is likely to be shoddy and fail inspection).
4. Supervisors do not have sufficient time to devote attention to individual performance. If the work requires a lot of supervision, it probably cannot be done quickly and easily, so the workers will not like the incentive payment plan.
5. Advance knowledge is available regarding the cost per unit. In this way, the owner/manager can estimate how high the incentive rate can go.

BENEFITS

Many types of employee benefits currently are provided by small businesses. Some are required by law, whereas others are voluntary. One required benefit is unemployment compensation, which is designed to provide subsistence payments for employees who are between jobs. The fund for these payments is supported by employer contributions. Depending on the state in which the firm is located and the amount of unemployment the firm has had in recent years, these contributions will vary.

Another required benefit is Social Security. Most firms are required to contribute to this fund and, along with employee contributions, serve to finance the system. When workers retire, they are entitled to a monthly pension.

A third benefit is workers' compensation, which is designed to help employees who have job-related illnesses or injuries and cannot work as a result. The employer pays the entire cost of workers' compensation, usually by participating in a private or state-run insurance plan.

Voluntary programs take many forms. Some of the most common include paid holidays, paid vacations, health insurance, life insurance, disability insurance, day care, educational programs, and recreational programs. The number of programs and the degree of employer participation vary, depending on how financially successful the firm is, the types of benefits employees most desire, and other factors.

One employee benefit for smaller businesses to develop is pension coverage. Less than 20 percent of employees in small firms have any type of pension, compared with 80 percent of employees in large businesses. A simplified employee pension (SEP), which operates like an individual retirement account (IRA) and a corporate profit sharing plan, may be one solution for small-business owners. The paperwork and administrative fees are minimal; any brokerage house or mutual fund company will set up a prototype SEP plan at no cost to the employer. The administrative fees, which range from $35 to $100 per account, are charged to the participating employees. Because SEP forms are standardized, all the business owner needs to provide is a list of qualified employees.

In an effort to examine the various types of compensation and benefit practices of small firms, researchers Jeffrey S. Hornsby and Donald F. Kuratko conducted a study of small businesses ranging from very small (1–50 employees) to larger firms (more than 150 employees).[19] Their results indicate that the compensation and benefit practices of small businesses are more sophisticated than generally believed. It is interesting to realize that small firms now use more sophisticated incentive plans, such as gain sharing, commissions, and bonuses. In addition, benefits such as health insurance, dental insurance, life insurance, and disability and pension plans now are offered by small businesses with more regularity than ever before.

EMPLOYEE DISCIPLINE AND COUNSELING

Employee discipline is based around two major activities: enforcing work rules and policies and ensuring that workers meet performance expectations. The major goal of discipline is to counsel and/or coach employees who have violated a policy or suffer from poor work performance. Early detection of problems can lead to positive corrective actions so that the employee can retain his or her job and the company does not have to hire additional human resources. Additionally, early and corrective actions are beneficial to reduce the risk the employer has for any violation or performance problem. Joseph Palermo recommends 11 activities to mitigate risk and improve performance. These activities are summarized in Table 11-3.

The key essentials for effective discipline appear to be documentation of job requirements, documentation of work rules and policies in an employee handbook, training managers on counseling techniques, and early counseling concerning problems.[20]

THE EMPLOYEE HANDBOOK: A KEY TOOL FOR EMPLOYEE ACCOUNTABILITY

Thus far, several employment-related issues have been discussed in this chapter. These issues are critical to employee attraction, development, and retention. However, as a company grows and emerges, communication between employees and management seems to become less effective. Employees lose touch with the ongoing feedback they received when the firm was small and supervisors had more time to provide hands-on management. The formalization of rules and policies is commonly one of the first steps to formalizing a human resource function. As the company grows and adds more managers, consistency in performance management and policy enforcement becomes problematic, and employees become

TABLE 11-3 Important Elements for an Employee Discipline

1. *Create an effective hiring process.* Standardize job descriptions and applications to ensure only candidates who meet the minimum stated qualifications are considered. Train staff on effective interviewing techniques. Utilize conditional offers to allow the organization to check references and other relevant background information and perform drug testing.

2. *Secure the support of administration.* Obtain support from the organization's leadership. Supervisors who refuse to discipline erode the validity of the discipline program.

3. *Work with a labor lawyer.* Utilize the services of an attorney with expertise in local labor law. The attorney should review every phase of the discipline program as well as the structure of an employee grievance process. Emphasis should be put on how to appropriately document disciplinary actions.

4. *Publish an employee manual.* Manuals should include policies or work rules concerning proper attire, offensive behaviors, use of vehicles, Internet and e-mail usage, and tardiness and absences. It should also outline the counseling, discipline and grievance processes. Once the manual is finalized, all employees should be required to provide written agreement to the terms outlined in the manual. This is usually accomplished at the time of worker orientation.

5. *Train managers and supervisors.* Managers and supervisors must understand all of the policies and disciplinary procedures because they will be responsible for explaining and enforcing the program. Management should be trained on coaching and counseling practices that are designed to help employees avoid the discipline system.

6. *Begin with counseling.* The goal of an employee discipline program should be to avoid disciplinary action. The purpose is to correct behaviors and fix problems before they escalate in to more serious issues. Most people respond well to an initial discussion and a definition of the conditions that would require further action.

7. *Establish an employee appraisal process.* Regular performance appraisal is an important component of an employee discipline program, especially in the detection and discussion of work-related problems. There should be no surprises in a yearly appraisal.

8. *Standardize documentation.* Create form letters that document when counseling has taken place, exactly what was discussed, and what will happen if the problem occurs again. This complete documentation accurately *informs* employees of an official discipline offense and protects the employer in case the employee alleges any illegal employment practices.

9. *Establish a grievance procedure.* Employees may not always agree with a supervisor's version of events, and must be provided with a forum for disputing disciplinary actions. Consult with a labor lawyer about specific state laws that could apply. If conducted appropriately, a grievance or appeals process could help the company correct any possible mistakes or misunderstandings regarding how an employee was treated.

10. *Obtain employment practices liability insurance.* Effective employee discipline programs are usually required to secure employment practices liability insurance coverage and other policies because they significantly reduce overall risk exposure.

Source: Adapted from Palermo, Joseph C. "Well-crafted worker discipline program diminishes risk." ***Business Insurance,*** 2007, Vol. 41, Issue 8.

frustrated and disgruntled over the inconsistent application of rules and favoritism. Moreover, many of the employment laws require formal communication of an employee's rights in a written document (e.g., family leave, sexual harassment, and dealing with disabilities). Documentation provided to employees that details an organization's policies and procedures makes it easier to take appropriate disciplinary action when necessary.

In any organization, the employee handbook summarizes the important human resource policies that every employee needs to know. In this chapter, all of the important functional areas of human resource management have been described (i.e., selection procedures, compensation, benefits, and performance appraisal). The goal of a handbook is to illustrate the relevant aspects of these functions to help orient new and existing employees to company practices. Essentially, the handbook serves as a guidebook to all the dos and don'ts of a particular company or organization. It is an effective way to communicate important information—such as a company's rules, procedures, and goals—to the company's workers, as well as more abstract things such as the company's expectations and philosophy. Employee handbooks help explain to new employees how the organization functions. A good employee handbook will provide a reliable source to which employees can turn when questions arise. When workers know their company's philosophy, goals, and motivations, they are likely to feel as if they are a part of the organization. In addition, because employee handbooks usually include disciplinary procedures, they can serve as an effective management tool for dealing with problem employees.

THE CURRENT STATE OF HUMAN RESOURCE MANAGEMENT PRACTICES

A generalization has persisted that small businesses are not large enough to employ any sophisticated human resource practices. However, current research demonstrates that small businesses do, in fact, use many of the latest practices and employ more sophisticated practices as they grow in size. Small businesses of all sizes have become more aware of the importance of attracting and retaining quality workers. For example, researchers Jeffrey S. Hornsby and Donald F. Kuratko conducted a study in this area in 1990.[21] The study was updated in 2000 to see the progression of human resource practices after ten years. Table 11-4 compares human resource management practices in 1990 to those in 2000. The same size categories (1–15 employees, 51–100 employees, and 101–150 employees) were utilized in both studies.

In the categories of benefits and compensation, an increase in company size affects the particular practices. However, in the categories of job analysis (assessment), recruitment, and selection, the sophistication level of the different practices does not vary too much with company size. For example, size does not determine the use of observation and interviews as job-analysis methods, although larger small businesses do seem more inclined to use questionnaires as a

TABLE 11-4	Use of Current Human Resource Practices in Small Ventures					
	1–50 Employees		*51–100 Employees*		*101–150 Employees*	
Human Resource Management Practice	*1990 Use (%)*	*Current Use (%)*	*1990 Use (%)*	*Current Use (%)*	*1990 Use (%)*	*Current Use (%)*
Job Analysis						
Observation	50	33	63	52	69	60
Questionnaires	10	9	21	14	46	37
Interviews	31	23	42	34	50	51
Recruitment						
Newspaper	50	44	62	65	63	64
Government employment agency	27	18	38	25	50	28
Private employment agency	23	23	38	34	25	62
Referrals	67	73	75	73	69	71
Walk-ins	58	57	67	64	66	69
Radio	2	6	0	11	0	14
Selection						
Application blanks	88	73	100	90	100	93
Reference checks	90	80	100	88	98	90
Interviews	100	90	100	97	100	93
Drug tests	3	27	9	34	24	48
Psychological tests	25	16	25	31	30	35
Aptitude tests	25	30	23	37	43	35
Compensation						
Market rate	30	36	40	38	44	46
Performance appraisal	18	17	22	20	18	29
Job requirements	21	10	38	8	12	15
Experience/seniority	34	27	33	32	28	22
Minimum wage	19	5	20	3	5	5
Union contract	2	2	6	2	12	7
Incentives	9	9	2	6	10	4
Benefits						
Health insurance	68	66	95	89	100	100
Dental insurance	15	21	33	49	34	60
Vision insurance	5	16	22			
Life insurance	54	41	85			
Disability	37	28	73			
Pension	19	24	53			
Sick leave	27	37	55			
Vacation plan	72	76	98			

TABLE 11-4   (*Continued*)

Human Resource Management Practice	1–50 Employees		51–100 Employees		101–150 Employees	
	1990 Use (%)	Current Use (%)	1990 Use (%)	Current Use (%)	1990 Use (%)	Current Use (%)
Incentive Plans						
Commissions	31	38	36	34	39	40
Bonuses	48	50	55	68	54	63
Profit sharing	17	13	31	28	26	31
ESOP	3	2	9	6	6	9
Piecework	4	1	16	6	5	0
Standard hour	3	5	16	10	15	6
Gain sharing	12	1	12	1	13	3
Performance Appraisal						
Rating scale	35	26	49	59	59	49
Narrative essay	29	33	49	48	59	37
Goal setting	32	31	49	48	59	37
Training						
On the job	96	93	100	96	100	97
Apprenticeships	24	17	43	42	33	31
Coaching	79	67	85	70	69	69
Seminars	50	34	60	46	59	45
Computer-aided instruction	16	21	25	27	21	41

Source: Jeffrey S. Hornsby and Donald F. Kuratko, "Human Resource Management in Small Business: Critical Issues for the 1990s," *Journal of Small Business Management* (July 1990): 13; updated in Jeffrey S. Hornsby and Donald F. Kuratko, "Human Resource Management in U.S. Small Businesses: A Replication and Extension," *Journal of Developmental Entrepreneurship* 8 (2003): 73–92.

job-analysis method. Size does appear to be a factor in whether or not the business has written job descriptions.

Newspaper advertisements, government employment agencies, private employment agencies, employee referrals, and walk-ins are used extensively as recruiting tools by small businesses. However, as expected, smaller firms are more likely to rely on the less expensive newspaper advertisements, referrals, and walk-ins. With regard to selection, larger firms are apt to use application forms, reference checks, and interviews, as well as drug testing, personality tests, and aptitude tests, more frequently than the smaller firms. This indicates that small-business owners are responding to the need for improved human resource practices to gain a competitive edge in hiring the best possible employees.[22]

CRITICAL ISSUES FOR THE FUTURE

The entire function of effective human resource management is one that small-business owners need to develop and improve as they expand and grow.[23] In many firms, the owner must personally handle all human resource practices; thus, inefficiencies may occur because of other activities that the owner has to perform. This situation creates the danger that small-business owners might fail to recognize or understand critical issues regarding human resources.

Regardless of the size of the small business, it is clear that owner/managers need to obtain and retain a quality workforce. Owners perceive benefits, retention, training, and child care, along with the availability of quality workers, to be the critical issues for the new millennium (see Table 11-5 for a complete breakdown of these and other issues ranked by importance in each size category). Thus, it is apparent that small-business owners recognize what issues must be continually improved on if a quality workforce is desired.

EMPLOYEE MORALE

Although human resource management issues have been recognized and are being improved on, certain questions about employees must be addressed. Are workers doing what they should be doing? Is morale good? Are the personnel content? Do they feel they are being treated properly?

When answering these questions, owner/managers often find their attention turning toward such behavioral topics as communication, motivation, and leadership. These concerns fall within the control process because they affect a company's overall performance. The major reason for employee problems can be traced to lack of job satisfaction.

JOB SATISFACTION

Job satisfaction determines how employees view their work. When they view it favorably, the likelihood of high productivity is much greater, although the two are not directly related. For example, in some organizations, workers are very satisfied, but their output is no higher than that of firms in which average satisfaction is reported.

Nevertheless, by remaining alert for signs of dissatisfaction, the owner/manager can assess when job satisfaction is within acceptable bounds. Keeping in mind that what is considered *acceptable* varies based on the type of business and industry, the following are indicators of job satisfaction levels:

- *Labor turnover.* Is the number of people leaving the organization for jobs elsewhere increasing?
- *Productivity.* Is the cost per unit rising because of worker inefficiency?
- *Waste and scrap.* Is the amount of material discarded higher than it should be?
- *Product quality.* Are customers returning goods because they have been made improperly or do not perform as expected?

TABLE 11-5	Human Resource Management Issues Perceived to Be Important for the Next Millennium
Ranking	*Issues*

Company Size 1–50

1	Availability of quality workers
2	Benefits
3	Training
4	Competitive wages
5	Government regulations
6	Flexible scheduling
7	Motivation
8	Technology
9	Employee relations
10	Ethics
11	Attendance
12	Teamwork

Company Size 51–100

1	Benefits
2	Retention
3	Availability of quality workers
4	Child care
5	Flexible scheduling
6	Effective employee evaluations
7	Employee relations
8	Competitive wages
9	Safety issues
10	Training
11	Government relations
12	Attendance

Company Size 101–150

1	Availability of quality workers
2	Benefits
3	Government relations
4	Attendance
5	Retention
6	Competitive wages
7	Training
8	Motivation
9	Labor/employee relations
10	Work conditions
11	Overtime/compensation
12	Scheduling

Source: Jeffrey S. Hornsby and Donald F. Kuratko, "Human Resource Management in Small Business: Critical Issues for the 1990s," *Journal of Small Business Management* (July 1990): 13; updated in Jeffrey S. Hornsby and Donald F. Kuratko, "Human Resource Management in U.S. Small Businesses: A Replication and Extension" *Journal of Developmental Entrepreneurship* 8 (2003): 73–92.

- *Service quality.*　Are customers complaining about the service they receive?
- *Tardiness and absenteeism.*　Are employees corning to work late or staying home more frequently than before?
- *Accidents.*　Have more accidents or injuries occurred in the workplace than usual?
- *Complaints or grievances.*　Is the owner/manager hearing more worker complaints, especially about minor things? If the firm has a union, are more grievances being filed than usual?
- *Suggestions.*　If a suggestion box exists, is the number of suggestions for improving morale or working conditions beginning to increase?
- *Exit interviews.*　When individuals who are quitting are asked why, do they indicate dissatisfaction with the work environment?

These are not the only indexes of employee morale, but they are some of the primary ones. When poor morale is indicated, the owner/manager needs to take appropriate action.

IMPROVING EMPLOYEE PERFORMANCE

Two control-related areas warrant the owner/manager's special attention because they are related to employee morale. The first is the link between pay and performance, and the second is the spirit of teamwork.

EXAMINE THE PAY/PERFORMANCE LINK

One of the most common causes of poor morale can be tied to the pay/performance link. Do those who do the best work receive the highest salaries? In many small businesses, the minimum wage is paid to beginning personnel, and all salaries are kept secret. Only the owner and the respective employee know how much the employee makes.

Over time, however, raises usually are given to those who stay, and they are not uniform; some people get more money than others. This can create a morale problem when employees feel that raises are arbitrary and not tied to performance. When this is the case, two things can happen. First, those who can make more money by going elsewhere will take advantage of such employment opportunities. Second, those who stay will do less work, reasoning that "I may not be paid what I'm worth, but I'm not putting forth as much effort as I used to, either."

How should this problem be handled? First, the manager should try to tie raises to performance whenever possible (as discussed in the previous section on management by objectives). Not everyone's job is quantifiable. It may be easy to evaluate a salesperson's performance simply by looking at how much the person sold, but a stock clerk's performance may call for a highly subjective evaluation. This is why some kind of evaluation system should be used. Second, the owner/manager should remain alert to locally competitive salaries. What are other firms paying? Some businesses are unable to match the salaries of other employers, but they must come close or risk losing key personnel. Overall, however, few people leave their jobs just because of dissatisfaction with their pay. In many cases, that is just one of the reasons. Another important reason is dissatisfaction with the work environment—for example, when it has no feeling of teamwork—so personnel simply do not like it there.

DEVELOP TEAMWORK

Teamwork occurs when everyone in the organization acts in a cooperative way. Individuals pitch in to help one another out, and any competition is of a friendly, constructive nature. Although some owner/managers believe that they encourage teamwork, they actually promote competition. For example, the owner who goes overboard in praising and rewarding the best salesperson soon will find the other salespeople working to undermine that individual. The secretary may slow down processing paperwork for this star salesperson's orders, and other salespeople probably will stop passing leads to the person for fear that they might increase his or her sales even more. The result is infighting among the personnel.

How can the owner/manager ensure that teamwork develops? The best way is to reward those who are team players and, most important of all, to reprimand (and in some cases fire) those who refuse to cooperate for the overall good.

Remember that money is an important work variable. No employee will continue to work for the small-business owner/manager who pays low salaries when higher-paying jobs are available. However, the work climate is also important. People want to be happy in their jobs. Research shows that attending to the psychological side of the work environment—including aspects such as a feeling of importance, creating an opportunity to do meaningful work, and the belief that workers are contributing to the business—is often more important to employees than salary and working conditions. When these good feelings are present, morale tends to be high and performance good.

Summary

Human resource management is one of the most important management functions, and the government regulates many of its procedures. The complete human resource management process has several sub-functions, including assessing staffing needs, recruiting personnel, screening potential employees, selecting and indoctrinating employees, training employees, and providing compensation and adequate benefits. The current practices of small businesses vary according to the size category of firms (from companies with fewer than 50 employees to those employing more than 150 people). Critical issues in human resource management that small-business owners will confront in the new millennium include benefits, training, retention, child care, and availability of quality workers.

In most cases, employee morale problems can be traced to a lack of job satisfaction. Job satisfaction indicators include labor turnover, productivity, product quality, employee complaints or grievances, and exit-interview information. Two of the most effective ways to deal with these problems are to improve the pay/performance link and to develop teamwork within the organization.

Review and Discussion Questions

1. How would you describe the diversity in the American workplace?
2. List some recent regulatory legislation that affects human resources.
3. What are ADA and FMLA? Describe each.
4. What are some of the questions an owner/manager must ask to assess the firm's personnel needs?
5. How should the small-business owner recruit personnel? Include in your answer the four steps discussed in this chapter.
6. How should the owner/manager screen and select new employees? Explain.
7. What is performance appraisal? How do graphic rating scales work?
8. Define MBO and describe how it works. What are its benefits?
9. List some of the current human resource practices that small firms in all size categories use.
10. How are the human resource practices that small businesses currently use different from those used by larger businesses? Identify four critical human resource issues that small-business owners will confront in the new millennium.
11. How can the owner/manager tell when employee job satisfaction is declining?
12. What are some typical job satisfaction indicators? List and describe at least five.

NEW VENTURE CONSULTANT

A Quality Workforce?

For the past five years, Oakdon & Associates, Inc. has attempted to build its workforce into a productive, competitive group. For Oakdon, which is a medical laboratory (processing blood samples that help doctors in their diagnoses), efficiency, effectiveness, and quality performance are mandatory. Turnaround time also must be as short as possible (within hours) so that doctors can make their diagnoses effectively. In addition, three shifts of workers are needed because the laboratory operates on a 24-hour basis.

Eighty-five people are employed by Oakdon, and turnover is high. Employee morale is very low because the workers have no benefits other than five sick days, five vacation days, and a life insurance policy. The hourly wages are competitive, yet the workers believe that they should move elsewhere once they gain some experience.

Dr. George Branam is the president and owner of the laboratory. He believes that his operation is too small to offer any sophisticated benefits. He also believes that turnover and poor morale are impossible to deal with in his type of business. Because his understanding of human resource management is limited, Dr. Branam has sought the assistance of a consultant.

Your consultation: As the consultant to Oakdon & Associates, Inc., explain to Dr. Branam the various human resource practices his business could use, even though it is small. In addition, relate the importance of employee morale and outline some specific steps that could improve the situation at his laboratory.

Endnotes

1. See: Jeffrey S. Hornsby & Donald F. Kuratko, *Frontline HR,* (Thomson Publishing, 2005); Karen Roberts, Ellen Kossek, and Cynthia Ozeki, "Managing the Global Workforce: Challenges and Strategies," *Academy of Management Executive* 12, no. 4 (Nov. 1998): 93–106; see also: Robert Gatewood, Hubert S. Field, Murray Barrick, *Human Resource Selection* 6th Ed., (Thomson/SouthWestern Publishers, 2008); and Richard M. Hodgetts, Kathryn W. Hegar, *Modern Human Relations at Work* 10th Ed., (Thomson/SouthWestern Publishers, 2008).
2. United States Small Business Administration Office of Advocacy (2006). Characteristics of small employers and owners. www.sba.gov/advo.
3. Heneman, R. L., Tansky, J., W. and Camp, S. M. (2000), "Human resource management practices in small and medium-sized enterprises: Unanswered questions and future research perspectives." *Entrepreneurship Theory and Practice,* 25: 11–26.
4. Davermann, M. "HR=Higher Revenues?" *Fortune Small Business,* July 2006, Vol. 16, 80–81.
5. W. W. Burk, "What Human Resource Practitioners Need to Know for the 21st Century," *Human Resource Management* 36, no. 1 (1997): 71–79; and Jeffrey S. Hornsby & Donald F. Kuratko, *Frontline HR,* (Thomson Publishing, 2005).
6. Paul Gibson, "Sexual Harassment Rulings Less Than Meets the Eye," *HR Magazine* (Oct. 1998): 136–143; and Robert K. Robinson, William T. Jackson, Geralyn McClure Franklin, and Diana Hensley, "U.S. Sexual Harassment Law: Implications for Small Business," *Journal of Small Business Management* (April 1998): 1–12.
7. See B. Becker, and B. Gerhart, "The Impact of Human Resource Management in Organizational Performance: Progress and Prospects," *Academy of Management Journal* 39 (1996): 779–80 I.
8. Pursell, E.D., Campion, M.A., and Gaylord, S.R. (1980), "Structured interviewing: Avoiding selection problems." *Personnel Journal,* 59: 908.
9. Bill Leonard, "SHRM Leads Fight for State Reference-Checking Laws," *HR News* (Oct. 1995): www.shrm.0rglhrmagazinearticles.
10. See Robert D. Gatewood and Hubert S. Field, "A Personnel Selection Program for Small Business," *Journal of Small Business Management* (Oct. 1987): 16–24.
11. James W. Fairfield-Sonn, "A Strategic Model for Small Business Training and Development," *Journal of Small Business Management* (Jan. 1987): 11–18.
12. See McRae C. Banks, Allen L. Bures, and Donald L. Champion, "Decision-Making Factors in Small Business Training and Development," *Journal of Small Business Management* (Jan. 1987): 19–25.
13. Richard M. Hodgetts and Donald F. Kuratko, *Management.* 3rd ed. (Ft. Worth: The Dryden Press, 1991), 602–612.
14. M. Michael Markowich, "Response: We Can Make Performance Appraisals Work," *Compensation and Benefits Review* (May–June 1995): 25. See also Julie Barclay and Lynn Harland, "Peer Performance Appraisals: The impact of Rater Competence, Rater Location, and Rating Correctability on Fairness Perceptions," *Group and Organization Management,* (March 1995): 39–60.
15. French, W. L. Human Resources Management (2007 6th ed.). Boston: Houghton Mifflin Company, p. 383.
16. "Traveling Beyond 360-Degree Evaluations: UPS Delivers Feedback with Role-Playing, Training," HR *Magazine* (Sept. 1999): 82–91.

17. Mark A. Mallinger and Tom G. Cummings, "Improving the Value of Performance Appraisals," *Advanced Management Journal* (spring 1986): 19; see also Jon Werner and Mark Bolino, "Explaining U.S. Courts of Appeals' decisions Involving Performance Appraisal: Accuracy, Fairness, and Validation," *Personnel Psychology* 50 (1997): 1–24.

18. See Dawn S. Carlson, Nancy Upton, & Samuel Seaman, "The Impact of Human Resource Practices and Compensation Design on Performance," *Journal of Small Business Management,* 44 (4) 2006. pp. 531–543.

19. Jeffrey S. Hornsby and Donald F. Kuratko, "Human Resource Management as Small Businesses Grow," *Mid-American Journal of Business* (spring 1990): 31–38.

20. Palermo, Joseph C. "Well-crafted worker discipline program diminishes risk." *Business Insurance,* 2007, Vol. 41, Issue 8.

21. Jeffrey S. Hornsby and Donald F. Kuratko, "Human Resource Management in Small Business: Critical Issues for the 1990s," *Journal of Small Business Management* (July 1990): 9–18; and updated in Jeffrey S. Hornsby and Donald F. Kuratko, "Human Resource Management in U.S. Small Businesses: A Replication & Extension" *Journal of Developmental Entrepreneurship,* 8 (1), 2003, pp. 73–92.

22. J. Duberley and P. Walley, "Assessing the Adoption of HRM by Small and Medium-sized Manufacturing Organizations," *International Journal of Human Resource Management* 6, no. 4 (1995): 891–909.

23. Bernice Kotey & Peter Slade, "Formal Human Resource Management Practices in Small Growing Firms," *Journal of Small Business Management,* 43 (1), 2005. pp. 16–40.

CHAPTER 12

GROWING VENTURES
THE FUTURE

INTRODUCTION

Growth is seemingly what every entrepreneur desires. However, the challenges that come with growth can be overwhelming if the entrepreneur is not prepared. Thus, the desire for growth can differ greatly from the actual ability to manage growth. Many entrepreneurial ventures have failed because of the entrepreneur's inability to manage growth; it is truly the entrepreneurial challenge of the 21st century.

Growing ventures differ in many ways from larger, more structured businesses. Several unique managerial challenges involve smaller ventures in particular. These challenges may seem insignificant to the operation of a large business, but they are important to many owner/managers of smaller, growing ventures.[1]

UNIQUE CHALLENGES OF GROWING VENTURES

THE DISTINCTION OF SMALLER SIZE

The distinction of *smallness* gives newer ventures and smaller firms certain disadvantages. The limited market, for example, restricts a business. Because a new venture has fewer employees and other resources, it is limited in its ability to geographically extend throughout a region or state. Another disadvantage is the higher ordering costs that burden many newer ventures. Because they do not order large lots of inventory from suppliers, newer ventures usually do not receive quantity discounts and must pay higher prices. Finally, a smaller staff forces firms to accept less specialization of labor. Thus, employees and managers are expected to perform numerous functions.[2] One research study that reviewed case histories of smaller emerging firms found that newer and/or smaller ventures suffer from several impediments to growth. Specifically, the study cited the following:[3]

- Lack of financing
- Lack of the right mix of employee skills
- Lack of market knowledge
- Lack of innovation in new markets
- Lack of innovation in new products
- Lack of management expertise
- Poor business systems
- Technology constraints

Smaller ventures have some advantages that should be recognized and capitalized on. One of these is greater flexibility. In smaller firms, decisions can be made and implemented immediately, without the input of committees and the delay of bureaucratic layers. Production, marketing, and service are all areas that can be adjusted quickly for a competitive advantage over larger businesses in the same field. A second advantage is constant communication with the community.[4] The owner of a smaller venture lives in the community and is personally involved in community affairs. The special insight of this involvement allows the owner to adjust products or services to suit the specific needs or desires of the particular community. This leads to the third and probably most important advantage of closeness to the customer: the ability to offer personal service. The personal service that an owner of a smaller venture can provide is one of the key elements of success today. Major corporations work feverishly to duplicate or imitate the idea of personal service. Because the opportunity to provide personal service is an advantage that small firms possess by nature of their size, it *must* be utilized.

THE ONE-PERSON-BAND SYNDROME

Smaller ventures are started by the entrepreneur alone or with a few family members or close associates. In effect, the business is the entrepreneur, and the entrepreneur is the business.[5] However, a danger arises if the owner refuses to relinquish any authority as the smaller venture grows. Some owners fail to delegate responsibility to employees, thereby retaining all decision-making authority. One study revealed that most planning in smaller firms is done by the owner alone, as are other operational activities.[6] This syndrome often is derived from the same pattern of independence that helped the entrepreneur start the business in the first place. However, the owner who continues to perform as a one-person band may restrict the growth of the firm because the owner's ability is limited. How can proper planning for the business be accomplished if the owner is immersed in daily operations? Thus, the owner of a smaller, growing venture must recognize the importance of delegation. If the owner can break away from the natural tendency to do everything, the business will benefit from a wider distribution of that person's abilities.

TIME MANAGEMENT

Effective time management is not a challenge faced exclusively by smaller ventures. However, limited size and staff force the entrepreneur to face this challenge most diligently. It has been said that a person never will *find* time to do anything but must, in fact, *make* the time. In other words, owners of smaller, growing ventures should learn to use time as a resource and not allow time to use them.[7] In order to perform daily managerial activities in the most time-efficient manner, owner/managers should follow four critical steps:

1. *Assessment.* The business owner should analyze his or her daily activities and rank them in order of importance. (A written list on a notepad is recommended.)
2. *Prioritization.* The owner should divide and categorize the day's activities based on his or her ability to devote the necessary time to the task that day. In other words, the owner should avoid procrastination.
3. *Creation of procedures.* Repetitive daily activities can be handled easily by an employee if instructions are provided. This organization of tasks can be a major time-saver for the owner, thereby allowing the fourth and final step to be put into effect.
4. *Delegation.* Delegation can be accomplished after the owner creates procedures for various jobs. As mentioned previously, delegation is a critical skill that smaller-venture owners need to develop.

All of these steps in effective time management require self-discipline on the part of owners seeking to grow their ventures.

COMMUNITY OBLIGATIONS

Proximity to the community has already been mentioned as a size advantage for smaller ventures. However, unlike major corporations with public relations departments, the owner of a smaller, growing venture is involved with community activities directly. The community presents unique challenges to smaller ventures in three ways: participation, leadership, and donations.

Each of these expectations from the community requires owners to plan and budget carefully. Many community members believe that an owner has excess time because he or she owns a business. They also believe that an owner possesses leadership abilities that are required for various community activities. Although the latter may be true, the owner usually does not have excess time. Therefore, owners of growing firms need to plan carefully the activities they believe would be most beneficial. One consideration is the amount of advertising or recognition the business will receive for the owner's participation. When the owner can justify his or her community involvement, both the business and the community benefit.

Financial donations also require careful analysis and budgeting. Again, because consumers have access to the owner of a smaller venture (as opposed to the chief executive officer of a major corporation), he or she may be inundated with requests for donations to charitable and community organizations. Although each organization may have a worthy cause, the owner cannot support every one and remain financially healthy. Thus, the owner needs to decide which of the organizations to assist and to budget a predetermined amount of money for annual donations. Any other solicitations for money must be placed in writing and submitted to the venture owner for consideration. This is the only way owners can avoid giving constant cash donations without careful budget consideration.

The critical fact to remember is that time and money are extremely valuable resources for a growing, smaller venture. Therefore, they should be budgeted in a meaningful way. Owners need to analyze their community involvement and continuously reassess the costs versus the benefits.[8]

CONTINUING MANAGEMENT EDUCATION

A final unique concern for the owner of a growing venture is the continuation of management education. All of the previously mentioned concerns leave very little time for owners to maintain or improve their managerial knowledge. However, the environment of the late 1990s produced dramatic changes that can affect the procedures, processes, programs, philosophy, and even the product of a smaller venture. The ancient Greek philosopher Epictetus once said, "It is impossible for a man to learn what he thinks he already knows." This quote illustrates the need for smaller-venture owners to dedicate time to learning new techniques and principles for their business. Trade associations, seminars, conferences, publications, and college courses all provide opportunities for smaller-venture owners to continue their management education. Staying abreast of industry changes is another way for growing entrepreneurs to maintain a competitive edge.

OTHER ISSUES IN THE FORMATIVE YEARS

Smaller-venture entrepreneurs confront many other managerial issues in the formative years of the business. Growth can demand huge inputs of cash at a time when the venture is simply *cash strapped*. The unique stress that this situation presents can be another managerial challenge for the entrepreneur (see Chapter 10 for the important financial gauges that every entrepreneur needs to be aware of during a period of rapid growth).

Table 12-1 provides a list of the 10 most crucial issues identified by smaller-venture managers.[9] As shown in the table, those issues focus on internal problems that require traditional managerial skills. Marketing, human resource planning, finance, and legal concerns summarize the issues most often cited.

The unique managerial concerns of smaller ventures presented in this section directly impact the growth period throughout which many smaller ventures evolve. The next section examines some of the key elements of the growth stage.

The Challenges Ahead

When trying to establish the most crucial challenges that confront new business ventures, *Entrepreneur* magazine, in conjunction with PricewaterhouseCoopers, polled 281 fast-growing firms. The sample firms included 125 product companies and 156 service companies; 129 were considered high-tech, and 152 low-tech. Seventy-seven percent employed fewer than 100 people, so the survey touched the newer-ventures market. The poll was intended to find out what challenges were perceived by the venture owners to be the most significant for 2007. Following are some of the summary results:

Top 10 Perceived Challenges

1. Retaining key employees
2. Hiring qualified employees
3. New product (or service) development
4. Expansion of U.S. market
5. Cost reductions
6. Productivity increases
7. Business alliances
8. Technology upgrades
9. Cash flow management
10. Merger or acquisition

The survey also posed questions regarding the most feared events that could harm the venture (as perceived by the venture owners). Following is a summary of the results:

Top 10 Damage Factors

1. Shortage of qualified workers
2. Unstable economy
3. Increased competition
4. Health care costs
5. Weaker capital spending
6. Shrinking profit margins
7. Interest rates
8. Government regulations
9. Weak consumer spending
10. Energy costs

Source: Adapted from Mark Hendricks, "A Look Ahead," *Entrepreneur* (January 2007): 70–76.

TABLE 12-1	The Most Critical Problems Firms Encounter in Their Formative Years

1. Finding new customers
2. Obtaining financing
3. Recruiting and hiring new employees
4. Recruiting and hiring new managers
5. Dealing with current employee problems
6. Product pricing
7. Planning for market expansion
8. Handling legal problems
9. Determining and maintaining product quality
10. Dealing with various governmental agencies

Source: Adapted from Guvenc G. Alpander, Kent D. Carter, and Roderick A. Forsgren, "Managerial Issues and Problem Solving in the Formative Years," *Journal of Small Business Management* (April 1990): 12.

KEY ELEMENTS OF GROWTH

Five key managerial actions come into play during the growth stage: control, responsibility, tolerance of failure, change, and flexibility.

CONTROL

Growth creates problems in the areas of command and control. To solve these problems, management must answer three critical questions: Does the control system imply trust between managers and employees? Does the resource allocation system imply trust? Is it easier for an employee to ask for permission than to ask for forgiveness? These questions reveal a great deal about the control of a venture. If they are answered positively, the venture is moving toward a good blend of control and participation. If they are answered negatively, the reasons for each response should be closely examined.

RESPONSIBILITY

As the smaller venture grows, the distinction between authority and responsibility becomes more apparent. Authority always can be delegated, but it is also important to create a sense of worker responsibility. It is through responsibility that flexibility, innovation, and a supportive environment are established. Because people tend to look beyond the ordinary limits of their job if a sense of responsibility is developed, the growth stage is better served by the innovative activity and shared responsibility of all of the business's members.

EFFECTIVE DELEGATION

In the operations of a new venture during a growth stage, *effective delegation* is a key component of success. This process entails three steps: (1) assigning specific duties, (2) granting authority to carry out these duties, and (3) creating the oblig-ation of responsibility for necessary action. Why is delegation so essential to growth-oriented ventures? Because to continue growth and innovation, the en-trepreneur needs to free up his or her time and rely on others in the enterprise to carry on the day-to-day activities.

TOLERANCE OF FAILURE

Even if a venture has avoided the initial start-up pitfalls and has expanded to the growth stage, it is still important to maintain a tolerance of failure. The level of failure that the entrepreneur experienced and learned from at the start of the venture should be the same level expected, tolerated, and learned from during this stage. Although no business should seek failure, continual innovation and growth will require a degree of tolerance of—as opposed to punishment for—failure. Three distinct forms of failure should be distinguished:

- *Moral failure:* a violation of internal trust. Because the firm is based on mutual expectations and trust, this violation can result in serious negative consequences.

- *Personal failure:* brought about by a lack of skill or application. Usually, responsibility for this form of failure is shared by the firm and the individ-ual. Normally, those involved attempt to remedy the situation in a mutually beneficial way.

- *Uncontrollable failure:* caused by external factors and the most difficult to prepare for or deal with. Resource limitations, faulty strategic direction, and market changes are examples of forces outside the control of employees. Top management must carefully analyze the context of this form of failure and work to prevent its recurrence.

CHANGE

Planning, operations, and implementation all are subject to continual changes as the venture moves through the growth stage and beyond. Retaining an innova-tive and opportunistic posture during growth requires variation from the norm. It should be realized, however, that change holds many implications for the enterprise in terms of resources, people, and structure. It is therefore important that flexibility regarding change be preserved during growth. This allows for faster managerial response to environmental conditions.

FLEXIBILITY

One of the most powerful assets a smaller venture possesses is flexibility. During the growth stage, the ability to access and accumulate resources is needed. *Networking* is a method of using external resources that the smaller ventures does not own.[10] Only by remaining flexible can entrepreneurs establish the net-work of relationships they need for assistance during growth periods.

THE TRANSITION FROM ENTREPRENEUR TO MANAGER

The transitions between the various stages of a venture are complemented (or, in some cases, retarded) by the entrepreneur's ability to make a transition in style. Entrepreneurial style relates to the creativity, innovation, and risk-taking ability needed to start up a venture, whereas managerial style emphasizes the planning and organizational ability needed to operate the business. A key transition occurs during the growth stage, when the entrepreneur shifts into a managerial style. This is not easy to do. As Hofer and Charan have noted, "Among the different transitions that are possible, probably the most difficult to achieve and also perhaps the most important for organizational development is that of moving from a one-person, entrepreneurial managed firm to one run by a functionally organized, professional management team."[11]

A number of problems arise during this transition, especially if the enterprise is characterized by factors such as (1) a highly centralized decision-making system, (2) an overdependence on one or two key individuals, (3) an inadequate repertoire of managerial skills and training, and (4) a paternalistic atmosphere.[12] These characteristics, although often effective in the start-up and survival of a new venture, pose a threat to the firm's development during the growth stage. Quite often, these characteristics inhibit the venture's development by detracting from the entrepreneur's ability to manage the growth stage successfully.

To bring about the necessary transition, the entrepreneur must plan carefully, and gradually implement the transitional process. Hofer and Charan have suggested a seven-step process:

1. The entrepreneur must want to make the change and must want it strongly enough to undertake major modifications in his or her own behavior.

2. The day-to-day decision-making procedures of the organization must be changed. Specifically, participation in this process must be expanded. Greater emphasis also should be placed on formal decision techniques.

3. The two or three key operating tasks that primarily are responsible for the organization's success must be institutionalized. This may involve the selection of new people to supplement or replace those "indispensable" individuals who have performed these tasks in the past.

4. Middle-level management must be developed. Specialists must learn to become functional managers, and functional managers must learn to become general managers.

5. The firm's strategy should be evaluated and modified, if necessary, to achieve growth.

6. The organizational structure and its management systems and procedures must be modified slowly to fit the company's new strategy and senior managers.

7. The firm must develop a professional board of directors.[13]

BALANCING THE FOCUS (ENTREPRENEUR AND MANAGER)

When managing the growth stage, owner/managers must remember two important points. First, an adaptive firm needs to retain certain entrepreneurial characteristics to encourage employee innovation and creativity while making a transition toward a more managerial style.[14] This critical entrepreneur/manager balance is extremely difficult to achieve. As Stevenson and Gumpert have noted, "Everybody wants to be innovative, flexible, and creative. But for every Apple, Google, and Papa John's Pizza, there are thousands of new restaurants, clothing stores, and consulting firms that presumably have tried to be innovative, to grow, and to show other characteristics that are entrepreneurial in the dynamic sense— but have failed."[15]

The ability to remain entrepreneurial while adopting administrative traits is vital to a venture's successful growth. Table 12-2 compares the entrepreneurial and administrative characteristics and pressures of five major factors: strategic orientation, commitment to seize opportunities, commitment of resources, control of resources, and management structure. Each of these five areas is critical to the balance needed for entrepreneurial managing.

At the two ends of the continuum (from an entrepreneurial focus to an administrative focus) are specific points of view; Stevenson and Gumpert have characterized these in a question format.

THE ADMINISTRATIVE POINT OF VIEW

- What sources do I control?
- What structure determines our organization's relationship to its market?
- How can I minimize the impact of others on my ability to perform?
- What opportunity is appropriate?

THE ENTREPRENEURIAL POINT OF VIEW

- Where is the opportunity?
- How do I capitalize on it?
- What resources do I need?
- How do I gain control over them?
- What structure is best?[16]

A recent study conducted by Donald Sull suggests that entrepreneurs practice "disciplined entrepreneurship." Even when the venture is up and running, the owner continuously faces the entrepreneurial challenge of dealing with risk and uncertainty when deciding on new products, markets, and so forth. Based on a review of the case histories of several entrepreneurial ventures, Sull recommends an approach similar to the scientific method when pursuing entrepreneurial activities. He uses the analogy that entrepreneurial ideas

TABLE 12-2 The Entrepreneurial Focus Versus the Administrative Focus				
	Entrepreneurial Focus		*Administrative Focus*	
	Characteristics	*Pressures*	*Characteristics*	*Pressures*
Strategic Orientation	Driven by perception of opportunity	Diminishing opportunities Rapidly changing technology, consumer economics, social values, and political rules	Driven by controlled resources	Social contracts Performance measurement criteria Planning systems and cycles
Commitment to Seize Opportunities	Revolutionary, with short duration	Action orientation Narrow decision windows Acceptance of reasonable risks Few decision constituencies	Evolutionary, with long duration	Acknowledgment of multiple constituencies Negotiation about strategic course Risk reduction Coordination with existing resource base
Commitment of Resources	Many stages, with minimal exposure at each stage	Lack of predictable resource needs Lack of control over the environment Social demands for appropriate use of resources	A single stage, with complete commitment out of decision	Need to reduce risk Incentive compensation Turnover in managers Capital budgeting systems Formal planning systems
Control of Resources	Episodic use or rent of required resources	Increased resource specialization Long resource life compared with need Risk of obsolescence Risk inherent in the identified opportunity Inflexibility of permanent commitment to resources	Ownership or employment of required resources	Power, status, and financial rewards Coordination of activity Efficiency measures Inertia and cost of change Industry structures

TABLE 12-2 *(Continued)*				
	Entrepreneurial Focus		*Administrative Focus*	
	Characteristics	*Pressures*	*Characteristic*	*Pressures*
Management Structure	Flat, with multiple informal networks	Coordination of key noncontrolled resources Challenge to hierarchy Employees' desire for independence	Hierarchy	Need for clearly defined authority and responsibility Organizational culture Reward systems Management theory

Source: Reprinted by permission of the *Harvard Business Review.* An exhibit from "The Heart of Entrepreneurship," by Howard H. Stevenson and David E. Gumpert (March/April 1985): 89. Copyright 1985 by the President and Fellows of Harvard College. All rights reserved.

are like experiments. Based on this analogy, Sull suggests the following three steps:[17]

Step 1: Formulate a Working Hypothesis

- Keep it fluid and change your hypothesis as the facts come in.
- Be sure you have the right to an opinion by gaining the appropriate expertise.
- Identify deal killers.

Step 2: Assemble Resources

- Raise enough financing for the next round of experiments.
- Stabilize the business model before making key hires.
- Outsource functions that are distracting to your experiments.

Step 3: Design and Run Experiments

- In the initial stages of the venture, conduct partial experiments by testing small parts of the business model.
- Conduct holistic experiment when several variables must be tested at once.
- Stage partial experiments before undertaking more expensive holistic experiments.
- Avoid *experiment creep* by not letting the experiments drag on too long and exhaust your resources.

OUTSIDE MANAGERIAL ASSISTANCE

Because smaller ventures are limited with regard to size and employees, assistance from outside of the venture can be helpful. One study identified the impact of outside assistance on the performance of small firms.[18] The findings supported the fact that smaller ventures benefit from outside assistance, especially in the areas of administration and operations.

Another suggested source of assistance is a board of advisers. *Quasi-boards* are composed of volunteers who serve in an advisory capacity to a venture's owner.[19] This group could comprise professionals, such as accountants, lawyers, or consultants, with whom the smaller-venture owner is familiar. The board would provide an outside view of the business and make recommendations for the smaller-venture owner. The quasi-board avoids some of the legal responsibilities associated with formal boards of directors.[20] However, as the venture grows, it is advisable to formalize a structure with an actual board of directors.

THE CHALLENGE OF ETHICAL PRACTICES IN GROWING VENTURES

Innovation, risk taking, and venture creation form the backbone of the free enterprise system. The qualities of individualism and competition that have emerged from this system have helped to create new jobs and to generate enormous growth in new ventures. However, these same qualities also have produced complex trade-offs between economic profits and social welfare. On one hand, the success rate is measured in profits, jobs, and efficiency; on the other hand is the quest for personal and social respect, honesty, and integrity. Ideally, society would provide one ethical norm to calculate the greatest good for the greatest number and, thus, would help resolve such ethical dilemmas. However, developing an *ethical code* that suits all people in all situations is nearly impossible. To illustrate, a study by researchers Longenecker, McKinney, and Moore examined the ethical concern of entrepreneurs regarding specific business issues.[21] The left side of Table 12-3 provides a list of the issues that owners believed needed a strong ethical stance. However, the right side of Table 12-3 lists the issues that the same owners viewed with greater tolerance in regard to demanding ethics. The contradictory nature of these findings proves that ethical decision-making is a complex challenge because of the nature and personal perception of various issues.[22]

TABLE 12-3 Ethical Views of Entrepreneurs	
Issues That Smaller Venture Owners Believe Require a Strong Ethical Position	*Issues That Smaller Venture Owners View with Greater Tolerance in Regard to Ethical Position*
1. Evaluating faulty investment advice	1. Padded expense accounts
2. Favoritism in promotion	2. Tax evasion
3. Reporting dangerous design flaws	3. Collusion in bidding
4. Misleading financial reporting	4. Insider trading
5. Misleading advertising	5. Discrimination against women
6. Cigarette smoking on the job	6. Copying computer software

Source: Justin G. Longenecker, Joseph A. McKinney, and Carlos W. Moore, "Ethics in Small Business," *Journal of Small Business Management* (January 1989): 30.

However, general public perception stereotypes *business ethics* as a contradiction in terms. This is a stereotype based on three principal misconceptions that dominate society. The first is that profit and morality are necessarily incompatible. In other words, the pursuit of wealth is a barometer of success, yet it is believed that wealth tends to corrupt individuals. The second is that all ethical problems have simple solutions: They always have a right and wrong answer. This misconception is based on an assumption that an absolute standard exists for judging moral conduct. The third is that ethics is simply a matter of compliance with laws and regulations. Although laws and regulations often emerge from ethical concerns, they are not always considered ethical. In spite of these misconceptions, the fact remains that unethical behavior does take place. Why? A few explanations are possible:

- Greed
- An inability to distinguish between activities at work and activities at home
- A lack of foundation in the study of ethics
- Survivalist (bottom-line) thinking
- A reliance on other social institutions to convey and reinforce ethics

Ethical decision-making is a challenge faced by small and large businesses alike. These challenges are only compounded as a venture grows.[23]

ETHICAL CODES OF CONDUCT

In the broadest sense, ethics provides the basic rules or parameters for conducting any activity in an acceptable manner. More specifically, ethics represents a set of principles prescribing a behavioral code that explains what is good and right or bad and wrong; ethics may, in addition, outline moral duties and obligations.[24] The problem with most definitions of ethics is that they are static descriptions that imply that society agrees on certain universal principles. Because society operates in a dynamic and ever-changing environment, however, such a consensus does not exist. Continual conflict over the ethical nature of decisions is quite prevalent. Therefore, a code of conduct within a business is a statement of ethical practices or guidelines to which an enterprise adheres. A variety of such codes exists; some relate to the industry at large and others relate directly to corporate conduct. These codes cover a multitude of subjects, ranging from misuse of corporate assets, conflict of interest, and use of inside information, to equal employment practices, falsification of books and records, and antitrust violations.

Two important points on codes of conduct should be kept in mind. First, codes of conduct are becoming more prevalent in all firms. Management is not just giving lip service to ethics and moral behavior; it is putting its ideas into writing and distributing these guidelines for everyone in the organization to read and to follow. Second, in contrast to earlier codes, more recent ones are proving more meaningful in terms of external legal and social development, more comprehensive in terms of their coverage, and easier to implement in terms of the administrative procedures for enforcing them.[25]

Tips for Organizational Integrity

When establishing a culture of integrity within a growing organization, numerous elements need to be considered. Researchers have been working with companies to figure out the most crucial elements for organizational leaders to develop. One recent research article noted that organizations with true integrity display the following four characteristics:

1. *The language of ethical decision-making is used.* The employees will openly and confidently discuss the ethical implications of decisions and actions.

2. *Structural supports and procedures that facilitate ethical decision-making have been developed.* Employees have a clear channel to air and discuss problems or issues and to explore the gray areas of compliance.

3. *A culture of openness, responsibility, and commitment to multiple business goals has been created and sustained.* Employees can articulate several business goals beyond the bottom line, such as the organization's responsibility to society, employees, the profession, or ideals.

4. *Employee development is valued.* Employees experience regular opportunities to learn and develop, including personal and career development opportunities within the organization. This commitment makes employees feel that they are a valuable part of the organization and ties individual success to organizational success.

There needs to be an understanding of deeply held assumptions for organizations to build a culture of integrity. One example is a three-phased approach, as follows:

Phase 1: *Understand the "why" of integrity.* Organizations need to educate employees on the importance of ethics and integrity in all aspects of the job. This helps everyone understand why integrity is crucial to the organization as a whole.

Phase 2: *Understand the "why not" of integrity.* Clearly spelling out the rewards for ethical actions and the consequences of unethical actions is important for all employees. This is the phase where employees commit to the processes and behaviors that are rewarded.

Phase 3: *Understand the "practices" of integrity.* Provide employees with the knowledge and tools necessary to resist unethical actions and adopt the appropriate behaviors. Coaching and intensive feedback are recommended.

Finally, all of these ideas can only be sustained through a concerted effort by the executive team of the venture. There must be a true business integration of all of the espoused policies and desired actions. In addition, organizations need to measure the progress and success in these areas. Ultimately, the key component is for executive support to be a strategic priority.

Source: Adapted from D. Christopher Keyes, David Stirling, and Tjai M. Nielsen, "Building Organizational Integrity," *Business Horizons* 50 (2007): 61–70.

ETHICAL LEADERSHIP BY ENTREPRENEURS

Although ethics and social responsibility present complex challenges for owners of growing ventures, the entrepreneur/owner's *value system* is the key to establishing an ethical organization. An owner has the unique opportunity to display honesty, integrity, and ethics in all key decisions. The owner's behavior serves as a model for all employees to follow.

In one study of 282 smaller-venture owners, four specific ethical concepts were examined: business development/profit motive; money-related theft; administrative decision-making; and accession to company pressure. The researchers found underlying dimensions of these concepts that were broader than simple adherence to the law. The study refuted the stereotypes of *ethics equating only to law* or *the law is ethics' only guide*. In other words, smaller-venture owners rely on considerations beyond the legal parameters when making decisions. Their value systems were demonstrated to be a critical component in business decisions.[26]

In smaller ventures, the ethical influence of the owner is more powerful than in larger corporations because his or her leadership is not diffused through layers of management. Owners are identified easily and are observed constantly by employees in a smaller venture. Therefore, smaller-venture owners possess a strong potential to establish high ethical standards for all business decisions.[27] (See Table 12-4 for guidelines that smaller-venture owners can distribute to all managers.)

TABLE 12-4   Twelve Questions for Examining the Ethics of a Business Decision

1. Have you defined the problem accurately?
2. How would you define the problem if you stood on the other side of the fence?
3. How did this situation occur in the first place?
4. To whom and to what do you give your loyalty as a person and as a member of the corporation?
5. What is your intention in making this decision?
6. How does this intention compare with the probable results?
7. Whom could your decision or action injure?
8. Can you discuss the problem with the affected parties before you make your decision?
9. Are you confident that your position will be as valid over a long period of time as it seems now?
10. Could you disclose without qualm your decision or action to your boss, your CEO, the board of directors, your family, and society as a whole?
11. What is the symbolic potential of your action if understood? If misunderstood?
12. Under what conditions would you allow exceptions to your stand?

Source: Reprinted by permission of the *Harvard Business Review.* An exhibit from "Ethics without the Sermon," by Laura L. Nash (November/December 1981). Copyright 1981 by the President and Fellows of Harvard College. All rights reserved.

A recent 20-year longitudinal study on ethical attitudes in smaller firms and large corporations found that ethical decisions are improving across all organizations, regardless of size. The researchers also found that leaders of smaller ventures appeared to respond more ethically in 2005 than they did when the study began in 1985.[28]

THE QUALITY MOVEMENT

The *Quality Movement* refers to an all-encompassing, quality-focused approach to managing a firm's operations. A smaller venture that adopts a philosophy of total quality management must be dedicated to the pursuit of excellence in all aspects of its activities. This philosophy sometimes is described as a cultural phenomenon—an adoption of basic values related to quality. Building a quality program that produces a superior-quality product or service takes dedication and the best efforts of the entire organization. Specifically, an organization adopting a quality strategy must provide significant training and incentive-based compensation to its employees.[29]

To encourage quality management of U.S. businesses, Congress created the Malcolm Baldrige National Quality Award. Each year, up to two awards can be given to applicants in each of three categories: manufacturing, service, and smaller ventures. Insights gained from smaller ventures that have won the Baldrige Award may be key to establishing a total quality approach.[30] (See Figure 12-1 for the Baldrige Award criteria framework.) A complete description of the quality standards can be found at the Malcolm Baldrige Web site: www.quality.nist.gov.

INVOLVE TOP MANAGEMENT

A characteristic common to all Baldrige Award winners is that top managers are involved actively in the total quality effort. In some cases, this has been more a result of operational necessity than of formal planning.

Informal meetings of employees can generate a host of ideas about how to streamline the business's processes as well as demonstrate the commitment of top management to the effort.

FOCUS ON CUSTOMER NEEDS

For a quality process to work, it needs a complete focus on the customer. If a company waits for consumer complaints before initiating improvements, it has waited too long. In addition, customers must believe that management is serious about responding to their needs, requests, suggestions, and so forth. Being customer driven is the heart of quality.[31] Baldrige Award winners in the smaller-venture category focus on customer needs in a number of ways; the two most common are data gathering and data analysis. Data gathering includes surveys, telephone interviews, and face-to-face meetings. The most common of these are

FIGURE 12-1   Baldrige Award Criteria Framework

```
                    ┌──────────────┐
                    │ Management   │
                    │ of process   │
                    │ quality      │
                    │         5.0  │
                    └──────────────┘
                                            ┌──────────────┐          ┌──────────────────┐
                    ┌──────────────┐        │ Customer     │          │   Goal           │
                    │ Human        │        │ focus and    │          │ • Customer       │
                    │ resource     │        │ satisfaction │          │   satisfaction   │
┌──────────────┐    │ development  │        │         7.0  │          │ • Customer       │
│ Senior       │    │ and          │        └──────────────┘          │   satisfaction   │
│ executive    │    │ management   │        ┌──────────────┐          │   relative to    │
│ leadership   │    │         4.0  │        │ Quality and  │          │   competitors    │
│         1.0  │    └──────────────┘        │ operation    │          │ • Market share   │
└──────────────┘                            │ results      │          └──────────────────┘
                    ┌──────────────┐        │         6.0  │          ┌──────────────────┐
                    │ Strategic    │        └──────────────┘          │ Measures of      │
                    │ quality      │                                  │ progress         │
                    │ planning     │                                  │ • Product and    │
                    │         3.0  │                                  │   service quality│
                    └──────────────┘                                  │ • Internal quality│
                    ┌──────────────────────┐                          │   and productivity│
                    │ Information & analysis│                          │ • Supplier quality│
                    │                   2.0 │                          └──────────────────┘
                    └──────────────────────┘
```

Source: Richard M. Hodgetts, Donald F. Kuratko, and Jeffrey S. Hornsby, "Quality Implementation in Small Business: Perspectives from the Baldrige Award Winners," *SAM Advanced Management Journal* (Winter 1999): 39.

company-initiated surveys. When data analysis detects problems, procedures are then developed to analyze and resolve them.

TRAIN EMPLOYEES

Training programs that Baldrige Award-winning firms use share a number of characteristics: (1) strong commitment and involvement by top management, (2) training that is practical and closely linked to the company's objectives and major programs so that trainees can quickly apply much of what they learn to the job, and (3) a consistent training message communicated to all levels and functions so that everyone is working in consonance. In most quality companies, statistical process control (SPC) training begins by first teaching the method to the employees and then giving them the opportunity to apply it in the workplace. This is followed by discussing the results and providing assistance and advice for dealing with any problems or issues that arise when employees use the technique. Additionally, if the company is providing a course or series of programs on SPC tools, the early sessions address simple applications, and the later ones cover more sophisticated tools and techniques.

EMPOWER EMPLOYEES AND GENERATE NEW IDEAS

Empowerment is the authority to personally take control and make decisions. Baldrige Award-winning firms invest a great deal of time and effort in teaching and encouraging their employees to become more personally involved and to use their empowered authority to accomplish tasks.[32] Solectron, for example, gives its line workers the authority to stop the production line any time they feel this is necessary. Customer-service employees at the firm have full authority to return or replace products without obtaining approval from their bosses. Meanwhile, engineers and sales representatives are trained to deal effectively with customers and to make whatever decisions are necessary to meet the needs of these buyers.

Thus, closely linked with the concept of empowerment is the goal of generating new ideas. In addition to giving employees the authority to make decisions, Baldrige Award winners encourage employees to think up new ways to accomplish tasks and to submit these ideas for review and implementation.

RECOGNIZE EMPLOYEES

Employee recognition takes a number of forms, including financial rewards, days off, vacation trips, choice parking spots (typically for a week or a month), "Employee of the Month" pictures placed on the wall, and names added to a plaque of distinguished employees. The latter often are displayed prominently in one area of the building and typically are referred to as "walls (or halls) of fame." Each company has its own recognition system, although the best systems have a handful of similar characteristics. These are that (1) recognition is always positive and is given to actions that have resulted in success; (2) recognition is given openly and tends to be publicized throughout the company or division; (3) recognition is tailored carefully to the needs of employees so that everyone is motivated to pursue the reward; (4) rewards are given soon after they have been earned; and (5) the relationship between achievement and the reward is clearly understood by employees.[33]

CONQUER FEAR

People fear dealing with change, expressing opinions (especially negative ones), taking the initiative on projects, making decisions, and failing. Primarily these fears arise from perceived outcomes the employee might face. Although this human characteristic is never reported directly in Baldrige Award data, it nevertheless has an impact on successful quality programs and should be recognized and addressed whenever possible.

THE CONTINUOUS-IMPROVEMENT CHALLENGE

Baldrige Award winners approach total quality management differently, but they all share a common desire: continuous improvement. By waging an ongoing, incremental battle to do tasks better and better, they ensure that they remain on the cutting edge in providing competitive goods and services.[34] An interesting aspect of the continuous improvement process is that it typically is viewed as incremental and additive rather than explosive and earth shattering. It is characterized more by rapid inching than by dramatic, revolutionary progress. Total quality companies would rather move a foot each day than remain where they are for an indefinite period while waiting to make a giant leap forward.

Baldrige Award winners report a number of benefits from their emphasis on incremental improvements, including (1) increased quality of output, (2) greater competitiveness, (3) higher profitability, (4) a lower operating breakeven point, (5) the opportunity to use a participative management approach that allows employees to play a role in decision making, and (6) a way of learning from past experience and using this information to set realistic, attainable goals.

To achieve these objectives, companies can take either or both of two routes: They can lead with strength by doing what they do best, or they can work to correct mistakes and deficiencies. Baldrige Award winners rely on both of these approaches, although they focus on the first—identifying processes or systems at which they are most successful and working to improve them further. In a manner of speaking, they follow the *attack yourself* rule by aiming to get better and better. In the process, they become or remain quality leaders.[35]

It is imperative that smaller firms develop new methods for quality improvement. Whereas idea generation is critical for a company's revitalization, so, too, are creative quality efforts for overall quality improvement.

TEAMWORK

Today's workplace requires fast movers and fast thinkers to stay on top of the market and ahead of the competition. Total quality goes beyond good ethical standards and customer service by including the lifeblood of the organization: the employees. Using teams and other collaborative efforts to synthesize ideas and finish projects efficiently is commonplace among companies that strive for quality standards. The dynamics of teams and teamwork performance are uniform regardless of the size of the corporation, so hiring employees with the ability to work well on team projects is both a necessity and an advantage. Following are the basic factors of human processing that affect the success or failure rate of the problem-solving tools used by a team, and the seven-step model commonly used to improve team performance in the workplace. Human information processing factors include:

- Generally, people can hold only seven bits of information in their memory at a time.
- The mind has filters that distort incoming information, affecting the interpretation and use of that data.
- Individuals tend to be overconfident.
- People tend to base decisions on incorrect original data.

- People do not learn well enough from past experiences and fail to process useful information.

To improve team performance, specific emphasis should be put on the following seven steps for quality decision-making:

1. **Define the problem.** A problem statement should incorporate observable and measurable data, and should be as exact as possible. The primary purpose of problem statements is to clearly define the gap between the current situation and the desired result. This step can be made easier by using mind maps, brainstorming, or problem questioning.

2. **Decide on the process to use.** Once the problem has been defined, the team must decide on the process or model by which it will find a solution. Without an agreed-upon process, the team may create overlapping work efforts and become aggravated. Key questions to answer when deciding on the process include the following:
   - Who should be involved in the problem-solving process? Who are the critical stakeholders or experts the team needs to be part of the process?
   - What tools or equipment will the team need to make a decision?
   - What information and data will the team need?

3. **Gather information.** Several important issues need to be addressed during this step:
   - Does the team have accurate data that are readily available?
   - Does the team need help understanding and interpreting the data?
   - Is there information the team needs that is considered private or confidential?

4. **Make the decision.** Three questions to answer before reaching the conclusion are:
   - Will the whole team work on the whole problem, or will sub-teams do some of the work?
   - What decision-making style will the team use?
   - What are the criteria for the solution?

5. **Develop an action plan.** An action plan is similar to a business plan in that it is used to track progress. It also serves to track how well the chosen solution worked. A standard action plan will answer the following questions:
   - What action is required?
   - Who is responsible?
   - Is there a completion date?
   - Does the plan contain space for marking when the action has been completed?

6. **Audit and evaluate the decision and process.** The learning does not end when the decision has been made. Team self-analysis and feedback allow for

a review of the results and the ability to learn more about both the team's own cognitive processes and the problem-solving process. Future performance can be improved by answering the following questions as a team:

TEAM SELF-ANALYSIS

How well did we define the problem?
How well did we gather information?
What would we do the same way next time?
What would we not do the next time?

7. **Record and share learning.** Prior to activating team dynamics in the workplace, mechanisms should be put in place to permit teams to learn from one another and to ensure that vital information is not lost. A foundation of intellectual capital is priceless and will allow any company to remain afloat and competitive.[36]

THE CHALLENGES OF GLOBAL EXPANSION

For many years, U.S. entrepreneurs shuddered at the thought of "going international" because it was just too big a step, too risky, and too uncertain. On the other side of the ocean, Lenin wrote that foreign investment represented the final stage of capitalism. It is therefore ironic that the world's greatest boom in foreign investment took place in the dying years of Lenin's communism. During the 1980s and 1990s, foreign investment grew four times faster than world output and three times faster than world trade. Entrepreneurs rushed enthusiastically to those countries that were blighted by communism, state socialism, or authoritarian, isolationist governments. Prime targets included Japan, China, India, and other parts of Asia, Latin America, and Eastern Europe.[37]

WHY GLOBALIZE FOR GROWTH?

Countries vary with respect to the quantity and proportion of resources they possess, which forms the basis for a competitive advantage of nations. Resource-rich countries (those with extractive assets) include the Organization of the Petroleum Exporting Countries (OPEC) block nations and many parts of Africa. Labor-rich, rapidly developing countries include Brazil, Sri Lanka, India, the Philippines, and South and Central America. Market-rich countries such as Europe, Brazil, Mexico, and the United States have purchasing power, in contrast to India or China, which possess large populations but suffer from a lack of purchasing power. Each country has something that others need, thus forming the basis of an interdependent international trade system.

Internationalization can be viewed as the outcome of a sequential process of incremental adjustments to changing conditions of a firm and its environment. This process progresses step by step as risk and commitment increase and entrepreneurs acquire more knowledge through experience. The entrepreneur's impression of the risks and rewards of internationalizing can be determined by feasibility studies of the potential gains to be won.

An entrepreneur's willingness to move into international markets is also affected by whether he or she has studied a foreign language, has lived abroad long enough to experience culture shock, and is internationally oriented. Another factor is the entrepreneur's confidence in the company's competitive advantage in the form of price, technology, marketing, or financial superiority. This advantage might include an efficient distribution network, an innovative or patented product, or possession of exclusive information about the foreign market.

Deteriorating market conditions at home may propel entrepreneurs to seek foreign markets to help offset declining business, or a countercyclical market may be sought to balance the fluctuations of a single market subject to one set of local economic conditions.[38] Some growing ventures internationalize immediately and do not wait to expand their horizons. Multinational from inception, these companies break the traditional expectation that a business must enter the international arena incrementally, becoming global only as it grows older and wiser. (See Table 12-5 for proactive and reactive reasons to globalize.)

According to researchers Oviatt and McDougal, seven characteristics of successful global start-ups are: (1) global vision from inception; (2) internationally experienced management; (3) a strong international business network; (4) preemptive technology or marketing; (5) a unique intangible asset; (6) a linked product or service; and (7) tight organizational coordination worldwide.[39]

As global opportunities expand, entrepreneurs are becoming more open-minded about internationalizing. The primary advantage of trading internationally is that a company's market is expanded significantly and its growth prospects are greatly enhanced. Other advantages include utilizing idle capacity, minimizing cyclical or seasonal slumps, getting acquainted with manufacturing technology used in other countries, learning about products not sold in the United States, learning about other cultures, acquiring growth capital more easily in other countries, and having the opportunity to travel for business and pleasure.[40]

TABLE 12-5 Major Reasons to "Globalize" a Growing Venture	
Proactive Reasons	*Reactive Reasons*
Increased profit	Competitive pressures
Unique goods or services	Declining domestic demand
Technological advantage	Overcapacity
Exclusive market information	Proximity to customers
Owner-manager desire	Counterattack foreign competition
Tax benefits	
Economies of scale	

Source: Adapted from Donald F. Kuratko and Richard M. Hodgetts, *Effective Small Business Management,* 7th ed. Wiley Publishers, 2001, p. 364.

RESEARCHING THE GLOBAL MARKET

Before entering a foreign market, it is important to study the unique culture of that market's potential customers. Concepts of how the product is used, demographics, psychographics, and legal and political norms are usually different from those in the United States. Therefore, it is necessary to conduct market research to identify these important parameters. The following market characteristics should be studied:

1. **Government regulations:** Must you conform to import regulations or patent, copyright, or trademark laws that would affect your product?

2. **Political climate:** Will the relationship between government and business or political events and public attitudes in a given country affect foreign business transactions, particularly with the United States?

3. **Infrastructure:** How will the packaging, shipping, and distribution system of your export product be affected by the local transportation system—for example, air, land, or waste?

4. **Distribution channels:** What are the generally accepted trade terms at both wholesale and retail levels? What are the normal commissions and service charges? What laws pertain to agency and distribution agreements?

5. **Competition:** How many competitors do you have and in what countries are they located? On a country-by-country basis, how much market share does each of your competitors have, and what prices do they charge? How do they promote their products? What distribution systems do they use?

6. **Market size:** How big is the market for your product? Is it stable? What is its size individually? Country by country? In what countries are markets opening, expanding, maturing, or declining?

7. **Local customs and culture:** Is your product in violation of cultural taboos?

How can a growing venture learn about international cultures and thus know what is acceptable and what is not? A number of approaches can be employed; one of the most helpful is international business travel. This provides the individual with firsthand information regarding cultural dos and don'ts. Other useful methods include training programs, formal educational programs, and reading the current literature.

GLOBALIZING YOUR PRODUCT: ADAPTATION

Every smaller business would like to sell the same product on a worldwide basis. However, this is not always possible. In many cases, the good must be adapted for different local markets. Two basic reasons for this are the nature of the product and the culture.

In some cases, a product will need little adaptation. An industrial good, such as a factory robot, will need only minor adaptation because the most important factor is the way the machine works. The company may need to rewire the unit to meet local electrical standards, but usually very few other changes are necessary.

In contrast, consumer goods often require much more adaptation. For example, in some countries in the Middle East, toothpaste is given a spicy taste, and, in Latin countries, some soft drinks are sweeter than they are in the United States.

Culture affects product adaptation because the basic product has to be changed to meet the values and beliefs of the local culture. For example, in Japan, Levi's jeans are snugger than they are in the United States because the Japanese like tighter-fitting pants. Similarly, in Japan, the McDonald's trademark character's first name is Donald (not Ronald) because it is easier for the Japanese to pronounce this word. Inside the McDonald's franchise in Germany, beer is sold; in France, wine is sold.

Another factor of product adaptation is governmental regulation. For example, in many countries, imported liquid products must identify their contents in metric measurements, such as liters. Many nations also regulate the content of products and do not allow aerosol spray containers or food processed with particular chemicals. Some of these regulations are designed to provide consumer or environmental safety. In other cases, regulations are formulated to provide protection to local industries. Auto exporters, for example, often find they must modify their cars to sell them in most other countries. Japan carefully regulates the import of all pharmaceutical products, which must be tested in Japanese laboratories. In Europe, many countries require that all postal and telecommunication equipment be developed according to uniform standards, thus forcing all exporters to modify their machines.[41]

Understanding where to find information on a selected foreign market may be the most important step. Some of the most common sources of secondary research include the U.S. government and foreign governments, international organizations, service organizations, trade organizations, directories and newsletters, and databases. The U.S. Government Printing Office publishes *Country Studies* for more than 100 nations. Each of these publications offers a wealth of information to small ventures interested in doing business abroad. The government also provides information through the Department of State, Department of the Treasury, U.S. Trade Department, and the American embassies abroad. Other countries also offer information, such as trade data and information related to domestic industries. This information often can be obtained from the respective country's embassy or consulate in the United States.

Some international organizations provide statistical data on trade and specific products exported and imported on a country-by-country basis, as well as population and other demographic information. Examples include (1) the *Statistical Yearbook*, published by the United Nations; (2) the *World Atlas*, published by the World Bank and providing information on population, growth trends, and gross national products; (3) the Organization for Economic Cooperation and Development, which publishes quarterly and annual trade data on its member countries; and (4) the International Monetary Fund and the World Bank, which publish periodic staff papers that evaluate region- or country-specific issues in depth. A large number of service organizations, such as accounting firms, airlines, universities, and banks, provide data on international business practices, legislative and regulatory requirements, political stability, and trade.

GLOBAL THREATS AND RISKS

Capturing global markets is not as simple as it may seem. Dangers exist and must be monitored carefully. Ignorance and uncertainty, combined with lack of experience in problem solving in a foreign country, top the list. Lack of information about resources to help solve problems contributes to the unfamiliarity, and restrictions imposed by the host country often contribute to the risk. Many host countries demand development of their exports and insist on training and development of their nationals. They can also demand that certain positions in management and technological areas be held by nationals. Many seek technologically based industry rather than extractive industry. In other instances, the host country may require that it own controlling interest and/or limit the amount of profits or fees that entrepreneurs are allowed to take out of the country.

Political risks include unstable governments, disruptions caused by territorial conflicts, wars, regionalism, illegal occupation, and political/ideological differences. Economic risks that need to be monitored include changes in tax laws, rapid rises in costs, strikes, sudden increases in raw materials, and cyclical/dramatic shifts in the gross national product (GNP). Social risks include antagonism among classes, religious conflict, unequal income distribution, union militancy, civil war, and riots. Financial risks incorporate fluctuating exchange rates, repatriation of profits and capital, and seasonal cash flows.

Foreign government import regulations can affect a company's ability to export successfully. These regulations represent an attempt by foreign governments to control their markets, to protect a domestic industry from excessive foreign competition, to limit health and environmental damage, or to restrict what they consider excessive or inappropriate cultural influences. Most countries have import regulations that are potential barriers to export products. Exporters need to be aware of import tariffs and consider them when pricing their product. Although most countries have reduced their tariffs on imported goods, other major restrictions to global trade exist, such as non-tariff barriers (NTBs). These include prohibitions, restrictions, conditions, or specific requirements that can make exporting products difficult and sometimes costly.

Most entrepreneurs avoid international trade because they believe it is too complicated and fraught with bureaucratic red tape. They also believe that international trade is only profitable for large companies that have more resources than smaller businesses. Some other perceived drawbacks of international trade include becoming too dependent on foreign markets; foreign government instability that could cause problems for domestic companies; tariffs and import duties that make it too expensive to trade in other countries; products manufactured in the United States that may need significant modification before they are accepted by people in other countries; and foreign cultures, customs, and languages that make it difficult for Americans to do business in some countries.[42]

International marketing research is critical to the success of a new venture's efforts to sell goods and services in overseas markets. Although venture owners can tap a host of sources to obtain the needed information, these efforts should be directed toward answering the following three questions.

1. *Why is the company interested in going international?* The answer to this question will help the firm set its international objectives and direct the marketing-research effort. For example, if the entrepreneur wants to establish and cultivate an overseas market, the firm will be interested in pinpointing geographic areas where future market potential is likely to be high. If the business owner wants to use the market to handle current overproduction, the company will be interested in identifying markets that are most likely to make immediate purchases. Regardless, the firm will have established a focus for its marketing-research efforts.

2. *What does the foreign-market assessment reveal about the nature and functioning of the markets under investigation?* The answer to this question, which often is comprehensive in scope, helps identify market opportunities and provide insights regarding the specific activities of these individual markets. For example, if the firm identifies potential markets in Spain, Italy, and Mexico, the next step is to evaluate these opportunities. This can be done by gathering information related to the size of the markets, the competition that exists in each, the respective government's attitude toward foreign businesses, and the steps that will have to be taken to do business in each location. Based on this information, a cost/benefit analysis can be conducted and a decision made regarding the market(s) to be pursued.

3. *What specific market strategy is needed to tap the potential of this market?* The answer to this question involves a careful consideration of the marketing mix: product, price, place, and promotion. What product should the firm offer? What specific features should it contain? Does it need to be adapted for the overseas market, or can the firm sell the same product it sells domestically? At what stage in the product life cycle will this product be? How much should the firm charge? Can the market be segmented so that a variety of prices can be used? How will the product be moved through the marketing channel? What type of promotional efforts will be needed: advertising, sales promotion, personal selling, or a combination of these?

Once these questions have been answered, the owner of a growing venture will be in a position to begin implementing the global phase of the firm's strategy.

Summary

A growing venture presents unique managerial challenges for owners to consider. Understanding the disadvantages as well as the advantages of their smaller size helps the entrepreneur/venture manager gain a better focus on strategies for success. The one-person-band syndrome occurs when a smaller venture begins to grow and the entrepreneur is accustomed to doing everything alone. Learning to delegate and share responsibilities is essential for the venture to expand. Effective time management through assessment, prioritization, and delegation will help the venture owner avoid wasting valuable time on needless activities and concentrate more on critical areas. Community involvement by the entrepreneur is a distinctive advantage in one sense, but it must be handled carefully. Time, as well as money, is a valuable resource that must be meaningfully budgeted. Finally, continuation of management education is essential if the owner wants to remain current in both knowledge and abilities.

The key elements of the growth stage are control, responsibility, tolerance of failure, change, and flexibility. The entrepreneur's evolution during this stage requires a transition in style from that of an entrepreneur to that of a manager. Differences in focus can be understood by reviewing the five major factors in Table 12-2. Outside assistance is recommended for growing firms. Additionally, quasi-boards can be developed, in which professionals volunteer to assist in an advisory capacity.

The chapter described the challenges of ethics that face newer and smaller ventures today. The complexity of ethical decisions was discussed, along with the misconceptions society has in regard to business and ethics. Codes of conduct are statements of ethical practices or guidelines to which a business adheres. These codes of conduct are becoming more prevalent in businesses, and owners are emphasizing their importance to the business more than ever. Business owners can provide ethical leadership through their personal involvement with the business. The owner's value system can permeate the business and become a standard of ethical performance.

The quality movement was covered in relation to ventures as they grow and develop. Taking insights from the smaller ventures that have won the Malcolm Baldrige Quality Award, we discussed factors such as top management involvement, customer focus, employee training, empowerment, idea generation, employee recognition, and conquering fear, all of which contribute to an overall quality program committed to the smaller venture's continuous improvement challenge.

Finally, the global expansion challenge was explored. The chapter examined the reasons for global expansion, the research needed to extend beyond domestic borders, and the threats that need to be understood.

Review and Discussion Questions

1. Identify five unique managerial concerns of smaller ventures.
2. What are some of the advantages and disadvantages associated with the distinction of small size?
3. Define the *one-person-band syndrome*.
4. Describe the five key elements involved in the growth stage of a business.
5. Explain the transition a smaller-venture owner must make from entrepreneur to manager.
6. How can a *quasi-board* help smaller ventures?
7. Explain the misconception that society has regarding business and ethics.
8. What is a code of conduct, and how can it assist ethical practices?
9. What are the three levels of social responsibility a business could exhibit?
10. How can smaller-venture owners assume an ethical business leadership position?

11. What is the quality movement?
12. Outline the key factors identified from the Baldrige Award winners that contribute to meeting the continuous improvement challenge.
13. Why should growing ventures globalize their operations?
14. What are some of the major threats and risks associated with foreign markets?

NEW VENTURE CONSULTANT

A Case of Growing Pains

When he first opened his own business, Richard Jacobs loved it. He went to work early in the morning and did not leave until after 9:00 P.M. To spend time with his family, he would take off a few hours in the afternoon and then return to the store after supper, staying until closing time. When he was away from the store in the late afternoon, part-time personnel handled the operation.

That was five years ago. Since then, Richard's business has grown tremendously. Now he employs eight full-time people and sells seven times as much as he did originally. With this increase in business, however, have come a lot of headaches. In particular, Richard has to make many more decisions than he did before. Additionally, although he wants to get his employees involved in the decision-making process and not do all of the work himself, he feels he must do many tasks on his own. He does not believe he can delegate much authority. For example, Richard still makes all of the decisions regarding purchasing, pricing, advertising, hiring, firing, and merchandise display, and he still sells goods in the store.

Recently, Richard went to the doctor for his annual physical. The doctor told him he was working too hard and had to start slowing down. "You've been running that store single-handed for as long as I can remember," the doctor said. "You've got lots of help in the store. Start relying on them to help you out."

Richard did not disagree. The doctor offered good advice, and Richard knows he has to start delegating more authority and getting out of the actual hustle-bustle of daily activity. However, this worries him. A few months ago, he tried turning over more work to his employees and staying in the background. During that time, he concerned himself with the overall operation of the store and left the minor day-to-day business to the staff. But Richard was bored with this side of the operation. He wants to be actively involved for two reasons: First, he believes that the owner/manager's job is to play an active role in the business, not just to sit on the sidelines. Second, he wants to be in the forefront of the action, like he always has been.

Richard does not know how to resolve this dilemma. He would like to maintain his level of involvement at the shop but realizes that, for health reasons, this is inadvisable. However, to be a manager in the true sense of the word seems boring to him.

Your consultation: Help Richard by explaining the key aspects of growing a venture and how important delegation is for growth. Next, explain the key elements in the growth stage that Richard should understand. Finally, recommend a way that Richard can avoid the one-person-band syndrome.

Endnotes

1. See Donald F. Kuratko and Richard M. Hodgetts, *Entrepreneurship: Theory, Process, Practice*, 7th ed. (Mason, OH: Thomson/South-Western, 2007), 609–46.
2. See Michael H. Morris, Nola N. Miyasaki, Craig R. Watters, and Susan M. Coombes, "The Dilemma of Growth: Understanding Venture Size Choices of Women Entrepreneurs," *Journal of Small Business Management* 44 (2006): 221–44.
3. Rob Sims, John Breen, and Shameem Ali, "Small Business Support: Dealing with the Impediments to Growth," *Journal of Enterprising Culture* 10 (2002): 241–56.
4. See Jerry R. Cornwell, "The Entrepreneur as a Building Block for Community," *Journal of Developmental Entrepreneurship* (Fall/Winter 1998): 141–48.
5. David E. Gumpert and David P. Boyd, "The Loneliness of the Small Business Owner," *Harvard Business Review* (November/December 1984): 19–24.
6. Charles B. Shrader, Charles L. Mumford, and Virginia L. Blackburn, "Strategic and Operational Planning, Uncertainty, and Performance in Small Firms," *Journal of Small Business Management* (October 1989): 45–60.
7. Charles R. Hobbs, "Time Power," *Small Business Reports* (January 1990): 46–55; and Jack Falvey, "New and Improved Time Management," *Small Business Reports* (July 1990): 14–17.
8. Terry L. Besser, "Community Involvement and the Perception of Success Among Small Business Operators in Small Towns," *Journal of Small Business Management* (October 1999): 16–29; and Rhonda Walker Mack, "Event Sponsorship: An Exploratory Study of Small Business Objectives, Practices, and Perceptions," *Journal of Small Business Management* (July 1999): 25–30.
9. Guvenc G. Alpander, Kent D. Carter, and Roderick A. Forsgren, "Managerial Issues and Problem Solving in the Formative Years," *Journal of Small Business Management* (April 1990): 9–18.
10. J. Carlos Jarillo, "Entrepreneurship and Growth: The Strategic Use of External Resources," *Journal of Business Venturing* 4 (1989): 133–47.
11. Charles W. Hofer and Ram Charan, "The Transition to Professional Management: Mission Impossible?" *American Journal of Small Business* (Summer 1984): 3; see also Michael J. Roberts, "Managing Growth," in *New Business Ventures and the Entrepreneur* (New York: Irwin/McGraw-Hill, 1999), included in *Annual Editions, Entrepreneurship (2000/2001)*, 170–72.
12. Hofer and Charan, 4.
13. Hofer and Charan, 6.
14. Donald F. Kuratko, Jeffrey S. Hornsby, and Laura M. Corso, "Building an Adaptive Firm," *Small Business Forum* (Spring 1996): 41–48.
15. Howard H. Stevenson and David E. Gumpert, "The Heart of Entrepreneurship," *Harvard Business Review* (March/April 1985): 85.
16. Stevenson and Gumpert, 86–87.
17. Donald N. Sull, "Disciplined Entrepreneurship," *MIT Sloan Management Review* (Fall 2004): 71–77.
18. James J. Chrisman and John Leslie, "Strategic, Administrative, and Operating Problems: The Impact of Outsiders on Small Business Performance," *Entrepreneurship Theory and Practice* (Spring 1989): 37–49.
19. Harold W. Fox, "Quasi-Boards-Useful Small Business Confidants," *Harvard Business Review* (January/February 1982): 64–72.

20. Fred A. Tillman, "Commentary on Legal Liability: Organizing the Advisory Council," *Family Business Review* (Fall 1988): 287–88.
21. Justin G. Longenecker, Joseph A. McKinney, and Carlos W. Moore, "Ethics in Small Business," *Journal of Small Business Management* (January 1989): 27–31.
22. Elisabeth J. Teal and Archie B. Carroll, "Moral Reasoning Skills: Are Entrepreneurs Different?" *Journal of Business Ethics* (April 1999): 229–40; and Shailendra Vyakarnman, Andy Baily, Andrew Myers, and Donna Burnett, "Toward an Understanding of Ethical Behavior in Small Firms," *Journal of Business Ethics* (November 1997): 1625–36.
23. Charles R. Stoner, "The Foundation of Business Ethics: Exploring the Relationship between Organization Culture, Moral Values, and Actions," *SAM Advanced Management Journal* (Summer 1989): 38–43.
24. Verne E. Henderson, "The Ethical Side of Enterprises," *Sloan Management Review* (Spring 1982): 38–46.
25. For more on this topic, see Donald R. Cressy and Charles A. Moore, "Managerial Values and Corporate Codes of Conduct," *California Management Review* (Summer 1983): 121–27; Steven Weller, "The Effectiveness of Corporate Codes of Ethics," *Journal of Business Ethics* (July 1988): 389–95; and Nancy J. Miller and Terry L. Besser, "The Importance of Community Values in Small Business Strategy Formation: Evidence from Rural Iowa," *Journal of Small Business Management* (January 2000): 68–85.
26. Jeffrey S. Hornsby, Donald F. Kuratko, Douglas W. Naffziger, William R. LaFollette, and Richard M. Hodgetts, "The Ethical Perceptions of Small Business Owners: A Factor Analytic Study," *Journal of Small Business Management* (October 1994): 9–16; see also Justin G. Longenecker, Carlos W. Moore, J. William Petty, Leslie E. Palich, and Joseph A. McKinnney, "Ethical Attitudes in Small Businesses and Large Corporations: Theory and Empirical Findings from a Tracking Study Spanning Three Decades," *Journal of Small Business Management* 44 (April 2006): 167–83.
27. Neil Humphreys, Donald P. Robin, R. Eric Reidenbach, and Donald L. Moak, "The Ethical Decision-Making Process of Small Business Owner/Managers and Their Customers," *Journal of Small Business Management* (July 1993): 9–22; see also Donald F. Kuratko, Michael G. Goldsby, and Jeffrey S. Hornsby, "The Ethical Perspectives of Entrepreneurs: An Examination of Stakeholder Salience" *Journal of Applied Management and Entrepreneurship* 9 (October 2004): 19–42.
28. Justin G. Longenecker, Carlos W. Moore, J. William Petty, Leslie E. Palich, and Joseph A. McKinney, "Ethical Attitudes in Small Businesses and Large Corporations: Theory and Empirical Findings from a Tracking Study Spanning Three Decades," *Journal of Small Business Management* 44 (2006): 167–83.
29. Gaylen N. Chandler and Glenn M. McEvoy, "Human Resource Management, TQM, and Firm Performance in Small and Medium-Size Enterprises," *Entrepreneurship Theory and Practice* (Fall 2000): 43–56.
30. Richard M. Hodgetts, *Measures of Quality and High Performance* (New York: AMACOM, 1998): 177–78; see also Jason A. Briscoe, Stanley E. Fawcett, and Robert H. Todd, "The Implementation and Impact of ISO 9000 among Small Manufacturing Enterprises," *Journal of Small Business Management* 43 (July 2005): 309–30.
31. Peter Tarasewich and Surest K. Nair, "Designing for Quality," *Industrial Management* (July/August 1999): 18–21.
32. Fred Luthans, Richard M. Hodgetts, and Sang Lee, "New Paradigm Organizations: From Total Quality to Learning to World-Class," *Organizational Dynamics* (Winter 1994): 5–19.

33. Fred Luthans, Richard M. Hodgetts, and Brett C. Luthans, "The Role of HRM in Sustaining Competitive Advantage into the 21st Century," *National Productivity Review* (Winter 1997): 80.

34. Quentin R. Skrabee, Jr., "Quality Assurance Revisited," *Industrial Management* (November/December 1999): 6–9.

35. Richard M. Hodgetts, Donald F. Kuratko, and Jeffrey S. Hornsby, "Quality Implementation in Small Business: Perspectives from the Baldrige Award Winners," *SAM Advanced Management Journal* (Winter 1999): 37–47.

36. Helene F. Uhlfelder, "It's All About Improving Performance," *Quality Progress* (February 2000): 47–52.

37. See Donald F. Kuratko and Harold P. Welsch, *Strategic Entrepreneurial Growth*, 2nd ed. (Mason, OH: Thomson/South-Western, 2004); see also Hiroyuki Okamuro and Nobuo Kobayashi, "The Impact of Regional Factors on the Startup Ratio in Japan," *Journal of Small Business Management* 44 (April 2006): 310–14.

38. B. Oviatt and P. McDougal, "Global Start-ups," *Inc.* (June 1993): 23.

39. Patricia P. McDougall and Benjamin M. Oviatt, "Defining International Entrepreneurship and Modeling the Speed of Internationalization," *Entrepreneurship Theory and Practice* 29 (2005): 537–54.

40. Shaker Zahra, James Hayton, Jeremy Marcel, and Hugh O'Neill, "Fostering Entrepreneurship during International Expansion: Managing Key Challenges," *European Management Journal* 19 (2001): 359–69. See also Dianne H. B. Welsh, Ilan Alon, and Cecilia M. Falbe, "An Examination of International Retail Franchising in Emerging Markets," *Journal of Small Business Management* 44 (2006): 130–49.

41. Richard M. Hodgetts and Donald F. Kuratko, *Effective Small Business Management*, 7th ed. (New York: John Wiley & Sons, 2001), 379; see also Edmund Prater and Soumen Ghosh, "Current Operational Practices of U.S. Small- and Medium-Sized Enterprises in Europe," *Journal of Small Business Management* 43 (April 2005): 155–69.

42. Lance E. Brouthers and George Nakos, "The Role of Systematic International Market Selection on Small Firm's Export Performance," *Journal of Small Business Management* 43 (October 2005): 363–81.

GREEN FUEL ALTERNATIVES

Evan Gady, Founder & CEO

I. EXECUTIVE SUMMARY

A. POTENTIAL

Green Fuel Alternatives will enter the biodiesel industry as a mid-level producer of soy-based B100 biodiesel. The biodiesel market is still in its infancy in the United States, with regard to both production and consumption. Currently, the biodiesel industry is explosive and on the rise. The current market demand is an estimated 150 million gallons per year. However, in the last year only 40 million gallons were produced, leaving room for an additional 110 million gallons of production capacity. Figure A-1 illustrates the estimated growth of the biodiesel industry through 2012.

Recently, the Renewable Fuels Association (RFA) and the National Biodiesel Board (NBB) praised state representatives for introducing a renewable fuels standard (RFS) bill. This bill would require the use of 8 billion gallons of renewable fuels like ethanol and biodiesel by 2012.[1]

B. FUNDING NEED

With contributions of $8 million from private investors, *Green Fuel Alternatives* will have enough capital to fund start-up costs. This portion is illustrated as "Remaining Need" in Table A-1.

C. MANAGEMENT

An exceptional management team and organizational structure are keys to success for *Green Fuel Alternatives*. Mr. Evan Gady is the founder and initial chief

FIGURE A-1 Biodiesel Industry Growth (estimated from 1999–2012)

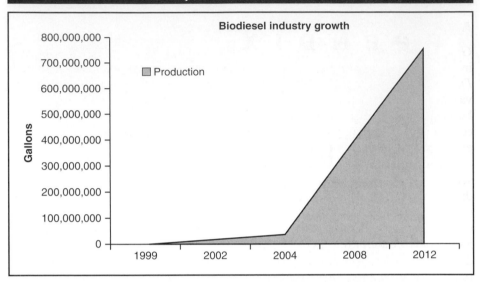

Source: Frazier, Barnes, & Associates.

TABLE A-1 Funding Needed for *Green Fuel Alternatives*

Source	Amount Needed
Land	$447,000
Working Capital	$5,000,000
Plant (Design-Build)	$20,000,000
TOTAL NEEDED	***$25,447,000***

Source	Contribution Amount
Mr. Gady	$5,089,400
Bank Loan	$12,357,600
REMAINING NEED	***$8,000,000***

executive officer (CEO) of the company. The company will be managed by an experienced general manager who will be hired. In addition to Mr. Gady, there are five other important team members in management: general manager, operations manager, office manager, logistics/marketing manager, and lab manager/chemist. With an industry expert in the position of general manager, the company will be poised for success in the biodiesel industry across the Midwest and especially in Indiana.

II. BUSINESS DESCRIPTION

A. GENERAL DESCRIPTION OF BUSINESS

Green Fuel Alternatives will be a fuel refinery of soy biodiesel that will be sold in bulk quantities and to fuel distributors and suppliers in the Midwest. The *Green Fuel Alternatives* refining plant will be built by Renewable Energy Group in the vacant lot at 8101 W. Morris St. in Indianapolis, Indiana. This location was chosen because of its excellent access to I-465, U.S. highways 40 and 36, and on-site rail access. This business has been named *Green Fuel Alternatives* so that customers can easily identify what the product is and know that it is beneficial to the environment.

A growing number of organizations, such as departments of transportation; school corporations; farmers; federal, state, and local governments; and even traditional diesel vehicle drivers, are using biodiesel to meet future sulfur emissions standards (2006 Environmental Protection Agency [EPA] mandate) and to become more environmentally responsible. The United States currently imports 58 percent of its oil, with fuel prices continually trending upward. This creates a demand to utilize cheaper and more efficient natural resources to help reduce fuel costs and the dependency on foreign oil. Biodiesel has been tested in labs and has passed all necessary tests required by the EPA. The American Society for Testing and Materials (ASTM) has even given biodiesel a standard (ASTM D6571) to be used as an acceptable diesel fuel alternative.

Several states around the country have already initiated biodiesel promotion programs; three examples are the programs in Minnesota, Arkansas, and Texas. The state of Minnesota has mandated the use of B2 (2 percent blend of biodiesel with diesel) in all petroleum diesel consumed in the state by the year 2005, subject to availability. Arkansas, on the other hand, is providing a 10-cents-per-gallon incentive for biodiesel production for the first 5 million gallons up to a period of five years. Texas now provides a net grant of 16.4 cents per gallon to producers of biodiesel for a period of 10 years, but the grant is capped at $3.6 million per plant.[2]

Currently, *Green Fuel Alternatives* is in the conceptual stage of development. Any co-op or other fuel distributor that wants to sell biodiesel to its customers must currently transport it from Ralston, Iowa; Cincinnati, Ohio; Kentucky; Minnesota; or farther. *Green Fuel Alternatives* will build a 15 million gallon per year (gpy) plant to provide enough B100 biodiesel for all of the distributors in Indiana, some outside sales, and some private sales.

The biodiesel that will be manufactured by *Green Fuel Alternatives* is very unique in the fact that it is made from soybean oil only, which benefits local soybean farmers. Many other biodiesel refineries are considered multi-feedstock refineries, and they offer soy biodiesel as well as waste grease and many other types of oils. *Green Fuel Alternatives* will offer soy biodiesel in an effort to support the local farmers and utilize the largest vegetable oil source. In order to extract the oil from the soybeans, a *cracking* or *crushing* plant is used to heat the soybeans to a temperature at which the soybean oil will come off of the soybeans in a gas form; next, it is filtered through a coil to cool it down and revert it to its liquid form. *Green Fuel Alternatives* will receive its soybean oil from ADM in Frankfort, Indiana. This oil will then be mixed with methanol to create B100, or *neat* biodiesel. B100 biodiesel is essentially 100 percent biodiesel—other blends, such as B5 or B20, contain 5 percent and 20 percent biodiesel, respectively, and the remainder is petroleum diesel. *Green Fuel Alternatives* will only manufacture and sell B100 to fuel distributors who will mix blends to satisfy each customer.

The mission statement for *Green Fuel Alternatives* will be to make soy bio-diesel more easily accessible in Indiana and strive for a low-cost alternative.

B. INDUSTRY BACKGROUND

Green Fuel Alternatives will be part of the fuel refining industry, which comprises businesses that refine petroleum and any other distillate fuel or oil. The petroleum refining industry (NAICS 324110/SIC 2911) is a $497.9 billion dollar industry annually in the United States.[3] Table A-2 illustrates the estimated market size statistics for the United States, the state of Indiana, and the metropolitan area of Indianapolis.

The petroleum refining industry is growing by approximately 5 percent each year because of the steady production of heavy machinery and vehicles that use fuel. Fuel alternatives are already being considered by owners of equipment and vehicles that use petroleum diesel to help decrease their dependence on imported petroleum and, in some cases, increase the efficiency of their engines. This is be-ginning to change the petroleum refining industry in an acceptable way. Produc-ers and distributors are researching alternative fuels that can provide the same power and efficiency as petroleum diesel but are safer for the environment and can be created with renewable resources. In 2000, renewable fuels only account-ed for 8 percent of the total U.S. energy consumption.

According to the National Biodiesel Board, there is an immediate production capacity for U.S. plants that produce nothing but biodiesel or can switch to biodiesel immediately. Current immediate production capacity is estimated to be 150 million gallons per year (gpy). A capacity of this magnitude illustrates a major inflection point for biodiesel because past production and capacity have remained under 80 million gpy. This capacity is mostly modular and can be doubled or

TABLE A-2 National and Local Industry Data (SIC 2911)

	Number of Businesses	Total Employees	Total Sales (in millions)	Average Employees	Average Sales per Establishment (in millions)
U.S.	1,462	107,336	497,940	95	821.7
Indiana	15	1,686	63.4	169	9.1
Indianapolis	4	18	1.5	6	0.8

Source: Dun & Bradstreet Market Size Statistics.

tripled in a short time frame (less than 12 months). In addition, it has been reported that an additional 200 million gallons of production capacity are available through long-term production agreements with existing biodiesel marketing firms. *Green Fuel Alternatives* recognizes the demand for alternative fuels and will help to integrate biodiesel into the current diesel market with the help of ADM and World Energy Alternatives. Several factors, such as low sulfur regulations both on the national scale and in California, will be a major driving force in increasing the consumption of biodiesel. The current energy bill being debated in Congress also has favorable provisions for biodiesel, and its enactment would provide a boost to biodiesel. Technology will play a major role in lowering the cost of biodiesel production and finding alternative, higher-value uses for the primary process byproduct, glycerin. Legislative incentives may not be necessary if biodiesel is competitive with petroleum diesel on a cost basis alone. Increased used of biodiesel will also require a massive education effort to inform the public about the benefits of this relatively new renewable fuel.[4]

C. Competition Analysis

Many plants currently use a variety of feedstocks such as waste grease from restaurants, poultry fat, and rapeseed oil (canola). The major competition in this area is from out-of-state companies who refine biodiesel and transport it to co-op plants in Indiana. These companies are able to sell 100 percent of production because, in the virtually untapped biodiesel industry, not many other refineries exist. Current fuel cooperatives are trucking in B100 biodiesel from Peter Cremer in Cincinnati, Ohio, and from West Central Soy in Ralston, Iowa. Even though *Green Fuel Alternatives* will be competing with these biodiesel refineries, it will be beneficial to the Indiana co-ops because they won't have to pay as many freight costs to have their biodiesel shipped to them. In addition, *Green Fuel Alternatives* has a slight edge over other biodiesel refineries because it only refines soy biodiesel and will be the farthest northern plant, with better proximity to possible customers in the northern part of the United States who might not have tried biodiesel because there weren't any plants close enough. As described, the target market for *Green Fuel Alternatives* would be the wholesalers and distributors of fuel, such as Countrymark Co-op. Countrymark has blending facilities in Peru, Jolietville, and Switz City. The fuel cooperatives with Countrymark travel to these three terminals and bring fuel back to their facilities to blend. Each cooperative provides different blends, depending on the demand from their farmers and other customers. *Green Fuel Alternatives* will be able to satisfy the needs of these customers by producing an environmentally friendly fuel source that helps them to meet upcoming emissions requirements and to increase the demand for soybeans to keep Indiana soybean farmers in business.

D. Products and Services

Green Fuel Alternatives will provide B100 biodiesel that will be refined by ADM in Frankfort, Indiana using a cracking plant to extract soybean oil feedstock.

B100 biodiesel is known as pure (or neat) biodiesel because it is 100 percent biodiesel. Some customers prefer B100 because of its increased lubricity and cleansing characteristics. However, B100 does have trouble in cold weather because of an increased cold flow test and cloud point. As a result, it has become an industry standard, when transporting fuel, to heat it to avoid gelling in climates below 40 degrees Fahrenheit. The American Society of Testing and Materials has tested biodiesel and uses a standard test for biodiesel called ASTM D 6751.

E. STRATEGY TO DIFFERENTIATE

Green Fuel Alternatives will have a competitive advantage in Indiana compared to other biodiesel providers because current providers are located hundreds of miles away, out of state. *Green Fuel Alternatives* will be a fuel refinery. Currently, there are 40 biodiesel providers or fuel co-ops in Indiana, but they only blend the fuel to make biodiesel and then distribute it to the end user or to a fuel station. *Green Fuel Alternatives* will provide the B100 (100 percent biodiesel) to customers such as Countrymark, who will blend it with diesel fuel at its terminals to create a biodiesel blend. Countrymark currently has B100 biodiesel transported in from Iowa, Kentucky, and Ohio, and they blend the fuel usually using various methods. Some facilities such as the Countrymark Co-op in Jolietville and Peru, Indiana, use a state-of-the-art direct injection method to blend the biodiesel proportionately with petroleum diesel. Currently, the B100 fuel is received at these terminals (places where co-ops pick up fuel to distribute) to be blended and is then picked up for disbursement. *Green Fuel Alternatives* can get fuel to these terminals quicker than competitors because of its convenient location in Indianapolis, Indiana. Because of this, the fuel cooperatives will have constant access to biodiesel. *Green Fuel Alternatives* will attempt to establish a good relationship with Countrymark and other providers in Indiana—and eventually elsewhere—that distribute biodiesel. This relationship will enable *Green Fuel Alternatives* to develop long-term contracts with the distributors. These contracts will be a safeguard in the even that soybean oil prices unexpectedly rise and *Green Fuel Alternatives* has to keep prices at a higher level to maintain profitability.

F. KEY DYNAMICS

1. Biodiesel is 100 percent renewable and can be made in the United States, thereby reducing our dependency on foreign oil.
2. Engine life is increased with the use of biodiesel.
3. The EPA is requiring the sulfur emissions in 2006 to be reduced from 500 ppm to 15 ppm.
4. Biodiesel has the highest positive energy balance of any renewable fuel to date (3.24 units produced per unit of energy used).
5. Biodiesel can reduce toxic air emissions by as much as 90 percent (B100 compared to petroleum diesel).[5]

III. MARKETING

A. Economics

In 2004, the state of Indiana harvested an estimated 74.0 million acres of soybeans, a 2 percent increase from 2003. Biodiesel can be made from soybean oil, as well as other feedstock such as waste grease and other vegetable oils. Biodiesel can be blended with conventional diesel and used in engines with no modifications. When biodiesel is blended, it is referred to by the letter B and the percentage of its blend with diesel fuel (e.g., B100, B20, B5, and B2). B2 and B20 are the blends most commonly used by fuel cooperatives. The following are among the most prevalent reasons why substituting petroleum diesel with biodiesel makes sense:

- Biodiesel can reduce toxic air emissions by as much as 90 percent (B100 compared to petroleum diesel).[6]
- Biodiesel is homegrown and renewable, reducing our dependence on foreign oil. The United States currently imports 58 percent of its oil.[7]
- Markets are expanded for U.S. farmers.
- Engine life is increased (higher lubricity).
- Requirements were mandated in 2006 to reduce sulfur emissions in air from 500 parts per million (ppm) to 15 ppm.
- Biodiesel has the highest positive energy balance of any renewable fuel to date (3.24 units produced per unit of energy used).

Researchers believe that the 20 percent blend is the best blend for general use without encountering any major issues. Higher blends often cause problems in winter and with nitrogen oxide emissions. The EPA has stated that the 20 percent blend is "basically a trade off between cost, emissions, cold weather, material compatibility and solvency issues."[8]

B. Market Analysis

Currently, the United States consumes approximately 55 billion gallons of diesel fuel annually. Highway usage accounts for 32 billion gallons and off-road usage (agriculture and other uses) accounts for 23 billion gallons. Current diesel demand is growing at 5 percent annually, and the primary driver is government regulations. A 2 percent blend of biodiesel is currently the most common blend used. If a 2 percent blend of biodiesel were used with the 55 billion gallons consumed annually, that would represent a market size of approximately 1.1 billion gallons annually. In 1999, only 500,000 gallons of biodiesel were produced; in 2002, the number climbed to 25 million; and, by 2004, the number had grown to over 30 million gallons.[9] It is projected that the industry will produce 400 million gallons by 2008 and 700–800 million gallons by 2012 (see Figure A-2).[10]

FIGURE A-2 Biodiesel Growth History and Projections

Biodiesel growth history and projections

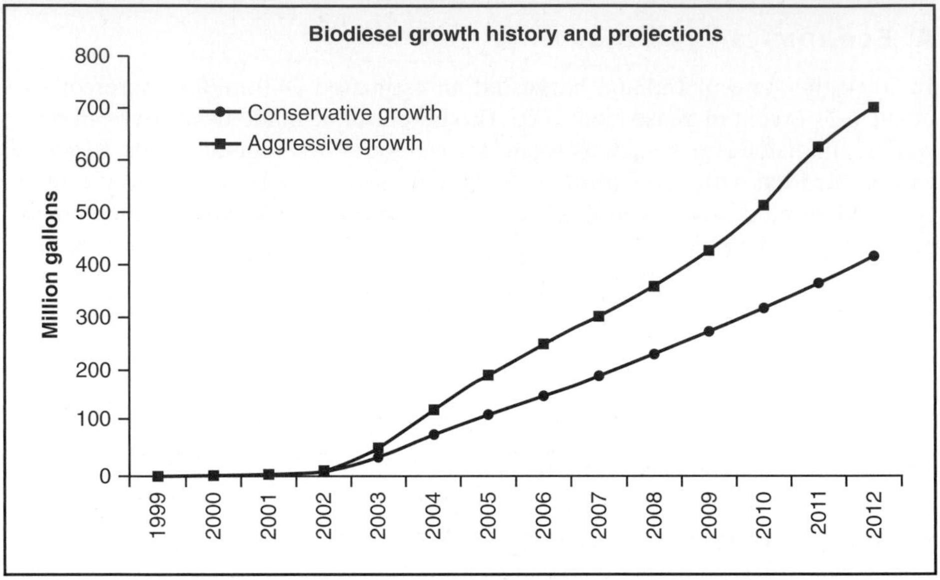

Source: Frazier, Barnes, & Associates.

Several states have considered mandating the use of a 2 percent blend of biodiesel in all diesel engines. North Dakota and Minnesota have already passed legislation that mandates the use of a 2 percent biodiesel blend with all diesel. The mandate in Minnesota alone will generate demand for 16 million gallons of biodiesel (equal to the oil from 11 million bushels of soybeans). Currently, 17 states have laws that set mandatory state fleet usage of alternative fuels.[11] For the mandate to become effective in North Dakota and Minnesota, two out of three of the following conditions must be met:

1. Eight million gallons of biodiesel production capacity must be in place in the state.
2. Eighteen months must have passed after the federal or state government enacts, through taxes imposed, tax credits or otherwise creates a 2 cent or higher per-gallon reduction in the cost of diesel fuel containing at least 2 percent biodiesel.
3. The date June 30, 2005, must have passed.

A reasonable production goal for the biodiesel industry would be to produce 350 million gallons annually of the current 35 billion gallons of on-road diesel used. These 350 million gallons of biodiesel will use approximately 2.6 billion pounds of soy oil or the equivalent of oil from 235 million bushels of soybeans. That amount of oil is nearly equal to the amount of surplus oil in 2001, which was 2.8 billion pounds.

C. Barriers to Entry

It has been determined that building a 15-million-gallon-per-year plant for *Green Fuel Alternatives* will utilize the oil from approximately 10.5 million bushels of soybeans each year, or 15 million gallons of soybean oil.[12] *Green Fuel Alternatives* will face several barriers to entry in the biodiesel market. Because of the capital-intensive nature of a start-up biodiesel refinery, scaling operations quickly will help *Green Fuel Alternatives* when faced with challenges in both raising capital and breakeven status. Approximately $26 million is needed as start-up capital to build a quality biodiesel production facility that can produce 15 million gallons per year (gpy). To overcome the barrier of high capital cost, *Green Fuel Alternatives* will establish relationships with all necessary industry professionals, such as Countrymark and Crystal Flash, to maintain commitment and profitability. In addition to these relationships, a membership to the National Biodiesel Board will also aid *Green Fuel Alternatives* with free advertising. These relationships will help overcome barriers to entry because *Green Fuel Alternatives* will have all the necessary knowledge to gain market share. Shipping costs and time can also be a barrier to entry. However, with *Green Fuel Alternatives'* central Indiana location, northern biodiesel distributors will have fuel closer to customers for quicker delivery. If a producer has sole access to a pipeline or other mode of transportation, the producer may have a competitive advantage for that particular area. To overcome this barrier, *Green Fuel Alternatives* will lease trucks and purchase used tankers to maintain low costs and a competitive nature; if fuel can be shipped from the plant, it won't always have to be picked up by the customer.

Government regulations will change in the near future to help promote the use of alternative fuels in fleets and the statewide use in all diesel engines. For example, the EPA recently mandated that, for 2006, the sulfur emissions in the air must be reduced from 500 ppm to 15 ppm. As mentioned earlier, Minnesota has already mandated the use of B2 in all diesel engines, and many other states are projected to do so in the near future.[13] New regulations that are implemented will promote the reduction in emissions and the long-term benefits of biodiesel. The biodiesel industry has seen exponential growth since the introduction of biodiesel in the mid- to late 1990s. Growth in the biodiesel industry will take place with the addition of new plants across the United States and around the world.

D. Product

Green Fuel Alternatives will produce B100 (100 percent biodiesel) made from soybean oil. This fuel has several features and benefits that make it suitable for use. The main benefits of biodiesel are:

- *Renewable fuel source.* Unlike fossil fuels, biodiesel is made from vegetable oilseed crops grown in America, which replenishes the market annually with renewable feedstock.

- *Well-established distribution infrastructure.* Biodiesel is compatible with the existing petroleum diesel infrastructure. In fact, biodiesel can be blended with any percentage of diesel fuel.

- *No new vehicles or engine modifications.* Biodiesel works in today's engines. No special vehicles or engine modifications are needed to comply with the Energy Policy Act of 1992 (EPAct) using biodiesel. The EPAct was set forth to encourage fleet use of alternative fuels.

- *Performance.* Recent studies show that biodiesel actually increases engine efficiency through a higher cetane rating and extends engine life via added lubricity.

- *Biodegradable and less toxic than table salt.* Biodiesel is far less damaging to the environment than petroleum diesel, particularly in environmentally sensitive areas or in the event of a spill or leak.

- *Dramatically reduces emissions.* Diesel engines account for 79 percent of all particulate matter emitted by vehicles.[14] Biodiesel reduces lifecycle CO_2 emissions by over 78 percent compared to petroleum diesel. In fact, even when it is blended with petroleum diesel, biodiesel significantly reduces emissions.

- *Made in the U.S.A.* Biodiesel benefits American farmers, businesses, and the national economy. Job creation, new markets for domestic agricultural products, and keeping our energy dollars domestic are just a few of the many economic benefits gained by using biodiesel instead of petroleum diesel.

- *Safe to use.* Not only is 100 percent of biodiesel biodegradable, biodiesel also has a higher flashpoint than diesel. The flashpoint (defined as the temperature at which a substance will ignite) of biodiesel is 300°F compared to 125°F for petroleum diesel. This means that biodiesel is safer to transport and store than petroleum diesel.[15]

- *Energy balance.* According to a report by the U.S. Department of Energy and the Department of Agriculture, the "energy yield of biodiesel is (3.2/0.83) 280 percent greater than petroleum diesel fuel. Biodiesel yields 3.2 units of fuel product energy for every unit of fossil energy consumed in its life cycle. By contrast, petroleum diesel's life cycle yields only 0.83 units of fuel energy per unit of fossil energy consumed."[16]

The dominant features of biodiesel are its increase in performance, efficiency, and improved lubricity. As far as benefits are concerned, clearly the environmental impact is the most significant. *Green Fuel Alternatives* will provide a steady supply of approximately 1.25 million gallons of B100 biodiesel each month to its customers once full capacity is reached. The fuel can either be delivered by *Green Fuel Alternatives* or the customer can pick up the fuel at the plant. Most fuel will be shipped via rail because the cost is lower than shipping via truck ($0.03 per gallon by rail versus $0.07 per gallon by semi).

E. Customers

The targeted customers for *Green Fuel Alternatives* are fuel distributors that are able to or currently distribute blends of biodiesel to fleets and end users. These customers need a steady supply of B100 so that they can blend it with the diesel fuel that they purchase to make certain blends for their customers. Countrymark, a division of the Indiana Farm Bureau, purchases about 400,000 gallons of B100 annually. They currently import the B100 from Peter Cremer North America in Cincinnati, Ohio, and a smaller portion from West Central Soy in Ralston, Iowa. Crystal Flash is a local Indiana fuel distributor that has 26 fueling stations around Indiana, 16 of which sell blends of biodiesel. Crystal Flash purchases approximately 100,000 gallons of B100 each year from Peter Cremer in Cincinnati. When speaking with Jerry Ban from Crystal Flash, Mr. Gady learned that if the fuel were closer it would help Crystal Flash because they wouldn't have to wait for the supply truck to arrive.[17] Many of the customers who will be using biodiesel produced by *Green Fuel Alternatives* are located in Indiana.

In order to sell 15 million gallons per year, *Green Fuel Alternatives* will establish an agreement with ADM and World Energy Alternatives. These businesses have marketing programs in place for biodiesel refineries. Each company will purchase a certain amount of B100 each year from *Green Fuel Alternatives* and will in turn sell it to previously established customers. This agreement is beneficial to *Green Fuel Alternatives,* as well as to ADM and World Energy Alternatives, because *Green Fuel Alternatives* will be able to operate a continuous batch sequence and sell nearly all gallons refined. The remaining gallons not purchased will be sold to various private customers by the sales and marketing staff at *Green Fuel Alternatives*. Using production agreements, ADM and World Energy Alternatives will have enough fuel to supply the increasing demand for alternative fuels. Many refineries, such as West Central Soy, already have all of their production purchased through August 2005, and they won't be taking any new orders until after that date. The large demand for biodiesel is constantly rising, and the need for increased production is imminent.

Green Fuel Alternatives will ship fuel to ADM/World Energy Alternatives via truck and railway. The future *Green Fuel Alternatives* site at 8101 W. Morris St. will have rail spurs and four loading/unloading spots, which are steam heated to make loading and unloading of feedstock and finished product easier. Depending on where the fuel is needed, *Green Fuel Alternatives* and ADM/World Energy will work together to decide the best freight methods.

F. Competition

Currently, there are 32 active biodiesel refineries in the United States; in addition to these, there are 23 plants proposed.[18] These refineries try to keep costs low by not having to ship all over the country—it is more convenient to focus on local customers. For this reason, *Green Fuel Alternatives* will be competing primarily with Peter Cremer in Cincinnati, Ohio; Griffin Industries in Butler, Kentucky; and West Central Soy in Ralston, Iowa (see Table A-3).

TABLE A-3 Main Competitors		
Peter Cremer, North America	*Griffin Industries, Inc.*	*West Central Soy*
3117 Southside Avenue Cincinnati, OH 45204	Corporate Headquarters 4221 Alexandria Pike Cold Spring, Kentucky 41076 USA	406 First St. Ralston, IA 51459

Many of the other production facilities, such as Ag Processing, Inc., make biodiesel for specific customers only and produce small amounts at a time (batch processing). *Green Fuel Alternatives,* however, has a key feature that they do not: All of the fuel made at *Green Fuel Alternatives* will be made solely with soybean oil, whereas the competition uses multiple feedstocks (waste grease, poultry fat, etc.).

Green Fuel Alternatives is poised to have a strong business and a good competitive advantage in comparison to Peter Cremer and West Central Soy. With its northern location, *Green Fuel Alternatives* will be able to supply fuel cooperatives quicker than the competition. In addition, with an excellent management team and committed personnel, *Green Fuel Alternatives* will be able to transition into the biodiesel market smoothly.

G. NICHE

Green Fuel Alternatives fits into the spectrum of biodiesel refineries well. With a location that can reach over 50 biodiesel distributors, its potential is great. In addition to a central location for reaching Indiana's distributors faster than most competitors, *Green Fuel Alternatives* also is unique in the fact that it only produces soy-based biodiesel. The main competitors in the biodiesel industry produce multi-feedstock biodiesel. *Green Fuel Alternatives* prefers to use only soybean oil to support the 28,000 soybean farmers of Indiana.

H. MARKETING STRATEGY

Green Fuel Alternatives will focus its attention on providing enough B100 biodiesel for the current distribution of the Indiana fuel cooperatives. Countrymark and Crystal Flash are Indiana's main fuel distributors. Both Crystal Flash and Countrymark currently import and blend B100 at their facilities and then disburse it to their cooperatives or to fleets of vehicles. In 2004, Countrymark marketed more than 14 million gallons of soy-blended biodiesel to end users.

There are over 400 diesel fleets nationwide that currently use biodiesel. Among these are Eli Lilly Pharmaceuticals, Marion County Highway Department, Ball State University, Purdue University, and Indiana University. In addition to the current markets available to market biodiesel, marine diesel use and smog-risk cities are new potential markets. *Green Fuel Alternatives* will be actively involved in new market research for biodiesel to capture a portion of these markets in their early stages.

PROMOTION

Green Fuel Alternatives will rely heavily on two groups to get the word out about its B100 biodiesel: the marketing team, and ADM and World Energy Alternatives. The marketing team for *Green Fuel Alternatives* consists of a vice president of marketing and a five-person team of sales representatives. This group will identify potential new customers for *Green Fuel Alternatives* and keep in contact with current customers to see if their quantity of fuel needs have changed. This will not only be important to the steady revenue for *Green Fuel Alternatives,* it will help lead to growth and expansion of the business.

PRICING

According to the Indiana Soybean Board, blended biodiesel has historically cost about 1.5 percent more than straight petroleum fuels.[19] Prices for B100 fuel are basically set by current market prices. Using the Chicago Board of Trade, *Green Fuel Alternatives* will be able to monitor prices for the soybean oil that will be purchased from Archer Daniels Midland (ADM). In addition to this, the current market price for methanol will also be used. Incentives—such as the biodiesel tax incentive offering a one cent refund per percentage of biodiesel (which amounts to $1.00 per gallon for the B100 that *Green Fuel Alternatives* will produce)—will help mitigate production costs. This will allow consumers to purchase a blended version of biodiesel for nearly the same price as a gallon of diesel. Prices for biodiesel vary depending on the region of the United States.

PROPOSED LOCATION

Green Fuel Alternatives will purchase the vacant land at 8101 W. Morris St. in Indianapolis, Indiana. This is a 14.5-acre plot of land that has rail access and is zoned specifically for petroleum refining and storage. Close access to this rail—the Norfolk Southern railway—is important because Archer Daniels Midland will ship the soybean oil directly to the *Green Fuel Alternatives* site via rail from Frankfort, Indiana. In the biodiesel industry, it is good to have some distance from your close competition because then you have easier access to a specific area. This gives *Green Fuel Alternatives* better access to distributors in Michigan and northern Ohio and Illinois.

DISTRIBUTION CHANNELS

Green Fuel Alternatives will market fuel directly to the distributor, who in turn will disburse it among its fuel cooperatives. Finally, these cooperatives will allow their members to pick up fuel as they need it. In addition to this distribution method, *Green Fuel Alternatives* will also utilize the marketing expertise of ADM/World Energy Alternatives to sell additional B100 biodiesel to their current customers in various states. The sales force at *Green Fuel Alternatives* will be used to cultivate new prospective biodiesel fleet users and to make sure current customers are satisfied with their present allocation. Approximately 1.25 million gallons of B100 will be produced and disbursed by *Green Fuel Alternatives* each month via the continuous batch sequence method.

IV. MANAGEMENT SEGMENT

A. LEGAL STRUCTURE

Green Fuel Alternatives will be developed as a limited liability corporation (LLC). Mr. Gady is using this legal structure to utilize investors to raise the necessary start-up capital. Income will be taxed through personal income, and corporate investors can help with the necessary start-up capital.

B. OWNERSHIP

Mr. Gady will own 60 percent of the company. The remaining 40 percent will be given to the angel investors for providing the necessary $8 million for start-up. This money will be paid back at the exit time of the company, or after the debt has been paid down further. Disbursements, if made, would not be given until at least five years after start-up. The cash on hand will be made available for potential expansion and to pay off debt.

C. MANAGEMENT TEAM

Without a qualified staff, the plant will not be able to run efficiently and will lose customers. *Green Fuel Alternatives* will be owned by Mr. Evan Gady but will be managed by an experienced general manager who will be hired. Mr. Gady is the founder and initial CEO of the company. In addition to Mr. Gady, there are five other important team members in management: general manager, operations manager, office manager, logistics/marketing manager, and lab manager/chemist.

EVAN GADY, FOUNDER/INITIAL CEO

Mr. Gady will assume the position of founder and initial CEO. Mr. Gady will work with the general manager to help oversee all of the general business practices of *Green Fuel Alternatives* and handle key decisions regarding the company as a whole. Mr. Gady has received a degree in entrepreneurship and small business management from Ball State University. Mr. Gady has worked to support himself since the age of 15 in various jobs including professional salesperson, student sales manager, resident assistant, marketing representative, and business consultant. Mr. Gady will chair a weekly operations meeting with the management team to ensure that the business is meeting production and financial targets. Mr. Gady will spend the majority of his time overseeing the operations of the plant and maintaining a positive relationship with all employees. Some time will be spent outside of the plant visiting various distributors and going to biodiesel conferences. By visiting distributors, Mr. Gady will be able to see whether there is a current demand and also develop good relationships with his clientele. Mr. Gady will receive a salary of $50,000 in the first year of operation.

The salaries and compensation for employees of *Green Fuel Alternatives* are listed in Table A-4.

TABLE A-4 Organizational Compensation Structure	
Position	*Salary/Pay*
Founder/Initial CEO (1)	$50,000
General Manager (1)	$115,000
Operations Manager (1)	$58,000
Shift Foreman (1)	$13–$14/hr.
Process Operators (12)	$13–$14/hr.
Shipping Operators (3)	$13–$14/hr.
Office Manager (1)	$42,000
Clerical Assistant (1)	$40,000
Accounting Assistant (1)	$40,000
Logistics/Marketing Manager (1)	$40,000 + 15% commission
Lab Manager/Chemist (1)	$45,000
Lab Assistant (1)	$18/hr.

These salaries are industry specific and include medical, workers' compensation, and 401(k) benefits. Total payroll each year amounts to approximately $976,554 for 25 employees. This payroll also includes medical, workers' compensation, and 401(k) benefits.

D. COMPANY ADVISORS

Green Fuel Alternatives will have several business professionals who will aid in the development and growth process of the business. These people come from a wide variety of backgrounds, but can all help *Green Fuel Alternatives* in important ways.

Kellie Walsh is the executive director of the Central Indiana Clean Cities Alliance. She has constant contact with various fuel distributors, refineries, and end users. She will be an important asset to *Green Fuel Alternatives* because she can help to promote the use of biodiesel and maintain contact between *Green Fuel Alternatives* and the distributors and other suppliers.

Don Aquilano is the managing director of Gazelle TechVentures and the director of the Blue Chip Venture Company. Mr. Aquilano was Mr. Gady's mentor in the entrepreneurship program at Ball State University and helped him to develop and complete his business plan.

Steve Horn is the business development manager at Heritage Research Group. He currently helps to develop new businesses for Heritage and has close contact with Crystal Flash, a large fuel distributor in Indiana. Steve has helped Mr. Gady gain contacts within the industry and will continue to be an asset to the development of *Green Fuel Alternatives*.

Dan Leach is a successful entrepreneur in Wyoming. Mr. Leach owns a wind power company that has a field of windmills that generate power for the area. He also has developed several biodiesel refineries and is currently working on an 80 million gpy facility.

V. OPERATIONS

A. PLANT OPERATIONS

The *Green Fuel Alternatives* biodiesel refinery will operate approximately 330 days each year. However, constant production will be maintained using the continuous flow technology of the plant. The plant will need time each year for repairs and general maintenance on pipes, seals, valves, and so forth, resulting in the 330 days each year of operation. The Renewable Energy Group in Iowa will build the plant for *Green Fuel Alternatives* in a custom design-build fashion. This way, the plant can be built specifically for the lot at 8101 W. Morris St. in Indianapolis.

To produce biodiesel that complies with the American Society of Testing and Materials' ASTM D6751 standard, *Green Fuel Alternatives* will use the following inputs to create the necessary biodiesel and byproduct outputs (also illustrated in the following graph):

- Inputs
  - 9 gallons of soybean oil
  - 1 gallon of methanol
  - Small amount of sodium (potassium) hydroxide
- Outputs
  - 9 gallons of methyl ester/biodiesel
  - 1 gallon of glycerin (assumed to be 9.0 pounds)
  - Some residual wash water, alcohol, and catalyst

The process will work in the following order:

1. Receipt of crude oil from ADM via Conrail railways
2. Pretreatment and cleansing of feedstock
3. Biodiesel transesterification
4. Segregated storage
5. B100 blending
6. Biodiesel loadout

The plant will be monitored by state-of-the-art process controls, will eliminate the process of wastewater, and will utilize stringent process safety management. These features from the Renewable Energy Group are part of the design-build process and include training and start-up services assistance.

The most significant costs for *Green Fuel Alternatives* are in the feedstock (soybean oil). Soybean oil will be purchased at 27 cents per pound from ADM in Frankfort, Indiana. This cost could potentially be lower if *Green Fuel Alternatives* were to build its own crushing facilities for soybeans. However, the cost of building a crushing plant can range from $16 to $45 million, depending on its size. For the time being, *Green Fuel Alternatives* has decided to simply buy oil on the open market. After production and cash flow are steady and *Green Fuel Alternatives* begins to consider growth opportunities, a crushing plant may be feasible.

B. FACILITIES AND EQUIPMENT

The *Green Fuel Alternatives* plant will be built by Renewable Energy Group on the vacant plot of land at 8101 W. Morris St. in Indianapolis, Indiana. This is a long-term location because of the capital intensity involved in designing and building a biodiesel production and storage facility. The plot of land is approximately 14.9 acres and has additional acres adjacent to the land that can be acquired by Colliers International to purchase for future expansion. The building needed to house the plant would be approximately 5,000 square feet and about 60 feet in height. It would contain all of the processing equipment plus a laboratory for quality control and offices. The processing area would use approximately 3,400 square feet. The tank farm may utilize about 20,000 square feet and would contain tanks totaling approximately 650,000 gallon capacity, divided between holding tanks for feedstock and finished product. This plant would operate continuously and stop production only for maintenance and repair. Table A-5 outlines the estimated capital costs for a 15 million gpy plant.

The costs outlined in Table A-4 are approximate costs from Frazier, Barnes, & Associates, a reputable consulting firm for the renewable fuel industry. The numbers given are base numbers, and the cost for *Green Fuel Alternatives* is considerably higher (at $20 million) because the plant will be custom designed, built to specifications, and one company will handle all of the setup work. Renewable Energy Group will complete two phases to help *Green Fuel Alternatives* begin production. Phase I and II are outlined as follows:

PHASE I:

- Floor plan and flow diagrams are developed to illustrate process.
- Project timetable is provided (with milestones).
- Permit requirements that may affect the given project are met.
- Electronic visuals of what the plant will look like are provided.
- Plant layout is finalized, from input storage to final loadout.
- Skilled individuals for management are located.

TABLE A-5 Estimated Biodiesel Capital Cost for a 15 Million gpy Plant	
Equipment	$3,750,000
Buildings	$1,200,000
Utilities	$720,000
Civil/Mechanical/Electrical	$2,736,000
Land Prep/Trans Access	$192,000
Engineering/Permitting	$192,000
Setup Consulting	$3,000
Contingency (10%)	$1,000,000
Total Installed Cost	*$9,793,000*

Source: Frazier, Barnes, & Associates.

- Options for selling coproducts (glycerin) are explored.
- Potential new markets for new biodiesel uses are identified.

PHASE II:

- Total site is laid out with roads and rail spurs.
- Site grading and drainage plan is established.
- General arrangement drawings are made.
- Mechanical and electrical design schematics are completed.
- A 3-D color image of the project is rendered.
- Construction schedule is finalized.
- Contract price is finalized.
- Permitting assistance is obtained as needed.
- Cash flow projections are made.

Phases I and II are included in the total estimated price of $20 million to be paid to Renewable Energy Group. However, if either of these phases is completed without finishing the entire project, they must be paid as follows: Phase I, $50,000, paid after agreement is signed; Phase II, $150,000, paid one-third after agreement is signed, and the remainder upon completion.

C. ORGANIZATIONAL PLAN

There will be 25 workers at the *Green Fuel Alternatives* plant, including Mr. Gady. The management team will consist of Mr. Gady—the founder/initial CEO—and a general manager who oversees everything. Mr. Gady and the general manager will work in collaboration with four teams: the operations team, the office team, the logistics team, and the lab team. The operations team will be run by the shift foreman and three shipping operators. The shift foreman will oversee 12 process operators who will work on 12-hour shifts (three days on and four days off, then the reverse). The shipping operators will ensure that shipments are on time and that the flow of production to shipping is in sync. The office team will be run by the office manager, who will oversee a clerical worker and an accounting worker. These positions help to maintain the administrative work at *Green Fuel Alternatives*. The logistics team will consist of one sole logistics and marketing manager, who will be responsible for marketing the B100 biodiesel. The lab manager/chemist will work with a lab assistant to make sure that the biodiesel produced meets EPA and ASTM requirements and standards.

VI. CRITICAL RISKS

SOYBEAN OIL DEMAND

As a result of the steady use of soybean oil for various biodiesel plants nationwide, a shortage could occur. This could potentially hurt *Green Fuel Alternatives* because it is a single-feedstock plant. A way to avoid this problem could be to adopt multiple feedstocks before operations begin or to try to add them if a problem occurs. Even though soybean oil is the largest amount of oil available, it still tends to cost several cents more per pound than alternative feedstocks.

SOYBEAN RUST FUNGUS

According to the U.S. Department of Agriculture (USDA), soybean rust can be a major problem for the production of soybeans. Soybean rust fungus is an airborne fungus that can cause significant yield loss for farmers. It can even wipe out a field of soybeans and spread to other neighboring farms if preventative measures are not taken. This could be a problem for *Green Fuel Alternatives* if soybeans become a tight supply and soybean oil is limited.

BIODIESEL PROBLEMS

Biodiesel can be corrosive to rubber and liner materials. Biodiesel also cannot be stored in concrete-lined tanks. In some cases, the fuel intake orifices may need to be reduced in size to create higher cylinder pressures. Given current petroleum prices, biodiesel is more costly to produce than petroleum diesel. *Green Fuel Alternatives* understands the risks involved and the environments in which the fuel must be kept—these are common among most fuels. Although biodiesel might be more expensive to produce, the tax credits and incentives help to level the playing field with petroleum diesel.

MARKETER INFLUENCE

ADM and WEA may appear to control operations of *Green Fuel Alternatives* if they are the sole customer(s). For this reason, *Green Fuel Alternatives* has decided that all fuel will not be sold in one place. This is a protection measure for the company.

VII. EXIT STRATEGIES

Green Fuel Alternatives recognizes that it may be a small player in the market initially and could potentially be purchased by a larger biodiesel producer. Companies such as Peter Cremer, which operates under Procter & Gamble, have prime opportunities to become chain biodiesel producers because of their deep pockets and previously established customer base. Other potential buyers may include companies such as Countrymark or ADM, who do not currently own a biodiesel plant but would like to enter the market. ADM would be the most likely to do so, because they currently use their ethanol marketing group to purchase and sell biodiesel to various customers in different areas of the country.

In addition, after speaking with Mr. Dan Leach, the CEO of HTH Wind and PowerSHIFT Technologies, another potential exit strategy was developed. Mr. Leach was very interested in the progress that Mr. Gady had made on his business venture and mentioned the possibility of purchasing *Green Fuel Alternatives* in the future. This exit strategy is slightly different from a purchase by Countrymark or ADM because Mr. Leach is from Casper, Wyoming, and he already has a great deal of experience in the renewable technology industry—specifically, biodiesel.

VIII. FINANCIAL SEGMENT

A. START-UP PROPOSAL

The total start-up costs needed for *Green Fuel Alternatives* will be $25,447,000. This cost includes a design-build package with the Renewable Energy Group, cost of land, and working capital money. The start-up period will begin May 2005 and end August 2006. Production will begin in September 2006.

B. FINANCING PLAN

A total of $25,447,000 in capital will be needed to finance this venture. Tables A-6 and A-7 break down the start-up costs and sources of capital.

C. FINANCIAL ASSUMPTIONS

Exact financial calculations can be found in the financial appendix at the end of this plan.

Cost of goods sold: Figures are outlined on the COGS sheet in financial documents. COGS is based upon current market figures and averages in an industry. Mr. Dan Leach, an industry expert, was consulted for current information.

TABLE A-6 Sources of Funding

Source	Amount
First Merchants Bank	$12,357,600
Contributed Capital (Owner)	$5,089,400
Angel Investment	$8,000,000
TOTAL	**$25,447,000**

TABLE A-7 Uses of Funding

Source	Amount
Renewable Energy Group (Design-Build Package)	$20,000,000
Land	$447,000
Working Capital	$5,000,000
TOTAL	**$25,447,000**

Salaries and wages: Figures are based on industry norms for positions in a biodiesel refinery. A breakdown per position can be found in the operations section. Mr. Jim Venner of Western Iowa Energy provided information on a good structure for a refinery.

Payroll taxes: Calculations are based on the following standards:

Social Security: 7.65 percent for first $90,000
Federal unemployment: 0.8 percent for first $7,000
State unemployment: 2.7 percent for first $7,000

Payroll expense: ADP charges $102 biweekly for payroll processing; checks and pay-stubs are shipped overnight via FedEx.

Benefits: Industry average is 20 to 25 percent of pay; a 25 percent rate is used to establish basic benefits for workers' compensation, medical, and a 401(k).

Insurance: The yearly insurance premium is $249,500, or $20,792 per month. It is expected that the rate will be lower once established because of possible changes in what might need to be insured (e.g., trucks, exact property specs, insurance on building, etc.).

Sales expense: Sales expense is calculated using $2,000 per month for promotional items and an additional $2,500 for Web site updates and sales commission for the marketing manager as needed. It is understood that updates will not be required some months, and some months will have updates that may cost more than the allotted amount. This commission is typically 4 to 6 percent of the sale, depending on the size of the deal.

Office supplies: Figure is based on typical use in industry; $1,000 is used for start-up to account for basic filing cabinets and other office supplies.

Freight expense: Based on industry norms, approximately 3 to 8 cents per gallon is acceptable for freight costs (both rail and road); 8 cents per gallon was used.

Travel expense: A total of $500 is available monthly for Mr. Gady to travel to distributors or other potential customers.

Security expense: Gates, fences, and cameras are covered in the initial design-build of the plant and property. However, an additional $10,000 is figured in each year to account for upgrades and maintenance costs.

Maintenance expense: Cost is 5 percent of replacement capital ($3.75 million in equipment): $187,500 over seven-year life, $26,786/year, or $2,233/month.

Professional services: At start-up, expenses are high and an attorney must be used to set up the prospectus, articles of incorporation, nondisclosure agreement (NDA), and so forth. Thus, the attorney cost is $120,000, and the CPA is $30,000.

Depreciation: Depreciation is calculated based on the useful life of the item. Office equipment depreciates after 4 years, the building after an estimated 30 years, and the manufacturing equipment after 7 years. Industry experts claim that a plant and equipment will last longer than 30 years and 7 years, respectively, but these figures are used to determine approximates.

Property taxes: Property tax is figured on tax abatement. The tax is computed by adding the building, equipment, and land, and any depreciation, then multiplying by a 2.7 percentage rate and using whatever abatement rules for that year. For the three years calculated, abatement is 100 percent on the first year, 50 percent on the second, and 33 percent on the third.

Miscellaneous expense: This cost is estimated to be 3 percent of revenue; it will cover various expenses (e.g., postage) and serve as a cushion.

Inventory: Inventory is based on a 21-day supply from start-up. The cost of these goods is calculated by taking the amount of fuel produced, dividing it by 365, and multiplying by 21 days. The result is $621,945.

Equipment: Crown Ironworks in Minnesota builds all of the equipment for Renewable Energy Group. Crown estimates that the total equipment needed will total $3.75 million.

Notes payable (long term): First Merchants Bank in Muncie, Indiana, will loan Mr. Gady $12,357,600 for 20 years at a 6.25 percent rate.

Common stock: Common stock includes Mr. Gady's 20 percent investment of $5.09 million and the $8 million contribution from private investors.

D. START-UP BUDGETING

All costs and expenses outlined in the start-up budget were determined by contacting industry experts for approximations. For example, it will cost near or above $100,000 for professional services at start-up for an attorney and a CPA. These figures are based upon the industry average of approximately $90,000 to $150,000.

FINANCIAL APPENDIX

First Year Balance Sheet (12 months)
First Year Income Statement (12 months)
First Year Cash Flow Statement (12 months)
Summary Balance Sheets (3 Years)
Summary Income Statements (3 Years)
Summary Cash Flow Statements (3 Years)

Green Fuel Alternatives Balance Sheet as of August 31, 2007

	Opening	September	October	November	December	January	February	March	April	May	June	July	August
Assets													
Current													
Cash	$9,938,524	$9,840,926	$9,743,329	$10,133,660	$10,036,062	$9,938,465	$10,327,612	$10,230,014	$10,132,417	$10,522,477	$10,424,879	$10,327,282	$10,717,204
Inventory	621,945	621,945	621,945	621,945	621,945	621,945	621,945	621,945	621,945	621,945	621,945	621,945	621,945
TOTAL CURRENT ASSETS	10,560,469	10,462,872	10,365,274	10,755,605	10,658,008	10,560,410	10,949,557	10,851,959	10,754,362	11,144,422	11,046,825	10,949,227	11,339,149
Noncurrent													
Land	447,000	447,000	447,000	447,000	447,000	447,000	447,000	447,000	447,000	447,000	447,000	447,000	447,000
Building	10,250,000	10,250,000	10,250,000	10,250,000	10,250,000	10,250,000	10,250,000	10,250,000	10,250,000	10,250,000	10,250,000	10,250,000	10,250,000
Accumulated Depreciation Building		(28,472)	(56,944)	(85,417)	(113,889)	(142,361)	(170,833)	(199,306)	(227,778)	(256,250)	(284,722)	(313,194)	(341,667)
Office Equipment	7,500	7,500	7,500	7,500	7,500	7,500	7,500	7,500	7,500	7,500	7,500	7,500	7,500
Accumulated Depreciation Equipment		(156)	(313)	(469)	(625)	(781)	(938)	(1,094)	(1,250)	(1,406)	(1,563)	(1,719)	(1,875)
Manufacturing Equipment	3,750,000	3,750,000	3,750,000	3,750,000	3,750,000	3,750,000	3,750,000	3,750,000	3,750,000	3,750,000	3,750,000	3,750,000	3,750,000
Accumulated Depreciation Mfg. Equipment		(44,643)	(89,286)	(133,929)	(178,571)	(223,214)	(267,857)	(312,500)	(357,143)	(401,786)	(446,429)	(491,071)	(535,714)
TOTAL NONCURRENT ASSETS	14,454,500	14,381,229	14,307,957	14,234,686	14,161,415	14,088,143	14,014,872	13,941,601	13,868,329	13,795,058	13,721,787	13,648,515	13,575,244
TOTAL ASSETS	25,014,969	24,844,100	24,673,231	24,990,291	24,819,422	24,648,553	24,964,429	24,793,560	24,622,691	24,939,480	24,768,611	24,597,742	24,914,393

(Continued)

	Opening	September	October	November	December	January	February	March	April	May	June	July	August
Liabilities													
Noncurrent													
Notes Payable - LT	$11,925,569	$11,897,356	$11,868,997	$11,840,489	$11,811,833	$11,783,028	$11,754,073	$11,724,967	$11,695,709	$11,666,299	$11,636,736	$11,607,019	$11,577,147
TOTAL NONCURRENT LIABILITIES	11,925,569	11,897,356	11,868,997	11,840,489	11,811,833	11,783,028	11,754,073	11,724,967	11,695,709	11,666,299	11,636,736	11,607,019	11,577,147
TOTAL LIABILITIES	**11,925,569**	**11,897,356**	**11,868,997**	**11,840,489**	**11,811,833**	**11,783,028**	**11,754,073**	**11,724,967**	**11,695,709**	**11,666,299**	**11,636,736**	**11,607,019**	**11,577,147**
Equity													
Common Stock	13,089,400	13,089,400	13,089,400	13,089,400	13,089,400	13,089,400	13,089,400	13,089,400	13,089,400	13,089,400	13,089,400	13,089,400	13,089,400
Retained Earnings		(142,656)	(285,165)	60,402	(81,811)	(223,874)	120,956	(20,807)	(162,418)	183,781	42,476	(98,676)	247,846
TOTAL EQUITY	**13,089,400**	**12,946,744**	**12,804,235**	**13,149,802**	**13,007,589**	**12,865,526**	**13,210,356**	**13,068,593**	**12,926,982**	**13,273,181**	**13,131,876**	**12,990,724**	**13,337,246**
TOTAL LIABILITIES AND EQUITY	**25,014,969**	**24,844,100**	**24,673,231**	**24,990,291**	**24,819,422**	**24,648,553**	**24,964,429**	**24,793,560**	**24,622,691**	**24,939,480**	**24,768,611**	**24,597,742**	**24,914,393**
CHECK TOTAL	$-	$-	$-	$-	$-	$-	$-	$-	$-	$-	$-	$-	$-

Green Fuel Alternatives Pro Forma Income Statement for the 12 Months Ending August 31, 2007

	Start-up	September	October	November	December	January	February	March	April	May	June	July	August	Total
Sales														
Subsidies	$-	$-	$-	$655,700	$-	$-	$655,700	$-	$-	$655,700	$-	$-	$655,700	**$2,622,800**
Biodiesel/ Glycerin Sales		1,128,800	1,128,800	1,128,800	1,128,800	1,128,800	1,128,800	1,128,800	1,128,800	1,128,800	1,128,800	1,128,800	1,128,800	**13,545,600**
Cost of Goods Sold		900,833	900,833	900,833	900,833	900,833	900,833	900,833	900,833	900,833	900,833	900,833	900,833	**10,810,000**
Gross Margin		227,967	227,967	227,967	227,967	227,967	227,967	227,967	227,967	227,967	227,967	227,967	227,967	**5,358,400**
General and Administrative Expenses														
Design-Build Plant Cost	20,000,000													
Land Cost	447,000													
Salaries and Wages	220,000	77,711	77,711	77,711	77,711	77,711	77,711	77,711	77,711	77,711	77,711	77,711	77,711	**1,152,528**
Payroll Taxes	15,898	6,296	6,296	6,296	6,296	6,296	6,296	6,296	6,296	6,296	6,296	6,296	6,296	**91,449**
Payroll Expense		204	204	204	204	204	204	204	204	204	204	204	204	**2,448**
Benefits	55,000	19,428	19,428	19,428	19,428	19,428	19,428	19,428	19,428	19,428	19,428	19,428	19,428	**288,132**
Insurance	20,792	20,792	20,792	20,792	20,792	20,792	20,792	20,792	20,792	20,792	20,792	20,792	20,792	**270,296**
Sales Expense	2,000	4,500	4,500	4,500	4,500	4,500	4,500	4,500	4,500	4,500	4,500	4,500	4,500	**56,000**
Office Supplies	1,000	450	450	450	450	450	450	450	450	450	450	450	450	**6,400**
Utilities	25,855	25,855	25,855	25,855	25,855	25,855	25,855	25,855	25,855	25,855	25,855	25,855	25,855	**336,109**
Internet	140	140	140	140	140	140	140	140	140	140	140	140	140	**1,820**
Telephone and Fax	800	800	800	800	800	800	800	800	800	800	800	800	800	**10,400**
Web Site	10,000	100	100	100	100	100	100	100	100	100	100	100	100	**11,200**
Freight Expense		33,200	33,200	33,200	33,200	33,200	33,200	33,200	33,200	33,200	33,200	33,200	33,200	**398,400**
Travel Expense		500	500	500	500	500	500	500	500	500	500	500	500	**6,000**
Conference Expense							1,500							**1,500**

(Continued)

	Start-up	September	October	November	December	January	February	March	April	May	June	July	August	Total
Security Expense		833	833	833	833	833	833	833	833	833	833	833	833	**10,000**
Maintenance Expense		2,233	2,233	2,233	2,233	2,233	2,233	2,233	2,233	2,233	2,233	2,233	2,233	**26,796**
Professional Services														
Attorney	120,000	4,167	4,167	4,167	4,167	4,167	4,167	4,167	4,167	4,167	4,167	4,167	4,167	**170,004**
CPA	30,000	4,167	4,167	4,167	4,167	4,167	4,167	4,167	4,167	4,167	4,167	4,167	4,167	**80,004**
Depreciation		73,271	73,271	73,271	73,271	73,271	73,271	73,271	73,271	73,271	73,271	73,271	73,271	**879,256**
Property Taxes		—	—	—	—	—	—	—	—	—	—	—	—	—
Miscellaneous Expense		33,864	33,864	53,535	33,864	33,864	53,535	33,864	33,864	53,535	33,864	33,864	53,535	**485,052**
Total G&A Expenses	20,948,484	308,510	308,510	328,181	308,510	308,510	329,681	308,510	308,510	328,181	308,510	308,510	328,181	**4,283,793**
Earnings Before Interest and Taxes	(20,948,484)	(80,544)	(80,544)	555,485	(80,544)	(80,544)	553,985	(80,544)	(80,544)	555,485	(80,544)	(80,544)	555,485	**(19,372,393)**
Interest Expense	1,013,172	62,112	61,965	61,818	61,669	61,520	61,370	61,219	61,068	60,915	60,762	60,608	60,453	**1,748,652**
Earnings Before Taxes	(21,961,657)	(142,656)	(142,509)	493,668	(142,213)	(142,064)	492,615	(141,763)	(141,611)	494,570	(141,306)	(141,152)	495,032	**840,612**
Income Taxes														
Federal		—	—	123,417	—	—	123,154	—	—	123,643	—	—	123,758	**493,971**
State		—	—	24,683	—	—	24,631	—	—	24,729	—	—	24,752	**98,794**
Shareholder Distributions														—
Net Income	$(21,961,657)	$(142,656)	$(142,509)	$345,567	$(142,213)	$(142,064)	$344,831	$(141,763)	$(141,611)	$346,199	$(141,306)	$(141,152)	$346,522	**$247,846**

Green Fuel Alternatives Statement of Cash Flows for the 12 Months Ending August 31, 2007

	Start-up	September	October	November	December	January	February	March	April	May	June	July	August	Total
Beginning Cash Balance		$9,938,524	$9,840,926	$9,743,329	$10,133,660	$10,036,062	$9,938,465	$10,327,612	$10,230,014	$10,132,417	$10,522,477	$10,424,879	$10,327,282	
Cash Inflows														
Net Sales														
Subsidies		—	—	655,700	—	—	655,700	—	—	655,700	—	—	655,700	2,622,800
Biodiesel/ Glycerin Sales	12,357,600	1,128,800	1,128,800	1,128,800	1,128,800	1,128,800	1,128,800	1,128,800	1,128,800	1,128,800	1,128,800	1,128,800	1,128,800	13,545,600
Bank Loan	12,357,600													12,357,600
Common Stock	13,089,400													13,089,400
Total Cash Available	25,447,000	11,067,324	10,969,726	11,527,829	11,262,460	11,164,862	11,722,965	11,456,412	11,358,814	11,916,917	11,651,277	11,553,679	12,111,782	
Cash Outflows														
Design-Build Plant Cost	20,000,000													
Land Cost	447,000													
Cost of Goods Sold		900,833	900,833	900,833	900,833	900,833	900,833	900,833	900,833	900,833	900,833	900,833	900,833	10,810,000
Salaries & Wages	220,000	77,711	77,711	77,711	77,711	77,711	77,711	77,711	77,711	77,711	77,711	77,711	77,711	1,152,528
Payroll Taxes	15,898	6,296	6,296	6,296	6,296	6,296	6,296	6,296	6,296	6,296	6,296	6,296	6,296	91,449
Payroll Expense		204	204	204	204	204	204	204	204	204	204	204	204	2,448
Benefits	55,000	19,428	19,428	19,428	19,428	19,428	19,428	19,428	19,428	19,428	19,428	19,428	19,428	288,132
Insurance	20,792	20,792	20,792	20,792	20,792	20,792	20,792	20,792	20,792	20,792	20,792	20,792	20,792	270,296
Sales Expense	2,000	4,500	4,500	4,500	4,500	4,500	4,500	4,500	4,500	4,500	4,500	4,500	4,500	56,000
Office Supplies	1,000	450	450	450	450	450	450	450	450	450	450	450	450	6,400
Utilities	25,855	25,855	25,855	25,855	25,855	25,855	25,855	25,855	25,855	25,855	25,855	25,855	25,855	336,109
Internet	140	140	140	140	140	140	140	140	140	140	140	140	140	1,820

(Continued)

	Start-up	September	October	November	December	January	February	March	April	May	June	July	August	Total
Telephone and Fax	800	800	800	800	800	800	800	800	800	800	800	800	800	10,400
Web Site	10,000	100	100	100	100	100	100	100	100	100	100	100	100	11,200
Freight Expense		33,200	33,200	33,200	33,200	33,200	33,200	33,200	33,200	33,200	33,200	33,200	33,200	398,400
Travel Expense		500	500	500	500	500	500	500	500	500	500	500	500	6,000
Conference Expense							1,500							1,500
Security Expense		833	833	833	833	833	833	833	833	833	833	833	833	10,000
Maintenance Expense		2,233	2,233	2,233	2,233	2,233	2,233	2,233	2,233	2,233	2,233	2,233	2,233	26,796
Professional Services														–
Attorney	120,000	4,167	4,167	4,167	4,167	4,167	4,167	4,167	4,167	4,167	4,167	4,167	4,167	170,004
CPA	30,000	4,167	4,167	4,167	4,167	4,167	4,167	4,167	4,167	4,167	4,167	4,167	4,167	80,004
Property Taxes		–	–	–	–	–	–	–	–	–	–	–	–	
Miscellaneous Expense		33,864	33,864	33,864	33,864	33,864	53,535	33,864	33,864	53,535	33,864	33,864	53,535	485,052
Income Tax Expense		–	–	148,100	–	–	147,785	–	–	148,371	–	–	148,510	592,766
Total Cash Disbursements	20,948,484	1,136,072	1,136,072	1,303,844	1,136,072	1,136,072	1,305,028	1,136,072	1,136,072	1,304,114	1,136,072	1,136,072	1,304,253	14,807,303
Cash Surplus (Deficit)	4,498,516	9,931,252	9,833,654	10,223,985	10,126,388	10,028,790	10,417,937	10,320,339	10,222,742	10,612,802	10,515,205	10,417,607	10,807,529	
Loan Principle	1,445,203	28,213	28,360	28,507	28,656	28,805	28,955	29,106	29,258	29,410	29,563	29,717	29,872	348,423
Loan Interest		62,112	61,965	61,818	61,669	61,520	61,370	61,219	61,068	60,915	60,762	60,608	60,453	735,480
Ending Cash Balance	$3,053,313	$9,840,926	$9,743,329	$10,133,660	$10,036,062	$9,938,465	$10,327,612	$10,230,014	$10,132,417	$10,522,477	$10,424,879	$10,327,282	$10,717,204	

Green Fuel Alternatives Balance Sheet Summary for the Years 2007–2009			
	2007	*2008*	*2009*
Assets			
Current			
Cash	$10,717,204	$14,601,502	$21,401,961
Inventory	621,945	621,945	621,945
TOTAL CURRENT ASSETS	11,339,149	15,223,447	22,023,906
Noncurrent			
Land	447,000	447,000	447,000
Building	10,250,000	10,250,000	10,250,000
Accumulated Depreciation Building	(341,667)	(683,333)	(1,025,000)
Equipment	7,500	7,500	7,500
Accumulated Depreciation Equipment	(1,875)	(3,750)	(5,625)
Manufacturing Equipment			
Accumulated Depreciation Mfg. Equipment			
TOTAL NONCURRENT ASSETS	13,575,244	12,695,988	11,816,732
TOTAL ASSETS	**24,914,393**	**27,919,435**	**33,840,638**
Liabilities			
Noncurrent			
Notes Payable—L/T	11,577,147	11,206,313	10,811,626
TOTAL NONCURRENT LIABILITIES	11,577,147	11,206,313	10,811,626
TOTAL LIABILITIES	**11,577,147**	**11,206,313**	**10,811,626**
Equity			
Common Stock	13,089,400	13,089,400	13,089,400
Retained Earnings	247,846	3,623,723	9,939,612
TOTAL EQUITY	**13,337,246**	**16,713,123**	**23,029,012**
TOTAL LIABILITIES AND EQUITY	**24,914,393**	**27,919,435**	**33,840,638**
CHECK TOTAL	**$-**	**$-**	**$-**

Green Fuel Alternatives Income Statement Summary for the Years 2007–2009

	2007	% of Sales	2008	% of Sales	2009	% of Sales
Sales						
Subsidies	$2,622,800	16%	$4,303,092	14%	$5,966,667	13%
Biodiesel/Glycerin Sales	13,545,600	84%	27,199,989	86%	40,800,000	87%
Cost of Goods Sold	10,810,000	67%	21,145,000	67%	31,480,000	67%
Gross Margin	5,358,400	33%	10,358,081	33%	15,286,667	33%
General and Administrative Expenses						
Salaries and Wages	1,152,528	7%	932,528	3%	932,528	2%
Payroll Taxes	91,449	1%	75,551	0%	75,551	0%
Payroll Expense	2,448	0%	2,448	0%	2,448	0%
Benefits	288,132	2%	233,132	1%	233,132	0%
Insurance	270,296	2%	249,504	1%	249,504	1%
Sales Expense	56,000	0%	54,000	0%	54,000	0%
Office Supplies	6,400	0%	5,400	0%	5,400	0%
Utilities	336,109	2%	620,508	2%	930,762	2%
Internet	1,820	0%	1,680	0%	1,680	0%
Telephone and Fax	10,400	0%	9,600	0%	9,600	0%
Freight Expense	398,400	2%	800,000	3%	1,200,000	3%
Travel Expense	6,000	0%	6,000	0%	6,000	0%
Conference Expense	1,500	0%	1,500	0%	1,500	0%
Security Expense	10,000	0%	10,000	0%	10,000	0%
Maintenance Expense	26,796	0%	26,796	0%	26,796	0%
Professional Services						
Attorney	170,004	1%	50,004	0%	50,004	0%
CPA	80,004	0%	50,004	0%	50,004	0%
Depreciation	879,256	5%	879,256	3%	879,256	2%
Property Taxes	—	0%	170,802	1%	212,969	0%
Miscellaneous Expense	485,052	3%	642,420	2%	642,420	1%
Total G&A Expenses	4,283,793	26%	4,822,332	15%	5,574,753	12%
Earnings Before Interest and Taxes	(19,372,393)	−120%	5,535,749	18%	9,711,914	21%
Interest Expense	1,748,652	11%	713,068	2%	689,216	1%
Earnings Before Taxes	840,612	5%	4,822,681	15%	9,022,699	19%
Income Taxes						
Federal	493,971	3%	1,205,670	4%	2,255,675	5%
State	98,794	1%	241,134	1%	451,135	1%
Shareholder Distributions	—	0%	—	0%	—	0%
Net Income	$247,846	2%	$3,375,876	11%	$6,315,889	14%

Green Fuel Alternatives Statement of Cash Flows Summary for the Years 2007–2009

	2007	2008	2009
Beginning Cash Balance	$9,938,524	$10,717,204	$14,601,502
Cash Inflows			
Net Sales			
Subsidies	2,622,800	4,303,092	5,966,667
Biodiesel/Glycerin Sales	13,545,600	27,199,989	40,800,000
Bank Loan	12,357,600		
Common Stock	13,089,400		
Total Cash Available	51,553,924	42,220,285	61,368,170
Cash Outflows			
Cost of Goods Sold	10,810,000	21,145,000	31,480,000
Salaries and Wages	1,152,528	932,528	932,528
Payroll Taxes	91,449	75,551	75,551
Payroll Expense	2,448	2,448	2,448
Benefits	288,132	233,132	233,132
Insurance	270,296	249,504	249,504
Sales Expense	56,000	54,000	54,000
Office Supplies	6,400	5,400	5,400
Utilities	336,109	620,508	930,762
Internet	1,820	1,680	1,680
Telephone and Fax	10,400	9,600	9,600
Freight Expense	398,400	800,000	1,200,000
Travel Expense	6,000	6,000	6,000
Conference Expense	1,500	1,500	1,500
Security Expense	10,000	10,000	10,000
Maintenance Expense	26,796	26,796	26,796
Professional Services	—	—	—
Attorney	170,004	50,004	50,004
CPA	80,004	50,004	50,004
Property Taxes	—	170,802	212,969
Miscellaneous Expense	485,052	642,420	642,420
Income Tax Expense	592,766	1,446,804	2,706,810
Total Cash Disbursements	14,203,337	25,086,876	36,174,297
Cash Surplus (Deficit)	37,350,587	17,133,409	25,193,872
Loan Principle	348,423	370,834	394,687
Loan Interest	735,480	713,068	689,216
Ending Cash Balance	$36,266,685	$16,049,506	$24,109,970

Endnotes

1. Energy Management Institute (EMI), Alternative Fuels Index, April 15, 2005.
2. Frazier, Barnes, & Associates. Mississippi Biodiesel Feasibility Study, 2004.
3. Dun & Bradstreet Industry Reports, 2004, www.zapdata.com.
4. National Biodiesel Board, Biodiesel Quick Facts, 2004.
5. "An Overview of Biodiesel and Petroleum Diesel Life Cycles," U.S. Department of Energy, National Renewable Energy Laboratory (NREL), and the U.S. Department of Agriculture (USDA), May 1998–March 2004.
6. John Sheehan, Vince Camobreco, James Duffield, Michael Graboski, and Housein Shapouril, "An Overview of Biodiesel and Petroleum Diesel Life Cycles." A joint study by the U.S. Department of Energy, National Renewable Energy Laboratory, and the U.S. Department of Agriculture, Office of Energy, May 1998–March 2004, www.afdc.doe.gov/pdfs/3812.pdf.
7. "United States Country Analysis Brief." U.S. Department of Energy, Energy Information Administration. September 28, 2003, www.eia.doe.gov/emeu/cabs/usa.html.
8. Environmental Protection Agency (EPA), Alternative Fuels Data Center.
9. Grain Growers Cooperative, Inc. Biodiesel Analysis and Plant Feasibility, 2004.
10. Phone interview with Pete Moss at Frazier, Barnes, & Associates, LLC, April 10, 2007.
11. Energy Information Administration (EIA), 2004.
12. Frazier, Barnes, and Associates, Nashville, Tennessee, Biodiesel Feasibility Studies in GA.
13. Minnesota Department of Agriculture, www.mda.state.mn.us/ams/biodiesel/tfm2004july.htm.
14. Tom Cackette, "Diesel Engines: What Role Can They Play in an Emissions-Constrained World?" *California Air Resources Board,* August 29, 2004.
15. "Environmental and Safety Information," National Biodiesel Board, October 5, 2003, www.biodiesel.org/pdf_files/Envi&Safetyinfo.PDF.
16. Department of Energy (DOE) and U.S. Department of Agriculture (USDA).
17. Phone interview with Jerry Ban of Crystal Flash, March 30, 2005.
18. National Biodiesel Board.
19. Belinda Puetz, Indiana Soybean Board.

NAME INDEX

SUBJECT INDEX

A

Absentee management, 15
Accountants, 66, 78, 202–203
Accounts payable, 195
Accounts receivable
  collection on, 223, 225t
  defined, 193
  as purchase price factor, 41
  turnover of, 218–219
Accounts-receivable
  factoring, 179
Accounts-receivable loans, 177
Accrual system of accounting, 170
Accumulated depreciation of
  building, 194–195
Accumulated depreciation of
  equipment, 195
Acid-test ratio, 212
Action plan, 26–31
  entrepreneur's self-assessment,
    26–28
  financial picture, 28–30
  other factors, 30–31
ADA. *See* Americans with
  Disabilities Act
  (ADA, 1990)
Administrative expenses, 200
Administrative focus, versus
  entrepreneurial, 268–272,
  270–271t
Africa, 281
Ag Processing, 304
Allowance for uncollectible
  accounts, 194
American Association of
  Franchisees and Dealers
  (AAFD), 62
American Franchisee Association
  (AFA), 62
American Online (AOL), 136
American Society of Testing and
  Materials (ASTM), 295,
  298, 308
Americans with Disabilities Act
  (ADA, 1990), 232–233
Apple Computer, 1
Application forms, 238
Archer Daniels Midland (ADM),
  296, 297, 303, 305, 308,
  311–312
Asia, 281
Assets
  analysis of, as purchase
    consideration, 34

current, 170, 192–194
  defined, 170, 191
  fixed, 194–195
  intangible, 192
  as purchase price factor, 40–41
  value of, 192
Attorneys, 64
Auction value, 39–40
Australia, 57

B

Babson College, 2
Balance sheet, 191–198
  analysis of, 209–214
  components of, 192–196
  defined, 170, 191
  sample, 193t
  why it balances, 196–198
Baldridge Award, 276–279, 277f
Balloon loans, 177
Ball State University, 304
Bankers
  business plans and, 77
  financial advice from, 66
Bankruptcy, 14
Banks, as source of capital,
  176–178, 195
Banner ads, 136
Belgium, 2
Benefits, employee, 248–249
Betheboss.com, 65t
Biodiesel industry growth,
  294f, 300f
BMW, 153
Board of advisers, 272
Book value, 39
Bootstrapping, 169
Brain-Reserve, 23
Brand names, 58–59
Brazil, 281
Budgets, 222–226
Building. *See* Location/building
Business angels, 77, 175
Businesses, legal forms of, 95–118
  comparison of, 96t, 100f,
    112–113t, 116–117t
  considerations regarding, 96
  corporations, 107–114
  limited liability companies
    (LLCs), 114–115
  partnerships, 99–107
  sole proprietorships, 96–99
Businesses, purchasing. *See* Buying
  an ongoing business

Business failure, 13–15, 220–221
Business opportunities, 20t
Business plans, 73–92
  appearance/form of, 79
  assessment guidelines for, 82–88t
  components of, 77–79
  criticisms of, 74–75
  crucial questions for, 81, 88
  defined, 76
  development of, 79–91
  guidelines for effective, 89–91
  length of, 79
  new venture funding dependent
    on, 76–77
  resources for, 80–81t
  updating of, 91
  value of, 73–76
Business schools, recruitment
  from, 238
Business Source Premier, 81t
Business Week (newspaper), 131
Buying an ongoing business, 31–46
  advantages of, 31–32
  analysis prior to, 33–38
  dos and don'ts of, 45t
  negotiations for, 44–45
  price for, 32, 39–44

C

Capital
  defined, 170
  types of, 169
  working, 171, 211
  See also Start-up capital
Capital fund managers, 77
Cash, 192
Cash budgets, 223, 224f, 225
Cash Disbursement, Purchases,
  and Expense Journal, 201–202,
  202t
Cash discounts, 153
Cash flow, 40, 170
Cash planning, 223
Cash system of accounting, 170
Central America, 281
Certified Development Company
  Program, SBA, 184t
Certified public accountants, 66
Challenge, as entrepreneurial
  motivation, 10
Change, 267
Chicago Board of Trade, 305
China, 281